42

Core Themes in Geography

Human

Eddie Broadley
Depute Rector, Glen Urquhart High School, Drumnadrochit, Highland Region

and

Ritchie Cunningham
Rector, Inverness High School, Highland Region

99 000 1 01 002 2002

Oliver & Boyd

Acknowledgements

The publishers thank the following for permission to reproduce photographs or other copyright material:
British Library (1.3); Panos (1.29 Sean Sprague, 1.35 Barbara Cheney, 2.12a Patrick Knight, 2.13 and 2.14 Sean Sprague, 2.17 Cooper & Hammond, 2.18 Ron Gilling,4.63 Paul Harrison, 4.70 Patrick Knight, 4.71 Julio Etchart, 5.11 Bror Karlsson, 5.30 Heldur Jaaan Netocny, 5.40 Liba Taylor); Adrian Arbib (1.30); Mary Evans (1.31); Christine Osborne (1.34); Tony & Marion Morrison (2.10, 4.61, 4.64, 4.68); Hulton–Deutsch Collection (2.12b); Mark Edwards (2.12c, 2.12d, 5.37); Tony Waltham (2.15, 3.3, 3.33, 3.47); J. Allan Cash (2.23, 3.20b, 3.23, 3.24, 4.20, 4.37, 4.38, 4.40c, 4.47, 4.48); R. Cunningham (2.26);Ford (3.8, 3.46); Teesside Development Corporation (3.17); IBM Communications Library (3.19, 3.61, 3.62); P. Morris (3.20a); German Embassy (3.20c); AirFotos (3.20d); Digital Equipment Scotland Ltd (3.20e); Eric Kay (3.30, 3.54); Highland and Islands Enterprise (3.36, 3.40); Glasgow Herald and Evening Times (3.41); Camara de Comercio Industria y Navegacion de Bilbao (3.43); International Institute for Aerospace Survey and Earth Sciences (3.52); Inter Nationes (3.58); Bryce Creative Services, Meadowhall Centre (3.65); Sealand Aerial Photography (4.2 inset, 4.6, 4.17, 4.33); Salvation Army (4.34); Milton Keynes Development Corporation (4.40a); Zefa (4.40b); Geoslides (4.42); Andes Press Agency (4.53, 4.58, 4.65, 4.67, 5.18); Volkswagen AG (4.60); Hutchison Library (4.75 Richard House); WHO/C. James Webb (5.25, 5.32a, b, c); © Health Education Authority (5.35, 5.36); Oxfam/Geoff Sayer (5.46)

The authors and publishers would like to thank the following sources which were used as a basis for figures:
M. J. Readman & F.M. Mayers, *The Dynamic World*, Oliver & Boyd (1.2); *Challenge of the Human Environment,* Longman (1.6, 1.21, 1.26, 1.27, 1.28, 1.32, 1.40, diagram, p.138); Population Concern, *Global Snapshots* (1.9, 1.24); Gemini New Service (1.11,1.12, 1.13, 1.33, 5.1); Population Division of the Department of International Economic and Social Affairs of the United Nations Secretariat (map 3, p. 15); J.I. Clarke, *Population Geography*, Pergamon 1970 (1.17); E.E. Simpson, *The Developing World – an Introduction*, Longman (1.22); *Geographical Magazine*, April 1989 (1.23), December 1989 (1.36); Population Concern, 1988 World Population Data Sheet (1.38); Geography Higher Grade Exam Paper II, 1987 (1.39); J. Jowett, 'China: The Population of the People's Republic', *SAGT Journal*, 1989, no 18 (1.41); H. H. McCarty and J. B. Lindberg, A *Preface to Economic Geography*, Prentice Hall, 1966 (2.2); B. Knapp et al.,*Challenge of the Economic Environment*, Longman 1989 (2.4, 2.8, 2.16, 2.19, 2.24, 3.1, 3.9, 3.10); K. Briggs, *Human Geography*, Hodder & Stoughton 1982 (2.5); E. Jones, *Human Geography*, Chatto & Windus 1969 (2.27); A. Adam & S. Dunlop, *Village, Town and* City, Heinemann (2.28) *Sunday Times,* 14 January 1990 (3.7); A-Level Revision Guide, Longman (3.11, 3.12); *New Internationalist* (3.13); Geocom 9, Alan Doherty, Linlithgow Academy (3.20); Hull, Jones & Terry, *Geographical Issues in Western Europe*, Longman (diagram 1, p. 70, and 3.26); D. Waugh, *Europe*, Nelson (3.29); Minshull, *The New Europe* (diagram 2, p.71, 3.32, 3.50); Horsfall, *Manufacturing Industry*, Blackwell (diagram 1, p.96); *Sunday Times*, 7 July 1987 (4.1); Knapp, *Systematic Geography* (4.8, 4.10, 4.12, 4.13, 4.14, 4.28); Gordon & Dick, *Settlement Geography* (4.9); D. Burtenshaw, *A-level Revision Guide* (4.15, 4.18, 4.21, 4.22, 4.24); Graves & White, *Geography of the British Isles* (4.27); *The Social Atlas of London* (4.29); B. Lenon, *London* (4.32, diagram 2, p.124);P. Hall, *London 2001* (4.45,4.49); Reed, *Brazil*, Unwin Hyman (4.51); *National Geographic*, Feb. 1978 (4.52); D. Waugh, *The World*, Nelson (4.64); E. Broadley and R Goring, *Studies in Geography 2*, Oliver & Boyd (5.16); *New Internationalist*, Oct. 1989 (5.17, 5.26, 5.45), June 1990 (5.18); *The Development Data Book* (5.19); *New Internationalist*, Aug. 1989 (5.22);*World Health Statistical Quarterly*, 41, 1988 (5.31); *New Internationalist,* March 1987 (5.38, 5.41); *Aspects of Social Geography* (5.43); *Gaia Peace Atlas* (5.44);Higher Geography Exam Paper II, 1985 (diagram 1, p. 171); Higher Geography Exam Paper II (diagram 2, p.171).

E. Broadley would also like to thank the following organisations and individuals: Ruth Bankhead, Librarian, Plockton High School; Andrew Ramsay, IBM Edinburgh;, Dave and Joy Short , Leicester; Paul Clarke, Leicester City Council; Mr Tipping, London & Edinburgh Trust; Dr Susan Cunningham, São Paulo; Peter Flynn, Director of the Institute of Latin American Studies, University of Glasgow; Margaret Harrison, Cheltenham & Gloucester College; Paul Singer, Municipal Planning Secretary, City of São Paulo; Roberto Schmidt de Almeida, Rio de Janeiro; Geografia Ltd, Rio Claro; and Fay Broadley for all the coffee, and Jenny, David and Douglas Broadley for their infinite patience.

Figures 1.7, 1.10, 1.15, digram 1, p.14, cartoon 2, p.15, diagram p.49, cartoon p.139, 5.5, 5.6, 5.12,diagram p. 151,5.14,5.15, diagrams 3 and 4, p.155, 5.27 were supplied by Gemini New Service, 9 White Lion Street, London N1 9PD (Tel. 071 833 4141). Figures 1.4, 1.5, 1.8 , 1.20 and 5.3 are from M. J. Readman and F. M. Mayers, *The Dynamic World 1*, Oliver & Boyd. Figures 1.25 and 5.4 are from W.E. and V. M. Marsden, *World in Change*, Oliver & Boyd. Figure 2.11 is from E. Broadley and R. Goring, *Studies in Geography 2*, Oliver & Boyd. Figure 2.22 is from *GCSE Geography Copymasters: Industry, Agriculture and Recreation*, Oliver & Boyd. Figure 2.21 is from M.J. Readman & F. M. Mayers, *The Dynamic Landscape*, Oliver & Boyd.The map on p.173 is an extract from OS 1:25 000 Pathfinder 1192 Orpington map, reproduced with the permission of the Controller of Her Majesty's Stationery Office, © Crown Copyright.The map on page 174 is an extract from the National Topographic System map sheet number 72-IRegina © 1974. Her Majesty the Queen in Right of Canada with permission of Energy, Mines and Resources Canada.The map on p.175 is an extract from the National Topographic System map sheet number 72-I/7 Regina © 1984. Her Majesty the Queen in Right of Canada with permission of Energy, Mines and Resources Canada. The map on p.176 is an extract from1:21 500 map of Sao Paulo, Sistema 'Falk', patente depositada no. 56.898, GR-Editora & Publicidade.

Every effort has been made to trace copyright owners; the publishers apologise if there are any omissions.

Cover and book design by Lynda McNee. Cover photograph by R.J. Pipes.

Illustrated by Bob McAllister and Swanston Graphics, Derby

Oliver & Boyd
Longman House
Burnt Mill
Harlow
Essex CM20 2JE
An Imprint of Longman Group UK Ltd

ISBN 0 05 00 4557 1
First published 1992
Fourth impression 1994

©Oliver & Boyd 1992. All rights reserved; no part of this publication may be stored in a retrieval system, or transmitted in any form or by any means, electronic, mechanical, photocopying, recording, or otherwise, without either the prior written permission of the Publishers or a licence permitting restricted copying in the United Kingdom issued by the Copyright Licensing Agency Ltd, 90 Tottenham Court Road, London, W1P 9HE.

Typeset in 10pt Helvetica Narrow on the Apple Macintosh. Styled by Word Power, Berwickshire
Produced by Longman Singapore Publishers Pte Ltd
Printed in Singapore

The Publisher's policy is to use paper manufactured from sustainable forests.

CONTENTS

CHAPTER 1

POPULATION

World Population Distribution

Population density (crude) is a measure of the average number of people per unit area (usually 1 square kilometre). The average population density of Europe is 88 persons per km^2 but this hides wide variations on either side of the average: from 13 persons per km^2 in Norway to 395 persons per km^2 in the Netherlands.

The **population distribution** within any given area is usually uneven, with large numbers of people living in some parts and very few in others. The world's population is very unevenly distributed as is shown in map 1.1.

The most densely populated areas are in Eastern Asia, Southern Asia, Europe and eastern North America; there are also significant concentrations of people in Africa (areas such as the Nile valley) and coastal South America. More than half of the world's population lives in Asia but Europe is the most densely populated part of the world. Densely populated areas tend to be relatively flat with a moderate climate. Hot deserts, mountainous regions, very cold regions and wet tropical forests support relatively few people (1.2). The contrast between population densities can be seen on many different scales. Even the most densely populated regions can contain relatively empty forests or deserts.

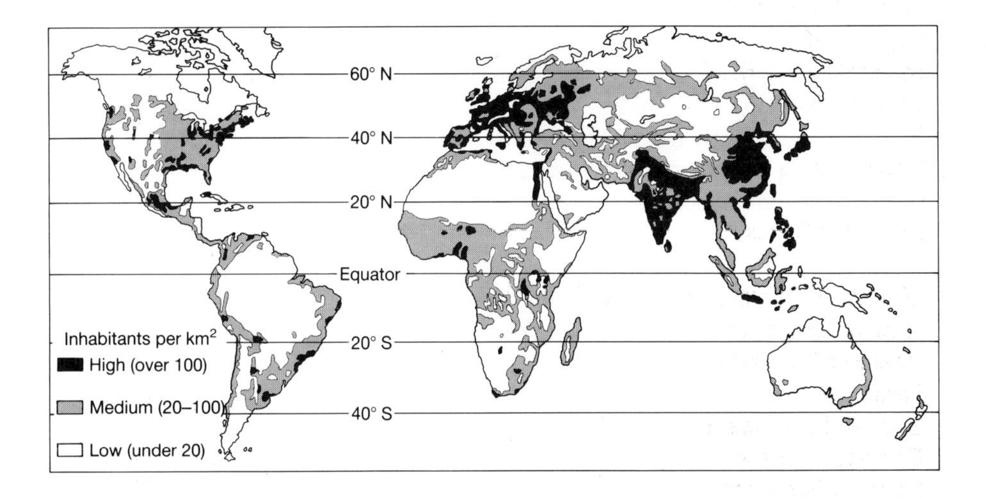

1.1 World population density map. This map shows how population density varies over the world, from population densities over 100 people per km^2 in urbanised areas of the world and in the alluvial lowlands of Asia to less than 1 per km^2 in the hot deserts and tropical rainforests.

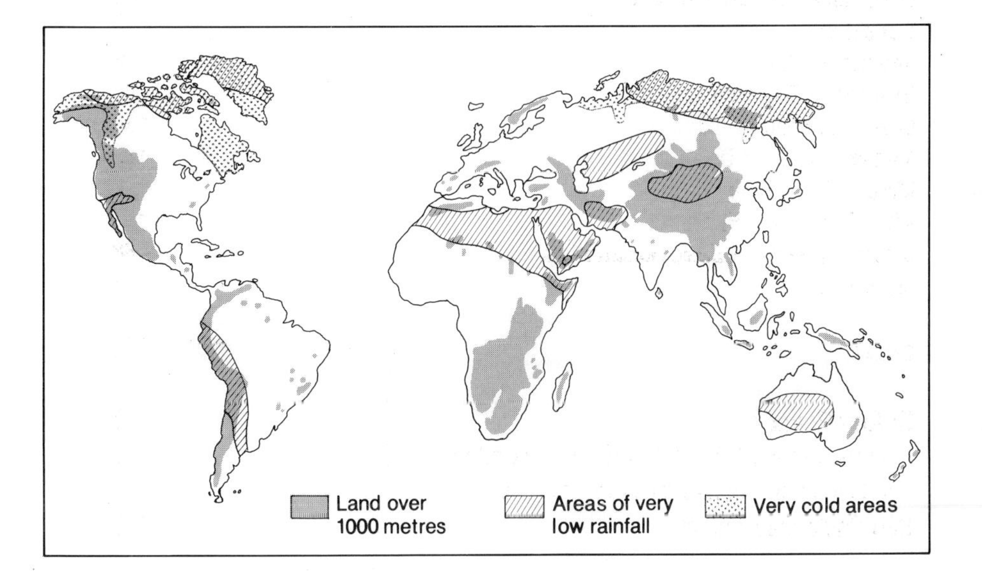

1.2 Positive and negative environments: low-lying areas tend to be attractive for settlement, while upland areas tend to discourage settlement. People also tend to avoid very cold areas and very dry areas.

CHAPTER 1

Factors Influencing Population

There are a number of factors (human as well as physical) which influence population distribution. The influence of physical factors such as latitude, relief, continentality, water supply, soil quality, seasonal variations in temperature and precipitation, and availability of mineral resources is greater in some places than in others, but in all areas people exert some control over their habitat. The environment offers possibilities and opportunities which may or may not be exploited by the population. Human factors which might influence population distribution include type of economy, level of technology, disease, historic and social influences. Analysing the relative importance of human and physical factors is difficult because so many are involved, and because population distributions are constantly changing, as are the causes and effects. Factors which were important 100 years ago may now be relatively insignificant while new factors come into play as technology advances and economies change.

The interpretation of population distribution involves a careful analysis of all the physical and human factors. The world population density map (1.1) shows that the main concentrations of people are on the coastal margins of continents: over 60% of the world's population live within 450 km of the sea. Both physical and human factors are involved here. The range of temperatures and in particular the low winter temperatures of the interior of the Asian and North American continents has tended to discourage human settlement there. The economic importance of coastal locations for trade and communications is a factor which attracts people. However not all coastal locations are desirable and some continental interiors have attributes which are attractive for settlement.

Factors which were important in the past have influenced present-day population distribution but changes in their relative importance will have an influence on future patterns.

1.3 Medieval wheeled plough. This picture is taken from a monastic painting of a farming scene. This plough enabled medieval farmers to cultivate the clay vales which had been impossible to farm with lighter ploughs.

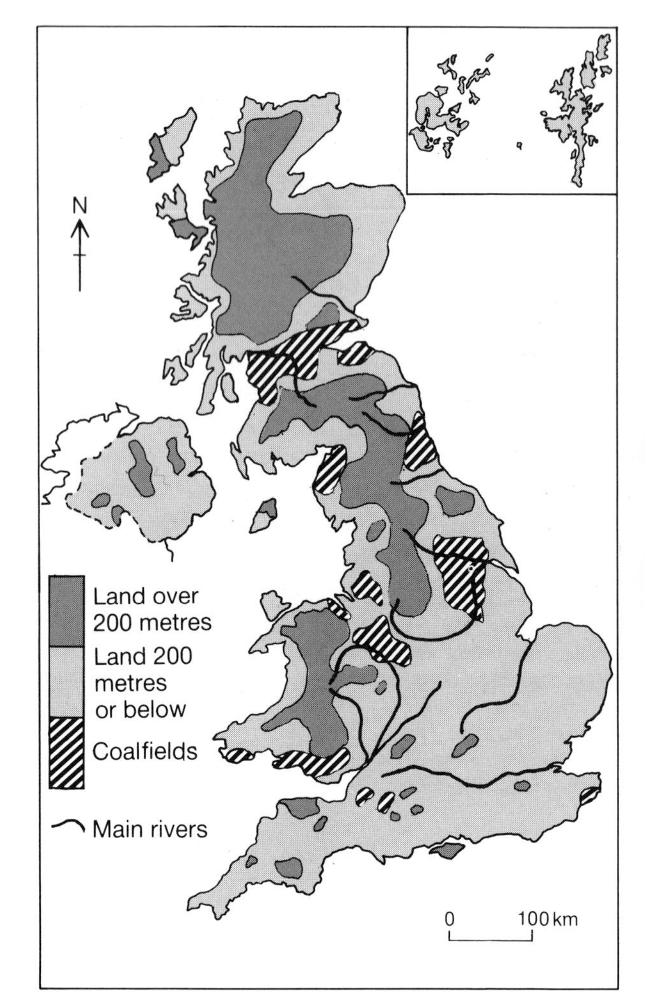

1.4 Coalfields and relief of the UK

Physical factors

The most comfortable climate for people to live in is probably within the temperature range of 10 °C to 30 °C but people have developed the means to protect themselves from uncomfortable features of their environment. This adaptability, combined with the different norms perceived by different cultures, makes it difficult to find a clear relationship between climate and people. Some very harsh environments such as the Sahel of Africa have relatively high populations. But, in general, people prefer to avoid harsh environments.

Other physical factors such as **soil fertility** can have an influence on population distribution. The fertile alluvial soils of South-East Asia and the Nile delta in North Africa support very dense agricultural populations. Areas which suffer from **soil erosion** tend to repel people. The type of soil which attracts settlement can also vary through time and may be dependent on the technology available.

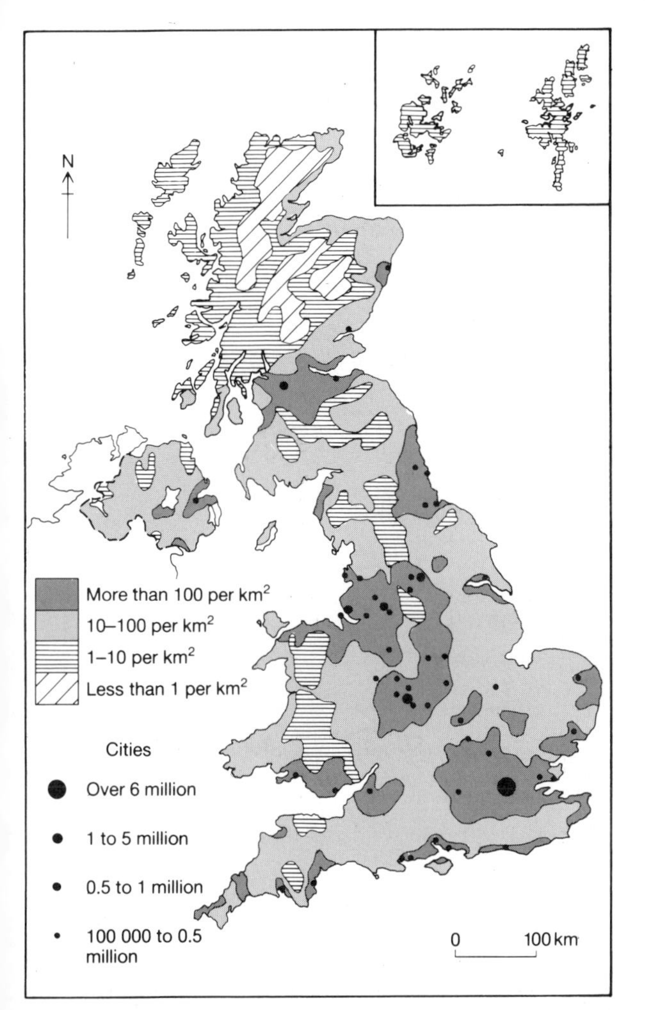

1.5 UK population density, 1990

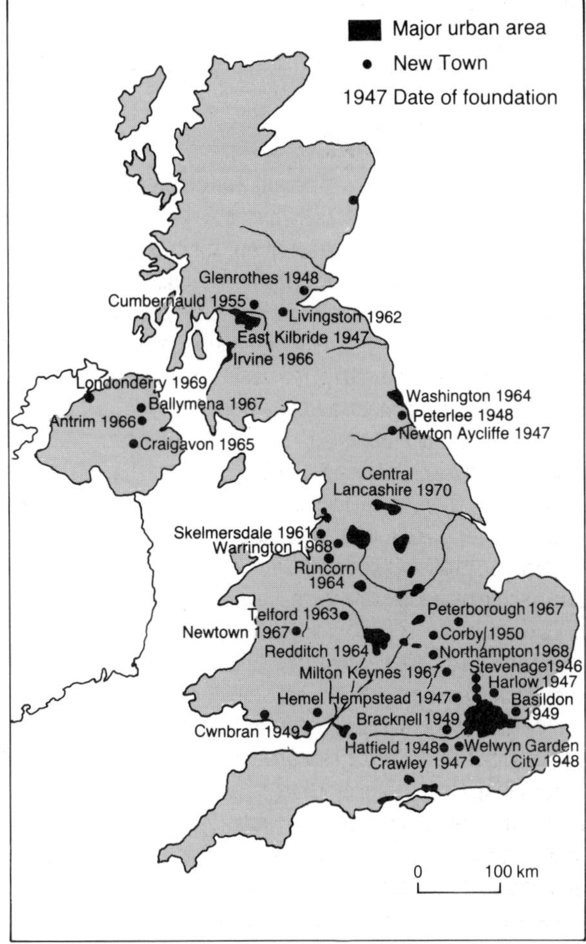

1.6 New Towns in relation to major urban areas

Human factors

Social disasters such as 'the holocaust' (the attempted extermination of Jews in the Second World War) can have long-lasting effects on population distribution, with many survivors migrating to new countries.

In agricultural economies the nature of the staple foods and productivity tend to influence population density. In general, livestock economies support a sparser population than high-yield grain crops. But the different technologies available in different economies tend to break down any relationship between types of agriculture and population distribution. The commercial farming of the Prairies is more of an industry than a rural activity and is less dependent on land quality for productivity than is subsistence farming. Pre-industrial agricultural populations tended to be more dependent on the type and scale of the agricultural activity than rural communities are today.

Changes in population distribution are often linked with advances in technology. The settlement of the clay vales of southern England is a good example. At one time settlement was restricted to the Downs because the technology couldn't cope with heavy clay soils. The heavy wheeled plough (1.3), which was capable of tilling clay soils, was brought to England in the Middle Ages and this technological advance changed the population distribution.

Changes in technology continue to influence the location of industry, and hence population. The settlement pattern established in the UK during the **Industrial Revolution** of the last century was influenced by the coalfield location of industries (1.4), and the importance of London as a commercial centre. This has been reinforced by the consumer-orientated industries of the twentieth century, which have to be sited near to population concentrations (1.5). Even the establishment of **New Towns** (1.6) to house overspill populations was in some way a response to the continuing pull of the cities which thrived in the Industrial Revolution. This population inertia means that most population distributions are only fully explained by reference to the past.

CHAPTER 1

World Population Change

There is a tendency to think of **population change** as **population growth** because this situation has dominated world history. However, today, as in the past, there are areas of population decline as well as population growth. The rapid growth in world population since the last century, with a doubling of world population between 1957 and 1990, is an issue of worldwide concern. Many have predicted disastrous consequences if population numbers outstrip resources.

World population reached 1000 million by about 1820 and has increased rapidly since then (see 1.7), reaching 2000 million in 1930, 3000 million in 1960, 4000 million in 1974 and 5000 million in 1987. Each year the world's population increases by more than 80 million, which is more than the population of the UK, and each month the world increase is more than the population of Scotland.

The accelerating rate of population growth is a relatively recent phenomenon with growth rates doubling between 1650 and 1850 and doubling again between 1850 and 1920 and again between 1920 and 1970. The accelerating growth rate has not been caused by any appreciable increase in **birth rates** but by progressive reductions in **death rates**. The terrible **pandemics** (worldwide epidemics) which have kept population in check through history have been almost absent in the twentieth century. One aspect of the rapid world population growth is that numbers are growing most rapidly in the developing nations which have the least developed agriculture and technology. Diagram 1.8 illustrates the growth in population for major regions of the world.

European countries have never grown at the rates currently experienced in the less developed countries. The peak **natural increase** (birth rate minus death rate) in England and Wales occurred in 1871. It was only 14 per thousand while the natural increase in many less developed nations is currently double that. European countries were also able to sustain the rapid population increases of the nineteenth century because their economies were expanding fast at the same time. The less developed nations have had to cope with rapidly falling death rates in a short space of time without a commensurate economic advance. India, for example, experienced an increase in **life expectancy** from 39 to 58 years between 1955 and 1985. Equivalent progress in many European nations had taken more than 100 years.

In this century growth rates in most European countries have slowed down to the point where some countries have experienced a drop in population. During the 1970s Scotland had a decrease of 0.5% per annum. However growth rates in Asia and Africa show little sign of slackening, Pakistan has a natural increase of

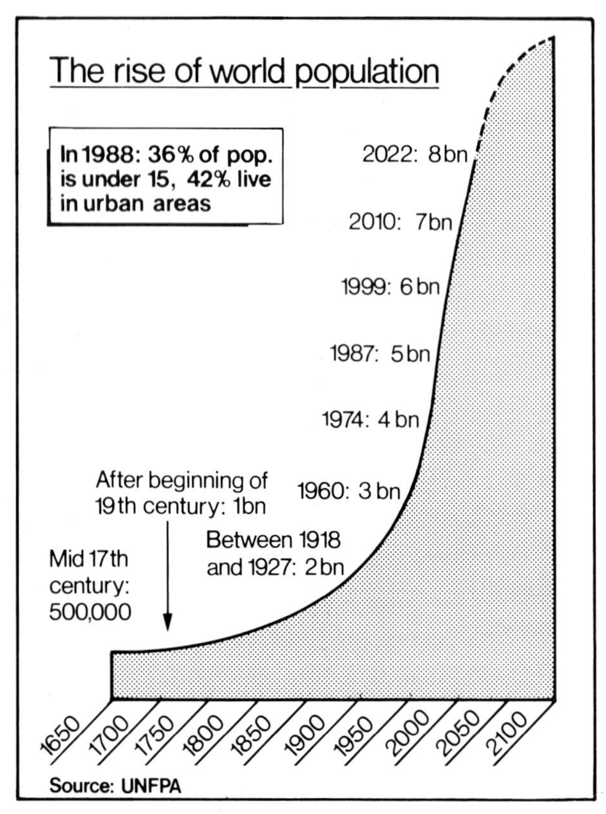

1.7 The march of the billions. The graph shows the growth in world population since 1650 with projections until 2100.

2.9%, and an increase of over 3.0% is common in the Middle East and North Africa. A growth rate of 3.0% does not sound serious but if maintained it will cause a doubling of population in 25 years.

The differential growth rates are causing a progressive shift in the distribution of world population. The share of world population in selected regions in 1920 and estimated for 2000 is as follows:

	1920	2000
Europe	18%	9%
Latin America	5%	10%
Africa	8%	13%
Asia	53%	58%

80% of the growth in world population over the last 30 years has occurred in the less developed nations and 95% of the growth over the next 20 years will also take place in these countries.

Population growth rates expressed as a percentage can sometimes convey the wrong impression: for example, a world growth rate of 2.04% between 1965 and 1970, falling to 1.67% between 1980 and 1985 could be taken to indicate a decline in total numbers, which is not the case.

There is an inbuilt population momentum since children and young people account for over 36% of world population (as high

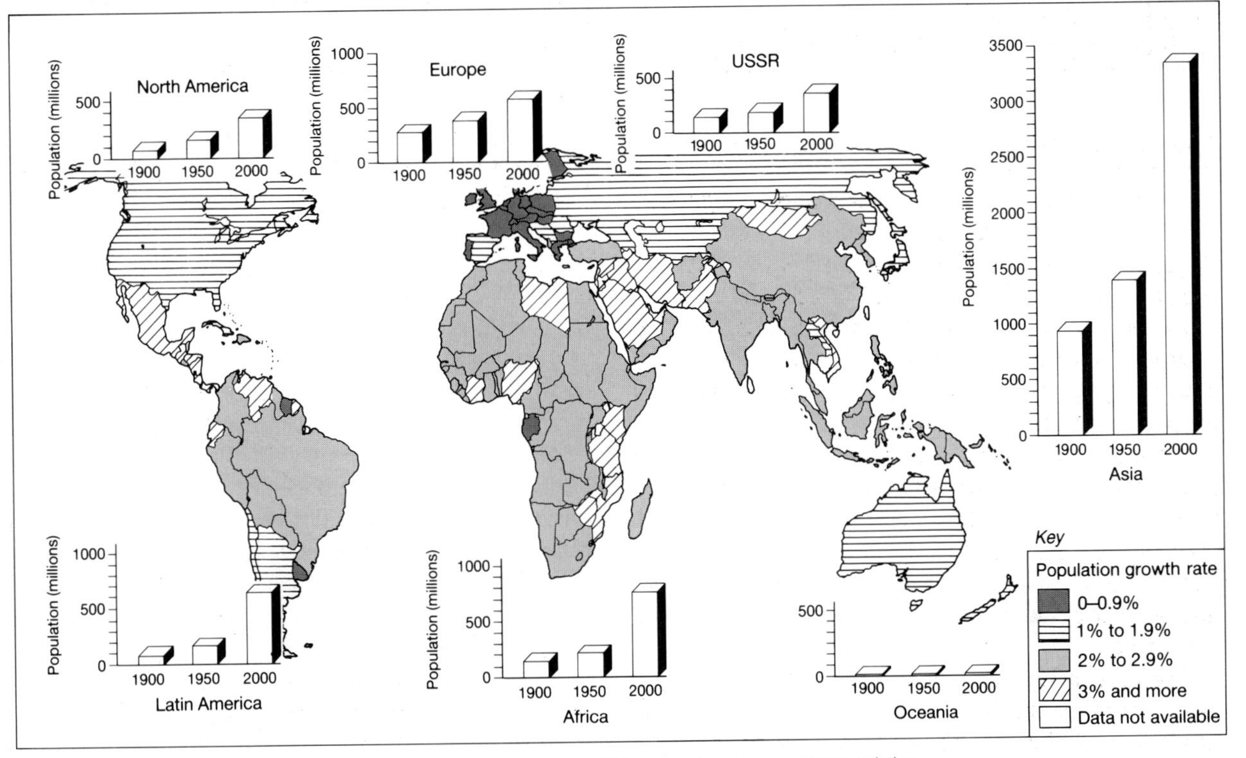

1.8 Population growth. This graphic illustrates the differences in growth rates of different regions by comparing population in 1900 and1950 with projected population in 2000.

as 44% in some less developed countries), and these children will in due course start families of their own. Even if the birth rate falls, world population is set to increase for the next 50 years, because the next generation of parents are already born.

Measuring population change

There are three factors which influence population change: the number of births over a given period of time (**fertility**), the number of deaths over the same period (**mortality**), and the number of persons moving in or out of the area (**migration**).

The **crude birth rate** is the number of live births per thousand people in one year; it is simply the ratio between the number of live births and the total population (usually a mid-year estimate). The crude birth rate is easy to calculate but it cannot always be used to compare countries since it does not take into account the effect of age structure (relative proportions of young and old people) on birth rates. The crude birth rate also cannot reveal any differences in the frequency of births among different reproductive age groups. To overcome this difficulty **fertility ratios** are more commonly used when comparing countries (see page 10). The **total fertility ratio** is calculated by dividing the number of children under 3 by the number of women between the ages of 15 and 44 years (childbearing age). This calculation gives a figure of 1.9 for Europe and 6.3 for Africa.

The **crude death rate** is the most widely used index of mortality; it is simply the number of deaths per thousand inhabitants in one year. It also takes no account of age structure and is therefore of limited use. Other indicators of mortality which are commonly used to compare countries are the **infant mortality rate** and the **average life expectancy at birth**. The infant mortality rate is the number of deaths of infants under one year old per thousand live births. It is a good indicator of the quality of health services and is usually the first mortality rate to be reduced when health services improve. Average life expectancy is the number of years people are expected to live. It is less at birth than after the first year because of infant mortality but it is a better measure of mortality than crude death rate because it is not affected by the age structure of the population.

Net migration is calculated by subtracting **emigration** from **immigration.** Total population change is arrived at by subtracting deaths from births (natural increase) and adding net migration.

Civil registration systems which record births, deaths and marriages tend to be much less reliable than national censuses. The problems of recording births and deaths in remote areas of developing countries, where a high proportion of the population is illiterate, are considerable. Many countries are attempting to improve civil registration with the help of the United Nations but censuses and sample surveys are likely to be the main source of **vital statistics** for some time to come.

Patterns of Fertility and Mortality

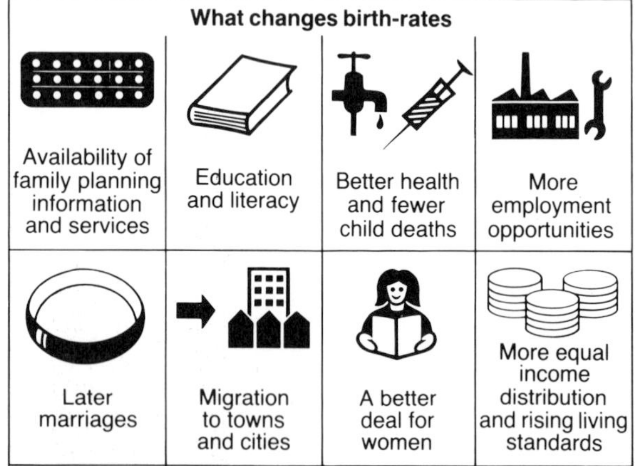

1.9 What changes birth rates: the main factors which promote a decline in fertility rates.

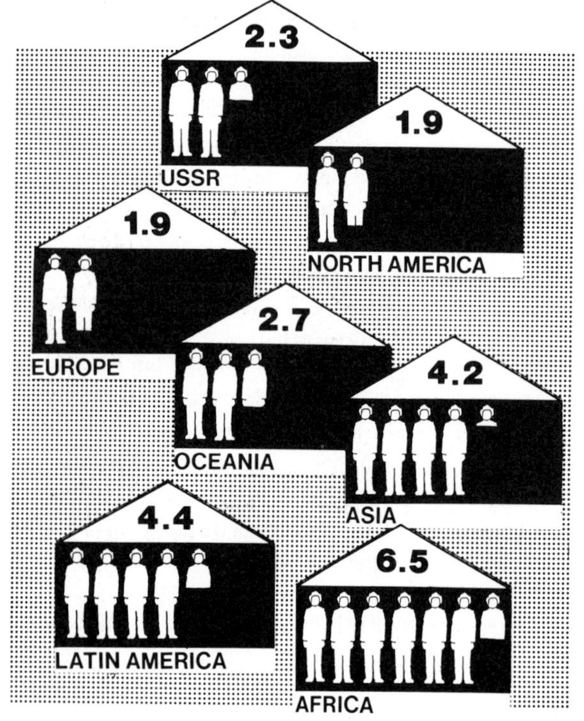

Fertility

In 1988 crude birth rates ranged from 55 per thousand in North Yemen to 10 per thousand in West Germany and Italy, with a world average of about 28 per thousand. Countries with a high birth rate (often over 40 per thousand) are found in parts of tropical Latin America, throughout Africa, much of southern Asia and the Middle East. Countries with a low birth rate (less than 20 per thousand) are found in Europe and North America, Australia, New Zealand, Japan and the USSR.

The crude birth rate is one characteristic which is usually a good indicator of whether a country is developed or developing. Most developed countries have seen a progressive reduction in birth rates since the late nineteenth century. There have been periods of higher birth rates such as that after the Second World War but the trend has been clearly downward. Developing countries have also seen a fall in birth rates in this century but the gap between the birth rates of developed and developing countries is still very wide. The crude birth rate for India, for example, fell from 47 per thousand in 1920 to 33 per thousand in 1988 but this was still more than three times that of West Germany.

In developed countries a wide variety of social and economic influences have induced a general decline in fertility. The main factors promoting this decline are probably later marriage, increased use of birth control methods, the desire for higher economic status, and the rise in status of women (1.9).The deliberate limitation of family size in developed countries is influenced by a range of factors including income, social class, education, race, religion, and economic prosperity. These social and economic differences can lead to regional patterns of fertility.

An examination of crude birth rates for the UK underlines the difficulty in predicting birth rates. Contrary to official predictions the birth rate fell steadily between 1964 and 1977, and in 1973 it was lower than the death rate. This resulted in a fall in UK population, in 1974, for the first time in recent decades. The introduction of the contraceptive pill in 1963 and the abortion act of 1968 were important factors in this decline.

Comparisons of birth rates ignore the importance of age structure. For example, China and Dominica both have a crude birth rate of 21 per thousand but the total fertility ratios and age structures are very different: China has a total fertility ratio of 2.4, 29% of the population under age 15 years and 6% over 65 years; while Dominica has a total fertility ratio of 3.0, 40% of the population under 15 years and 7% over 65 years of age.

1.10 illustrates the average number of children per family across the world, which is an indicator of fertility ratios.

1.10 How many children? The average number of children per family across the world illustrates the differences in fertility rates.

Mortality

Mortality differs from fertility as a component of population change in that it tends to be more stable and predictable. In most parts of the world, death rates are lower than birth rates thus leading to population growth. The decline in death rates throughout the world in this century has been largely responsible for the rise in world population (1.11).

The decline in death rates has resulted in dramatic changes in life expectancy. In 1900 life expectancy (world average) was about 30 years of age, by 1950 it was 46 years and by 1988 it had increased to 63 years. The life expectancy of 63 years in 1988 hides a difference between the developed and developing world. The developed world's average life expectancy in 1988 was 73 years while the developing world had an average life expectancy of 60 years (13 years difference). This difference has narrowed significantly since the beginning of the century (1.12).

In 1988 crude death rates ranged from 2 per thousand in Qatar to 28 per thousand in The Gambia with a world average of 10 per thousand (world average death rate in 1960 was about 18 per thousand). Countries with above average death rates are found mainly in West and Middle Africa and southern Asia. A high infant mortality rate in many of these countries accounts for up to one-third of the deaths. Lower than average mortality rates are found in North and South America, Europe, Oceania and East Asia.

Improved medical facilities and campaigns against infectious diseases have lowered death rates throughout the world. A lowering of infant mortality and consequent rise in life expectancy have been achieved worldwide but this has not always gone hand in hand with an improved quality of life. There is some debate about the extent to which improved standards of living have lowered death rates but most observers agree that public policy (e.g. providing public health care and organising campaigns) is effective in reducing death rates. Public policy aimed at lowering fertility has met with less success. The lowering of death rates means that there are more people to support and in some countries population growth has outstripped resources and economic growth, creating a further set of problems for their governments.

In developed countries the death rate is unlikely to fall further because the percentage of the population over 60 is increasing (an ageing population). Places such as Hong Kong, South Korea, Iceland and Puerto Rico have very low death rates because their populations are youthful (a high percentage of young people) with rising living standards. With world variations in death rates becoming less, fertility now appears to be the main determinant of future population growth.

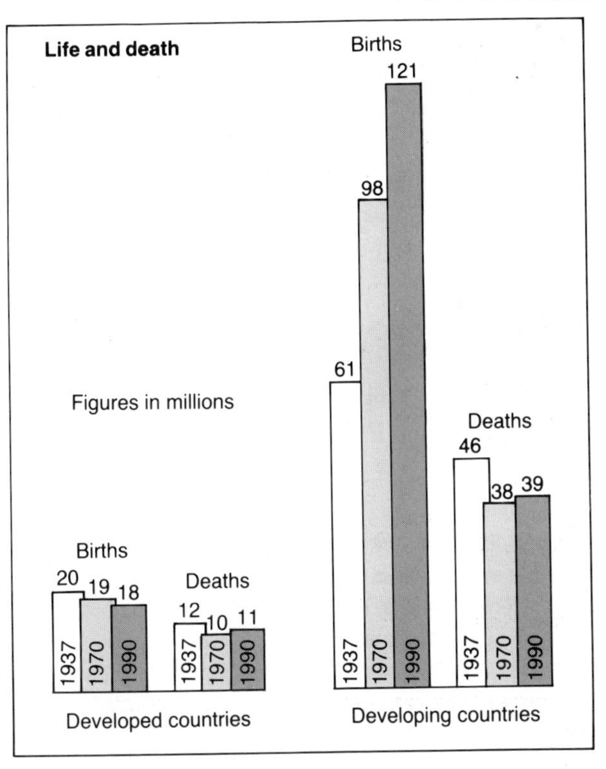

1.11 Life and death. Death rates have been consistently below birth rates in both developed and developing countries. But a comparison of birth and death rates between 1937 and 1970 shows that while both rates fell in developed countries the birth rate increased substantially in developing countries.

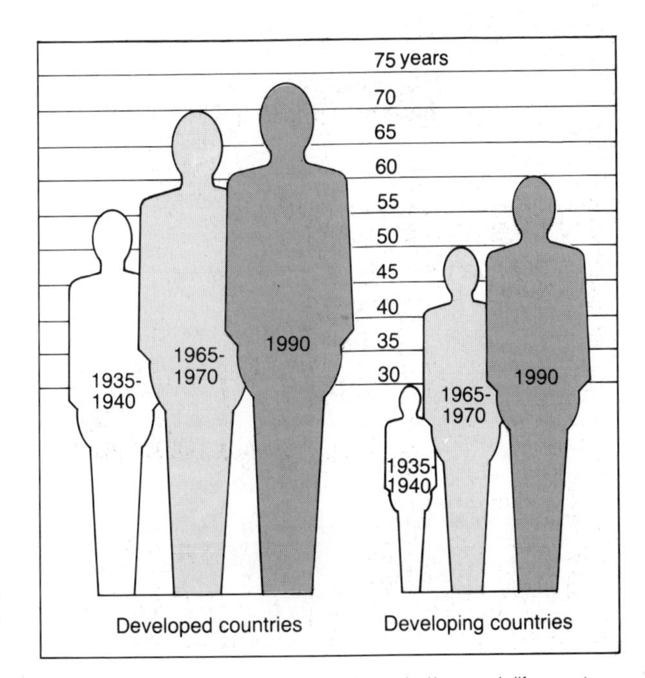

1.12 Life expectancy. This diagram shows the gradual increase in life expectancy, in both developed and developing countries, and the narrowing of the difference since 1935.

CHAPTER 1

Differential Mortality

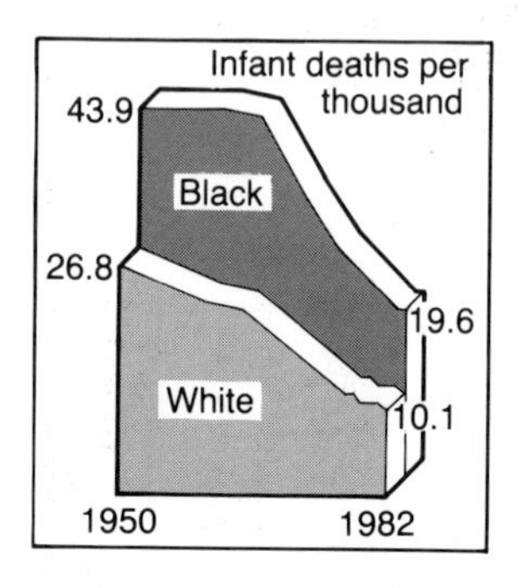

1.13 US discrimination at birth. As with overall mortality rates the infant mortality rates for blacks and whites in the US have fallen and although the rate for blacks is still significantly higher than that for whites the gap between the two rates is narrowing.

Although death rates are becoming more equal on a global level, there are still disparities within countries, determined by social class, economic status, racial group, and location of residence (urban or rural). In both developed and developing countries the poorest and most seriously underprivileged groups of people are forced to live in the lowest-quality and most overcrowded housing, and they are least able to afford a balanced diet and proper medical care. They are therefore more likely to develop illness and die. In the United States the black population has a higher death rate at all ages than the white population (1.13), and in the UK there is a close correlation between social class and mortality.

The gap between the death rates of blacks and whites in the United States has narrowed significantly in recent years and this has ruled out biological differences as the cause of **differential mortality**. It is obvious now that social, economic and environmental factors are the main causes.

In most countries the death rate of males is higher than that of females at almost every age. There are, however, exceptions: in countries where the status of women is low and they do much of the manual labour, their death rates are comparable and in some cases higher than for males.

Environmental causes of differential mortality are difficult to isolate. However, factors such as quality of water, frequent catastrophic events (such as floods, earthquakes and hurricanes), climatic variability, and levels of solar radiation all affect health and mortality. In the UK, January death rates are usually significantly higher than those of the summer months because of deaths from influenza and the cold weather. Many of these winter deaths are of elderly people or others whose health is already fragile.

Causes of death

Causes of death can be divided into two broad categories: **exogenetic** (environmental, i.e. from accidents or illness brought on by external factors) and **endogenetic** (degenerative, i.e. from illness that is not infectious). The environmental causes can be

1.14 Leading causes of death in developed and developing countries

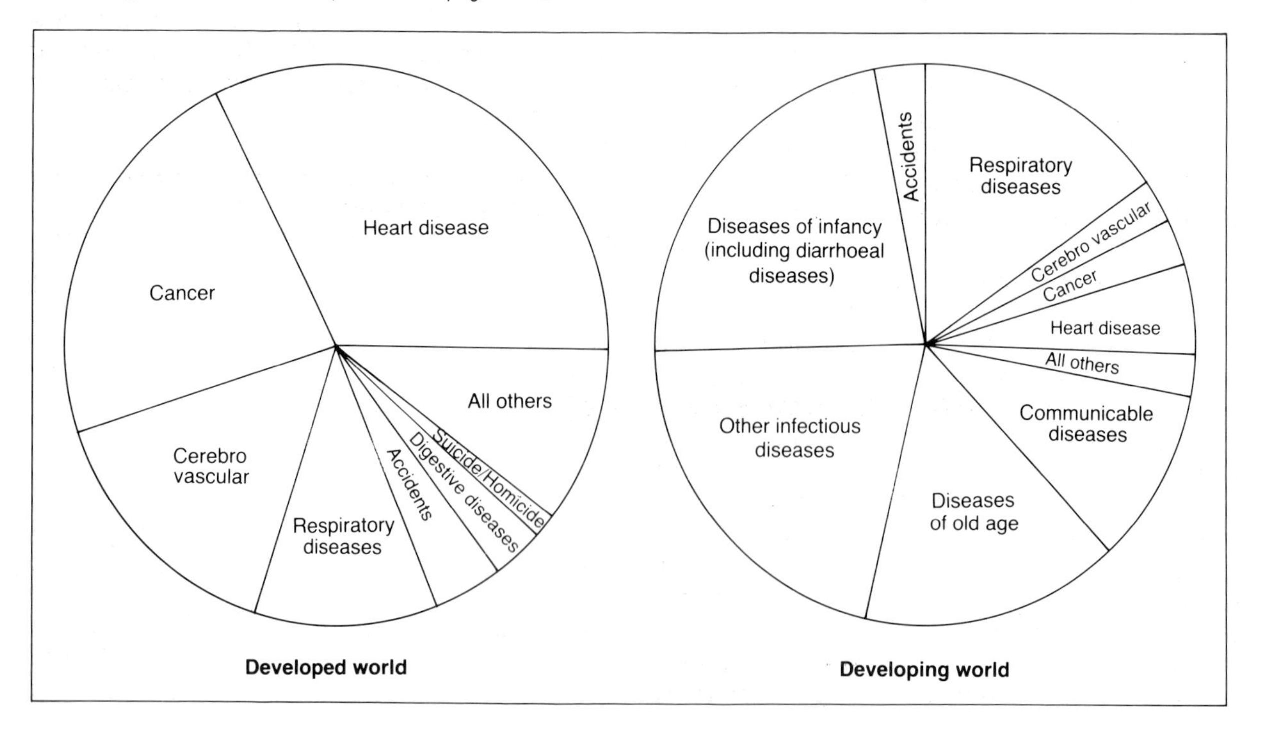

1.15 Cancer, the worldwide killer. The map illustrates that although cancer is a worldwide killer the death rate from cancer is much higher in the developed countries, where over half the deaths from cancer occur.

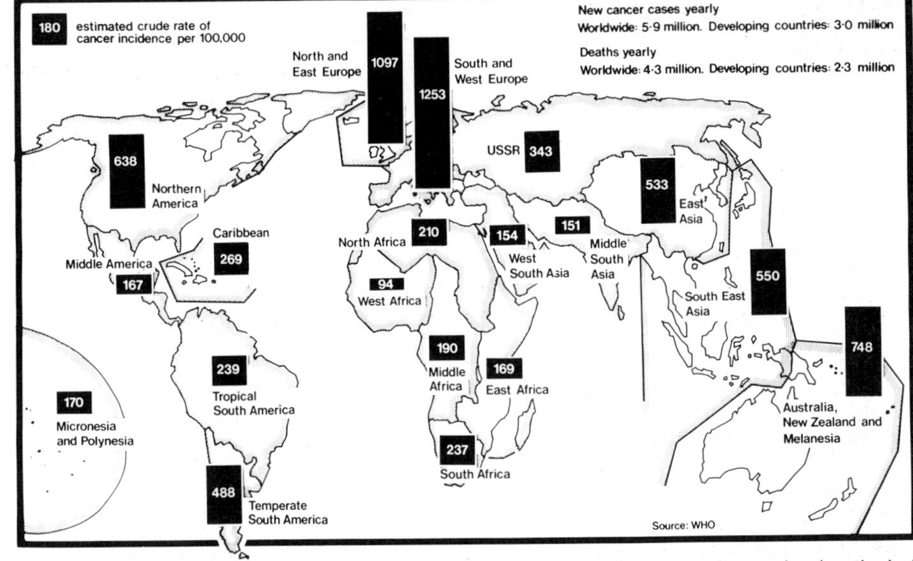

as diverse as illnesses brought on by contaminated food and water supply and inadequate housing. Infectious diseases such as malaria, typhoid and dysentery also fall into this category. In developed countries, where many of these infectious diseases are under control, degenerative causes of death are most common. Heart disease, cancer, pulmonary and vascular diseases fall into this category (1.14).

In developing countries with higher death rates many deaths are due to exogenetic causes but as death rates become lower these causes become less significant. The effectiveness of treatments and controls on respiratory and infectious diseases has been a major factor in lowering death rates worlwide. One hundred years ago about 30% of all deaths in the UK were due to infectious diseases, now this figure is about 0.5%. However the percentage of deaths from heart disease, cerebrovascular disease and cancer has risen to about 75% of all deaths in the UK. Historical comparisons can be misleading as some causes of death have only been diagnosed in the twentieth century and were formerly unknown. Even common influenza was only recognised as a disease in the 1880s.

Cancer, a worldwide killer, accounts for a greater proportion of deaths in developed countries than in developing countries, but in both the number of deaths from the disease is rising (1.15). Cancer is more common in middle and old age and therefore, as life expectancies rise in developing countries, cancer deaths will account for a greater proportion of the total. Increased tobacco smoking in the developing countries is also likely to lead to an increase in the deaths from lung cancer. Changes in diet may also be responsible for the increase in the number of deaths from cancer. It is thought that a diet rich in fatty and processed foods and low in fibre can increase the liklihood of developing cancer.

Deaths from diarrhoeal diseases are much more common in developing countries than developed countries, while respiratory diseases are more common in developed countries (particularly north-west Europe). These differences probably reflect differences in climate and sanitary conditions as well as economic level. Within regions the deaths from certain categories of disease can vary significantly: for example, diarrhoeal disease accounts for 3–30% of deaths in South American countries.

Although there is a correlation between life expectancy in a country and its economic wealth (per capita GNP: gross national product) the relationship is not as direct as one might expect (1.16). Some poor countries have achieved high life expectancies by devoting a large proportion of limited resources to improving health and lowering death rates. China has a life expectancy of about 66 years and a per capita GNP of only $300 (1988) while Saudi Arabia has a life expectancy of 61 years and a per capita GNP of $6930.

1.16 GNP and life expectancy correlated. This graph shows the relationship between life expectancy and gross national product (wealth).

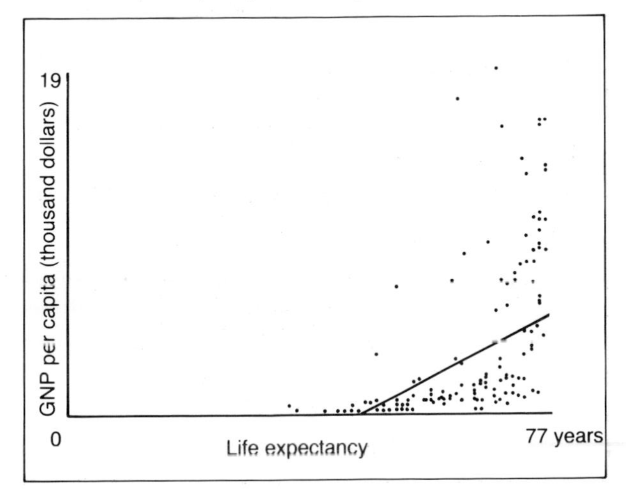

Questions

Q WORLD POPULATION DISTRIBUTION / WORLD POPULATION CHANGE

1 (a) Explain the difference between population distribution and population density.
(b) Describe the distribution of the world's population.
(c) What factors influence the distribution of population?
(d) Explain why reference has to be made to the past in order to understand present-day population distribution.
(e) Describe the growth in world population since 1650.
(f) Look at diagram 1. Describe change in the share of world population between 1900 and the projection for 2000.
(g) Explain what is meant by the term fertility ratio.
(h) Why is infant mortality rate a good indicator of the quality of health service?
(i) The following extract is from a letter to the *Scotsman* newspaper dated 1 August 1974.

> The figures given in 'The Scotsman' today for the population of Nigeria do not make sense. The reported census figures include total population 1963 - 55 million; 1973 - 79.76 million; Northern Nigeria 1963 - 29.8 million;1973 - 51.38 million. This implies an increase in the Northern Region of over 20 million in ten years. If 15 million northerners in 1963 were female and 10 million of these were of child bearing age then each woman would require to have two children a year (assuming no net immigration and the female population of child bearing age remained constant). This is almost biologically impossible.
>
> I lived in Nigeria at the time of the 1963 census. It was rumoured at the time that the 1963 census figures for the North were exaggerated in order to secure political representation for the North. If these figures were inaccurate as rumoured then the present figures become even harder to believe.

Explain why population data from some countries may often be incomplete or inaccurate.
(j) Make a list of factors which cause problems for those collecting population data.

Diagram 1

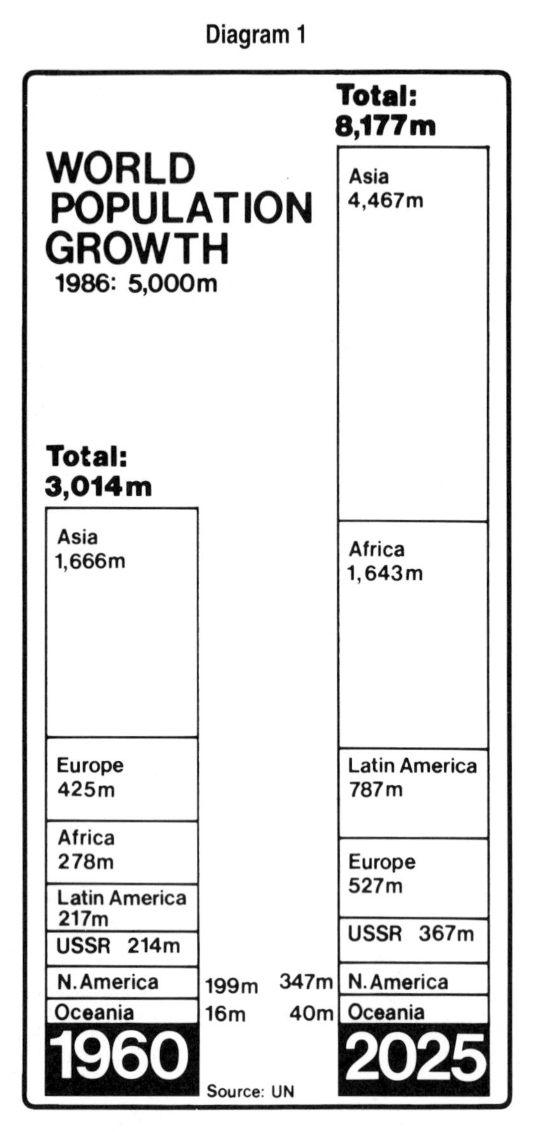

Q PATTERNS OF FERTILITY AND MORTALITY / DIFFERENTIAL MORTALITY

2 (a) Describe the differences in fertility rates between developed and developing countries.
(b) List the factors which are promoting a general decline in fertility.
(c) Why is crude birth rate a very limited measurement when comparing the fertility and population growth potential of countries?
(d) Why have death rates fallen steadily over the last 30 years?
(e) Describe the trends in life expectancy since 1940 and give reasons for this trend.

(f) What is meant by the term differential mortality?

(g) Why can biological differences be ruled out as a factor in differential infant mortality between blacks and whites in the United States?

(h) What is the difference between exogenetic and endogenetic causes of death?

(i) Account for the different causes of death in developed and developing countries.

(j) Look at cartoon 2.
What is the cartoonist saying about population policies in developing countries?

Cartoon 2

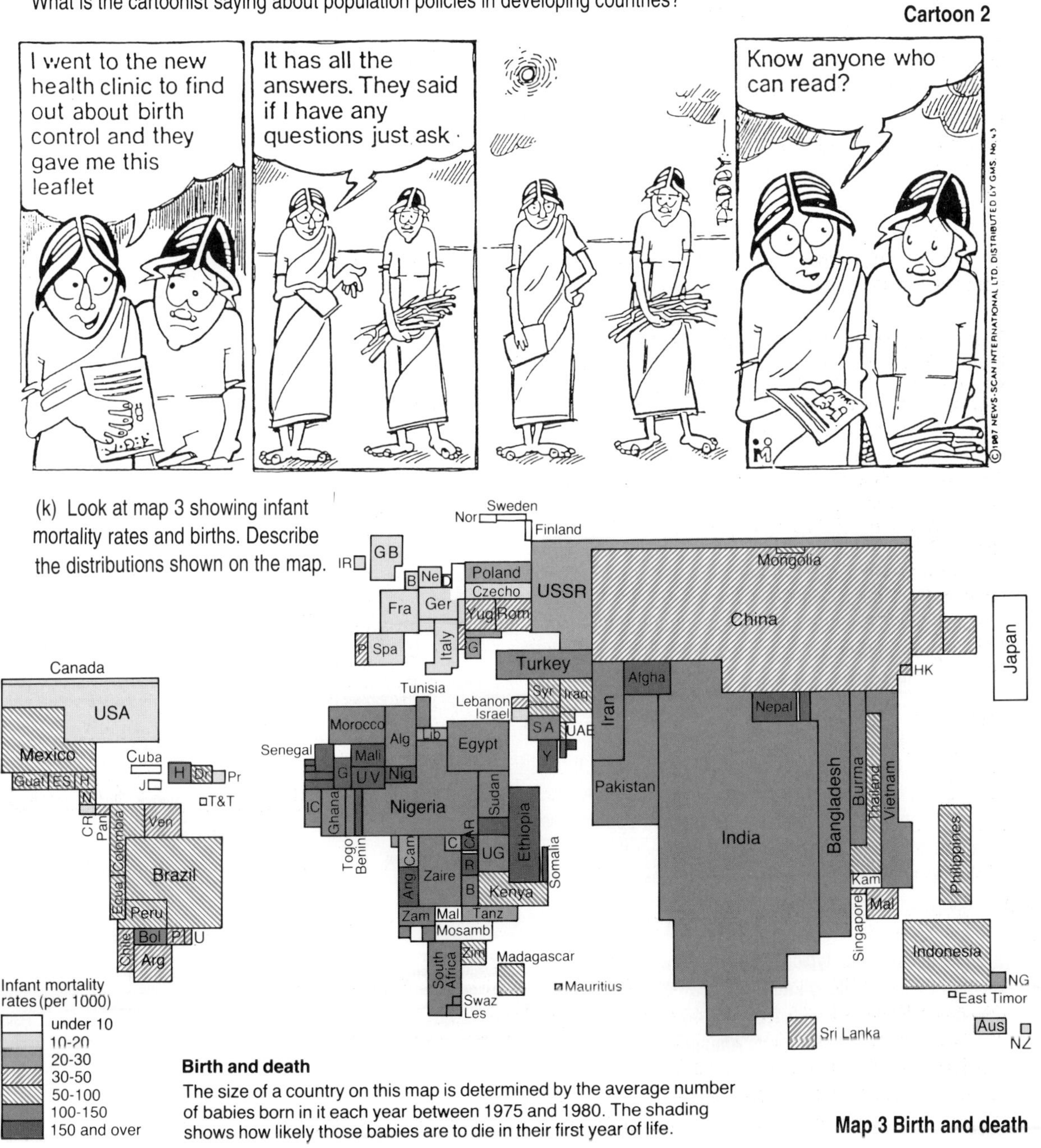

(k) Look at map 3 showing infant mortality rates and births. Describe the distributions shown on the map.

Birth and death

The size of a country on this map is determined by the average number of babies born in it each year between 1975 and 1980. The shading shows how likely those babies are to die in their first year of life.

Map 3 Birth and death

CHAPTER 1

Population Composition

The term **population composition**, or **population structure**, is used to describe population characteristics which can be measured, however inadequately. This tends to mean the aspects of population for which census data are available. Normally studies of population composition refer to the **age structure, sex composition, occupation structure** and **ethnic composition.** Sometimes a distinction is drawn between those aspects which are **innate**, such as sex, age and race, and those aspects which are **acquired** during life, such as marriage, family size and occupation.This section will deal mainly with age structure and sex composition as an introduction to population composition.

Age structure

The term **age structure** refers to the number of males and females in different age groups in a given population. The age structure of any population is a result of population change over the lifetime of the oldest member of the population and it is a demographic history of a population over that time period.

The age structure of a population is of considerable economic and social importance because almost every aspect of life is affected by age: for example, economic and social activities, political interests, mobility, and military service. The size, proportion and composition of the **economically active** labour force can be determined from the age structure. The type and range of health and welfare services required by a given population can also be inferred from its age structure.

Age structures are often analysed by comparing proportions of the three main **age groups** in the population:

- **infants and adolescents** (0–14 years),
- **adults** (15–64 years),
- **the aged** (65 and over).

The proportion of the total population in each of these three groups gives a quick and generalised picture of the age structure. Comparing the age structures of different countries' populations by this method shows that they fall into three general types.

1. A **developed type** where typically children make up 22% of the population, adults 64%, and the aged 14%. Example: Western European countries.
2. A **transitional type** with typically 36% children, 59% adults, and 5% aged. Example: many Latin American countries.
3. A **less developed type** with typically 45% children, 52% adults, and 3% aged. Example: many African countries.

The lowest proportion of adults is to be found in the less developed type where around 50% of the population is economically inactive. This is because these populations are youthful (they have a high proportion of children). This creates a considerable burden on the working population.

The economically inactive group is also growing in developed countries but in this case it is because populations are ageing as life expectancy increases. The increase in the proportion of the population over 65 years of age is a comparatively recent phenomena as 1.17 shows.

Age indices are sometimes used to illustrate the relationship between the three age groups. The **dependency ratio** is the most common age index; it is a ratio of the economically inactive population to the economically active and is calculated as follows:

$$\text{Dependency ratio} = \frac{\%\ \text{children} + \%\ \text{aged}}{\%\ \text{adults}}$$

The following are a selection of dependency ratios:
Switzerland 0.45, Brazil 0.67, Tanzania 1.04.
This means, for example, that for every adult in Tanzania there are on average 1.04 dependants to support.

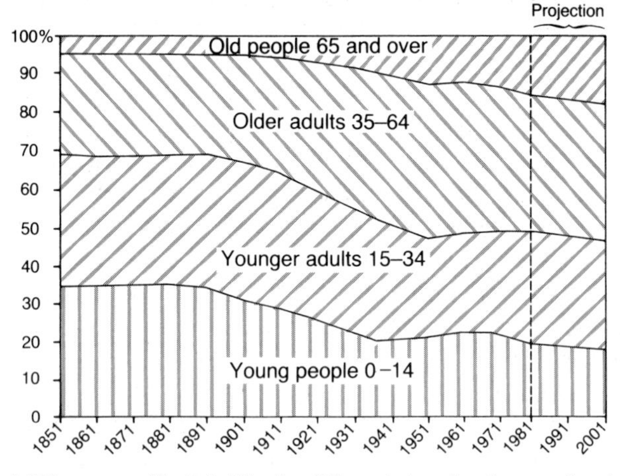

1.17 Age groups of the United Kingdom. This graph shows how the proportion of the major age groups has changed since 1851.

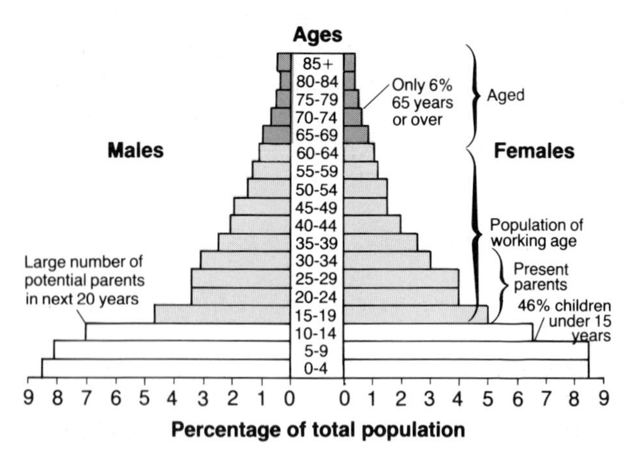

1.18 Population pyramid: Bangladesh. This pyramid, which is typical for many developing countries, shows that 46% of the population are children.

Population pyramids

Age structure can be studied in more detail by means of **population pyramids** (1.18). These are graphs in which a central vertical axis is divided into years or groups of years, usually five-year age groups. On either side of this vertical axis are horizontal axes which show the numbers (or percentages) of males and females in the different age groups. (Pyramids constructed using the percentage method are easier to compare.) Conventionally males are shown to the left of the horizontal axis and females to the right.

Population pyramids illustrate the age and sex compositions of a population at a given time and they can be used to derive a great deal of information about population change in the recent past. The pyramid can reveal changes in birth and death rates, the impact of migration, and events such as epidemics and wars.

Three basic types of population pyramid can be distinguished.

1. **Stationary**. If a population has relatively unchanging birth and death rates over a long time its population pyramid will be regular and tapering. 1.19a has a wide base indicating a high birth rate. The gentle slope to the apex indicates a mid-range death rate.
2. **Progressive pyramid**. If the birth rate increases from year to year the population type will become **progressive** and the pyramid will widen at the base. The sharply tapered point indicates that death rates are still relatively high (1.19b).
3. **Regressive pyramid**. A consistent decline in birth rates usually accompanied by lowering mortality rates will result in this type. The pyramid is bell shaped with a narrow base (1.19c). In this example the lowering of the death rate has not yet had an impact on the apex of the pyramid, which will widen with time.

Composite pyramid. Changes in birth and death rates will alter the shape of the population pyramid and result in a composite pyramid which will display attributes of two or more of the basic types. The composite example shown in 1.19d illustrates a population that had a period of declining birth rate followed by an increase in the birth rate. This results in a pyramid which is regressive in its upper part and progressive at its base. This type was typical of many developed countries after the Second World War. When a country has a long-established pattern of low birth and death rates, the bell-shape becomes quite wide at the top indicating the high proportion of aged people.

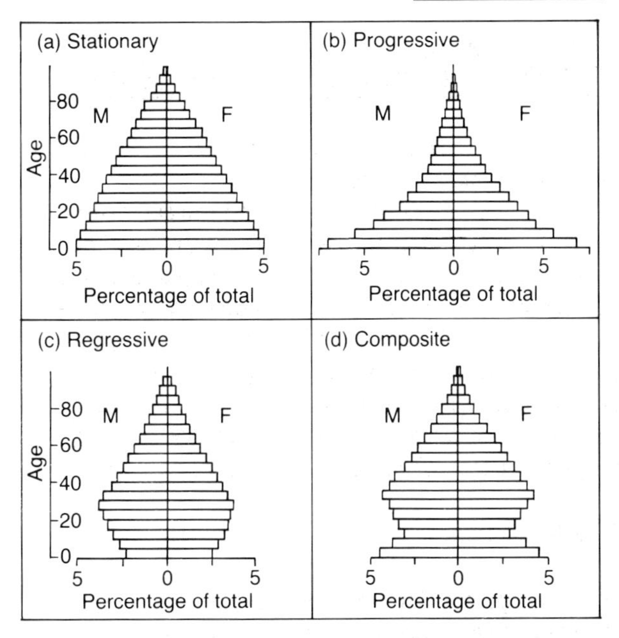

1.19 Types of population pyramid

Sex composition

The sex ratio of a population is usually expressed as the number of males per 100 females.

As with other mammals, human populations typically generate more male than female births. In developed countries there are usually between 104 and 106 male births to every 100 female births. Male stillbirths also outnumber those of females but improved pre-natal care is reducing the number of deaths at birth and consequently the male preponderance at birth is increasing slightly in developed countries.

There is some debate about whether male preponderance at birth is due to biological or social factors. Some social scientists suggest that in many societies families tend to be completed on the arrival of a male child and this could create the disparity. In developed countries this disparity in numbers at birth is gradually eliminated by about the age of 30, because male mortality is higher than female mortality at all ages. This results in a sex ratio of 94.2 (in 1985) for developed countries, projected to rise to 95.6 by 2000. The loss of males in the Second World War accounts for some of the disparity between the sexes. For example, the sex ratio in the USSR was only 78 in 1950 but this rose to 90 by 1985. However, much of the disparity is explained by the greater life expectancy of women in developed countries. This sex differential in mortality appears to be widening rather than narrowing.

In many countries of the developing world the sex ratios are reversed. This difference is probably due to the inferior position of females in these societies, which results in higher female mortality. Some of the higher mortality can be accounted for by high levels of maternal mortality (deaths of women during child-birth), but much of it is due to the hard physical labour which most women undertake in societies dominated by men. The sex ratio of developing countries in 1985 was 104.3 and this is projected to decline to 103.2 in 2000.

The sex ratio for any population is influenced by three main factors: the preponderance of male births, different mortality of the sexes, and sex-selective migrations (see 1.26 on page 23).

CHAPTER 1

The Demographic Transition

Although all theories of population evolution are flawed, the most useful model of this type is the so-called **demographic transition model**. This model suggests that any population passes through a series of stages as it develops from a 'primitive' agrarian society to an 'advanced' urban–industrial economy. The four stages of the demographic transition model are based on the pattern of population changes that took place in Europe between about 1700 and the present. The purely European basis for this model is one flaw in its universal application. During the period from 1700 Europe experienced changes in society and economy – moving toward an industrialised and urbanised society – which the model assumes are taking or will take place in other parts of the world.

The change from high birth and death rates to low birth and death rates over four stages is shown in 1.20a.

Stage 1 the 'primitive' society, is characterised by high and fluctuating birth and death rates, over 30 per thousand. Not even the most isolated of countries fits into this category today as death rates are falling in all parts of the world. This 'primitive' demographic regime is characterised by a slow or intermittent growth in population. In Britain this situation lasted until the mid eighteenth century.

Stage 2 represents the early expanding societies which still have high birth rates but have falling death rates, which leads to a rapidly increasing population. The death rate has been lowered by improved medical care and living standards but birth rates remain high because there hasn't been time for a cultural change which would bring down fertility rates. A danger for countries in this stage is that their population can increase faster than their wealth and thus they become poorer. In Britain this stage lasted for some 130 years until approximately 1880. Many developing countries are in this category today, with a marked excess of births over deaths. Examples include Mali with crude birth and death rates of 50 per thousand and 22 per thousand respectively and Afghanistan with crude birth and death rates of 48 per thousand and 24 per thousand respectively.

Stage 3 represents late expanding societies in which death rates remain low and birth rates also begin to fall, leading to a fall in population growth rates. However the population is still rising: the transition to low growth or static population is not complete. Britain went through this stage between 1880 and 1940. Some other developed countries have just completed this stage: for example, Yugoslavia with a crude birth rate of 15 per thousand and a crude death rate of 9 per thousand, giving a natural increase of 0.6%; and New Zealand with a crude birth rate of 16 per thousand and a crude death rate of 8 per thousand, giving a natural increase of 0.8%. Some developing countries are just entering this stage with a natural increase of around 2.0%. For example, Brazil with a crude birth rate of 28 per thousand and a crude death rate of 8 per thousand, giving a natural increase of 2%.

Stage 4 represents low stable or mature demographic societies which have low birth and death rates with very little difference between the two rates. This means that population growth is slight and in a few cases population numbers are in decline. With the exception of Japan, all the countries currently in this stage are European or are countries (such as the USA) that were settled by Europeans. In some countries which have just completed the demographic transition, population is still rising modestly as large youthful populations grow up to childbearing age. Other countries, such as Britain, which completed the transition around 1940, have a relatively stable population with periods of slight growth alternating with periods of population decline. In 1988 Britain had a crude birth rate of 13 per thousand and a crude death rate of 12 per thousand.

The demographic transition is often illustrated by graphs showing the changes in birth and death rates through time (1.20a) but the pattern typically illustrated is that of European countries which have completed the transition. Many developing countries have shown a different pattern of population change. Death rates have plummeted in a short time because of improvements in medical services, health care, hygiene and diet, as well as systematic campaigns to eradicate contagious diseases. Birth rates, however, have not fallen as fast and this has brought about rapid population growth. Population growth rates are higher than they were during the eighteenth and nineteenth centuries, when European countries went through the transition, and they are applied to a much larger base population.

It took some time in Britain before family sizes fell, mainly as a result of improvements in the economic and social status of women. Other changes in Britain encouraged the reduction in birth rates: for example, the state took over, from the family, the role of supporting people in old age (thereby removing the need for people to have children to support them); and it became illegal to use child labour to support the family.

With the reduction in birth and death rates the structure of the population changed. In 1871 England and Wales had a 'youthful' population with only a small proportion of elderly people, while by 1971 the population had a more significant proportion of elderly people and a smaller proportion of children (1.20d).

Developing countries have a difficult task in matching the European drop in birth rate because there is often great cultural resistance to change. Religious and social values which encourage people to have large families are difficult to influence. China has made significant progress by instigating a programme

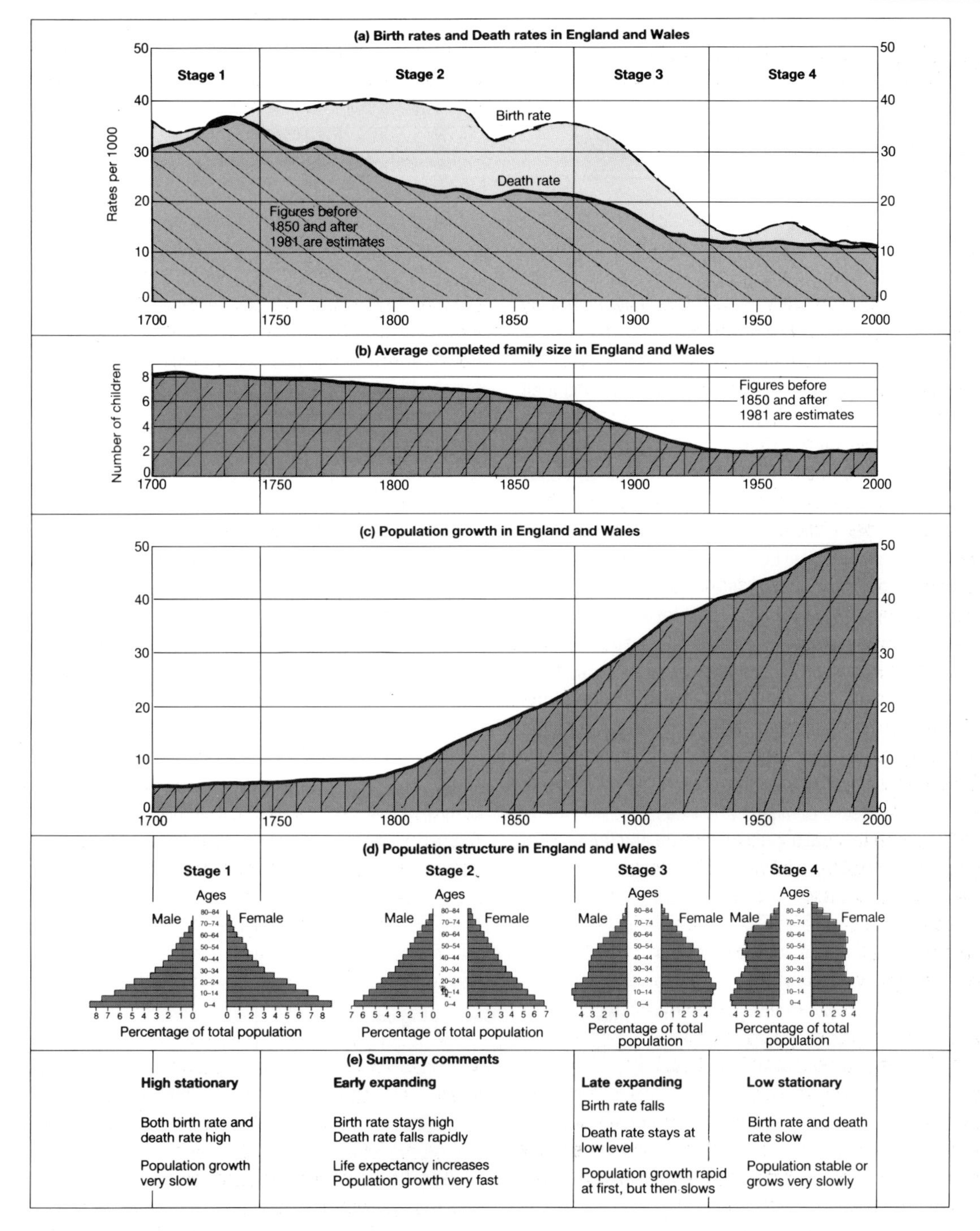

of contraception, education and communal pressure. But even in China there has been considerable resistance to family planning, and government programmes have had to be modified to maintain popular support. Other governments have found strong resistance to programmes of birth control, and consequently birth rates in most developing countries are declining very slowly, but they are falling.

1.20 The demographic transition in England and Wales. The birth and death rates for England and Wales trace the path through the demographic transition from an agrarian society with high birth and death rates to an industrialised society with low birth and death rates. The graph showing population illustrates how the different stages in the demographic transition influence population growth rates.

CHAPTER 1

Consequences of the Demographic Transition

There is a major problem in that the countries currently undergoing the demographic transition contain most of the world's population, and the population growth experienced by these countries is much faster than European countries experienced during their transition.

Concern about population growth is nothing new. In 1798 Thomas Robert Malthus published the first edition of his 'Essay on the Principle of Population'. Malthus studied at Cambridge, became a Church of England curate in 1793 and in 1805 was appointed Professor of Political Economy (economics). The first edition of his essay grew out of his interests in economics, politics, and demography. In it Malthus suggested that food supply increased at an arithmetic rate while population tended to increase at geometric rate (1.21); and that therefore, if population growth was unchecked, it would outstrip food supply. As the amount of food available per person fell, Malthus suggested that the population would be checked by either voluntary action or 'natural checks' such as war, starvation and disease (which he called the 'positive checks of misery and vice').

His essay suggested that population growth and the cycle of

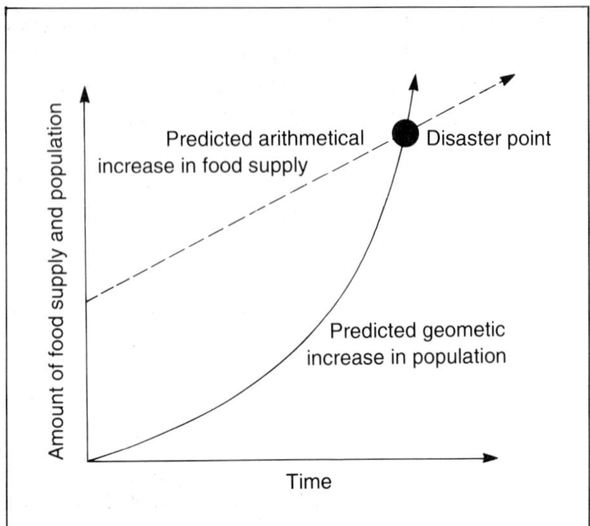

But the food to support the increase from the greater number will by no means be obtained with the same facility. Man is necessarily confined in room. When acre has been added to acre until all the fertile land is occupied, the yearly increase in food must depend upon the melioration of the land already in possession. This is a fund, which, from the nature of all sorts, instead of increasing, must be gradually diminishing,... It may be fairly pronounced, therefore, that considering the present average state of the earth, the means of subsistence under circumstances the most favourable to human industry, could not be made to increase faster than in an arithmetic ratio. (Malthus 1798)

1.21 Extract from 'Essay on the Principle of Population' by Thomas Malthus, 1798, and graph illustrating the limits to population growth

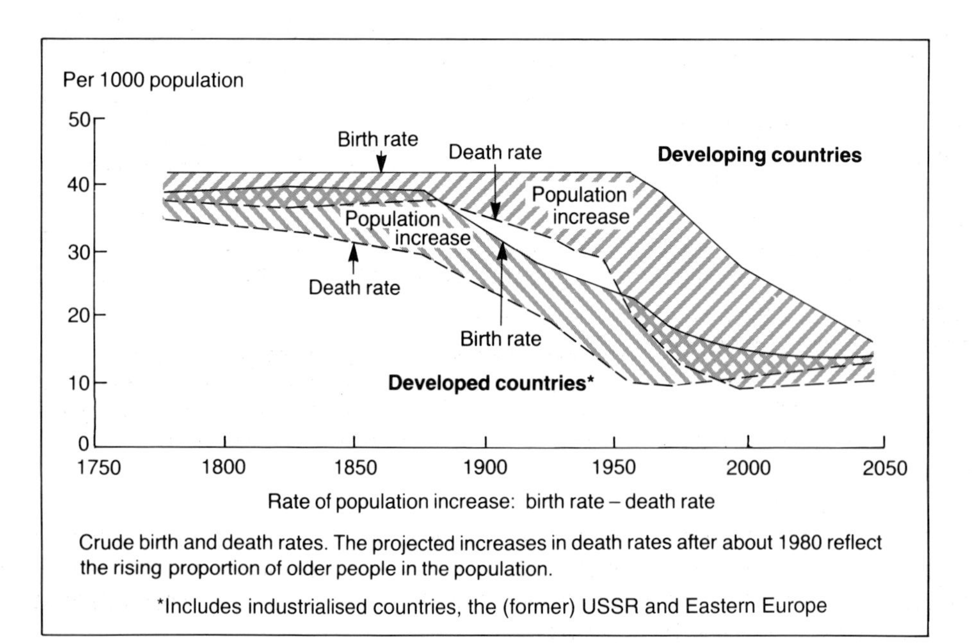

Crude birth and death rates. The projected increases in death rates after about 1980 reflect the rising proportion of older people in the population.

*Includes industrialised countries, the (former) USSR and Eastern Europe

1.22 The World Bank projection for the demographic transition. This indicates that the developing countries will not complete the demographic transition until 2050 and will have had to cope with a much larger population growth than did the developed countries.

poverty it sustained could be controlled by moral restraint and a strong economy. Some later academics have tended to take his model of population growth too literally and have accused him of undue pessimism. The enlarged second edition of his essay in 1803 gave a more detailed account of his views on population checks, backed up by some empirical evidence. His views on population growth were conditioned by the period he lived in, when Britain was moving from an agricultural to an industrial society. His essay therefore provides an insight into conditions during this transition and highlights the cultural factors of the time which had an influence on population growth.

Malthus was unable to foresee the technical and scientific advancements which have permitted agriculture in Britain to increase production at a greater than arithmetic rate. The drop in birth rate as Britain went through the demographic transition would also have surprised Malthus. In his day large families were the norm.

The rapid world population growth since 1940 led to fears of **overpopulation** (more people than the available resources can support) in the 1960s. By 1990 most projections for world population suggested that population growth will slow down by the year 2000. But growth rates in the developing countries will still be higher than in developed countries, and by 2100 the present developing countries could account for 86% of the world's population.

Some developing countries which are rich in resources do not see their population growth as the main problem facing them but seek greater progress with development. Although some developing countries have progressed from stage 2 to stage 3 of the demographic transition (1.22), others with growth rates of over 3% and limited resources may not be able to achieve a reduction in fertility before natural controls such as mass starvation significantly increase the death rate (see also page 30 'Population Projections and Policies').

The opening up of the New World in America relieved population pressure in Britain when population growth there was at its greatest, both because people migrated to the New World and also because it provided Britain with cheap imports of raw materials such as cotton. The countries of the developing world have to cope with faster population growth without an expansion in their resource base and without a migration escape route.

The demographic transition also has consequences for the developed world. Declining birth rates and rising life expectancy have led to an ageing population. In Britain, in 1900, those over 65 years old accounted for only 4.7% of the population; in 1990 they accounted for slightly over 15% and by 2040 they will probably account for 25% of the population. This ageing trend has significant implications for society in developed countries. The burden of state pensions will increase taxation on those of working age, and the cost of caring for an ageing population will rise significantly (1.23). Even with more women in work there is likely to be a shortage of people of working age. This shortage could be tempered by immigration from the rapidly growing developing nations, but this sort of solution is not likely to be popular.

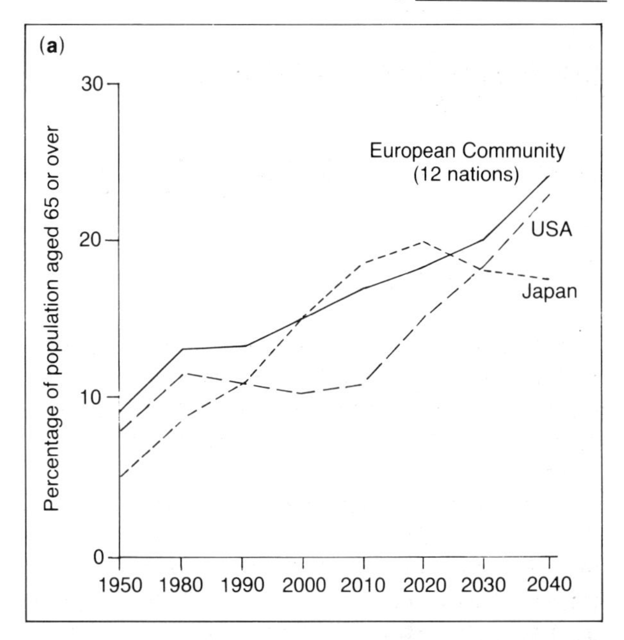

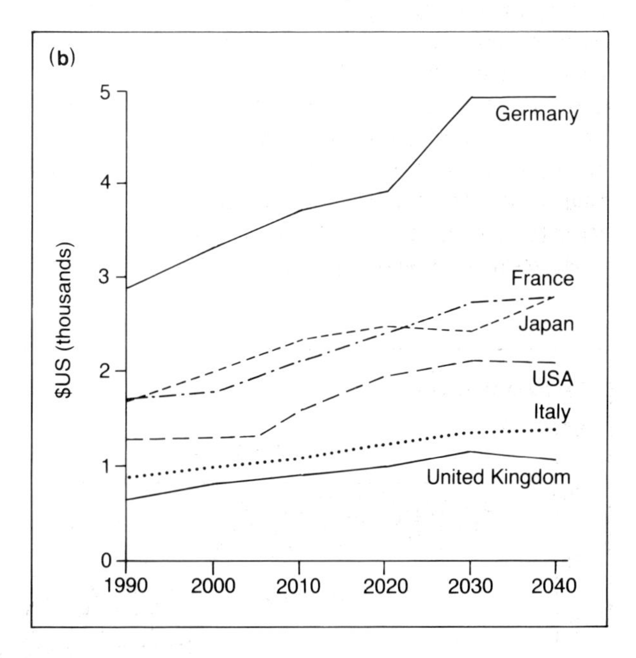

1.23 Grey future for Western populations. By 2040 the EC's population will have dropped by 30 million but the growing number of elderly people has serious economic implications for governments (a). Germany will have a four fold increase in pension costs if current projections are accurate (b).

CHAPTER 1

Migration

Migration is usually defined as being a movement of population involving a change of residence of a substantial duration. This definition excludes the constant movement of pastoral nomads or seasonal short-term movements such as transhumance (winter/summer movement), tourism or commuting. There might however be debate about how long a 'substantial duration' is and the study of migration is plagued by migration statistics which are calculated in different ways and using different methods of collection. Because of this, migration statistics have to be treated with a certain amount of caution.

The diversity of migrations in terms of duration, distance and organisation has resulted in a wide range of types. To simplify things, we will examine two main types: **international migration** which involves the crossing of national boundaries, and **internal migration** which is within a nation. These types will be looked at with reference to both **forced** and **voluntary migration.**

International and internal migrations are not necessarily different in terms of their causes or consequences but there is a specific terminology for international migration. **Emigration** means the departure from and **immigration** means the entry into a country to change permanent residence. The term 'permanent residence' in this context usually means more than one year.

Migration patterns can be selective in terms of both age and gender: apart from migration for retirement, most migration streams consist of young adults. The study of migration has thrown up generalistions which give a broad representation of migration patterns but these don't always hold true.

- In developed countries short-distance internal migrations are predominantly female.
- In developed countries long-distance internal migrations are predominantly male.
- In developing countries internal and international migrations are predominantly male.
- Professional classes in developed countries are more migratory than are skilled or unskilled workers.

Push and pull factors

The conditions which cause migration can involve both **'push'** and **'pull'** factors (1.24). The 'push' factors are adverse conditions in the sending area which stimulate individuals and families to change their place of residence. These factors could include: low income, poor employment prospects, housing shortages, inadequate social amenities, intolerance of political/racial/ethnic minorities, social upheaval/strife, natural disasters, adverse climatic conditions; and this list is by no means exhaustive. The 'pull' factors are real or imagined attractions of the destination and could include: high wages, employment opportunities, improved housing, wide range of amenities, tolerance of minorities, high standard of living, and physically attractive environment.

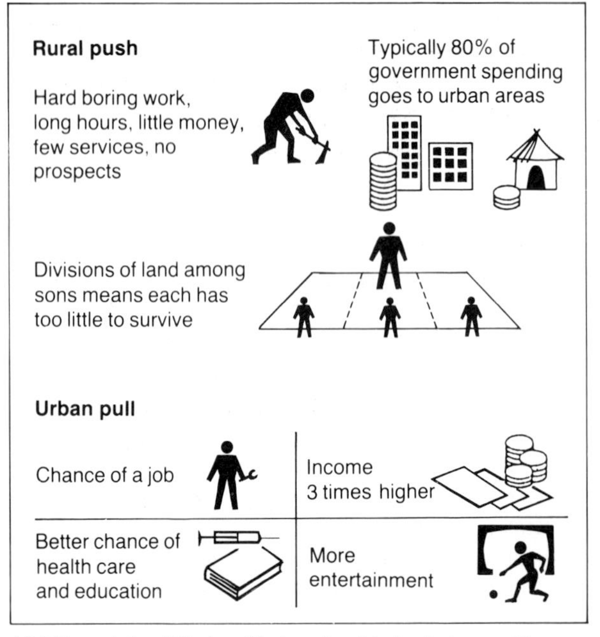

1.24 Why go to town? Push–pull factors at work in developing countries

Internal migration in the United States during the depression of the 1920s and 1930s illustrates 'push' and 'pull' factors. Poverty stricken farmers moved out of the 'Dust Bowl' states which had been ravaged by soil erosion and went to the growth areas of California, the Gulf coast and Great Lakes. Black workers from the 'Deep South' migrated northwards to try to find work in the industries of the northern cities, such as Detroit .

The 'push–pull' concept is particularly useful in studying internal migrations; international migration may involve a number of other factors and barriers, such as entry restrictions/quotas.

Internal migrations

Rural–urban migration. The most characteristic movement of people within their own country has been from rural to urban areas. The migrants move from areas of perceived deprivation to areas of perceived promise. During the Industrial Revolution in Europe, migration from country to town changed the character of society, and Europe's urban population now accounts for 75% of the total (in the UK 91% of the population lives in urban areas). In developing countries migration to large cities has long been a feature and in some countries this migration causes acute problems (such as large numbers of homeless people). The migration from rural to urban areas is not always direct and it is common for migrants to move in stages: for example, from farm to market town, to regional centre, to large city.

Counterurbanisation. In the most developed countries where urban populations are a very high proportion of the total, inter-urban migration and urban to rural migration are gaining in significance. This **counterurbanisation**, where people move away from cities to areas that appear more rural, is not simply a rejection of an urban lifestyle, because often these people still choose to live within range of urban areas for jobs and services. It is a way of relieving pressure on overcrowded cities and overused urban amenities. The rapid growth of major cities has created stress not only on the urban fabric (roads, houses, services, etc.) but also on urban society (poverty, vandalism, rising crime rates). The problems created by excessive rural–urban migration have stimulated governments throughout the world to adopt strategies to deal with them, for example (see also Chapter 3):

- New Towns in the United Kingdom, created to house the 'overspill' population from major urban areas;
- regional development in Greece and Italy;
- subsidies for industrial relocation in France, Sweden and the UK to move jobs (and therefore people) to areas outside cities;
- a tax on living in the capital city (e.g. in Seoul, South Korea) to encourage people to move out.

Migration in the UK

The British population is highly mobile with the average person making a move every seven years, usually over relatively short distances. Migration can have an impact on both the sending and the receiving areas. **Depopulation** in some rural areas of the United Kingdom has resulted in the closure of some local services such as schools and post offices, and the withdrawal of public transport. Even the migration of retired elderly to rural areas does little to improve services and in some popular retirement towns the imbalance between the level of social services required by the elderly and the income received from local taxes places a great strain on the resources of local government.

Migration in developing countries

Migration can also have an impact on both the sending and the receiving areas in developing countries. The influx of population in the cities of developing countries has posed great problems in housing, public transport, water supply, sewerage, and severe social problems (1.25). The shanty towns of makeshift homes, which grow up on the outskirts of developing cities, are evidence of rural–urban migration which failed to live up to its promise.

Many governments of developing countries believe that migration is the main reason for urban growth and have looked for ways to slow it down. However only the centrally planned nations such as China have attempted direct controls on migration and the effects of these schemes tend to be short lived. Tanzania on the other hand has concentrated on a programme of rural development in an attempt to persuade people to stay in their rural communities, rather than add to the overcrowded urban centres. The 1988 census showed a slowing down of urban growth rates for the first time.

It would be wrong to give the impression that all aspects of rural–urban migration in developing countries are negative. Migration can play a positive role in relieving population pressure in rural areas and improving the standard of living of the migrants.

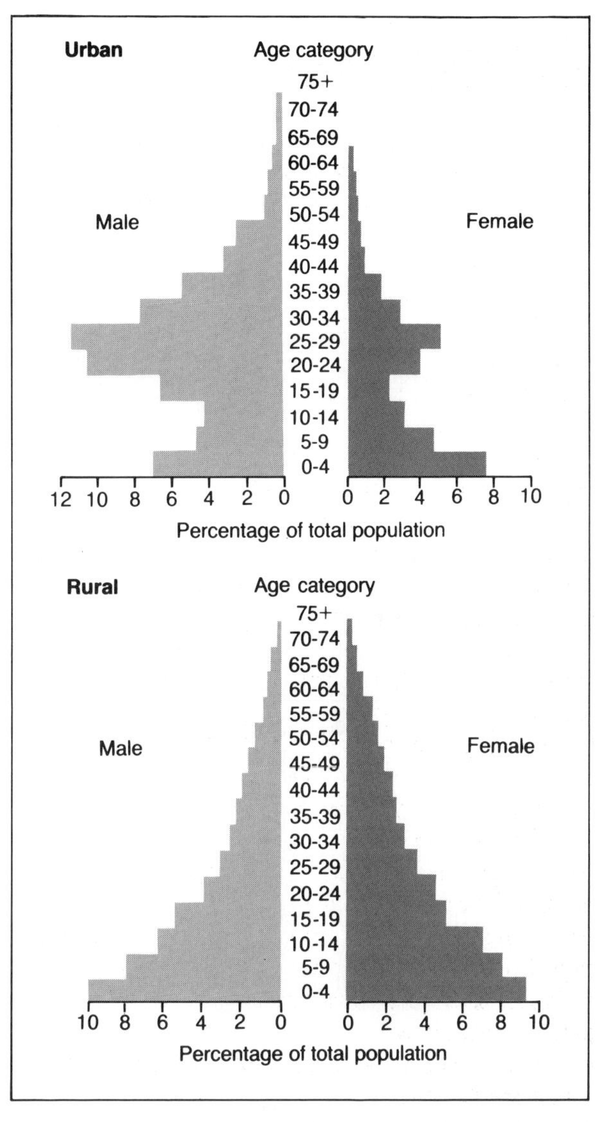

1.25 Population pyramids showing the impact of rural–urban migration in Zambia. Migration of young adults (mostly male) into urban areas distorts the population pyramid for urban areas. The effect on the rural pyramid is less noticeable because the total population in rural areas is much higher than in towns.

CHAPTER 1

Transmigration in Indonesia

The background

The **transmigration** programme in Indonesia has been the largest government-sponsored voluntary re-settlement scheme in the world. The programme was announced in 1949 and originally envisaged the migration of 48 million people from Java, the most populous island of the Indonesian archipelago, over a 35 year period. This figure was later modified to a target of 2 million every five years. The transmigration programme was embarked on by Indonesia primarily to relieve overpopulation in the inner islands of Java, Madura and Bali which occupy only 7% of Indonesia's land area but support 65% of the population. Despite the very fertile volcanic soils on Java, Madura and Bali, which can often sustain three crops each year, the agricultural population are in great difficulty. Land holdings have become progressively smaller, by subdivision, as families have grown. The average size of a land holding is down to a quarter of a hectare, which is too small to support a family.

80% of Java's 100 million population live in the countryside and of these 40% have no land. This overcrowded countryside has fuelled migration to the towns and in particular Jakarta, the capital. Jakarta's population increases naturally by about 200 000 each year and a further 80 000 landless migrants arrive annually adding to the city's overcrowding problem. Over 65% of the city's labour force is unregistered and barely able to earn enough to survive.

The population problem

Indonesia had an estimated 165 million population in the 1985 census, making it the world's fifth most populous nation, with an annual growth rate of 2.2% (1990 estimate: 180 million population and a 1.7% growth rate). The population is also very youthful with 40% of the population under 15 years of age (1990 estimate). While the inner islands support most of Indonesia's population giving very high population densities such as 758 per km^2 in Java and 486 per km^2 in Bali, the outer islands have relatively low population densities: for example, Irian Jaya 3 per km^2 and Kalimantan 15 per km^2 (1.26).

The idea of encouraging mass migration from the overcrowded inner islands to the outer islands at first seemed a simple and workable solution to Indonesia's overpopulation. However the outer islands have supported much smaller populations because the land is not as fertile and not suitable for intensive farming. The outer islands' capacity for settlement has been greatly overestimated by the Indonesian government.

History of the migration

About 1905, when the Dutch held Indonesia (Dutch East Indies) as a colony, migration from Java to the outer islands began. Most of the early migration was to provide labour in the rubber, coffee and tobacco plantations of Sumatra. The policy of encouraging migration was continued when Indonesia became independent in 1945 and by 1968 about 600 000 people had migrated. In 1969 the scale of migration was increased when the government introduced the first of its five-year development plans (*repelitas*), which was linked with the transmigration programme. World Bank funding was made available to assist the programme and

1.26 Indonesia: population density, showing the uneven distribution of people

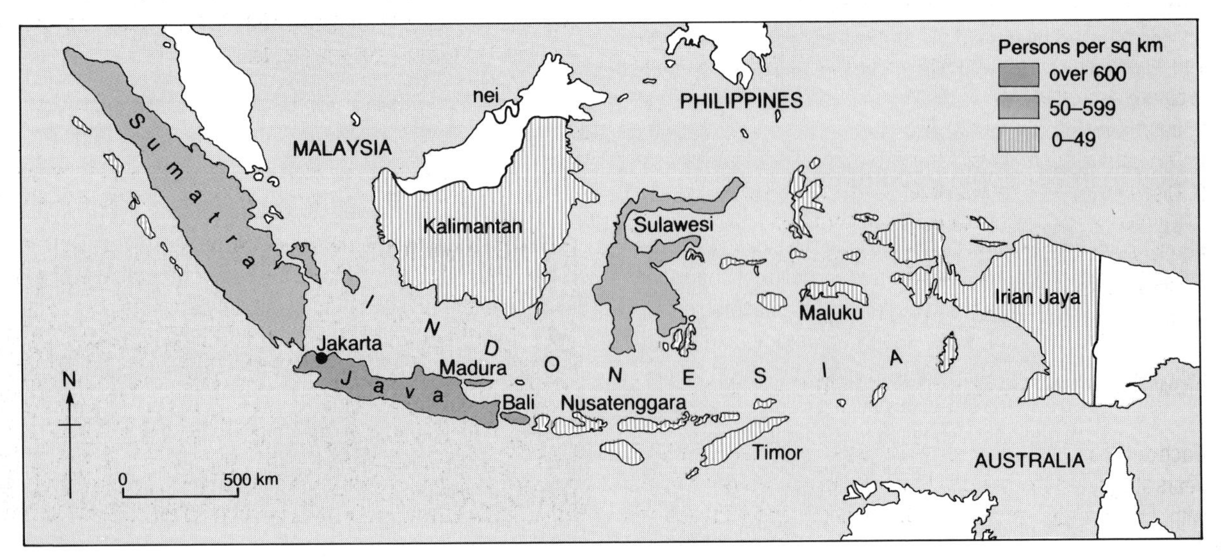

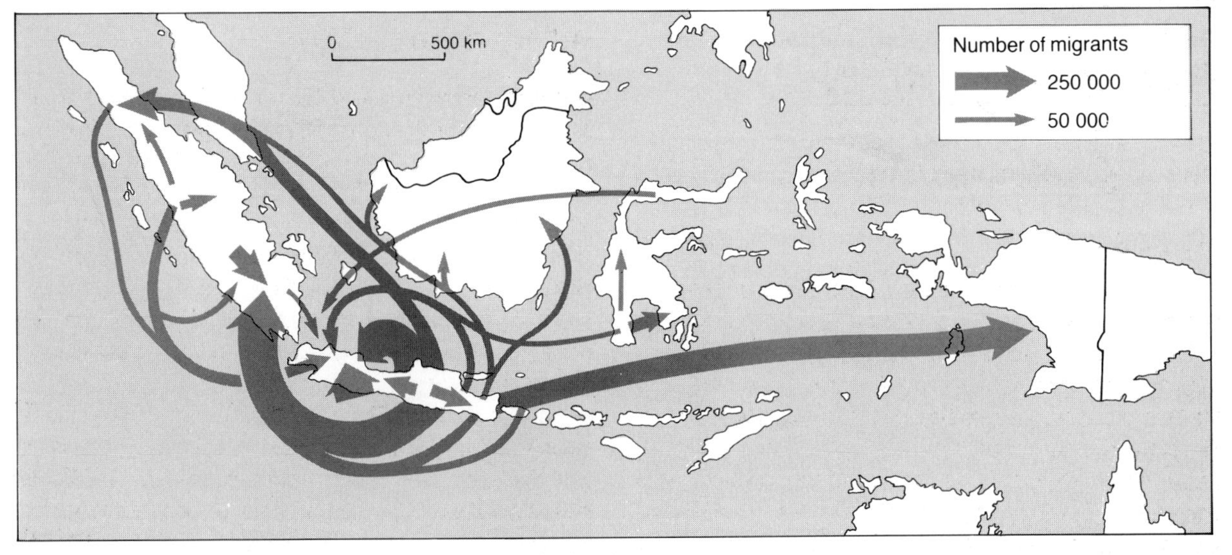

1.27 Main migration routes from the densely populated inner islands of Indonesia

still continues, despite the fact that the World Bank has a stated policy for the protection of tribal peoples and their lands, and the Indonesian government has disregarded the tribal rights of indigenous people in their outer islands.

Approximate transmigration figures since 1969 are:

1969–74	240 000 people
1974–79	465 000 people
1979–84	1 500 000 people
1984–89	750 000 people

Since 1905, figures suggest that over 3 million people have migrated, but the actual number of migrants may be 2 or 3 times as great because the government's recent figures are for migrants assisted by the programme and many people have migrated without government assistance (1.27).

Aims of the transmigration programme

The Indonesian government has seven aims for the transmigration programme to meet.

1. Improve living standards
2. Promote regional development
3. Disperse population from overcrowded regions
4. Equalise development throughout Indonesia
5. Harness and use natural resources and human labour
6. Unify the nation
7. Strengthen defence and national security

How the transmigration programme works

Each applicant for the government programme must be under 40 years of age, healthy, preferably married with two to four children, with no criminal record and have some previous farming experience (1.28). Migrants are given one week's training before being sent mostly by air to their new homes. The government provides each family with a four-roomed wooden house on at least 2 hectares of land, with seed and provisions for one year. About 10% of settlers receive a cow or water buffalo and others get some tree crops and a few small livestock. The government aim is to establish transmigrant settlements each with a population of about 2000 in population. In 1985 the cost of moving one family under the scheme was about $12000.

Since the fall in price of Indonesian oil in 1986 the government has had to cut its transmigration budget severely and this has led to a re-assessment of priorities. More emphasis is now placed on assisting and encouraging spontaneous migrants (people who choose to migrate without inducement), with investment concentrated on existing sites. However the 1989–94 plan still intends to develop over 1000 new sites for migrants. Current migration targets for 1989–94 are 180000 state assisted migrants and 370000 spontaneous migrants.

1.28 A Jakarta billboard advertises the promise of an idyllic life as a transmigrant, escaping overcrowded Java for a life of prosperity which few migrants achieve

CHAPTER 1

Impact of the Indonesian transmigration programme

The transmigration programme has caused considerable controversy both within and outside Indonesia, particularly since 1969. But, despite growing condemnation of some aspects of the programme, resettlement in south-east Sumatra has been succcessful. The draining of the coastal swamps in south-east Sumatra has created an environment with rich soils which are able to support the migrant communities. Furthermore the migrants are able to use the same rice cultivation techniques that they used in Java and they have been upgraded from landless peasants to landowners. The Indonesian government has, however, provided a lot of support for this region, as one might expect, since it is so close to Java and an unsuccessful migration would have brought adverse publicity.

There have also been some notable failures in the programme. Some 2500 families sent to central Kalimantan have had to be relocated because soils on the original site were both infertile and toxic. The most serious charges levelled at the Indonesian government are in relation to Irian Jaya (the Indonesian half of New Guinea). Human rights groups such as Survival International have suggested that migrants have been shipped from Java and Bali to Irian Jaya to replace the dissenting indigenous peoples who have consistently resisted Indonesian rule since the United Nations handed over control in 1963. Most of the indigenous people of Irian Jaya are Melanesian in origin with different customs from the Javanese. The Indonesian government has sought not only to swamp the indigenous population of Irian Jaya with outsiders but to change their way of life by moving them into permanent settlements. In the rush to secure Irian Jaya the Indonesian government has shipped 300 000 migrants to unsuitable locations where many live on the edge of starvation (1.29). Much of the soil is infertile and unsuitable for permanent cultivation. The migrants have had to contend with floods, plagues of mice and insects, a harsh climate, and attack from bitter indigenous tribal groups. Many migrants have fled to the towns, where they are destitute, but despite this the government still proposes to send a further 4 million migrants to Irian Jaya. Martono, the Minister for Transmigration, said on 20 March 1985 '... The different ethnic groups will in the long run disappear because of integration... and... there will be one kind of man...'.

The environment has also suffered as a result of the transmigration programme. 80% of transmigration sites were once rainforest and around 8 million hectares of virgin rainforest is likely to be cleared between 1988 and 1998, accounting for some 12.5% of Indonesia's remaining productive forest. Indonesia has one of the richest ecosystems in the world with around 500 native mammals, over 1500 species of bird, and an estimated 40 000 species of flora but the loss of habitat through transmigration is threatening many species with extinction.

The transmigration programme has cost the Indonesian government $8 billion but even at its peak it only managed to move about 20% of Java's annual increase in population and population growth rates remain high. This money might have been better spent on promoting birth control and development.

1.29 The conditions that greet many transmigrants in Irian Jaya are as bad if not worse than those they left in Java. The picture shows a crowded shanty in Sorong.

HERE AND THERE;
Or, Emigration a Remedy.

1.30 A nineteenth-century emigration cartoon. This cartoon points to migration as the solution for those who wish to avoid poverty.

International Migration

In most countries the natural increase in population is greater than the gain from inward migration, yet governments tend to make greater efforts to control immigration than they do to affect fertility. Immigrants from Commonwealth countries, particularly the West Indies, India and Pakistan, were encouraged to come to the UK in the late 1950s and 1960s, because there were jobs to be filled after the Second World War. But by the late 1960s the British government had begun to restrict immigration on the grounds that it would create social tension and exacerbate unemployment. Despite the regulation of immigration by many governments, statistics are notoriously unreliable.

As with internal migration, 'push–pull' factors determine international migration. Economic motives are particularly important. In general a nation gains migrants from a country less developed than itself. However, with immigration restrictions, many of the most developed countries accept very small numbers of migrants, and the oil-rich countries of the Middle East are emerging as the receiving nations of the 1990s.

The numbers involved in international migration are mostly small, with only 28 countries having a net number of migrants greater than 10 000 for the period 1980–85. The United States still receives the greatest number of immigrants annually but this number is only equivalent to 1.8 migrants per thousand total population. The United Arab Emirates has the highest immigration rate of 35 migrants per thousand total population.

Present migration numbers appear very small when compared with the vast numbers involved in the nineteenth and early twentieth centuries. The USA received around 50 million immigrants between 1840 and 1914. About 17 million people left the United Kingdom between 1825 and 1920, 65% to the USA (1.30). This tradition of emigration from the UK, encouraged by the fact that a large proportion of the world is English speaking, accounts for the fact that the UK is the only developed country in the top 12 sending countries, in terms of absolute numbers.

Since the Second World War, emigration from European colonies and former colonies in the developing world has brought waves of migrants to Europe seeking better opportunities. There have also been migration streams within Europe as people have crossed national borders in search of work (1.31).

Tens of millions of people were displaced during the Second World War. Wars and famines continue to stimulate migration: the number of refugees that were displaced during the 1980s increased by about a million a year and in 1988 stood at about 14.5 million worldwide.

1.31 Migration into and throughout Europe since the Second World War

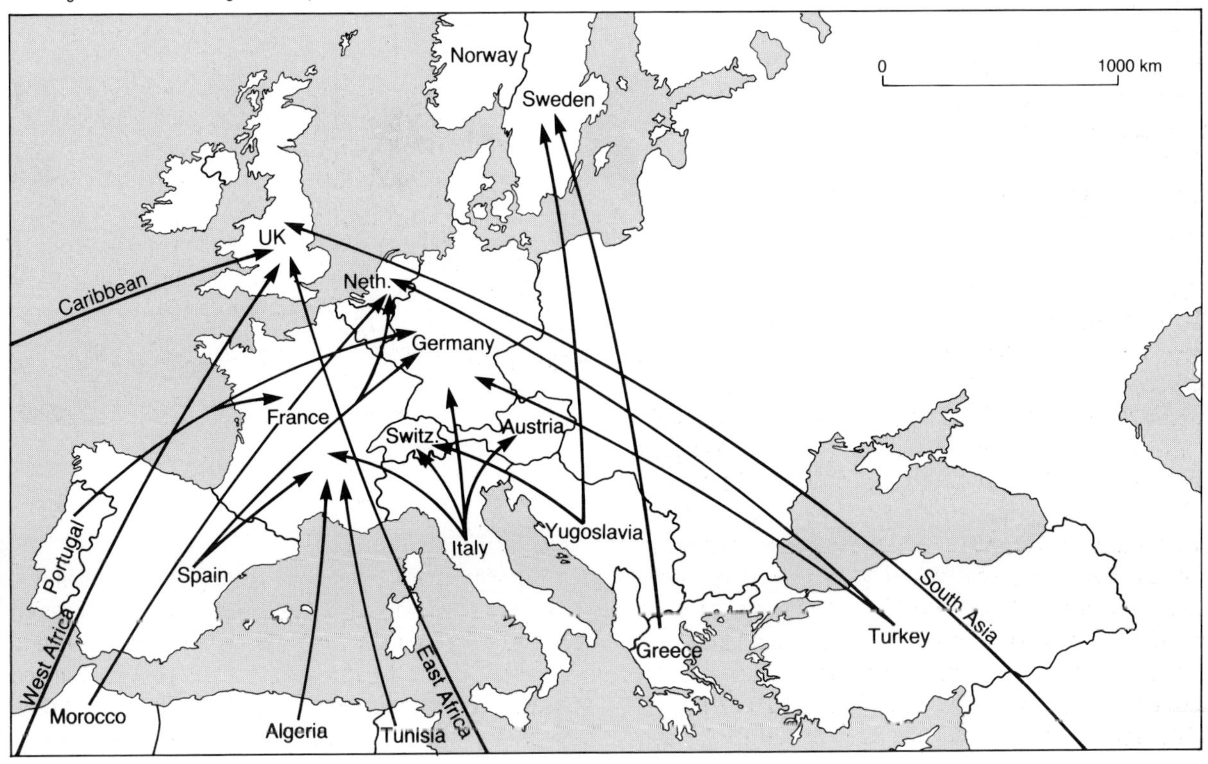

CHAPTER 1

Refugees

According to UNHCR (United Nations High Commission for Refugees) a refugee is a person 'who owing to well-founded fear of being persecuted for reasons of race, religion, nationality, membership of a particular social group or political opinion, is outside of his or her nationality and is unable, or owing to such fear unwilling, to avail himself/herself of the protection of that country'. Of the current 14.5 million refugees worldwide, 60% is made up of two main groups: 6 million Afghan refugees in Iran and Pakistan (1.32); and 2.3 million Palestinian refugees in Jordan, Syria, Lebanon and Israeli-occupied Gaza Strip and West Bank. The Palestinian refugees have been living in camps for 40 years (1.33). A further 4.5 million refugees are to be found in Africa (one million in each of Mozambique and Ethiopia) (1.34).

The very large numbers of refugees in the developing world have led to the developed countries adopting more restrictive definitions of who is and who isn't a refugee in order to restrict the numbers trying to enter these countries. This has meant that refugees have to compete for resettlement with all other categories of would-be migrants. The burden of housing refugees is being borne, in the main, by the developing countries while the developed countries tighten restrictions on migration.

1.33 A Palestinian refugee settlement in Jordan, 1980

1.32 The world's largest refugee population

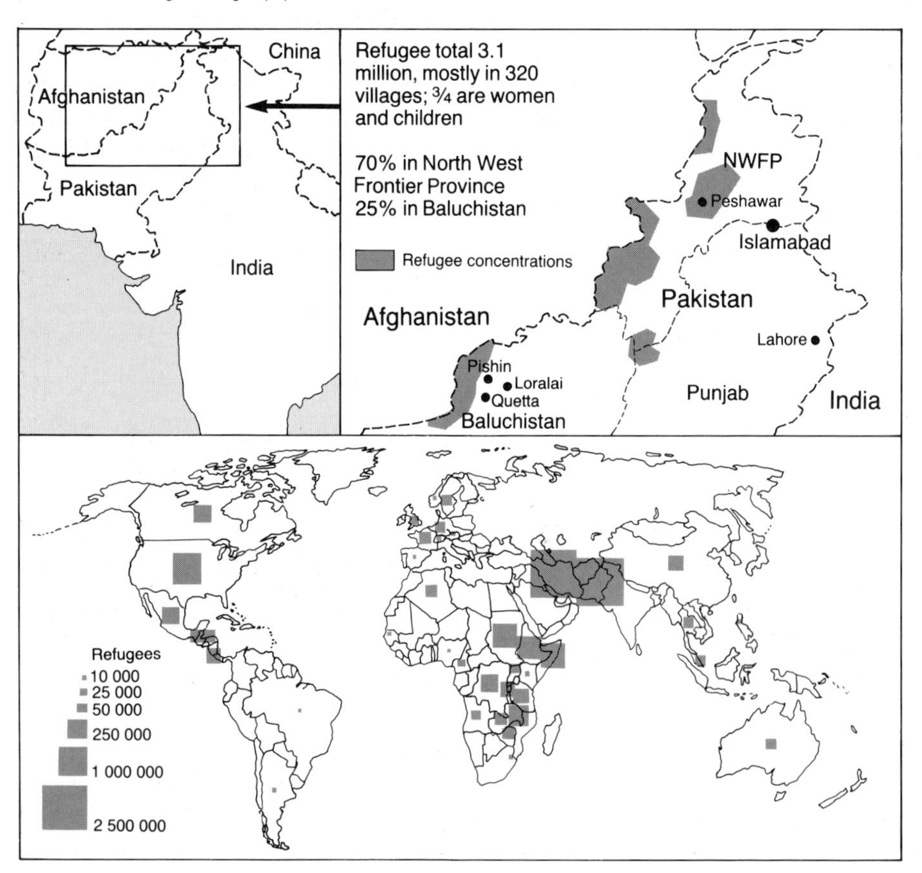

1.34 Ethiopian refugees heading for a relief camp. Famine, drought and civil war have forced the migration of large numbers of people in search of refuge in the drought stricken Sahel region of Africa.

Europe, which suffered from large refugee movements after the Second World War, had only 55 000 in 1988. The migrants from East to West Germany in 1989–90 were not considered to be refugees. Many of the post-war refugees have integrated into their host society, given up their original nationality and are therefore no longer considered to be refugees.

The war in Afghanistan (1978 onwards, easing after 1988) with the consequent bombing and mining of rural settlements caused about 6 million Afghans to flee as refugees to Iran (3.5 million) and Pakistan (2.5 million). Most of these refugees are women and children accompanied by elderly men and the wounded. Many refugees have been able to integrate into Iranian society and have dispersed throughout the country. In Pakistan most refugees end up in refugee camps and despite an agreement between Afghanistan and Pakistan there has been no major repatriation.

The refugee crisis in Africa

The number of refugees in Africa has risen sharply since the 1970s to a current estimate of 4.6 million, but this number only accounts for those displaced from their home country (1.35 and 1.36). Many others have been displaced from their homes by war and famine but are not technically classified as refugees because they have not crossed national boundaries. The large numbers of semi-nomadic migrants in Africa make the task of accurately calculating the refugee numbers very difficult.

Some refugees have been able to return home in a relatively short space of time: 40 000 Burundians who fled Rwanda in July 1988 returned by the end of the year. Other conflicts have been longer lasting and have displaced large numbers of people. The Sudan is host to more than 2 million displaced people, 1.5 million of its own citizens displaced by civil war, 70 000 from Chad, 5000 from Uganda and 630 000 Eritreans fleeing from the Ethiopian military. The large numbers of refugees in eastern Sudan have exacerbated the shortages of water and firewood in this marginal environment, causing severe ecological damage.

Over a million Mozambican refugees have fled the ferocious civil war between the Marxist government and the South African backed RENAMO guerrillas, with up to another 2 million internally displaced. Malawi has received 630 000 of the refugees and they now constitute over 8% of its total population.

UNHCR spent $150 million on African refugees in 1989, working out at about $30 per refugee. The budget is not, however, evenly spread. About $1000 per head was spent on small numbers of refugees in Morocco and Egypt, while $3 per head was spent in Malawi. The African refugee population is rapidly outstripping the resources allocated to alleviate it.

1.36 Africa's refugees

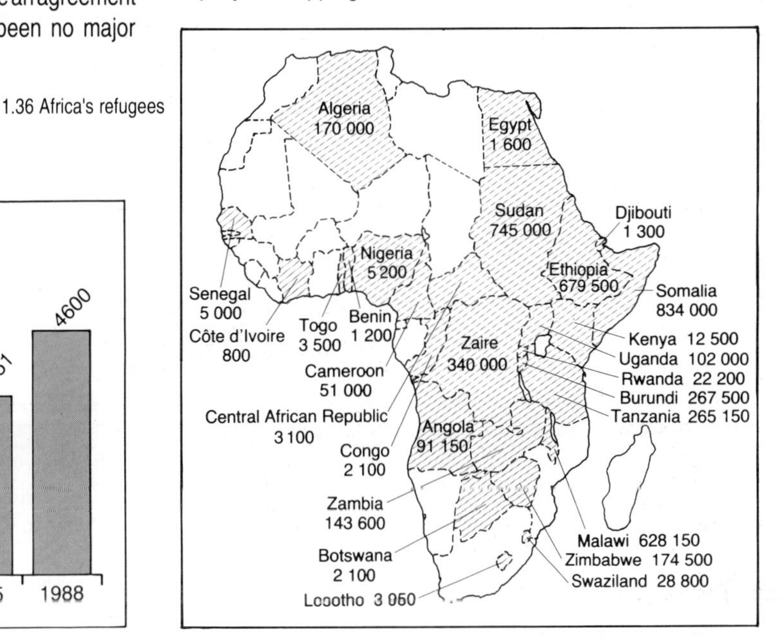

1.35 The growth of Africa's refugee population

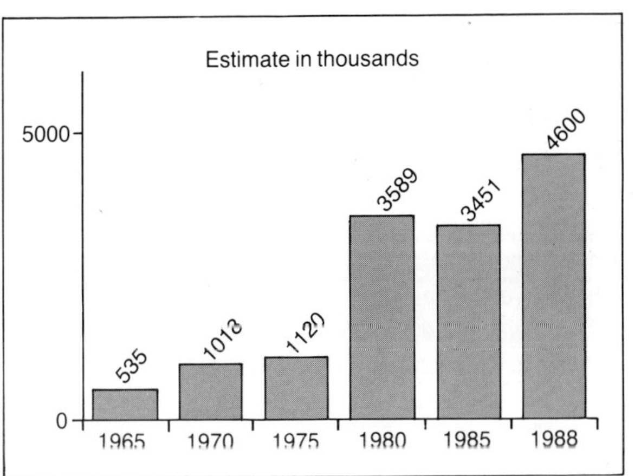

CHAPTER 1

Population Projections and Policies

Population projections

Governments and institutions find population projections both helpful and desirable when formulating long-term policy. To make any predictions, assumptions about future fertility, mortality, marriage and migration have to be made. The main difficulty is that of predicting future fertility. This has caused many projections made in the past to be widely inaccurate.

World population projections are made by various bodies including the World Bank and the United Nations. United Nations' projections are usually provided for a 40 or 50 year period. Three sets of projections are provided by the United Nations to take account of different trends in fertility (1.37). The low projection assumes that a 'two child' average will be reached by 2010, whereas the middle series assumes this will be reached by 2035, and the higher projection by 2065. This series of projections gives a total world population of between 7.5 billion and 14.2 billion in 2100. The World Bank projection for 2100 is 11.2 billion, a little above the United Nation medium forecast.

1.37 United Nations world population projections

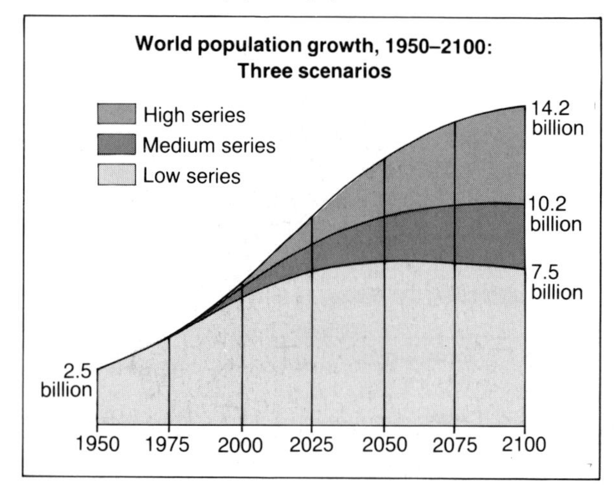

Within these projections there are predictions for individual countries and regions. By 2025 India is expected to overtake China as the world's most populous nation while Nigeria and Indonesia will overtake both the USA and the USSR. By 2100 it is estimated that Africa will have 25% of the world's population compared with 11.5% at present (1.38).

The bulk of the difference between the high and low world population projections is accounted for by Southern Asia, Latin America and Africa. Population policies which aim to reduce fertility in these regions could make a significant impact on the world's population over the next 100 years.

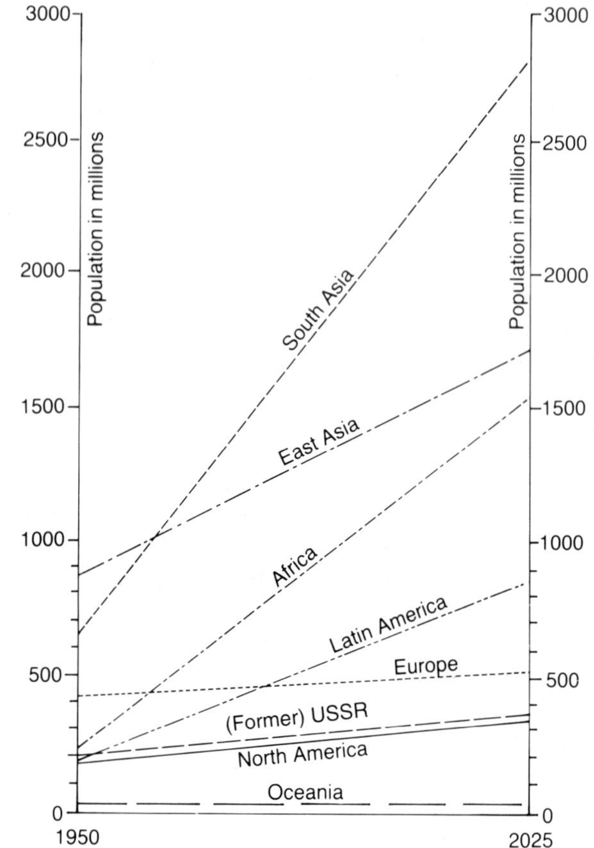

1.38 Population projections by region. These illustrate the different rates of growth in different parts of the world.

Projections cannot make assumptions about future wars, a changing environment, the impact of new diseases or technological advances in medicine. Even the assumption of a declining birth rate in developed countries is open to debate. Fertility rates can and have increased in developed countries under certain conditions and may do so in the future. Very slight errors in calculations could mean huge errors in 50 years time.

Population policies

Population projections often stimulate governments into introducing population policies. Population policies are concerned with influencing population growth, fertility, mortality, spatial distribution and migration.

Considerable attention is given to developing countries which are trying to reduce growth rates, and this gives the impression that population policies are aimed at reducing fertility. This is not universally true; around 23% of developing countries wish higher rates of population growth, including Iraq, Kampuchea, Laos,

Libya, Gabon, Bolivia, Uruguay and Israel. In Bolivia, in an attempt to increase fertility, family planning clinics have been closed and abortion has been made illegal.

Most developing countries do, however, wish to reduce population growth in order to assist social, economic and cultural development. Very few governments have attempted policies which intervene in only one part of the demographic process; most have attempted to modify fertility, mortality and migration in combination with economic development.

Governments seeking to reduce fertility have a number of possible options including (i) provision of contraceptive advice and facilities, (ii) legal measures such as legalising abortion and raising the age of marriage, (iii) economic and social measures to discourage large families, for example, taxing children or reducing state benefits.

Overpopulation in Japan after the Second World War resulted in a number of measures to curb fertility. The 'law of eugenic protection' introduced in 1948 legalised sterilisation and abortion, and encouraged contraception. The impact of this policy can be seen in Japan's population pyramid for 1970 (1.39).

China on the other hand has had several turnarounds in population policy since the Second World War. In an attempt to limit its population to 1.2 billion by the end of the century and complete its demographic transition, it introduced a policy of 'only one child per family' in 1979. The eventual aim of the Chinese government is to reduce the total population to around 750 million (1.40). This policy relies on strong social pressure and economic sanctions to enforce it. If a woman who already has a child becomes pregnant the whole community is notified and she and her husband become subject to daily visits in order to force the woman to have an abortion. If the woman insists on having the child the family will be taxed for the additional child and state benefits to the family will be reduced. Recently there have been signs that the strict one-child policy is being relaxed and a general two-child policy is being gradually introduced. Chinese demographers have calculated that, if a first pregnancy is delayed until the mother is 27 and there is a four-year gap before a second child, the population can still stabilise at about 1.25 billion.

While there is variation in fertility policies there is unanimity in goverments' approach to mortality. All governments seek to have higher life expectancies and improved quality of health.

Many governments see the distribution of people as a major obstacle to development. In particular many developing countries have policies to reduce rural–urban migration. Tanzania has a policy of deflecting population from urban areas to village communities (the ***Ujamaa Vijijini*** policy). As well as encouraging a better population distribution the Tanzanian government is attempting to spread education and health facilities to the entire population. These policies have given Tanzania the highest literacy rate in the region and a falling infant mortality rate. Population growth, though still high at 2.8%, is falling for the first time.

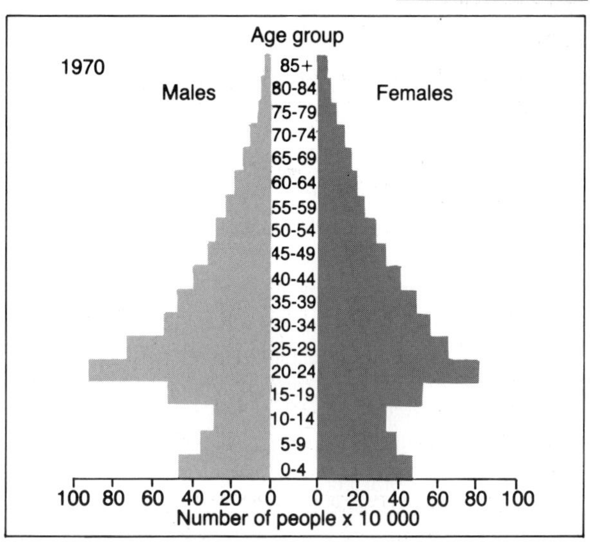

1.39 Population pyramid, Japan 1970. This shows the impact of twenty years of government policy promoting a fall in fertility.

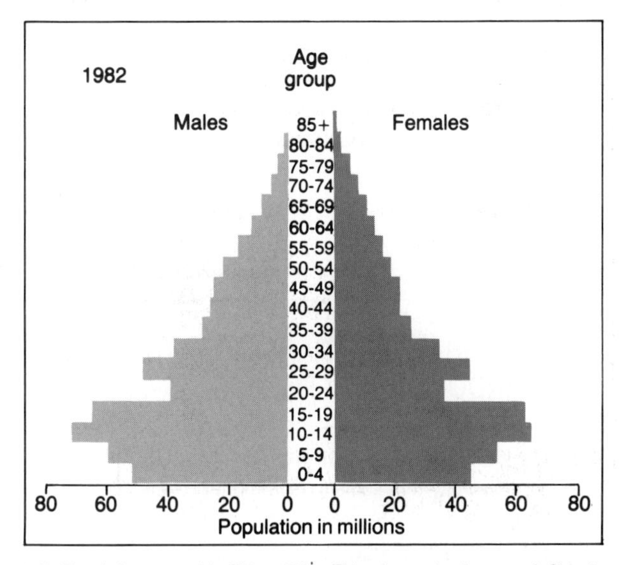

1.40 Population pyramid, China 1982. This shows the impact of China's population policies which since the 1970s have sought to reduce the birth rate radically.

Nearly all governments have policies on international migration and most wish neither emigration nor immigration. Only a few countries encourage immigration: for example, Israel, Bolivia, South Africa, Gabon, Saudi Arabia and Argentina. A few other countries encourage emigration, often temporary migration of manpower to employment in comparatively lucrative jobs: for example, Turkey, South Korea, Algeria and Pakistan.

Population policies in developing countries are often funded by aid from developed nations with much of this directed through the United Nations Fund for Population Activities (UNFPA).

Questions

Q POPULATION STRUCTURE / THE DEMOGRAPHIC TRANSITION

1 (a) Compare the age structure of developed and developing countries.
(b) Discuss the problems that a growing dependent population will cause Germany in the next 40 years.
(c) Explain the age structure in developed and developing countries in terms of birth and death rates.
(d) With reference to a country you have studied discuss how social and political factors have influenced the rate of natural increase.
(e) Describe the change in age structure of the United Kingdom as illustrated in 1.17.
(f) From graph 1.17 calculate the dependency ratios in 1851, 1941 and 1991.
(g) Describe the three main types of population pyramid.
(h) Account for the differences in sex ratios between developed and developing countries.
(i) Most commentators on ageing populations concentrate on the problems they bring. What positive contributions do the elderly make to the economy and society?

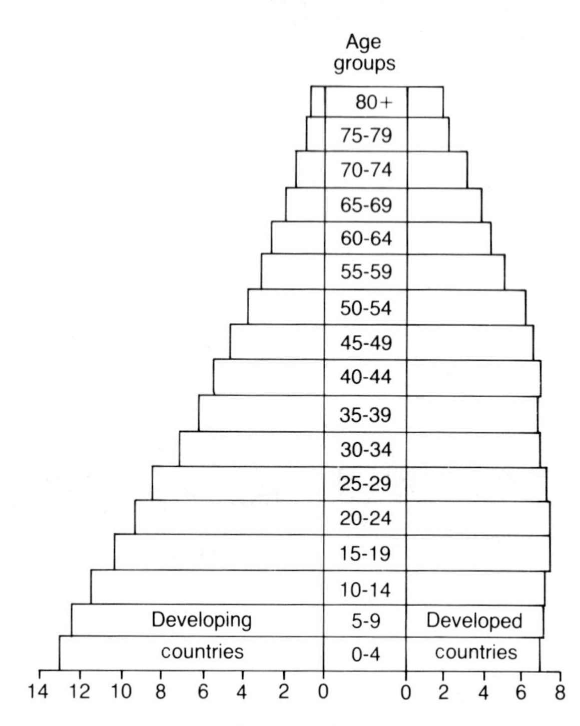

Q MIGRATION / TRANSMIGRATION IN INDONESIA / REFUGEES

2 (a) In the past, migration was dominated by the most disadvantaged in society. Comment on how this has changed.
(b) Comment on how the population pyramids for Zambia (1.26) have been distorted by migration.
(c) Why did the population of Indonesia become so concentrated on a few islands?
(d) What are the main objectives of the transmigration programme?
(e) Comment on the social, cultural and ecological effects of the transmigration programme.
(f) Would alternative policies have achieved some of the transmigration objectives?
(g) 'As mobility of population increases, migration decreases.' Comment on the validity of this statement.

Q POPULATION PROJECTIONS AND POPULATION POLICIES

3 Look at graph 1.39, showing population projections.
(a) Describe the differences between the projected population growth of the developed and developing worlds.
(b) Population projections are based on assumptions about future birth and death rates. What factors might cause the projections to be significantly inaccurate?
(c) Describe some of the ways developing countries are trying to reduce population growth and comment on the success or otherwise of their efforts.
(d) Discuss how a coercive population policy such as China's would be received in a developed country such as the UK.
(e) How will increasing numbers of people living in Asia and Africa have an impact on European countries?
(f) What measures could a government take to increase fertility?

Research and Further Work

(a) Find out about other aspects of population composition including occupation structure and ethnic composition.
(b) Research the views of some major religious groups on birth control.
(c) Research the impact of slavery on ethnic composition in the USA.
(d) Comment on the influence that Britain's colonial past had on both emigration from and immigration to Britain.
(e) Find out about the range of population data collected by local and national government in the UK.
(f) Research the medical and social advances which helped to reduce the death rate in the UK over the last 100 years.

Exam Style Questions

1 Look at the age-specific death rates for a rural area in a developing country, shown in the table.

(a) Describe the overall pattern shown and note any differences between male and female rates. (4)
and
(b) Explain the patterns in the death rate data, in terms of both social and environmental conditions. (5)
or
(c) Describe the normal pattern of age selective death rates in developed countries, quoting examples. (5)

Age	Male	Female
0 – 4	58.7	68.5
5 – 9	5.7	6.8
10 – 14	2.6	2.7
15 – 19	2.0	3.8
20 – 24	3.3	5.3
25 – 29	3.5	6.2
30 – 34	3.9	6.2
35 – 39	6.4	6.1
40 – 44	8.1	7.8
45 – 49	12.9	9.3
50 – 54	17.8	15.0
55 – 59	25.4	19.0
60 – 64	41.9	39.4
65 – 69	56.0	52.3
70+	118.4	115.5
all ages	17.8	19.5

2 Look at the diagram showing selected aspects of migration.
(a) Explain the terms forced and voluntary migration, giving an example of each. (3)
and
(b) Referring to specific areas you have studied, describe and explain the model of migration shown. (6)
or
(c) Describe and explain the problems migration can create for the areas of out-migration and in-migration. (6)

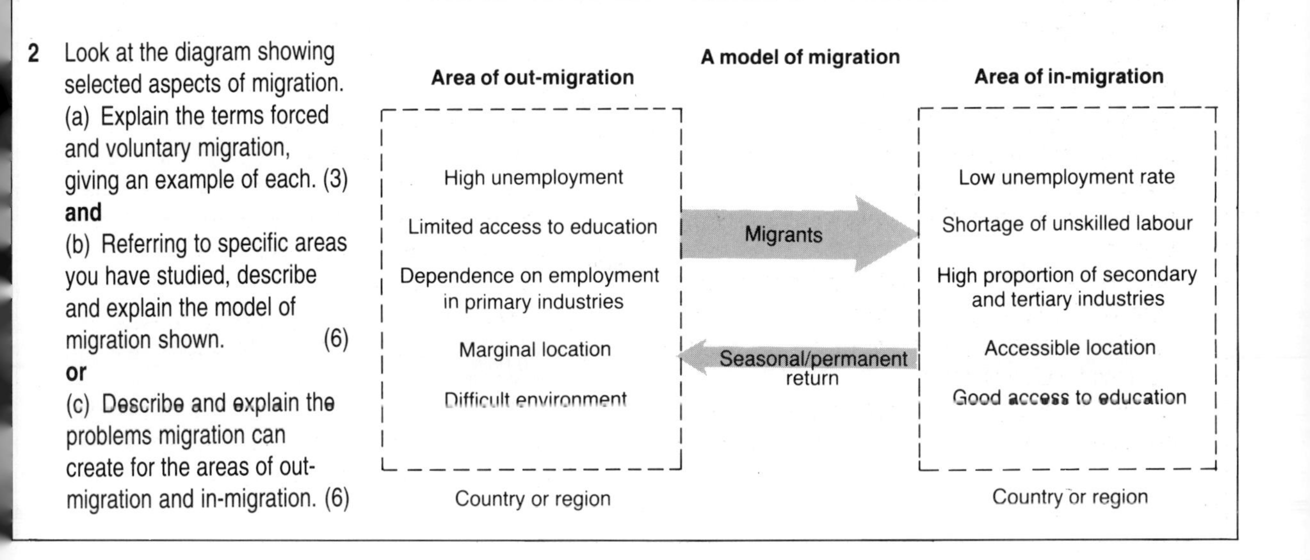

Exam Style Questions

3 Look at the three population pyramids below.

(a) Describe each pyramid in terms of its birth and death rates. (3)

and

(b) Choose **one** pyramid and explain its population growth characteristics, giving a named area/country which has similar characteristics. (6)

or

(c) With reference to specific examples discuss the problems associated with **either** expanding **or** contracting populations. (6)

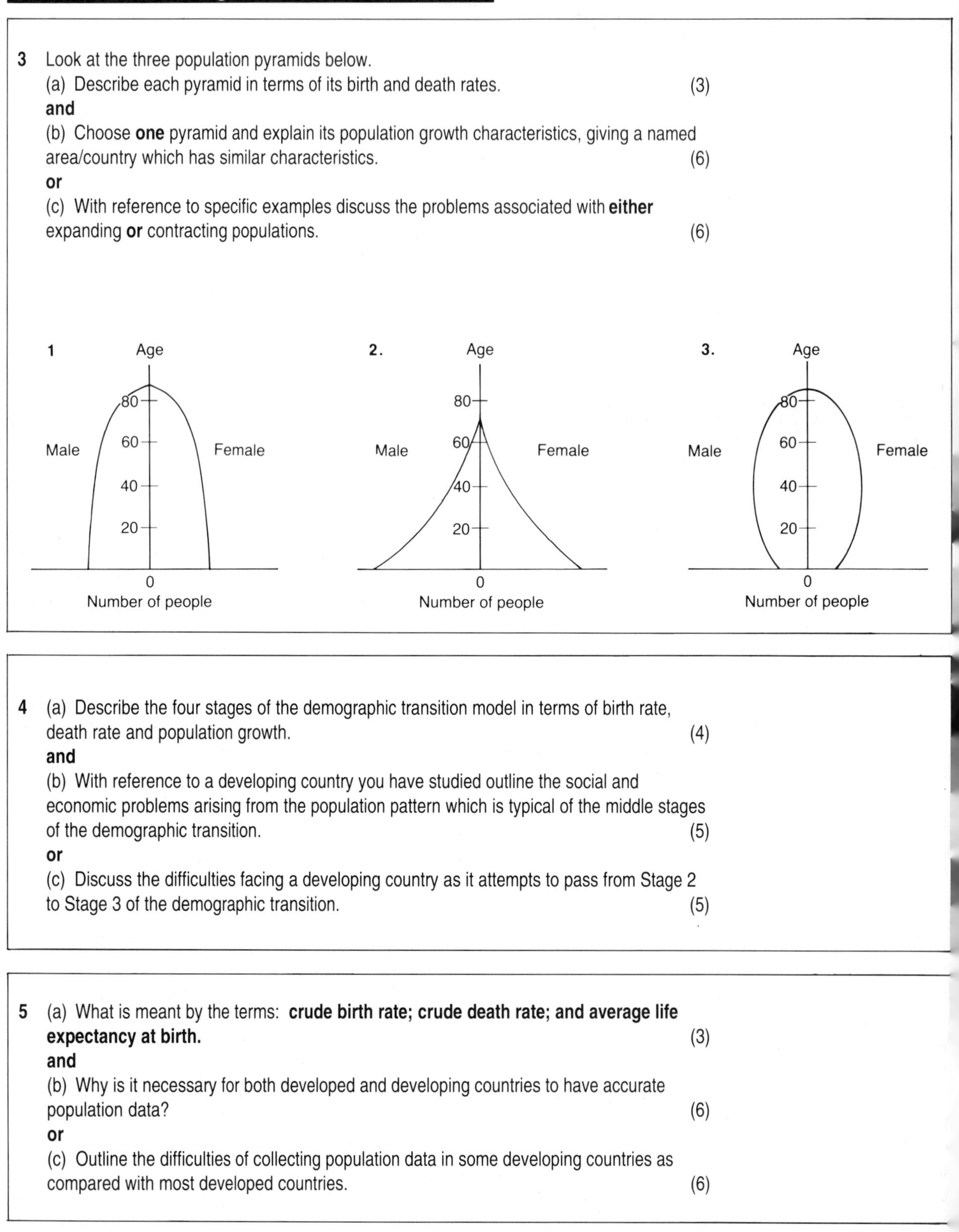

4 (a) Describe the four stages of the demographic transition model in terms of birth rate, death rate and population growth. (4)

and

(b) With reference to a developing country you have studied outline the social and economic problems arising from the population pattern which is typical of the middle stages of the demographic transition. (5)

or

(c) Discuss the difficulties facing a developing country as it attempts to pass from Stage 2 to Stage 3 of the demographic transition. (5)

5 (a) What is meant by the terms: **crude birth rate; crude death rate; and average life expectancy at birth.** (3)

and

(b) Why is it necessary for both developed and developing countries to have accurate population data? (6)

or

(c) Outline the difficulties of collecting population data in some developing countries as compared with most developed countries. (6)

RURAL GEOGRAPHY

Introduction

2.1 Some components of rural geography

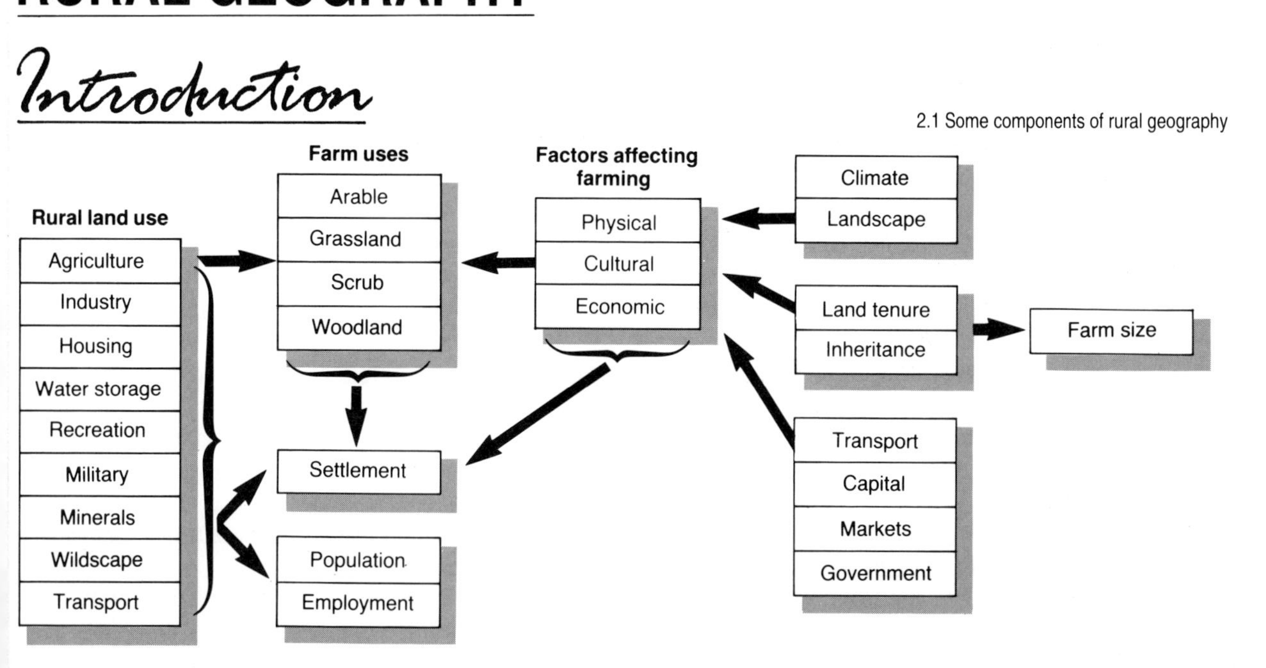

Rural geography is a broad subject which includes a variety of components, some of which are listed in 2.1. The subject generally includes the study of rural life in relation to agricultural production in varying physical, economic and social environments. To make a precise definition of the subject poses problems since even the term 'rural' is open to interpretation. For example, some areas, which to the eye appear to be rural, actually function as extensions of an urban settlement. A working definition of 'rural areas' might be 'less densely populated parts of the world where the landscape shows signs of recent agricultural activity'.

In this book the study of rural geography will be limited to three types of agricultural system: **shifting cultivation, intensive peasant farming**, and **extensive commercial farming**. In this chapter we will examine the social, economic and spatial changes that are taking place in these systems, and their implications.

Agriculture

The distribution of the different types of agriculture is determined by physical, economic and human (cultural) factors. Farmers need to understand the limitations and the opportunities presented by these three factors in order to select the most appropriate farming activities for their location.

Physical factors place limitations on the types of agricultural production possible in any area although some of the physical constraints can be partially compensated for by modern techniques. Every species (animal or plant) has an ecological optimum set of environmental conditions of temperature, humidity, sunshine, nutrients, slope, soils, etc. where it will flourish best.

McCarty and Lindberg produced an **optima and limits model** in 1966 which proposed that there was an optimum or ideal location(s) for each type of agriculture. The physical factors produced the optimum conditions for the type of agriculture and as conditions deteriorated away from this location (i.e. became too dry or cold, etc.) the profitability of this type of agriculture would be reduced, so it would be less attractive to farmers. Eventually the conditions would deteriorate to the point where this type of agriculture is no longer economically viable (2.2).

2.2 Optima and limits model (after McCarty and Lindberg)

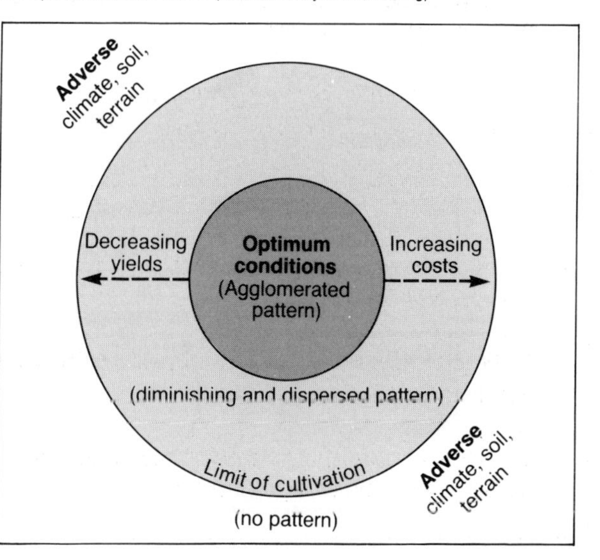

The Farming System

Farming can be viewed as a system with inputs, processes and outputs (2.3). The physical, economic and human factors form the inputs. In less developed economies physical factors may be the most important inputs whereas more developed cash-based farming systems rely more on economic and human factors. The decisions on what to produce and how to produce it are influenced by the inputs and past experience. The decisions will influence the eventual outputs of the system (animals, and crops). The outputs may exceed the inputs, resulting in a profit, but in many parts of the world farmers struggle just to match their inputs in order to survive.

Types of agricultural systems

Agricultural systems are difficult to classify precisely but they may be classified broadly according to whether they are:

- **arable** or **pastoral**
- **subsistence** or **commercial**
- **shifting** or **sedentary**
- **intensive** or **extensive**

Arable / pastoral. Arable is the growing of crops; it tends to occupy the best-quality and flattest land. Livestock rearing or pastoral farming is normally carried out in less favourable areas (i.e. too wet or too dry, etc. for arable farming). **Mixed farming**, involving both crops and animals, is more commonly practised in developed economies.

Shifting / sedentary. Shifting agriculture involves movement from one area to another. Shifting cultivation is still found in areas where soils are poor and there is a low population density. The cultivators have to move to new plots of land as poor soils become exhausted after only a few years of cultivation. Shifting pastoralists move around in order to find new pasture for their animals. Because only a small proportion of the land can be used at any one time, shifting agriculture supports a low density of population.

When farming becomes established in one place it is called sedentary. Sedentary farmers may have to use **crop rotation**, fertilisers, etc. in order to maintain the quality of their land.

Subsistence / commercial. Subsistence farmers usually produce only enough food for themselves and their families, without a surplus to sell. For subsistence farmers the priority is to produce enough to survive. Some try to reduce the risk of a failed harvest by growing a wide range of crops. Subsistence farmers are unable to increase output because they lack the land or technology to increase production.

Commercial farming is concerned with making a **profit.** Much commercial farming is on a large scale and, where conditions are suitable, this is done through producing one crop or rearing one type of animal because this makes the production cheaper and more efficient: for example, plantations in the Tropics, cattle ranching in Argentina. The commercial cash-based farming system has tended to have a high degree of political support from governments that wish to see agriculture contribute a larger share of national wealth (2.4).

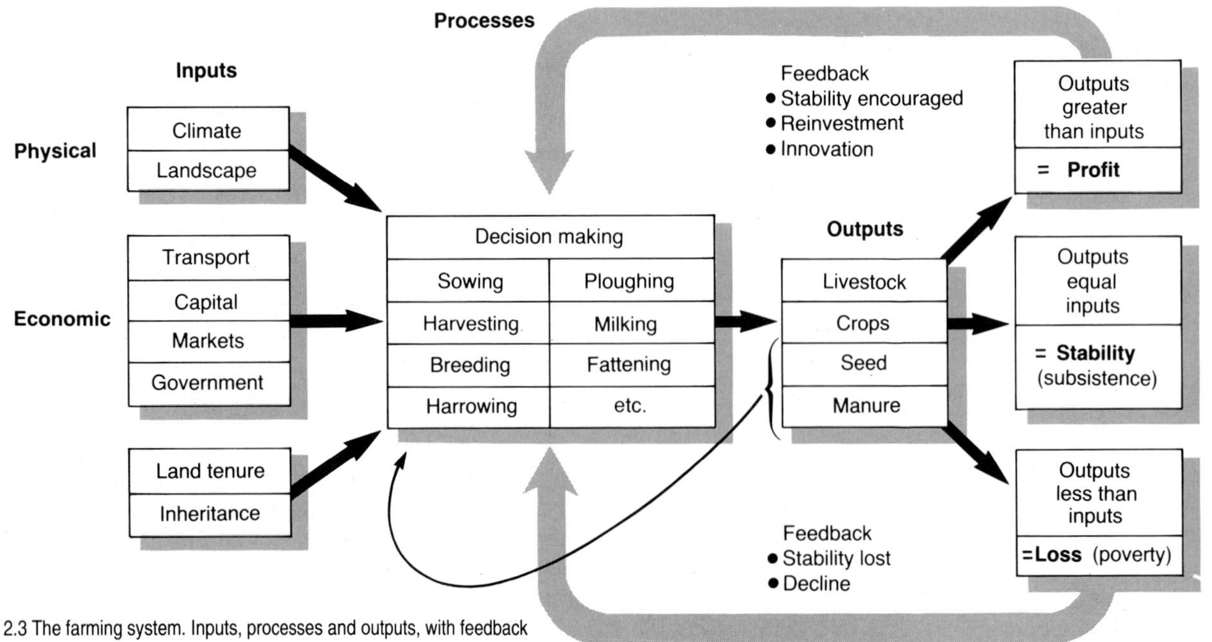

2.3 The farming system. Inputs, processes and outputs, with feedback loops, make up the basic model of a farming system.

Extensive / intensive. Extensive farming is carried out on a large scale utilising large areas of land, normally with relatively small amounts of **labour** and **capital**. (Labour is the workforce employed on the land while capital includes financial investment in buildings, machinery, irrigation/drainage systems, etc.) Intensive agriculture, on the other hand, involves the use of large amounts of labour and/or capital on a relatively small area of land. The distinction therefore mainly rests on the relationship between the size of the labour and capital inputs and the size of the land. 2.5 illustrates some examples of extensive and intensive agriculture.

2.4 Contrasts between cash-based and subsistence farming

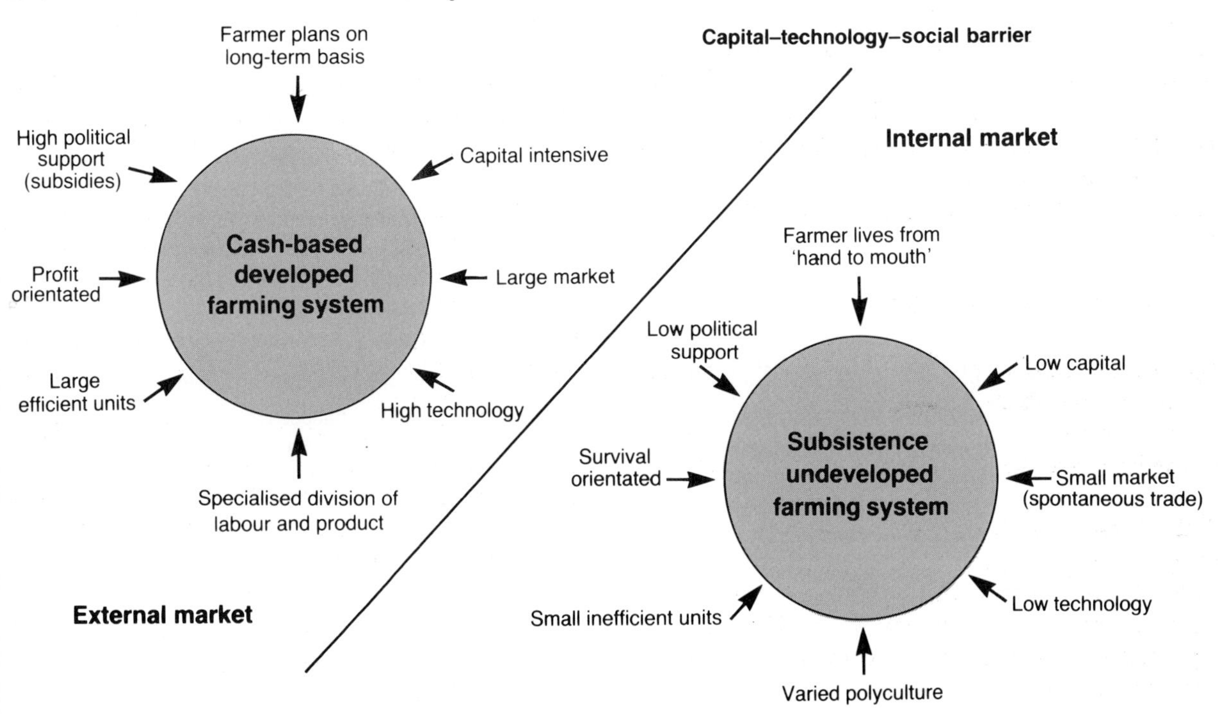

2.5 Contrasts in productivity between different extensive and intensive farming systems. These diagrams illustrate the relationship between land, labour and capital in four different farming systems.

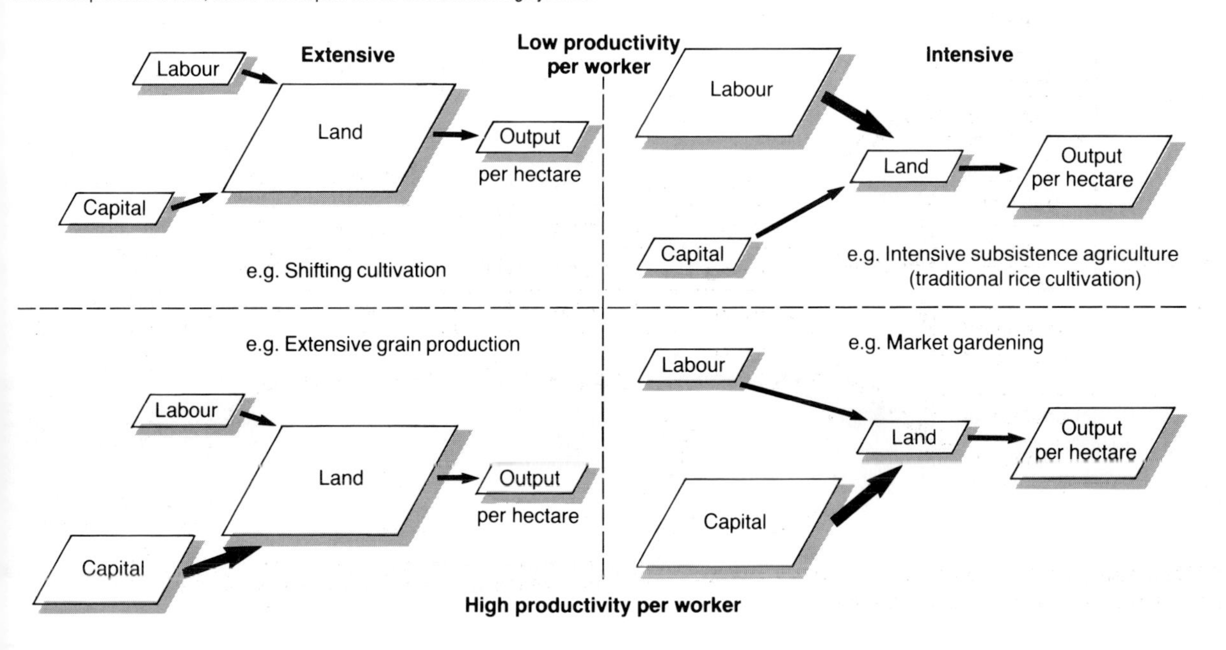

CHAPTER 2

Farming Types

There are a number of ways that farming can be classified and there is therefore no universally accepted classification. The number of types identified at a world scale will depend on the purposes of the classification. A simple classification using ten types as in 2.6 gives only a very generalised impression with many drawbacks. The boundaries on the map are very arbitrary: in reality boundaries are rarely rigid. Because of the small scale of the map it is not possible to show that a range of agricultural activites will be taking place in many of these areas.

Nomadic hunting/gathering

No crops are grown or domestic livestock reared in this type of farming; the hunter/gatherer relies on hunting animals and collecting fruit and other food to survive. The few remaining hunter/gatherer societies rely on their intimate knowledge of their environment to find food. Contact with the outside world is destroying this way of life. Examples of hunter/gatherers are the Bushmen of the Kalahari, Pygmies of central Africa and some tribes in the Amazon rainforest.

Nomadic herding

Nomadic pastoralists live in inhospitable arid or cold environments where pasture is sparse. They move in search of new pasture for their animals. In arid areas this movement is determined by the seasonal nature of the rainfall. In cold northern latitudes the nomadic pastoralists such as the Lapps move as pasture becomes covered in snow. Nomads may travel very long distances, often across national frontiers, in search of pasture. Recent droughts and increased human and animal populations in the Sahel region of Africa have caused many nomadic pastoralists to give up this way of life and move to small towns in order to survive.

Shifting cultivation

Shifting cultivation is largely limited to areas of tropical rainforest which tend to be relatively inaccessible. This type of agriculture is sometimes given the alternative name **slash and burn cultivation**. The shifting cultivators clear small areas of forest,

2.6 Distrtibution of the main farming types

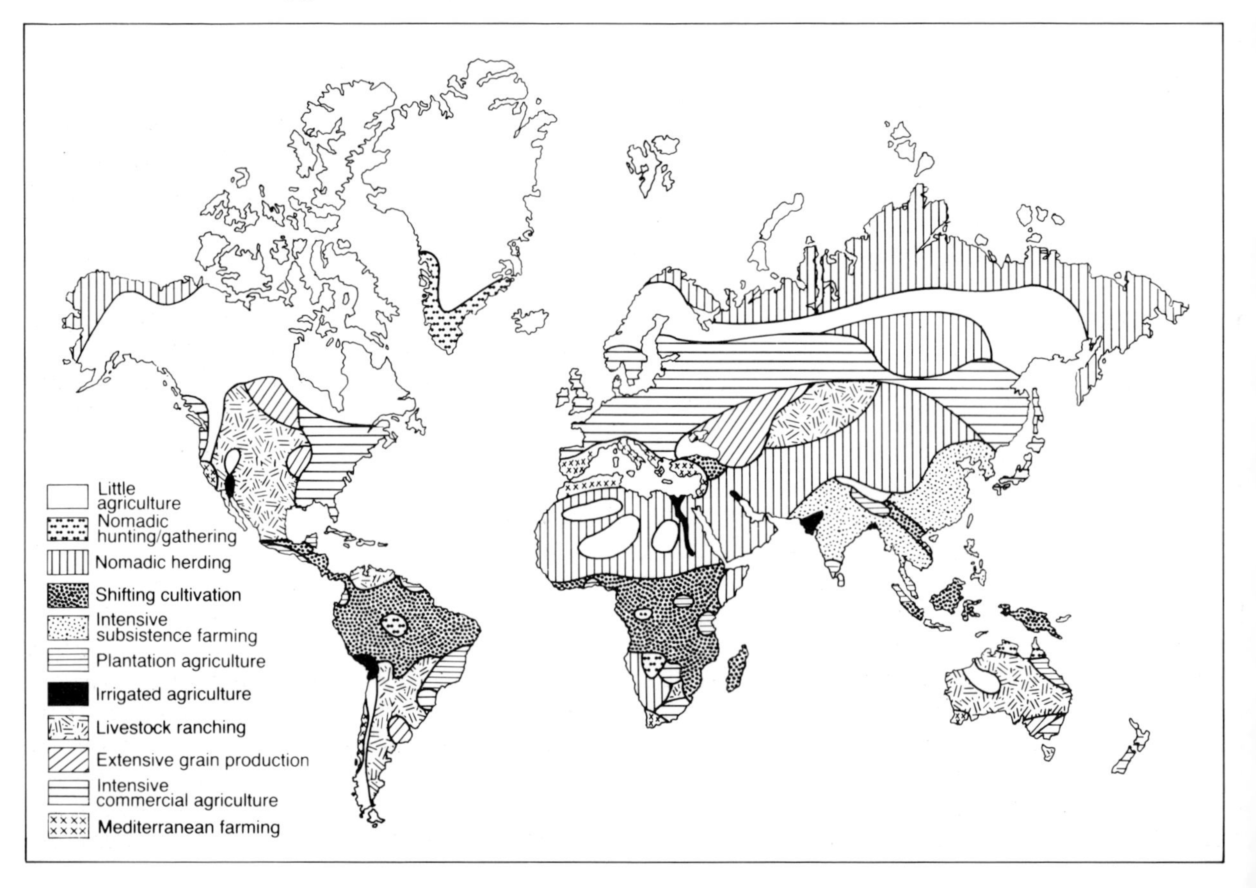

burn the felled timber and undergrowth, and then plant a range of crops for subsistence needs (in South America maize, cassava, yams, and bananas are basic crops, in Asia upland rice is an important crop). With the trees removed, the heavy rainfall **leaches** nutrients out of the soil, which therefore becomes less and less fertile. Within a few years the plot of land has to be abandoned and another is cleared.

Intensive subsistence farming

This type of agriculture is restricted to southern and eastern Asia. Traditionally the staple food crop has been rice. Farms are generally small with no wasted land or fallow. Inheritance customs, whereby the land is divided and passed on to children within a family, has led to fragmentation and reduction in size of holdings in many parts of Asia. Farms may be no more than 1 hectare in size. Because this type of farming is **labour intensive** and many fields yield two crops per year, **productivity per hectare** is high. In some parts of Asia rural population densities may be as high as 200 per km^2 but the standard of living is low.

Plantation agriculture

Plantations were developed in the Tropics by Europeans and North Americans. Large areas were cleared in the tropical forests and single crops were planted. Common plantation crops are cocoa, oil palm, sugar cane, rubber, bananas, tea, coffee and tobacco. Plantations required a large input of capital to clear the land and build an **infrastructure** (roads, buildings, irrigation, etc.). Plantations did not disappear with independence of colonies; most are now owned by either multinational companies or are state-run companies.

Irrigated agriculture

Irrigation is the provision of water to enable an area of land to be cultivated. Irrigation is needed in areas where:

- precipitation is low (e.g. Egypt)
- precipitation is seasonal (e.g. California)
- precipitation is unreliable
- the crops (e.g. rice) have special requirements

In developing countries traditional irrigation systems are slowly being replaced by major modern irrigation projects. Often much of the capital for these projects is provided by developed countries. These large projects are not without their environmental consequences. For example, the damming of the Nile at the Aswan High Dam has reduced the supply of silt to the Nile valley, requiring fertilisers to be used on fields. Irrigation channels have also enabled **bilharzia** (a tropical disease, spread by a freshwater snail) to spread to previously unaffected areas.

Livestock ranching (extensive commercial)

Livestock ranching earns the lowest profit per unit of land of any type of commercial farming. It tends to be found in relatively remote areas where other possible land uses are limited: for example, the Scottish Highlands and the Australian interior (sheep rearing); the Great Plains of the USA and Pampas of Argentina (cattle ranching). This type of agriculture requires relatively little capital investment and the output per farm worker tends to be high. European immigrants were largely responsible for the development of livestock ranching in the semi-arid grasslands of temperate latitudes, using European breeds.

Extensive grain production

Extensive grain production is found on the North American Prairies, the Steppes of the Soviet Union, some parts of Western Europe, south-east Australia and Argentina. Some state farms in northern China also fit into this category. These areas have a relatively restricted growing season with low precipitation. Characteristically farms are very large, often over 1000 hectares. In all regions except China very little labour is required as the production is very capital intensive. Productivity per hectare is low but per farm worker it is high.

Intensive commercial agriculture

This type of agriculture is found on a large scale in Europe, eastern North America, and parts of South Africa, South America, Australia and New Zealand. Smaller zones are also found in close proximity to many of the world's largest cities. The major regions have moderate precipitation throughout the year.

This category of agriculture covers a wide variety of agricultural activities including: crop cultivation, often in rotation; dairying; market gardening; and fruit production. A low input of labour and a large input of capital is typical, giving high productivity per farm worker. Farms are much smaller than those under extensive grain production, giving high productivity per hectare.

Mediterranean farming

The Mediterranean climate with its warm moist winters and hot dry summers has produced a distinctive type of farming, also adopted by other parts of the world with a Mediterranean type climate, such as central California, central Chile, south-west Australia and part of South Africa. Typically cereals and spring vegetables are grown in winter and harvested in spring and early summer. Vines, olives and citrus fruit production are widespread. Irrigation can permit a second crop to be grown on some land during the summer. On drier land goats and sheep are pastured.

CHAPTER 2

Shifting Cultivation

Although **shifting cultivation** is now regarded as a primitive form of agriculture, largely restricted to the Tropics, in the past it was practised by many different peoples in a wide range of natural conditions. Shifting cultivation was practised by the Indians of North America and until medieval times was common in Europe, when population densities were much lower than now.

Shifting cultivation is known by many other names including 'slash and burn' farming. It is known as 'milpa' in Mexico, 'roca' in Brazil, 'masole' in Zaire and 'ladang' in Malaysia. Throughout the humid Tropics the high temperatures and heavy rainfall result in rapid leaching of exposed soils. Once cleared of the original vegetation the soils quickly lose their fertility and crop yields fall rapidly. The poorest soils are not capable of an economic return under this system, and even the best soils provide adequate yields for only ten years or so (2.7).

Artificial fertilisers are not used and little animal manure is available so the natural fertility of the soil is recovered by **fallowing**: leaving the soil to **regenerate** naturally while crops are not grown. The regeneration is carried out by the natural plant life as it recolonises the abandoned clearing. Depending on the soil and local environment the soil recovery may take between 7 and 35 years. Forest environments tend to require longer fallow periods than grassland environments.

Under shifting cultivation only a small proportion of the land is used at any one time. This means that a large amount of land is required and the yields per hectare (for all land, in cultivation and in fallow) are tiny. Fallow periods tend to become reduced through population pressure or loss of land and when this happens the soil's productivity declines (2.8). Shifting cultivation

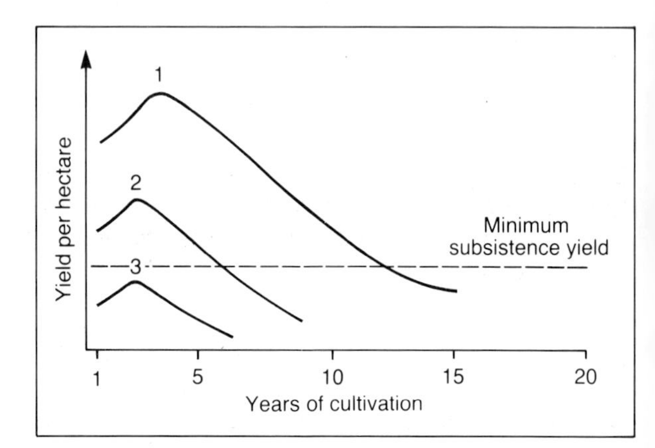

▲ 2.7 Declining fertility of tropical rainforest soils. Type 1, the most fertile, will produce at least minimum subsistence yields for 12 years, but the poorest soils, type 3, cannot produce subsistence yields for even one year.

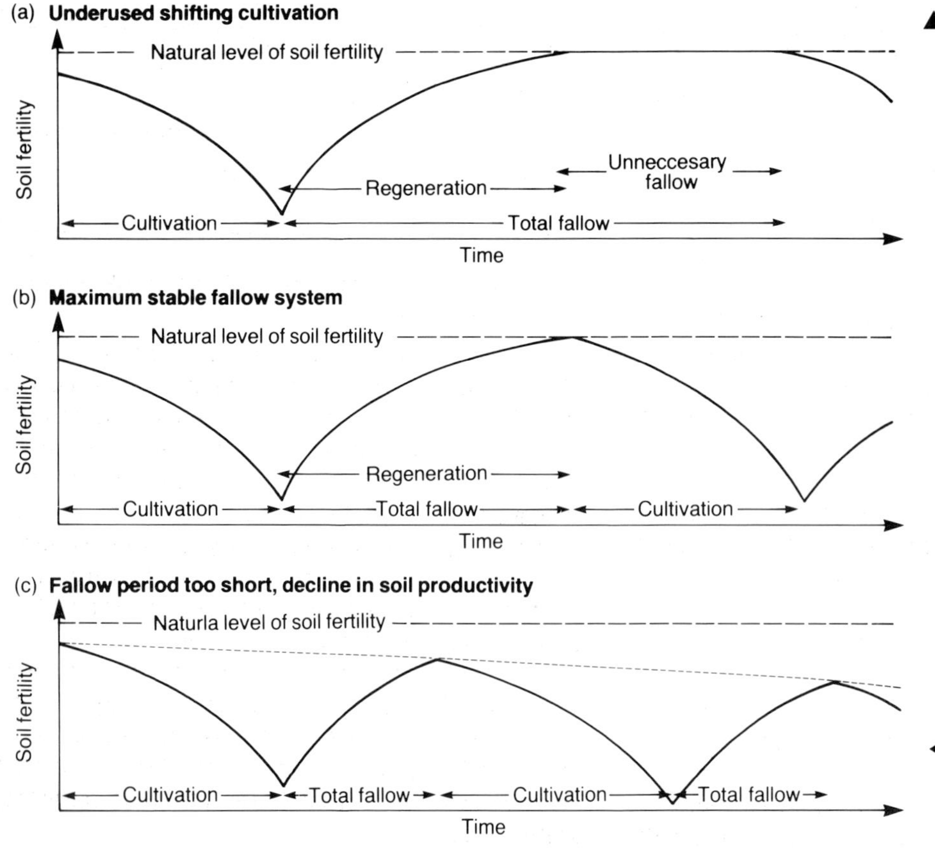

◀ 2.8 Soil fertility under different fallow regimes. When the fallow period is too short, soil fertility declines from its natural level.

as a system cannot cope with declining fallow periods. When the fallow period is radically reduced, stationary settlements tend to be the norm, with intensively cultivated land surrounding them and more distant land cultivated in rotation. This type of cultivation is known as **rotational bush fallowing** and is often distinguished from true shifting cultivation (2.9). Rotational bush fallowing has replaced true shifting cultivation in many parts of Africa, particularly West Africa. The distinction between shifting cultivation and bush fallowing is not clear-cut as the two systems merge into each other. Because they both rely on the rotation of land rather than the rotation of crops to regain fertility, they are often treated as one type of agriculture.

Components of shifting cultivation

Because shifting cultivation is practised on a range of tropical landscapes by a great variety of tribal groups, the exact details vary from place to place, but some essential aspects remain the same everywhere.

1. The natural vegetation is cleared. If the natural vegetation is forest some of the largest trees may be left standing because of the labour involved in felling them, and other trees are left because of their fruit. Clearing is usually a mixture of felling and burning. Clearings tend to have no clearly defined outline, to be untidy in appearance, and to be scattered throughout the area and not adjacent to each other.
2. Crops are planted in the ash of the cleared site. Most commonly a mix of crops are grown and only rarely will any single crop cover a large area. Very little cultivation is done and the crops are planted with the minimum of effort.
3. A succession of crops is grown in the clearing. Care is taken to plant the most demanding crops in the first years and concentrate on less demanding crops as the soil deteriorates. **Manioc** (cassava), a crop native to South America, is now widely grown throughout the Tropics, because it can be grown in depleted soils and can be left in the ground for long periods before use.
4. When yields fall to a low level, the clearing is abandoned to be recolonised by the natural vegetation.
5. A new clearing is chosen and prepared: this is often done before the previous clearing's fertility diminishes to a critical level. A village may actively use several clearings, at different stages of exhaustion, at any time.

A future for shifting cultivation?

Although this system of agriculture is regarded as primitive, the shifting cultivators display an intimate understanding of their environment. The practice of shifting cultivation is more sophisticated than it appears, and is not an unreasonable method of cultivation in areas of low population density and poor soils.

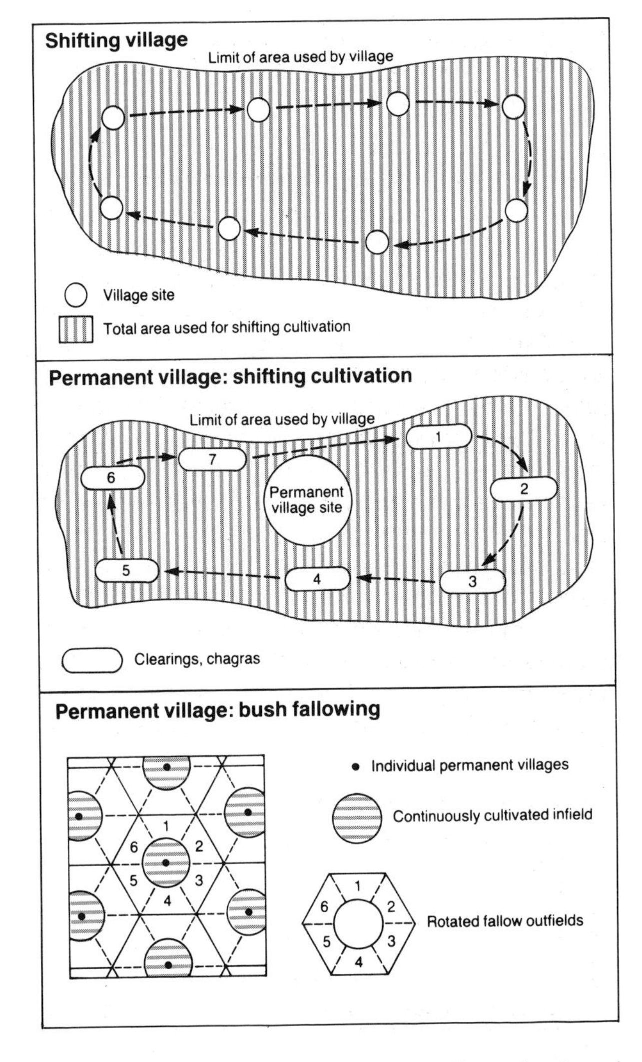

2.9 Shifting cultivation and bush fallowing. The diagrams illustrate three types of settlement/farming system.

Shifting cultivation however does have its critics, and the widespread destruction of forests in India and Thailand has been blamed on some shifting cultivators. Many tropical countries have taken steps to ban or modify the practices of shifting cultivators within their territory, with varying degrees of success. In India some shifting cultivators work with foresters: they clear the land and grow crops for one or two years then the foresters plant commercial timber and restore the land. In Indonesia and Fiji, government resettlement of shifting cultivators onto individual permanent farms has met with mixed results.

The inability of shifting cultivation to support an increasing population and assist in economic development is a problem for many developing countries. It also doesn't encourage the development of a transport infrastructure or other economic and social features which are present in permanent settlement (e.g. schools, shops, etc.).

CHAPTER 2

A Case Study: Shifting Cultivation in South America

Many tribes of Amerindians in the Amazon rainforest practise forms of shifting cultivation. The shifting cultivators make clearings of around 25 hectares and about three months after cutting down the trees the wood and undergrowth is burnt. These clearings are turned into cultivated gardens or **chagras** by the Indians (2.10).

2.10 Forest clearing. Chagra or garden cultivated by rainforest Indians.

The boundaries of the chagras aren't fired, to speed up regeneration after the chagra is abandoned. The chagras are mainly used to grow crops but fruit trees are also grown to provide more food and to attract birds and bats which leave seeds in their droppings. This also helps to speed up regeneration later.

The Indians are careful to choose the correct type of soil for their chagras by examining the natural vegetation. They prefer to clear fully developed forest which has little undergrowth and few surface roots. They also tend to aviod the fertile river banks because of flooding.

Subsistence crops such as yucca, peppers, tobacco, coca, beans, pumpkins, maize and manioc are grown in the chagras. Demanding crops such as yucca are grown for only one or two years before the soil loses its fertility and the weeds start to encroach. The Indians then make new clearings and return to collect fruit and harvest manioc (which is tolerant of poor soils) from the earlier clearing before it is finally abandoned, for the forest to reclaim. Manioc is often referred to as 'the bread of the Tropics' because it is used to produce a flour called cassava. Manioc can also provide sugar, beer, and poison for hunting darts. Cassava provides basic carbohydrate for the Indians' diet which is high in calories but low in protein.

A family group of 15–20 people may depend on four or five chagras (100 ha) in various stages of regeneration with only about 40 hectares suitable for active cultivation. If the land required for hunting, gathering and cultivating is taken into account, each person uses about 1000 hectares of land. The Indians live in a semi-permanent central clearing, where they set up their homes (**malocas**: see 2.11). From here they farm the various chagras that are in use (see 2.9b).

Apart from crops in the chagras, the Indians also cultivate an orchard of 2–3 hectares next to their communal homes on the semi-permanent site (see 2.11). Fruit trees such as avocado, papaya, mango, lemon and chontaduro palm are common. Some other crops may be grown on a small scale, fertilised by food remains, animal and human manure. Village or family clearings with their malocas may be inhabited for many years until they have to be moved because the actively cultivated chagras are becoming too distant. Clearings with abandoned malocas commonly remain in cultivation for a number of years because the soil is still fertile, having been manured and tended.

The Indians' view of nature shapes their use of the rainforest. They believe in the completeness of the forest and see each animal and plant species as having a necessary role. They believe that there is a balance between the species and if one increases at the expense of others it will lead to disaster and death. The Indians hunt or gather fruit under the guidance of their **shaman** (jaguar man or witch doctor – although this term does them an injustice – one of the community leaders, whose authority is inherited). He in effect acts like an ecologist managing the rainforest. This knowledge of the environment is embellished with rituals such as fasting and other restrictions. These rituals are seen as repayment for that which has been consumed and they maintain balance in the forest. The Indians' individual and social lives are based on a belief of giving and taking from the forest and each other.

In some parts of the Amazon forest the Indians have been forced onto reservations or into more remote areas deep in the interior of the forest. Hydro-electric schemes, mineral exploitation, cattle ranching and extension of the road system all increase contact with 'Western' culture, which threatens the Indians' traditional way of life (2.12). Population numbers have dropped through a lack of immunity to 'Western' diseases, and genocide (thousands of Indians have been killed by settlers over the last 30 years). There were perhaps up to 2 million indigenous people in the Brazilian Amazon 500 years ago; now numbers may be as low as 50 000. The destruction of the rainforest in Brazil is a serious threat to the existence of many Indian tribes. Poor Brazilian settlers who displace the Indians often have to practise some form of shifting cultivation. But these settlers don't have the Indians' knowledge of the forest or concern for the environment and are laying waste large tracts of the rainforest.

Shifting cultivators in the Amazon are not undergoing a slow change to sedentary (stationary) agriculture, as has taken place in other parts of the world, but are often experiencing the destruction of their environment and loss of their land.

In Colombia, however, the government has given recognition to the culture of the indigenous peoples, has given land back to them and recognised the authority of their traditional leaders. Without similar moves, in other countries, to preserve this way of life, shifting cultivation will become a thing of the past.

2.11 Forest clearing with settlement. The malocas are the houses of the rainforest Indians. The clearing is intensively cultivated and other chagras are cleared in the surrounding rainforest.

2.12 Contact with Western culture is disrupting the Indians' way of life: (a) new roads being constructed into the forest, (b) begging for food along the roadside, (c) cattle ranches replacing the forest, (d) new towns in the rainforest.

CHAPTER 2

Intensive Subsistence (Peasant) Farming

A change from shifting to sedentary cultivation does not necessarily mean that economic or social conditions are improved. Often such change has been brought about by the pressure of increased population on the land and has not been accompanied by significant food surpluses.

Within the category of intensive subsistence farming, which occupies much of southern and eastern Asia, there are two major types of farming system: one which relies on rainfall for its water supply and the other which is based on irrigation. The two types are not mutually exclusive as farmers will resort to forms of irrigation whenever possible.

Wet rice cultivation

In the wetter lowland areas of south-east Asia the main system of agriculture involves the cultivation of rice each year. A great variety of rice strains and methods of cultivation have been developed over the centuries. The lowland or 'wet' varieties of rice are by far the most important and are grown in flooded fields.

Wet rice requires a relatively short growing season of only 100 days or so and temperatures in excess of 20 °C. In parts of south-east Asia where rainfall or irrigation can supply water all year round, two or three crops of rice may be grown in a year. However on the best land it is usual to grow two crops of rice and one non-irrigated crop (e.g. wheat, maize, etc.) within one year. Sometimes the flooded paddy fields are stocked with fish to provide protein for the diet.

Typically the best type of soil for rice cultivation is medium to heavy with a relatively impervious subsoil to retain the water. The land has to be level and the fields are surrounded by banks of earth (called **bunds** in India) to hold the water. The small fields are called **sawahs** in south-east Asia and are sometimes referred to as **paddy fields**. In some parts of Asia, where population densities are high and there is limited flat land, **terraces** are created on the steep hill slopes (2.13). These terraced fields may only be a few metres in width.

The supply of water to the fields is of crucial importance in this form of agriculture and a range of methods are used throughout Asia. On river flood-plains and in deltas, annual flooding may provide water and nutritious silt to the fields. The regimes of most rivers are not reliable enough to guarantee flooding at the correct

2.13 Terraced rice fields

time so some form of irrigation is used in these areas. In some parts of India small reservoirs or **tanks** are used to retain some of the monsoon rains and this water is used to irrigate the fields. The irrigation water from the tanks is usually transferred to fields by gravity and the fields are monitored to ensure water levels are correct. Water is either drained from the fields or has evaporated before the rice is cut.

Method of cultivation

Although there are variations in the methods of cultivation of wet rice there are broad similarities between the methods. All are relatively simple processes with most work being done by hand.

1. The farmer has to make sure that the earth banks which surround the fields are in a good condition and capable of retaining the water.
2. In most cases seed is sown in nursery beds first and the seedlings are later transplanted into the paddy fields. The nursery beds are small areas where the soil is broken down into a fine mud in preparation for the seeds.
3. The paddy fields are prepared by flooding to a depth of several centimetres and then the land is hoed by hand or harrowed by oxen or water buffalo.
4. Seedlings are transplanted into the fields at a few weeks old. This process is very time-consuming, planting the seedlings the correct distance apart, but it ensures that the farmers obtain the maximum yield (2.14).
5. The water in the fields has to be kept at the correct level to ensure that the upper parts of the plants are not submerged. Water is fed in from feeder canals and can be drained by transferring water to adjacent fields by breaching the bunds. Once the rice matures, the fields are allowed to dry out to enable the crop to ripen.
6. Harvesting, like other practices, is done by hand, using a knife or sickle (2.15).

2.14 Transplanting rice

Soil fertility

Throughout much of Asia, rice has been cropped on the same land for centuries, without an appreciable drop in fertility. The soil fertility is maintained by the cultivation method (2.16). The water supplied to the fields provides nutrients as does any silt provided by river flooding. The rice stubble is ploughed back into the field adding organic material to the soil, and nitrogen-fixing algae enrich both the water and the soil. Algae grow on the soil and float on the water surface. Soil erosion is negligible as the fields are embanked. Some animal and human manure may also be added to the fields but this is not significant throughout the wet rice growing areas. The weathering of parent material (underlying rock) releases some nutrients, and leaching is negligible because the soils are relatively impervious. 2.16 illustrates the nutrient cycle: nutrients removed by the rice crop are replaced from various sources.

2.15 Harvesting rice by hand

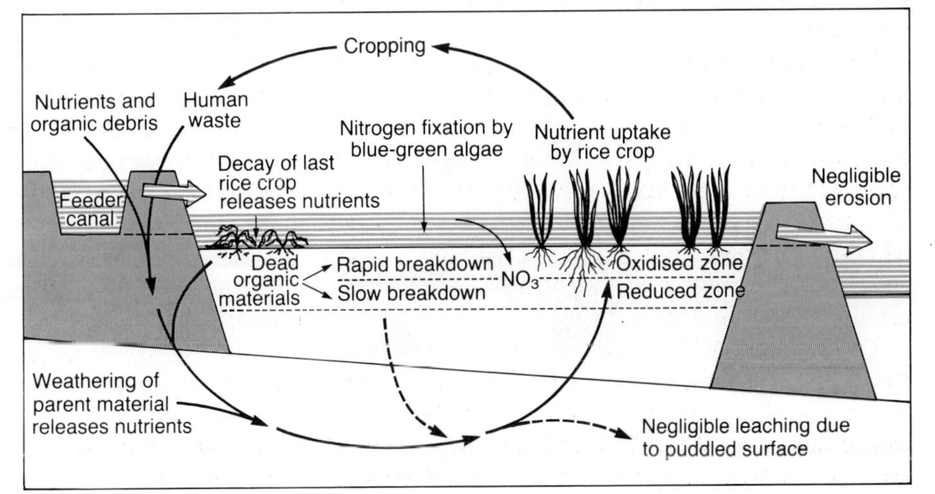

2.16 Maintenance of soil fertility in paddy fields

CHAPTER 2

Intensive dry-field farming

In the drier parts of south-east Asia, particularly the interior of the Indian sub-continent, the main system of farming is **intensive dry-field farming**. Unlike wet rice cultivation no single crop is dominant. In the driest areas wheat, millet and sorghum are the important cereal crops while wetter areas tend to grow rice and maize (2.17). Chick peas, groundnuts and sesame are also commonly grown throughout the dry farming areas in India, and cotton remains an important cash crop for farmers. Manioc has been introduced into the dry farming areas of India because it gives high yields in difficult conditions.

As with wet farming, in many areas farmers attempt the cultivation of two crops each year. A quick-growing crop is grown during the monsoon rains and a drought-resistant crop is planted once the rains have finished, often wheat, sorghum or chick peas. The crops grown during the monsoon are known in India as **kharif** crops and the crops grown during the dry season are known as **rabi** crops.

Cattle are used as draught animals (to pull ploughs, carts, etc.) in India but they are not eaten because this is prohibited by the Hindu faith (the Indian constitution forbids the slaughter of cattle). The cattle provide some manure but this is often used as fuel rather than to fertilise the land. Their milk yield is low because of inadequate feeding and poor quality of the stock. On the farms of the Deccan Plateau, in the drier interior of the Indian sub-continent, the yields from the volcanic soils are so poor that it has been calculated that cattle consume up to 30% of farm output (a smaller percentage would be consumed in more productive agricultural areas). This level of inefficiency suggests that cattle in India make a negative contribution to food production. However a lack of money for farm machinery and the expense of maintenance mean that mechanisation is not a realistic option for small farmers.

2.17 Wheat growing in the dry-field farming areas of India

The **Green Revolution** is the term used to label a range of modern techniques which have been applied to farming in developing countries. Its beginning can be traced to the **hybrids** (improved varieties) of wheat and maize developed in an attempt to solve Mexico's low domestic food production. Yields of wheat and maize increased by two to three times using the new varieties. This encouraged the introduction of these new techniques in developing countries to feed growing populations. 'Improved' varieties of rice have also been developed.

However, there have been some practical problems.

- Many of the improved strains can only sustain high yields by increasing use of fertilisers and pesticides.
- Fertilisers are expensive to make or import, and distribution from local factories or ports is often difficult.
- Local farmers need to be educated in the proper use of fertilisers, since wrong use can reduce yields.
- Many pesticides are highly toxic and dangerous to humans and the environment. Uneducated farmers may be unaware of the hazards involved.
- Often the innovations in rice cultivation have not been adopted by the peasant farmer because of the costs involved.
- Innovations have been developed without consulting the people they were intended for.

All evidence suggests that innovation will be accepted by small-scale farmers if (a) it solves a problem, (b) the recommended practices are demonstrated to them, and (c) the technology required is not too complex.

The high-yielding variety seed programme (HVP) (wheat and rice) was started in 1966, in India. It was an attempt to increase production in densely populated areas where land was already intensively cultivated. Traditional varieties of seed which had evolved over long periods of time were able to survive under less than ideal conditions but yields were low. The new high-yielding varieties (**HYVs**) have a shorter growing season and are very responsive to fertilisers. In the Indian Punjab region the uptake of the new varieties was rapid and by 1975 around 90% of wheat and rice cultivation used HYV varieties. This had more than doubled the yields for both grains. The success in adopting new HYV varieties in India changed its status from being a grain importer in the 1960s to a grain exporter in the 1980s. However, the new varieties were most successful on the larger farms and on the better-quality irrigated land. This has led to a widening of the gap between the most advantaged and the least well-off.

New seed varieties and cultivation methods have increased grain yields in south-east Asia, but the benefits have not been spread evenly among the rural population.

Case Study: Muda area of Malaysia

One area that has gained substantially from the Green Revolution is the Muda area of Malaysia. This is an area of about 100 000

2.18 Motorised plough in north-eastern Thailand. This enables the farmer to cultivate more land with less need for additional labour.

hectares of paddy fields near the coast. Irrigation (from a reservoir built with World Bank aid) and faster-ripening varieties of seed have allowed the cultivation of two rice crops a year as opposed to the previous single crop. Yearly yields have tripled in some farms and have provided the surplus necessary for farmers to buy machinery (2.18). The use of a motorised plough makes it possible for farmers to work four times as much land by themselves, reducing the need for additional workers.

The farmers have gained in wealth but they no longer require the services of the landless labourers, who are therefore worse off. However, the farmers' increased wealth allows them to buy more consumer goods and consume more electricity which creates a demand for more industrial jobs. The success of the scheme is to a large degree due to the improved provision of irrigation water. Without the guaranteed supply of water, the fast-ripening rice would be a much riskier proposition (2.19).

Land reform in south-east Asia

Many countries in south-east Asia have developed **land reform** policies in an attempt to share the land more evenly and maintain agricultural production. This is another aspect of the Green Revolution.

In India, for example, more than 160 million people live on farms smaller than 1 hectare which is the minimum size required to support an Indian family at subsistence level. Almost as many people are landless peasants. Land reform which concentrated on redistributing land to landless peasants was started soon after Indian independence but only some Indian states have succeeded in redistributing large areas of land. India's problem is that even if all rural land was equally distributed the average size of a family farm would still be less than 2 hectares.

In Thailand, land reform, started in 1974, concentrated on redistributing land from the large-scale absentee land owners to the small farmers and clearing some state land for leasing to farmers' groups. However the *coup d'état* in 1976 largely ended government interest in land reform, with little achieved.

The land reform attempts in India and Thailand are typical of many throughout south-east Asia which have met with very limited success.

2.19 Yield comparisons between the new 'miracle' seed and traditional varieties

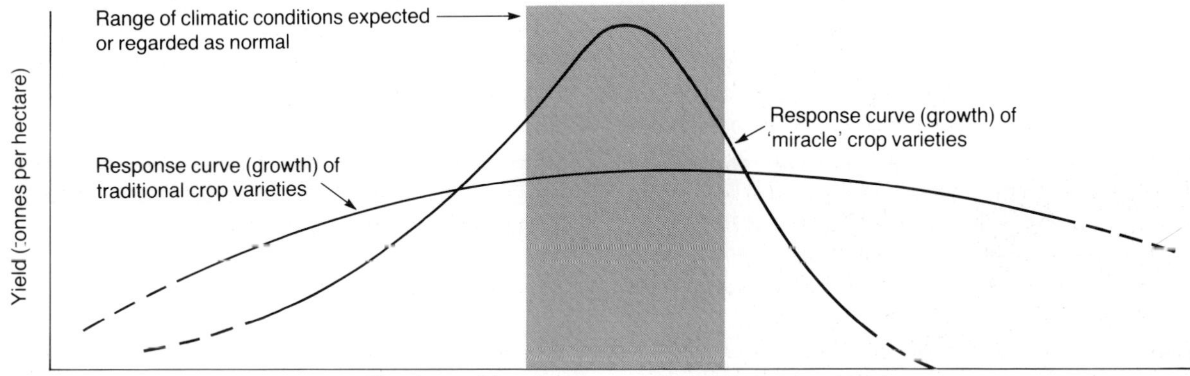

Q INTRODUCTION/THE FARMING SYSTEM

1 (a) What is a 'rural' area?
(b) What is meant by the term 'optimum condition' for a type of farming?
(c) Describe the optima and limits model (2.2).
(d) Explain the influences on the decision making processes in a farming system (2.3).
(e) What are the main differences between subsistence and cash-based systems of agriculture?
(f) Explain what is meant by the following terms:
intensive agriculture
extensive agriculture
sedentary agriculture
subsistence agriculture
(g) Copy the table below into your notebook.

Tick the boxes in the table which apply to each of the seven types of agriculture listed below.

1. Cattle ranching in Argentina
2. Rice farming in Thailand
3. Nomadic herding in northern Scandinavia
4. Coffee plantations in Brazil
5. Wheat growing in Canada
6. Shifting cultivation in Colombia
7. Bush-fallowing in Africa

	1	2	3	4	5	6	7
Arable							
Pastoral							
Shifting							
Sedentary							
Subsistence							
Commercial							
Intensive							
Extensive							

Q FARMING TYPES / SHIFTING CULTIVATION

2 (a) Describe the distribution of the following types of agriculture as shown on map 2.6:
(i) shifting cultivation *(ii)* intensive subsistence farming
(iii) extensive grain production *(iv)* livestock ranching
(b) Explain why shifting cultivation is practised in the humid Tropics.
(c) Why are some tropical soils not suitable for shifting cultivation?
(d) Why have fallow periods tended to become reduced in grassland areas of Africa?
(e) What happens to soil fertility as fallow periods are reduced?
(f) Describe the transition from shifting cultivation to bush fallowing.
(g) Describe the main components of shifting cultivation.
(h) Why is the future of shifting cultivation in the Tropics doubtful?

Q INTENSIVE SUBSISTENCE (PEASANT) FARMING /GREEN REVOLUTION

3 (a) Why is the supply of water the crucial factor in determining the system of agriculture for much of south-east Asia?
(b) Why are many rice fields terraced?
(c) Explain how soil fertility is maintained in paddy fields.
(d) Describe dry-field farming in the interior of the Indian sub-continent.
(e) Describe some of the advances in agriculture brought about by the Green Revolution.
(f) 'The Green Revolution has failed because it has merely widened the gap between rich and poor.'
Is this statement a fair reflection of the Green Revolution's success?
(g) Land reform has been attempted by many tropical nations. Why have so few attempts met with any success?
(h) List the advantages and disadvantages of growing the new HYV seeds.
(i) Look at the diagram below which illustrates the growth in grain production between 1970 and 1982 for different regions of the world. Population growth is illustrated for comparison.
(i) In which areas of the world has population growth outstripped growth in cereal output?
(ii) Why was there such a dramatic growth in cereal production in Asia?
(iii) How do these figures contradict the ideas of Malthus (Chapter 1)?

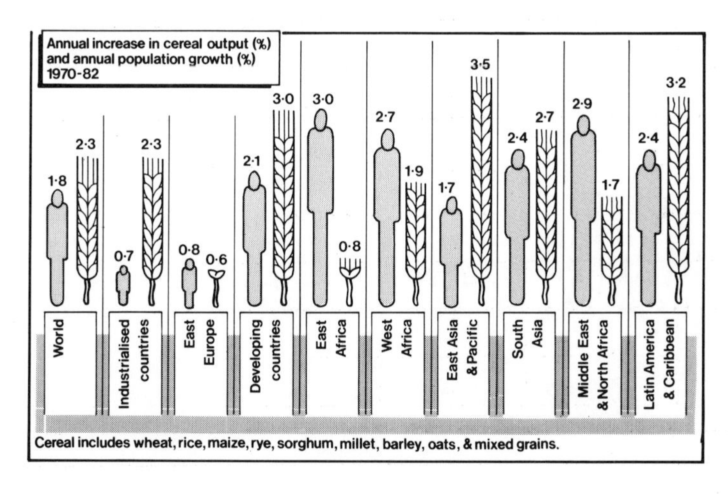

Research and Further Work

(a) Using an atlas attempt to define the optimum conditions for extensive wheat production in North America.
(b) Construct a diagram which explains the system of shifting cultivation.
(c) Find out what proportion of the world's cereal production is rice.
(d) Using the following table as a structure, find out more about the Green Revolution.

Type of change	Innovation	Success or failure
Biochemical	HYV seed	?
	Fertiliser	?
	Pesticides	?
Mechanical	Irrigation	?
	Farm machinery	?
	Improved infrastructure	?
Cultural	Agrarian reform	?
	Government loans	?

Extensive Commercial Farming

Commercial farming (livestock ranching and extensive grain production) spread into the temperate lands of the northern and southern hemispheres, notably the USA, Canada, New Zealand, Australia, Argentina, Uruguay and South Africa, with the emigration of European settlers.

Livestock ranching

In the USA livestock ranching originally began as an open range activity where the land was not divided by fences. Livestock had to be branded in order to indicate ownership. Fencing, improved transport and water supplies changed livestock ranching and made it possible to concentrate on producing high-quality beef. European pedigree bulls were brought over in the last century to improve local breeds, and now most cattle are European.

Livestock ranches in the USA are very large units: some are several thousand square kilometres in size. Large units are necessary because of the poor quality of grazing in this part of the Great Plains region which gets less than 500 mm of rainfall per year (2.20 and 2.21). Some irrigation water has made it possible for ranches to grow additional fodder crops. The workforce on most ranches is small and so productivity per worker is high.

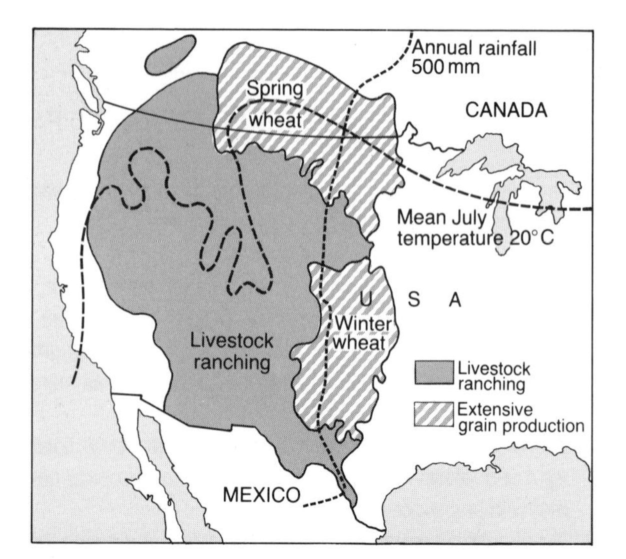

2.20 Extensive farming in the Great Plains and Prairies

Cattle are reared on the ranches for two years or so before being sent to the Corn Belt region for fattening, before slaughter.

The Pampas of South America (see 2.25) have between 500 and 1200 mm of rainfall per year which supports a better-quality grassland vegetation than in the USA and consequently the livestock ranches are smaller. Nevertheless, many ranches (*estancias*) are over 100 square kilometres, and keep around

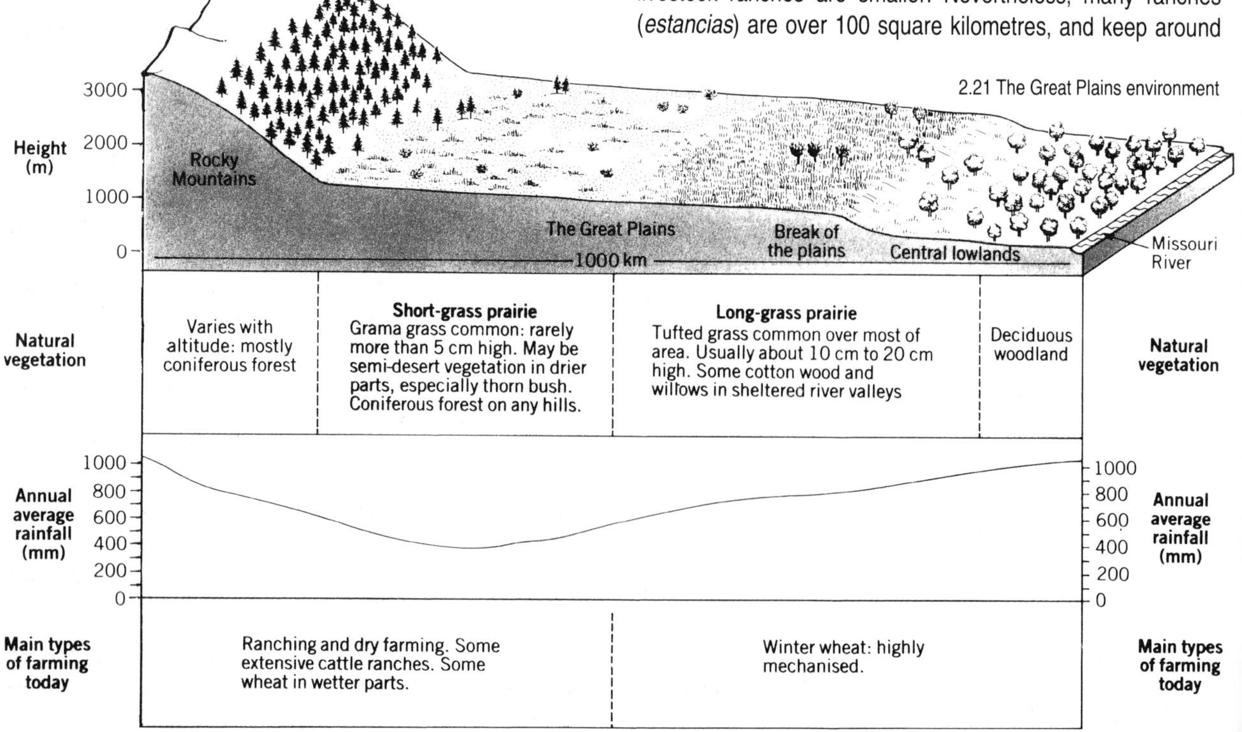

2.21 The Great Plains environment

2.22 Agricultural land use in the Prairies

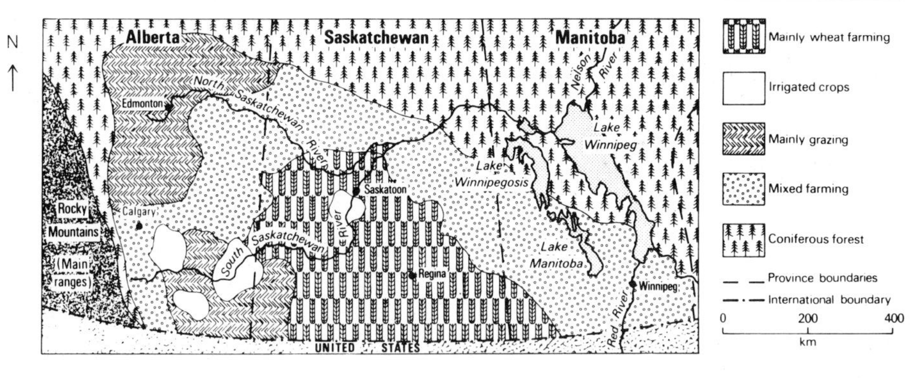

20 000 head of cattle, so they are still very large units. Most ranches are owned by large companies and the meat produced is largely for export.

The Pampas have other natural advantages for cattle ranching. The summers are warm and moist while the winters are mild and drier. This allows almost continuous plant growth. The land is flat and soils are deep and particularly fertile.

The introduction of alfalfa, a moisture-retaining legume, provides cattle fodder when the natural grasses die down in the drier winters. As in the USA, herds were improved by importing pedigree bulls both from Europe and Asia. Corned beef and Bovril are major meat products but refrigeration also allows the export of unprocessed meat.

Extensive grain production: the Prairies

The Canadian Prairies form the northernmost part of the interior grassland region of North America. The grasslands of the three Prairie Provinces, Alberta, Saskatchewan and Manitoba, are characteristically used for **spring wheat** (and cattle ranching in Alberta) but diversification into barley, sugar beet, beef and mixed farming has been noticeable since the 1970s (2.22). (Spring wheat is planted in the spring and harvested after a short growing season, while **winter wheat**, grown in warmer areas, is planted in winter and harvested in the autumn.)

The Prairies have physical characteristics which are advantageous for growing spring wheat.

- Although the summer growing season is short, it is long enough to give the 90 days minimum required.
- The short summer is warm (over 15 °C), sunny, with long hours of daylight.
- Precipitation, although light (about 500 mm), occurs mainly during the growing season.
- The black chernozem soils are deep and fertile.
- The land is relatively flat which aids mechanisation and transport (2.23).
- Severe winter frosts break up the soil.
- The warm chinook wind helps to melt the snow in the spring.

There are also some disadvantages.

- Droughts occur occasionally.
- Hail and early cold snaps can ruin crops.
- Summer tornadoes frequently damage crops.
- Without vegetation cover, the soil is vulnerable to erosion.

2.23 The farming landscape of the Prairies

In drier areas wheat may be grown by **dry farming** methods, which involve leaving the land fallow in alternate years, to regain soil moisture. Stubble is also left in the ground to trap moisture from the winter snow.

Wheat farming in the Prairies has tended to be capital intensive and therefore productivity per worker is high.

Yields in the Prairies have increased over the last 40 years thanks to a number of factors, including:

1. amalgamation of farms into larger more economic units (average size 400 hectares);
2. improved seed varieties which are drought and frost resistant, quicker maturing, and disease resistant;
3. more use of strip farming (land ploughed at right angles to the wind, sometimes with wheat and grass grown in alternate strips) and other measures to prevent erosion;
4. improved dry-farming methods (e.g. planting seeds deeper);
5. selective irrigation;
6. improved fertilisers and pesticides. (However, the modern practice of using artificial fertilisers and pesticides is harmful to wildlife, soil organisms, and the long-term productivity of the soil.)

While yields per hectare are relatively low in comparison with European farms, the high productivity per worker of extensive farming ensures that farms are very profitable.

CHAPTER 2

Von Thünen's rural land use model

The pattern of land use in many areas of extensive commercial farming has a broad similarity to the **von Thünen model** (2.24) because the landscape is fairly uniform.

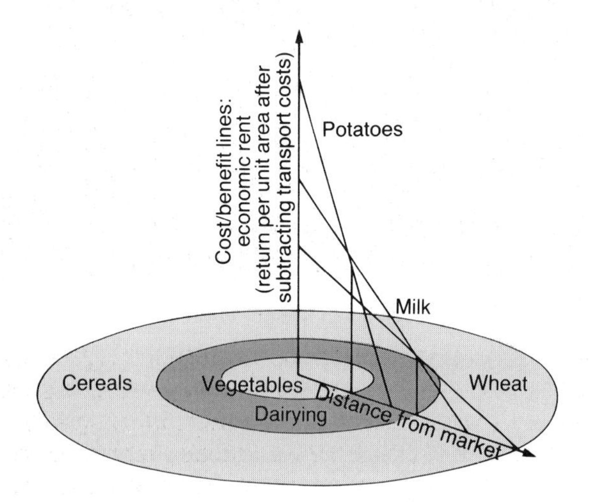

2.24 The von Thünen model. This illustrates the competition between cereals, dairying and vegetables

Henrich von Thünen, a German landowner, published a book called *The Isolated State* in 1826. In it he illustrated his ideas about patterns of agricultural land use by using a model. Von Thünen argued that, for farmers trying to sell to a single market, the land use they chose bore a relationship to the transport costs involved, the perishability and the value of the product.

Because the factors involved in the real world are too complicated, the von Thünen model, like all models, had to be based on several very simplistic assumptions.

1. The state or area is cut off from the rest of the world.
2. The state is dominated by one urban market.
3. All farmers seek to maximise profits and know the market equally well.
4. The physical environment (soil fertility, terrain, climate) is uniform throughout the state, i.e. it has an isotropic surface.
5. Transport is uniformly poor in all directions, and transport costs are proportional to distance, i.e. they are higher as distance from the urban centre increases.
6. Away from the central city the settlement pattern is one of strongly nucleated settlements (hamlets) of similar size.

The cost/benefit lines which delimit the zones in the model represent the value of the economic rent (profit for a unit of land under a particular crop) from the market to the periphery of the state.

Goods which are relatively cheap to buy but are heavy and bulky (e.g. potatoes) have a steep cost/benefit line because they are expensive to transport. They tend to be produced nearer to the market. Goods which are perishable (e.g. vegetables) can only be economic relatively near to the market, particularly if transport is poor. High-value goods (e.g. wheat), or those which are easy to transport and are not perishable, can be economically grown at some distance from the market.

In the real worl,. the pattern of land use in many areas follows roughly the pattern of the model, but obviously factors that contradict the general assumptions (e.g. uneven soil fertility, varying climate) alter the regularity. The assumptions of the model in relation to modern farming have less relevance today (since, e.g. transport links are much better and faster).

As an example, we shall look at how the pattern of land use in the Pampas of Argentina and Uruguay fits the von Thünen model. Map 2.25 indicates the main agricultural land uses, but is

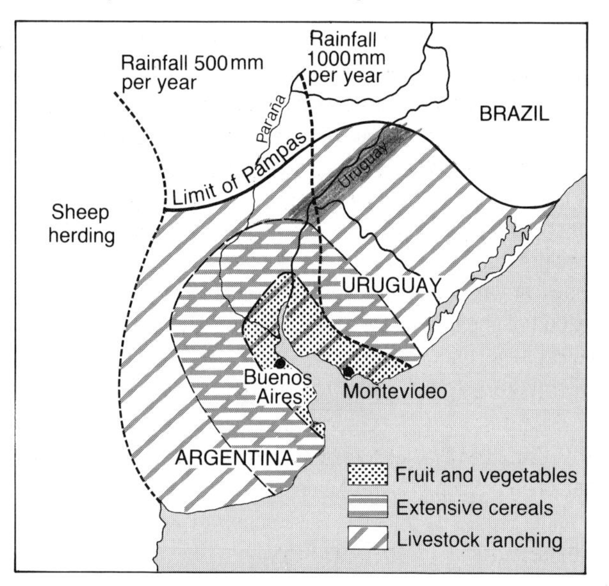

2.25 The Pampas of South America: main agricultural zones

much simplified. (In reality there are no clear boundaries between land uses and indeed cattle ranching is widespread and often intermingled with cereal cultivation.)

The zone closest to the urban markets of Buenos Aires and Montevideo concentrates on citrus fruit, potatoes, vegetables and dairying. Cereal cultivation is found in the next zone with wheat and maize being the two main crops. Further away from the urban markets, cattle ranching comes into its own with millet and sorghum grown as supplementary fodder. Cattle give way to sheep on the drier land to the south and also on the wetter land to the north, where tobacco is an important crop.

This zonal pattern of land use is similar to von Thünen's model, and the economic factors which are the basis for the model have been important determinants in farmers' decision making. The Pampas, being relatively uniform, are a good location to test von Thünen's model. Beyond the grassland environment, physical factors determine a change in land use.

Rural Settlement

The site, distribution and pattern of rural settlement, like the rural land use, are influenced by physical, economic and cultural factors. The site of a settlement is the land on which it is built and its relation to the immediate physical environment, while the pattern is the relationship of dwellings to each other. Rural settlement patterns fall into one of two main categories: dispersed (scattered) or nucleated (grouped together), with many different sub-divisions of each category.

Settlement: shifting cultivation

Human society involves group activity, and in simpler societies the tendency is to live in family, clan or tribal groups.The importance of social cohesion in groups of shifting cultivators is reflected in the type of dwellings they use. The Boro tribe of the Amazon rainforest tend to live in large groups with 3–6 families living under one roof. The large buildings they inhabit (malocas) are usually 20–30 metres long and about 10 metres high (see 2.11). Each family has its own fireplace, around which they sleep. Sometimes screening is erected inside the maloca to separate living areas. Other Amazon tribes have similar settlements, sometimes single dwellings and sometimes several large dwellings if the tribal group is large. These single malocas or villages are widely dispersed throughout the forest because about 1000 hectares of forest are needed to provide food for each person in the group (see 2.9).

Settlement: rice cultivation

The monsoonal rice-growing areas of south-east Asia are typically village landscapes. In some rural areas the population densities are very high and land is a precious commodity. Often canals are

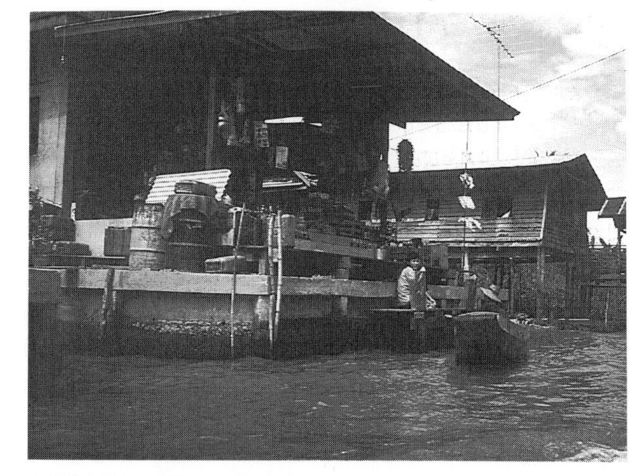

2.26 Canalside village in Thailand

the main streets and houses are on stilts (2.26). Although villages are common throughout south-east Asia there are some areas where settlement is dispersed. The villages also vary greatly in form and size. Typically they are nucleated settlements with houses surrounding a temple, school, market place and some shops. The need for communal co-operation over irrigation has been one factor which has encouraged nucleated villages in south-east Asia.

In India traditional villages are an untidy maze of paths without any recognised form. Socially the villages are segregated. The caste system, with divisions between the landowners and the landless, has tended to encourage settlement to be organised in villages, each caste occupying a separate part of the village and performing a particular function. The haphazard growth of the traditional nucleated village is very different from the planned villages which have tended to come hand in hand with irrigation schemes. These villages are rectangular canalside settlements with a central open space beside the temple and shops. They were planned by state agencies and their distribution is regular, and evenly dispersed along canals and roads (2.27).

2.27 Contrast between traditional and planned villages in the Punjab, India

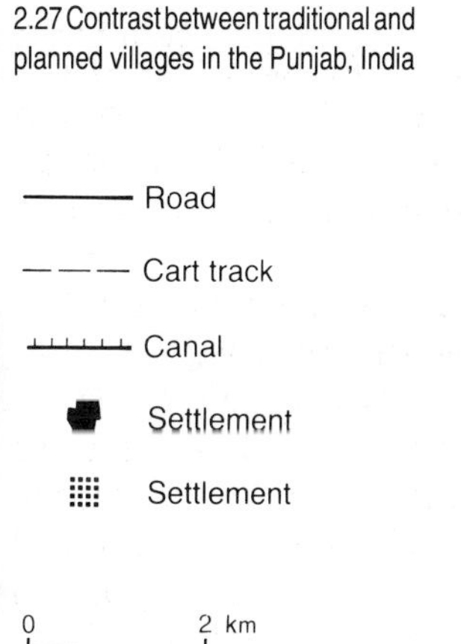

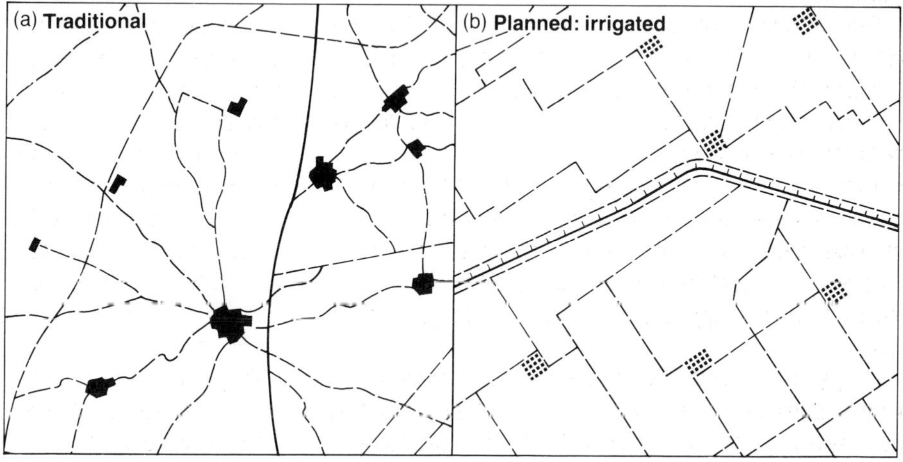

Settlement: The Prairies

The late colonisation of the Prairies (after 1872) allowed the settlers to benefit from the experience of their American neighbours in the Great Plains. In the early days, leases for cattle ranching in the dry Prairies could be cancelled in favour of cultivation. This priority for cultivation was largely responsible for today's land use patterns and settlement distribution.

The Park Belt (moister area of the Prairies) had better conditions for arable farming but the government encouraged mixed farming in this area in order to lessen the risk of any climatic hazard which might cause crop failure. This belt of mixed farming is still evident in the Prairie landscape.

Although settlers were allocated 160-acre (65 ha) farms the government encouraged farmers to acquire more land, often from the railway company. By 1920 farm sizes averaged 200 acres (81 ha) and by 1980 400 acres (162 ha) was the norm.

Settlement patterns are similar to those on the Great Plains with individual farms and villages dispersed along roads or railway lines. Farmers had to live close enough to the railway to deliver their grain and this created a linear pattern of settlement. The farms are more dispersed in the drier south and west, while the moister Park Belt has a higher density of population.

Because the Prairie Provinces are separated from the main population centres in eastern Canada by the coniferous forests of the Laurentian Shield (see 2.22), the Prairies have developed their own industries and service centres. The settlement hierarchy of the Prairies, from small hamlets to regional capitals (2.28), is

2.28 Rural settlement in the Prairies

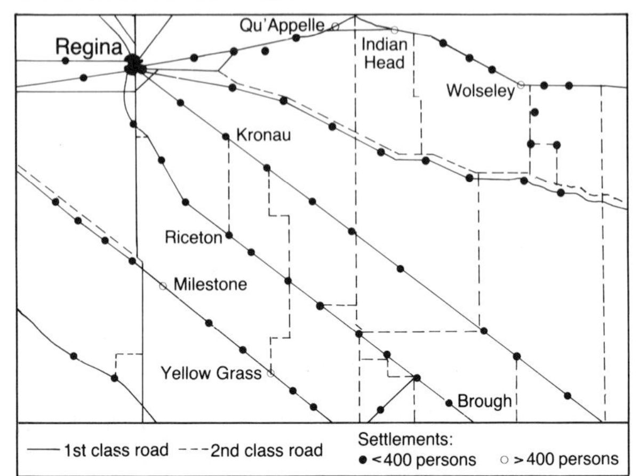

more fully developed than that of the Great Plains to the south. Although the cities of Edmonton (population 657 057 in 1981), Calgary, Winnipeg, Regina and Saskatoon are small by North American standards, they contrast with an absence of major regional centres in the northern Great Plains. Since the 1930s there has been an urbanisation of the Prairies population, with the towns and cities growing in population while many villages have declined or been abandoned. In 1931 61% of the population lived on farms; this percentage was halved by the mid 1960s.

Q EXTENSIVE COMMERCIAL FARMING/RURAL SETTLEMENT (SEE ALSO PAGES 174–5)

1 (a) Copy and complete the graph below by adding a further two lines. The line already drawn is the profit line for dairying which has a profit of £160 per hectare at the market and zero profit at 80 km from the market.
Draw on lines for wheat and sheep; wheat £120 profit at market and zero at 120 km from market; sheep £80 profit at market and zero at 160 km from the market.

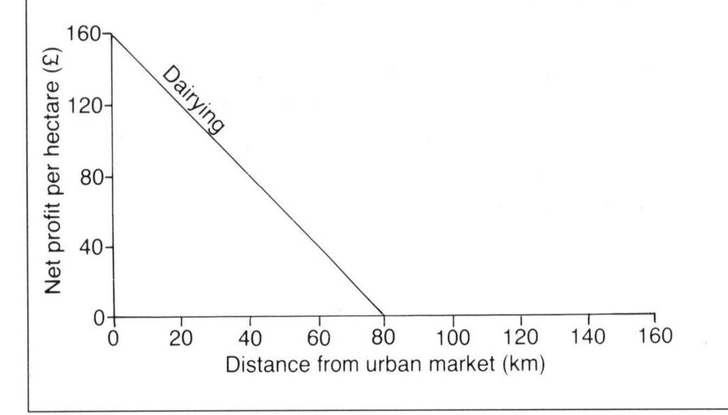

(i) At what distance from the market does wheat become more profitable than dairying?
(ii) At what distance from the market does sheep rearing become more profitable than wheat growing?
(iii) What would happen to the land use pattern if the market price of wheat were to rise sharply?
(iv) Why are patterns of land use that resemble von Thünen's model rarely found in reality?
(b) List the major differences in settlement patterns between intensive peasant farming in India and commercial grain production in the Prairies.
(c) What factors determine the limits of grain production and livestock ranching in The Great Plains and Prairies?
(d) Why does the land use pattern in the Pampas resemble von Thünen's model?

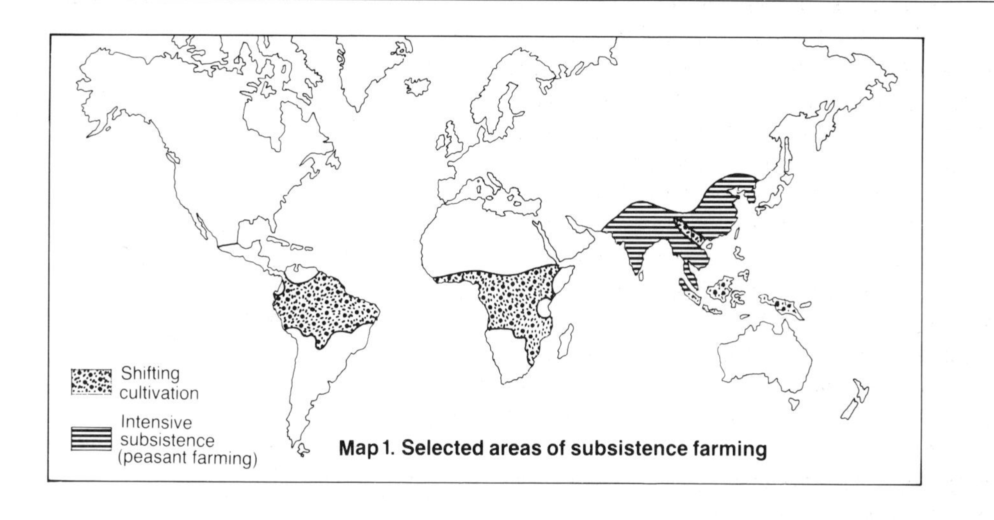

Map 1. Selected areas of subsistence farming

1 Look at map 1 which shows selected areas of subsistence farming.
(a) Name **one** area of 'shifting cultivation and **one** area of 'intensive (peasant) subsistence agriculture'. (2)
Either
(b) For one of the areas you have named in part (a):
(i) explain why subsistence farming is found there, (3)
(ii) describe and account for the farming methods used. (4)
or
(c) Shifting cultivation involves the rotation of fields rather than of crops. It is discouraged in some countries and illegal in others.
Describe this form of cultivation and explain why it may still be regarded as the best form of cultivation in some tropical, low population density areas. (7)

2 The table below gives approximate rice-production figures (million tonnes) in selected south-east Asian countries for 1966 and 1986.

	1966	1986
China	88.0	176.5
India	45.7	91.2
Indonesia	14.1	38.8
Pakistan	*16.4	4.8
Bangladesh		23.1
Thailand	11.8	19.7
Vietnam	8.8	15.8
Burma	6.6	14.8

* Pakistan figure for 1966 includes Bangladesh

Refer to the table if necessary.
Either
(a) Describe the traditional methods of rice cultivation in south-east Asia and comment on the developments which have led to increased production between 1966 and 1986. (9)
or
(b) In some parts of the tropical world shifting cultivation is changing into sedentary agriculture. Describe the impact this change is having on farming methods, the environment and settlement. Use named examples to illustrate your answer. (9)

Exam Style Questions

3 The agricultural system found in any area is influenced by a variety of factors, some of which are mentioned in diagram 2 below.

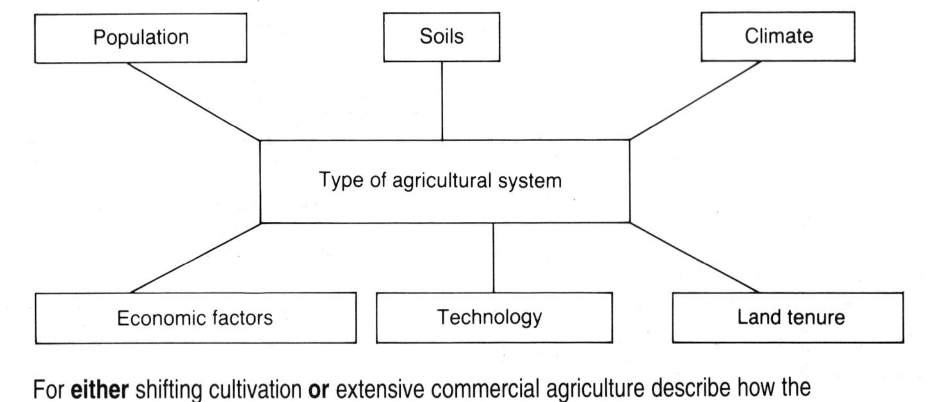

For **either** shifting cultivation **or** extensive commercial agriculture describe how the factors shown on the diagram above interrelate to influence the agricultural system. (9)

Diagram 3 Possible scenarios resulting from different management strategies on tropical ecosystems

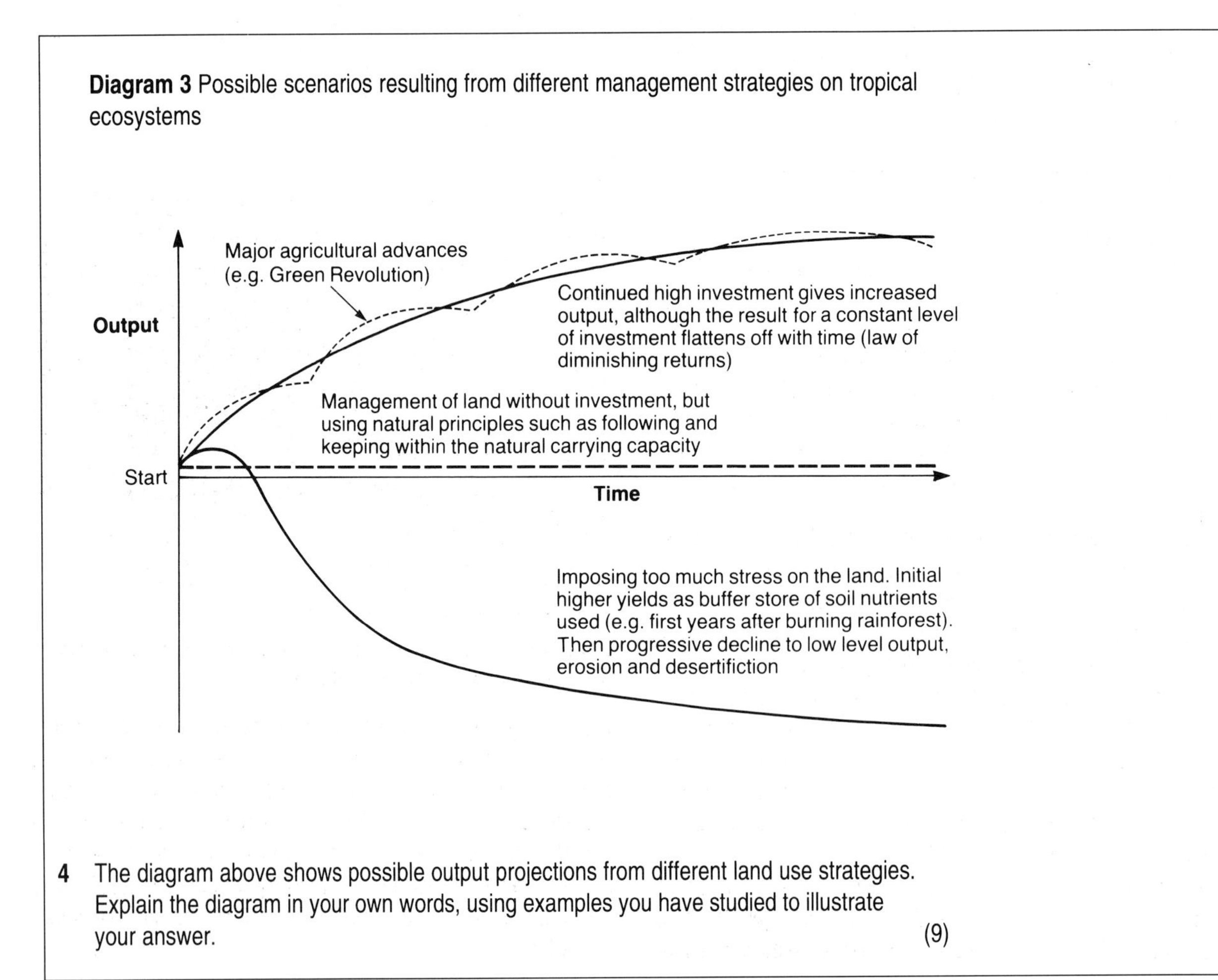

4 The diagram above shows possible output projections from different land use strategies. Explain the diagram in your own words, using examples you have studied to illustrate your answer. (9)

INDUSTRIAL STUDIES

The Industrial System

In its widest sense, industry is work performed for economic gain. For the purposes of geographical study, industry is usually classified into four main groups, as follows.

Primary industries are those which extract or collect raw materials direct from the earth (or sea) and do not involve any processing. Examples are mining, quarrying, farming and forestry. This type of activity must always take place at the source of the raw material.

Secondary industries involve the transformation of raw materials (or components) into consumable products. They include manufacturing, processing and assembly activity. All industries in this category add value to the raw materials they process, and their locations are very variable.

Tertiary industries are concerned with providing a service to customers rather than with raw materials or finished goods. They are always located near to the market they serve. Examples include transport, retailing, medical and other professional services.

Quaternary industries include such things as universities, research and development establishments, the media and political policy units. Their main output is information and expertise. Since such outputs can be transmitted electronically, these industries can, in theory, be located almost anywhere.

Chapter 2 considered various forms of agriculture as systems. Much the same approach can be applied to manufacturing, service and information industries (3.1). Inputs, consisting of various 'resources', are 'processed' to give a 'product' which is of value to the intended customer. (The 'product' may be a bus journey or education in the case of a service industry, where the 'processing' would be the management/operation of the service.) The value added in the processing must be sufficient to give a return on the capital invested and provide capital for future investment. The profit must also pay for raw materials, salaries, power and water supplies, and rent.

The relative sizes of the main sectors will change in a region or country as industrialisation leads to economic growth (3.2). Fourastie in 1964 suggested that, as mechanistion increases, the primary sector reduces and the secondary sector expands. As automation is applied in the secondary sector, levels of employment drop in that sector and increase in the tertiary industries. Contemporary economists now recognise that de-industrialisation, where the majority of a country's employment and economic output are provided by tertiary and quaternary sectors, leads to the **post-industrial** phase in developed countries.

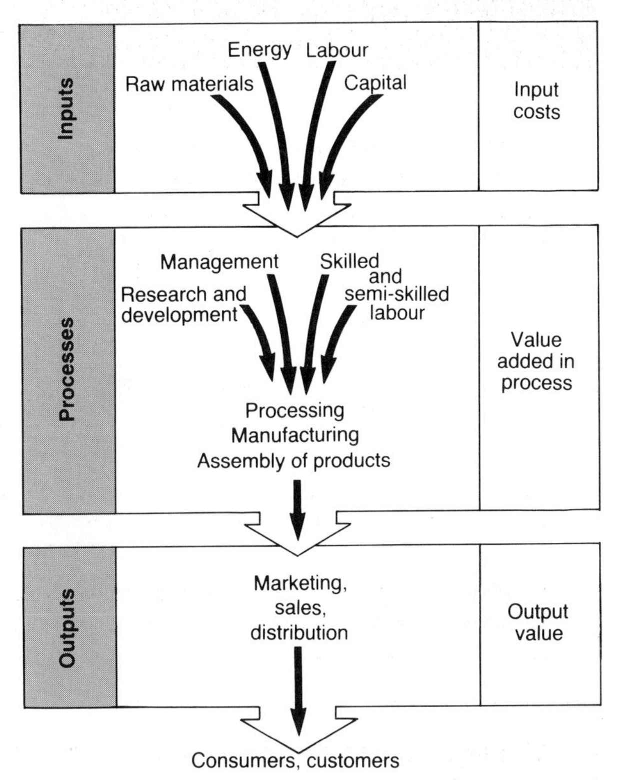

3.1 Industrial system

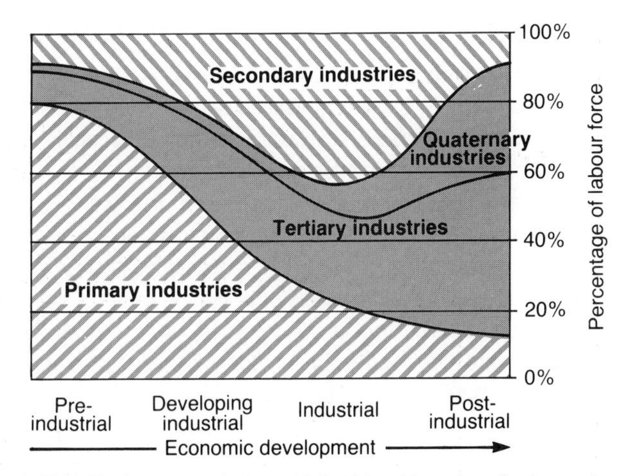

3.2 Transition from an agrarian to post-industrial society as shown by changes in the employment levels in each industrial sector

CHAPTER 3

Industrial Location

Physical factors

- Raw materials
- Energy/power
- Site/land
- Climate
- Natural routes

Human–economic factors

- Transport
- Labour
- Technology
- Capital
- Industrial inertia
- Markets
- Product life-cycles
- Linkages between associated industries
- Government policies

3.3 Factors influencing industrial location

The distribution pattern of Europe's industrial landscapes is still partly determined by the physical factors which influenced industrial location in the nineteenth century. Older, traditional industrial complexes were located in areas where raw materials and cheap energy were readily available. Today, however, other factors influencing industrial location across the continent have grown in importance. Expertise, efficient transport systems, proximity to markets for products and services (see Weber model, page 61), technology, product design and development, multinational companies and political intervention all contribute to the location of modern industry.

The factors which influence the location of all sectors of industry can be classified into physical factors and human–economic factors (3.3). In practice, the perfect location for any industry rarely exists. Companies seek out the most profitable location where the costs of labour, transport, raw materials, site and power are minimised and where there is a large market for their products or services.

Raw materials

In the nineteenth century, manufacturing industry was usually located near the source of a raw material (e.g. iron ore) or near a coalfield if coal was used as a source of power (3.4). Today most secondary industry is located near ports (for example, petro-chemical plants in Europoort, Rotterdam) because raw materials are often imported. There are relatively few new industrial plants which are tied to raw-material locations.

However, industrial location is strongly influenced by **inertia**: a traditional location may be occupied long after the original reason for choosing it has gone, especially where raw materials played a major role in the choice of original location. The inland

3.4 Europe's major industrial heartlands

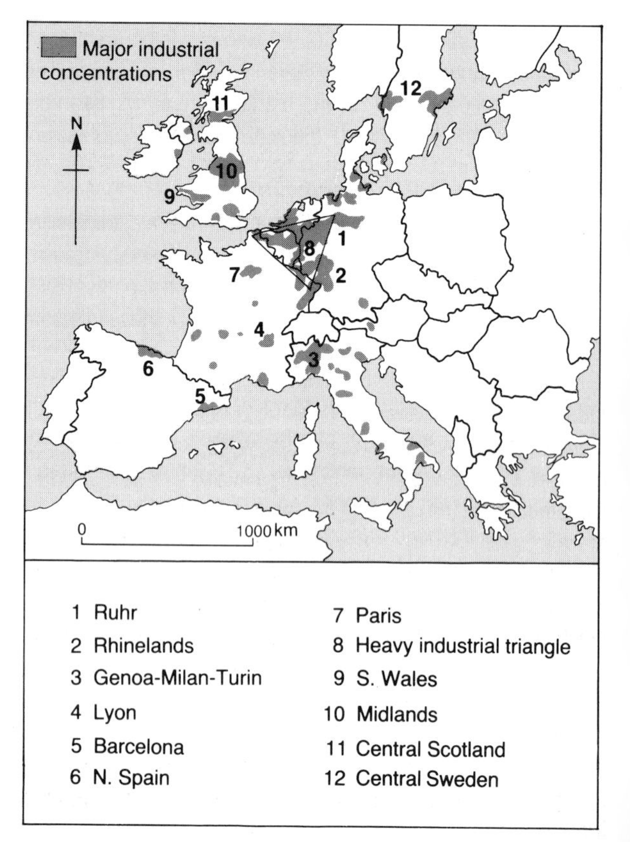

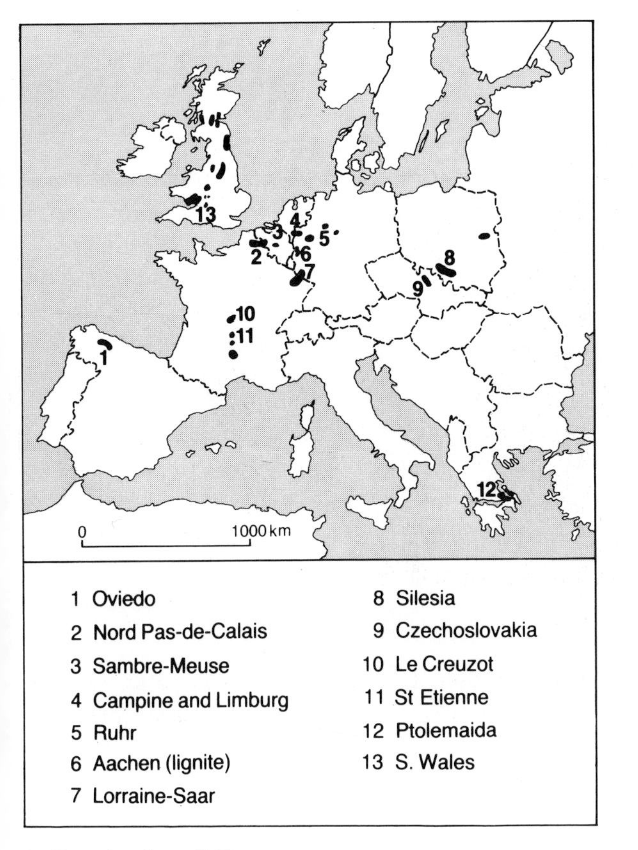

3.5 Europe's major coalfields

Charleroi iron and steelworks in Belgium is a classic example of industrial location on a worked-out coal and ironstone field. It is questionable whether its continued existence at this site is viable without direct government intervention and investment.

Energy/power

Early industrial locations were inseparable from sources of energy because power was the least transportable resource. Industries had to be located near fast flowing rivers or coal reserves (3.5). As technology developed, industrial location changed to suit new supplies of energy available. The metallurgy industries, such as iron and steel, are a good example of this. At first a location within a forest was essential for charcoal supplies to smelt the iron. Later, when steam technology developed, the steel industries had to move to coalfields. Once supplies of electricity were distributed through national grids across Europe, industry was no longer tied to sources of energy. Modern steel industries have relocated to coastal sites because the choice of location is now mainly influenced by distance from raw materials and markets. As electricity can be transported long distances cheaply, there has been an increase in the proportion of **footloose industries**: those which have a free choice of location.

Transport

Water transport has traditionally been the cheapest way to transport goods in bulk. Canal, riverport or coastal locations were therefore strongly favoured as locations for early secondary industries. With the gradual development of railway, road and air transport networks, the influence of transport on industrial location within Europe has become a very complex one. Companies strive to keep their transport costs as low as possible, whether transporting raw materials, products, personnel, or information. Minimising transport costs might mean selecting a central rather than a peripheral location within a country, region or urban area so that the factory is near the market, since costs increase with distance. But these costs must be very carefully considered. In many cases the raw materials may be bulkier or heavier than the finished product (e.g. iron ore processed into steel wire) so it may be cheaper to locate near the raw material source. **Economies of scale** may also play an important role since transport in larger vessels or lorries will reduce the overall transport costs. If there has to be a **break of bulk**, where for example large quantities of shipped goods must be off-loaded in smaller quantities onto barges for inland waterway transport, as at Europoort (3.6), this

3.6 Europoort: break of bulk point

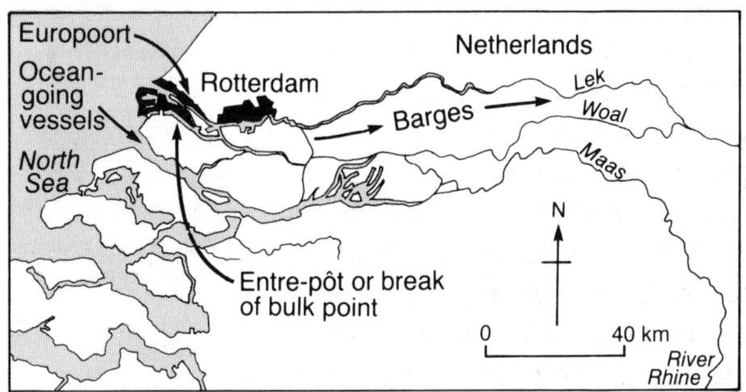

can be particularly expensive. Some industries have relocated to these break of bulk points in an attempt to reduce transport costs but the majority of industries must bear these and the other transport costs of storage, handling and distribution.

Labour

The costs of labour are a major factor in the profitability of industry and for this reason the supply of labour is extremely influential in most location decisions. For the more labour-intensive types of secondary industry and for all tertiary and quaternary activities, the supply, quality and skills of the labour force are vital to company success. Industry is not just concerned with locating near any supply of workers but also with their level of skills. Some types of worker have more influence on industrial location than others. In modern high-tech industries, for example, it is the research and development staff whose influence is strongest on location since their high-level skills are in short supply. Qualified sales staff are usually employed specifically to travel and therefore their locational influence is weaker. The majority of the workforce, the shopfloor personnel, are usually less well qualified but can be trained as skilled and semi-skilled workers. Suitable workers of this kind are available in most areas. Thus the locational influence of the majority of the workforce is weak unless they have specialised skills or an excellent reputation for productivity.

Despite the increased use of technology, robotics, computers, machinery, etc., which has reduced the number of shopfloor workers needed, the total wages bill is still a major factor in the production or service costs because new staff employed to operate the computers, etc. often have to be higher qualified and therefore have higher wages. The car industry provides interesting examples of the influence of labour on location. Many of Europe's newest car plants have been built in regions such as Spain where savings in labour costs attract foreign investment (3.7).

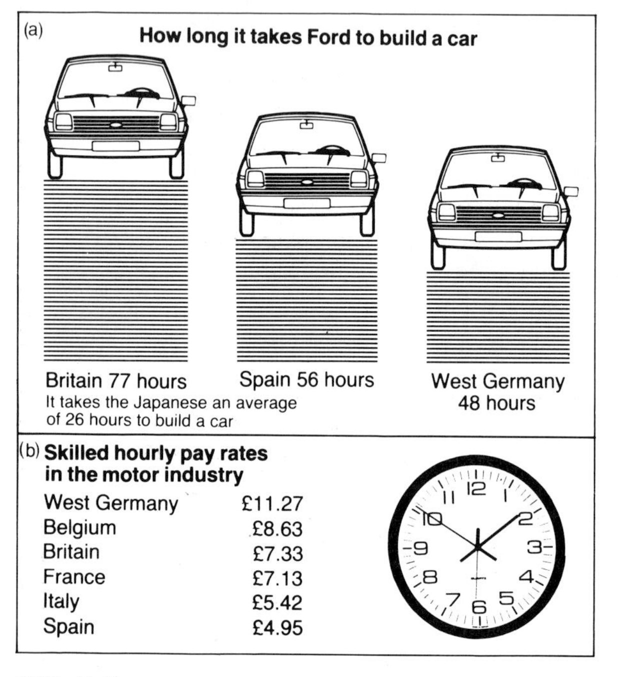

3.7 Ford in Europe

Technology

Improvements and developments in the technology used in industry have always created change with both positive and negative side-effects. Industries automate their production (of iron-ore, coal, polyethelene, cars, or whatever) or their services (e.g. cash dispensing machines) in an effort to maximise profits by becoming more efficient. New technology (3.8) has raised productivity and taken over many tedious repetitive tasks, but at a substantial cost in terms of job losses for manual workers, particularly skilled workers and craftsmen. Also, with many industries developing new product lines, the importance of research and development has increased. Universities and other centres for the development of applied technology are important influences in the location of modern industry such as micro-electronics or bio-engineering plants. While these establishments or branches of industries employ relatively few people, they often use large amounts of capital.

3.8 Robotics in car assembly

Capital

Early industrial developments depended heavily on investment of capital from wealthy entrepreneurs who oversaw the progress of the company. Companies therefore tended to locate factories near the investors. In the past a high proportion of the capital was tied up in the land, plant and machinery. Once industry became established it was very difficult for it to relocate because of industrial inertia. Today there are fewer problems since many industries lease land instead of buying it, releasing capital for relocation and for research and development. The rise of transnational corporations and the development of quaternary industries whose information is used for product research and design have only been possible because of the freeing of capital from land ownership.

Markets and models of industrial location

All industries attempt to minimise their costs and maximise their profits. In choosing a location they must consider not only costs of transport, labour, raw materials, land and plant but also the location of the markets for their products or services. There have been a number of important theories of industrial location which use costs as a basis for decision making.

Weber's model of industrial location (1909)

Weber suggested that the least-cost approach was the most relevant to industrial location. If transport costs of raw materials were the same as those of the finished products, then the location of manufacture should be equidistant between the source of the raw materials and the market. If the raw materials were heavier than the finished product (and therefore more expensive to transport), then the best location would be at or near the source of raw materials. This would be a **weight-losing industry** such as steel making. If the industry was **weight-gaining** (e.g. petro-chemicals), it should be located nearer to its market. Other influences would be labour costs and **agglomeration forces** (savings to be made by locating close to specialist or similar firms). Forces of **deglomeration** could have the opposite effect and discourage companies from locating in an area because of skills shortages, lack of space, etc.

Weber illustrated his theory using graphs to show how the least-cost location was found. **Isotims** are lines of equal cost of transport from a source of raw material and from a market (3.9). **Total** transport costs are found by adding the values where three circles intersect, as shown for two places in 3.9. Intermediate circles can be drawn of course to produce many more intersecting points. **Isodapanes** (3.10) are lines joining places with the same **total** transport costs. They form cost contours around the location of least-cost. Weber's ideas were based on the idea of an isotropic surface (i.e. assuming similar conditions existed everywhere).

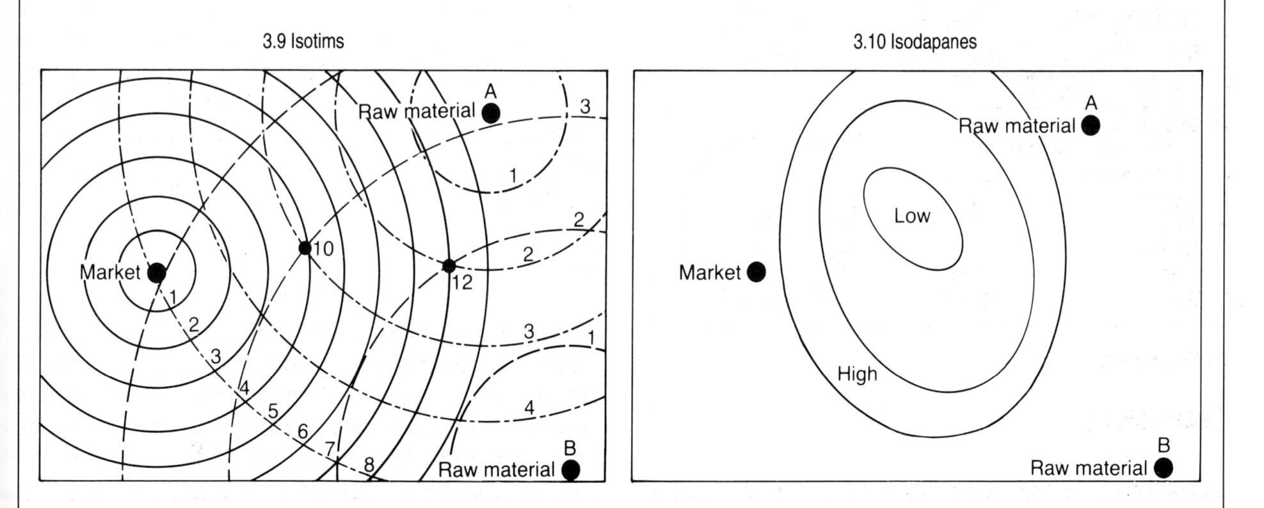

Weber's approach is useful as a starting point but it is outdated now and makes several assumptions: that there is no physical barrier or impediment to transport (costs simply increase with distance), and there is no preferred transport network. The model ignores revenue and political influences such as the pricing structures set by governments.

Losch's market area theory (1954)

Losch emphasised the role of demand from the market which would maximise revenue. Revenue would fall with increasing distance from the market (3.11). He recognised that industrial location is often not a simple matter of minimising transport costs to a single market location (as in Weber's model) but to an increasingly scattered market. For high-bulk, low-value products the costs of distribution are of overriding concern. For example, the transport costs of bottled beer are high compared with the product value. If a brewery delivers beer to markets some distance away, they may have to sell the beer at a higher price to cover the transport costs. The higher price will make the product less attractive and sales may decline with distance from the brewery until at some point the costs are so high that sales will cease. Competition from brewers nearer to the market will further restrict the trading area. This situation could lead to agglomeration, or to dispersal as each brewer seeks out its own market. Losch's market theory is based on simplistic assumptions about revenues and is valid mainly for baking and brewing industries.

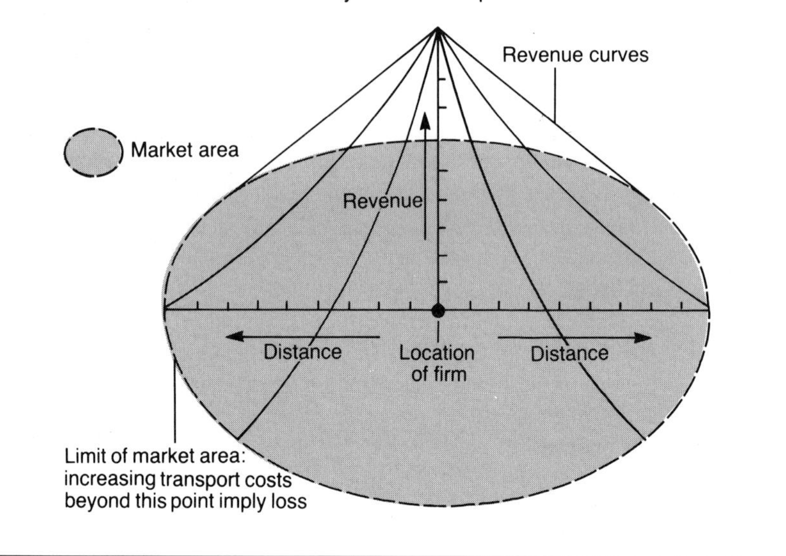

3.11 Losch's revenue cone

Smith's spatial margins model (1966)

This model, sometimes referred to as the space-cost curve, attempts to relate both revenues and costs to distance, showing the area over which profits can be obtained (3.12). Smith's theory recognises that locational knowledge is often imperfect but that, within a given area, any location will suffice in terms of potential profitability. For example, any choice of location within area 1 in 3.12 will result in profit for the business.

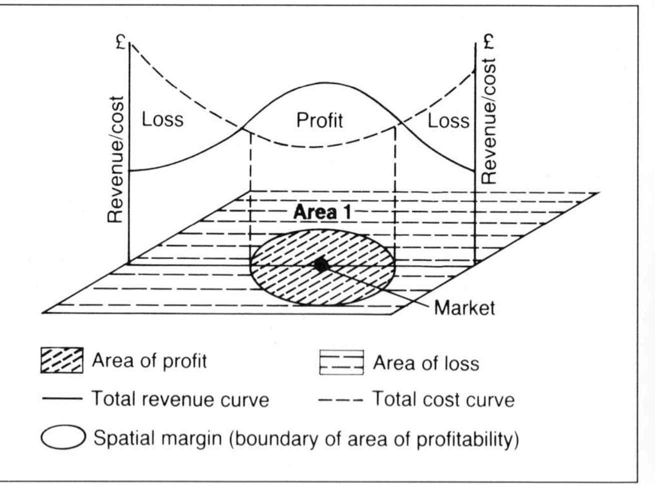

3.12 Spatial margins model

Most of the theories of industrial location tend to assume single-product companies. Today most companies have a market-orientation and are multi-product businesses receiving raw materials or components from a wide variety of sources as well as marketing their products in many areas. Many companies are multi-plant businesses, with a main factory and many satellite or branch plants. Therefore it is not only the market access of a single plant that has to be considered but the costs, revenues and distances for the overall company or group. This is why study and interpretation of market access in relation to industrial plant location has become an international and very complex issue. Multinational companies such as Unilever and ICI manufacture

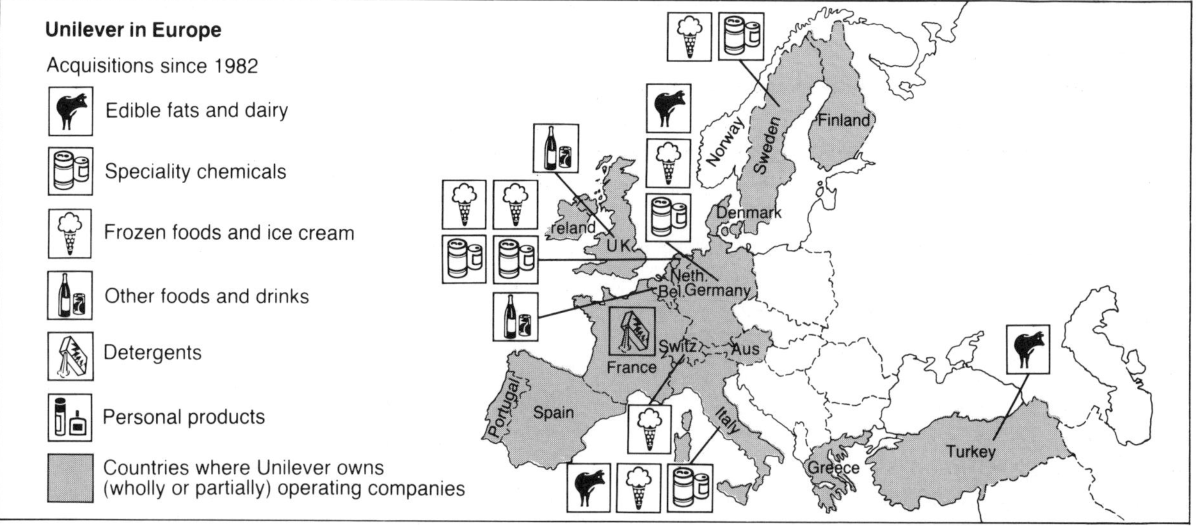

3.13 Unilever in Europe

goods or provide services in several countries while being administered from one country. Their decisions on industrial location must take into account not only market access within individual countries but also group profitability across many countries (3.13).

Product life-cycle

As products, for example hi-fi systems, go through their life-cycle (3.14), manufacturing companies assess how to achieve the best advantage from various locations. During **infancy**, when the product is a new design concept, research and development costs are high, and limited space is required. Production is therefore located close to or within company headquarters so that progress can be closely monitored. Headquarters are often near a large wealthy core market (such as London). In the **youth** stage, the product is ready for limited production based on a small, exclusive market. But as the market expands and competition increases, the **maturity** stage is reached and larger-scale production is necessary. At this stage, many companies try to minimise costs by relocating production at a low-cost peripheral site. Eventually **market saturation** stage is reached, where many competitors manufacture similar products and competition is intense. Continued profitability requires the lowest production costs with highest volume. The mature site may need to expand or be redesigned. Costs are often kept even lower by relocating production in either another developed or developing country where there are lower operating costs. Throughout this phase, company profits are amassed until sales decline or a new company product (for example, a compact disc system) result in production of the original product stopping altogether. Many companies operate on a planned **obsolescence** cycle where new products will inevitably replace existing ones to the benefit of the company. The entire production system may be sold to a competitor or overseas, and produced in a different location altogether.

3.14 Influence of product life-cycle on industrial location

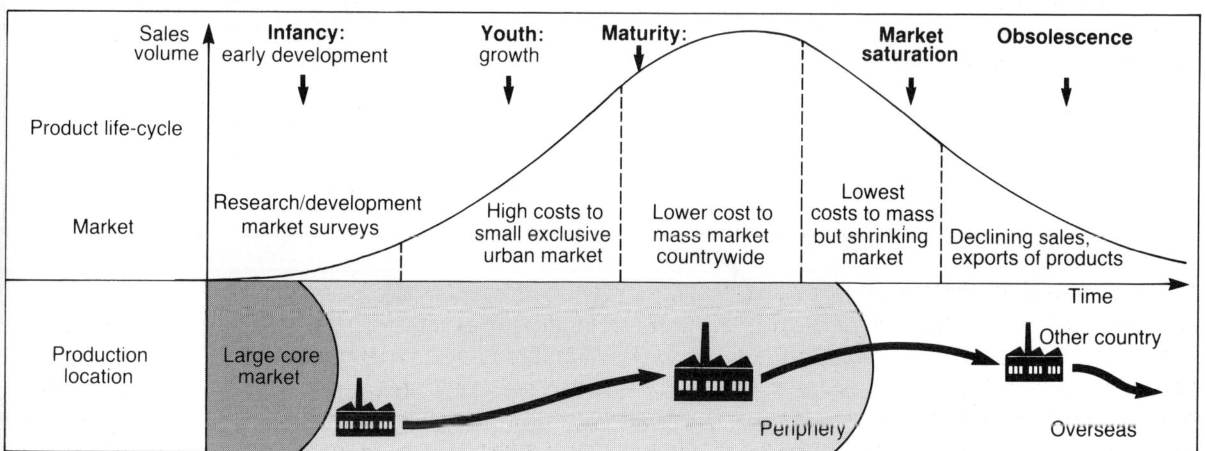

CHAPTER 3

Government intervention

The role of government is very often a crucial factor in decisions about industrial location. In Britain, **intervention** began as a response to the economic Depression of the 1930s. Since then, governments have recognised that the concentration of new industrial developments in the south-east is detrimental to older industrial areas in the north and west. Government policy has therefore been to redirect industry to areas of industrial decline or transition with above-average unemployment. As part of this policy, Industrial Development Certificates, needed to develop new industries, were only granted for areas undergoing industrial change outwith the south-east. Through the zoning of areas for new industry the government can directly influence the location of industrial developments under its statutory planning powers.

The government originally created three types of **Assisted Areas** (3.15) in which new firms received government grants for factory construction and worker-training schemes (among other things). Since November 1984 (3.16), assistance has concentrated on much smaller areas, and Special Development Areas have been phased out altogether. It was decided to retain the Development and Intermediate Areas because there was a possibility of receiving assistance from the European Regional Development Fund. 27 **Enterprise Zones** were established in 1980 to encourage industries to set up in derelict inner-city areas such as the Isle of Dogs (see pages 118–19), Clydebank and Hartlepool Docks (3.17), and thereby improve the economy of these areas.

The government is also a large employer and can exert direct control over the location of its many departments. Various **procurement policies** can also be used to aid and influence industries: for example, defence is the largest sector of government spending, and orders can be selectively placed to assist local economies.

Industrial linkages

These can influence industrial location in different ways. Large companies are often split into separate divisions for policy making, research and development (R&D), and production (3.18). This is usually sensible because each division will have different locational requirements: the headquarters and R&D divisions may be located in the core market area (see markets section p.61) while the production may be located in a low-cost peripheral area. However, all divisions of the company must be strongly linked to each other not only through transport networks but also through telecommunications systems.

3.15 Assisted Areas, June 1979

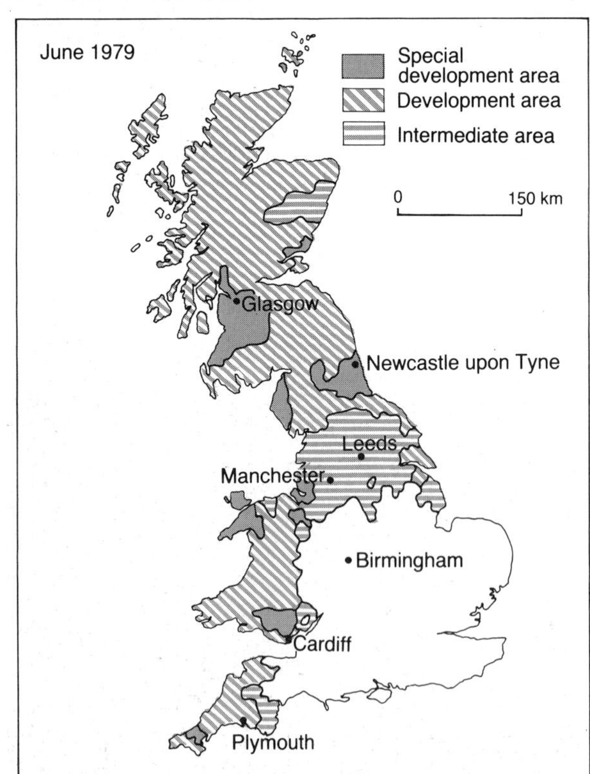

3.16 Assisted Areas, November 1984 onwards

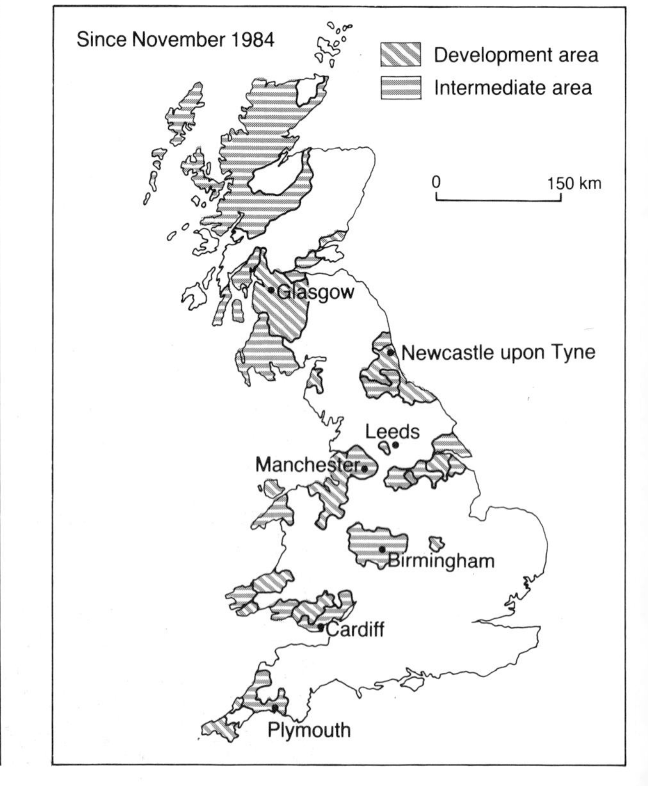

TEESSIDE

THE RESOURCEFUL GIANT

Skilled in meeting your working needs

People – the vital ingredient in making a business work. Teesside has an abundance of them; a working population of 200,000 in a conurbation of 600,000. With a reputation for loyalty and hard work, and a tradition of working in industry going back over many generations.

Teesside's well-established industries are still very important – in fact the area has one of the largest petro-chemical complexes in the world and many of the North Sea's oil platforms are built in its yards – but newer industries are also finding the skills and capabilities they need on Teesside. Backed by the education and training resources of Teesside Polytechnic and seven further education colleges, a plentiful supply of graduates, technicians, management-trained and craft-based people is readily available.

Teesside's rapidly-broadening economy now includes electronics, food processing, clothing manufacture, plastics, furniture, distribution and business services, in addition to well-established engineering and fabrication operations.

Teesside has many benefits to offer the growing business; a variety of premises and sites, financial assistance, good communications, and the vital ingredient – a dedicated workforce, skilled in meeting your working needs. To find out more contact: **Duncan Hall, Chief Executive, Teesside Development Corporation, Tees House, Riverside Park, Middlesbrough, Cleveland TS2 1RE. Tel 0642 230636. Fax 0642 230843.**

EDINBURGH
TEESSIDE
DURHAM
YORK
MANCHESTER
BIRMINGHAM
LONDON

3.17 Government-sponsored advertising aimed at influencing industrial location decisions

Linkages between different companies can also affect location, on the basis of the **agglomeration** principle. The separate divisions of a large company may be best located in areas where there are similar activities or interests. For example, the research and development division may be best located around other R&D establishments, while the production division is often located on industrial estates where there are external trade links and efficient transport services. In many cases smaller firms of similar profile are best located together as they can often attract cheaper services by creating a larger demand.

Industrial parks

Perhaps the most influential and innovative change in industrial location this century has been the development of **industrial estates** or **parks**. Many of the traditional, central industrial areas of large cities have been abandoned in favour of the modern peripheral industrial park (3.19).

Industrial parks offer many locational advantages since they are planned on an integrated basis, close to excellent communications, with flat land and room for expansion, as well as an attractive greenfield environment, now recognised as an important factor in increasing workers' amd therefore the company's efficiency.

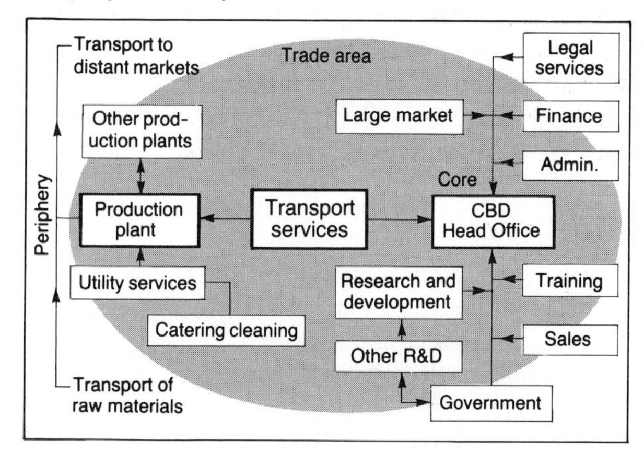

3.18 Industrial linkages

3.19

Trends

Industrial transition has had an enormous effect on industrial location and this pattern is set to continue throughout what some experts regard as the second Industrial Revolution, which is linked to the freeing of industry from specific locations through the application of electronic technology (3.20).

The rise of the great secondary sector in most European countries was accompanied by massive employment and consequent urban and transport developments. Indeed, secondary industries have formed the backbone of our economic development and material prosperity for most of this century. However, industry's requirements are changing. Companies need more floor space, preferably in single-storey buildings, on spacious sites close to excellent communications, with room for parking and easy lorry access. These needs are not easily met within Europe's large cities where sites are cramped and where multi-storey factory buildings are frequently ageing and designed for outdated processes. At the same time, the growth in importance of service industries, both tertiary and quaternary, has led to a decline in the great manufacturing regions such as the Ruhr, central Scotland and the Po basin.

The decline in manufacturing employment has been accompanied by major shifts in industrial location (3.20). Associated with these locational changes is the evolution of the industrial workforce from mainly agrarian based, through manufacturing to service employment in the post-industrial phase. Experts now recognise that there will be several important key trends in future industrial development. These are likely to include a growing **awareness of the environment** with more pleasant working conditions for employees and much stricter controls on location, building design and emissions. Higher **energy costs** will lead to cheaper peripheral locations beside good communications links. **Technological innovation** will continue to have the most influence on changes in location and company organisation.

3.20 Industrial trends

Type of location	Smokestack industries	Inner city/break of bulk
Development	Developed on the coalfields which soon became major industrial regions. Smokestack industries are traditional heavy industries dependent on bulky raw materials.	The Industrial Revolution was a great stimul urban industrial development. New 'textile' a 'steel' town grew; existing ports were extend Break of bulk points became very important industries that used bulky raw materials.
Examples	Central Scotland, Lancashire, West Midlands, Ruhr (Germany), Milan–Turin–Genoa, Nord, Lyon	Sheffield, Blackburn, Alsace-Lorraine, Ruhr, Lombardy, Marseilles, London, Charleroi, Ravenscraig, Europoort
	Steelworks, mining, heavy engineering, brick works, potteries	Iron and steel works, textile factories, food processing, engineering, shipbuilding
Industrial landscape	Agrarian society —— Industrial development —— Industrialisation — Canal; Railway; Coalfield	Canal; Riv; Tidewater estuary; Inn
Transport and labour	Originally dependent on canals, then railways, for bulk movement, especially in inland locations. Originally labour intensive, mainly male oriented.	Developed around urban canals and railhea Original ports at major bridging points of rive extensions on major estuaries and river mou Large workforces: mixed (inner cities); male
Technological and environmental impact	Invention of steam engine led to relocation of iron and textiles industries from water power sites to coalfields. Large workforce attracted to new plants from rural areas. Major environmental impact on air, water and landscape because of atmospheric and land-based pollution.	Major technological developments both in pr (e.g. steel production, building processes, shipbuilding) and in structural improvements ports, quays, dredging, viaducts, aqueducts) agglomeration. Major environmental impact rivers, air and general landscape.
Urban development	Work-oriented residential development of low-quality, terraced brick housing close to factories. (Walking to work necessary before days of public transport.)	High-density housing quickly developed bes factories and ports. Infamous 'back-to-back' tenements without basic services. Still base 'walk to work' principle.
Locational trends	Major industrial decline as most profitable reserves of raw materials became exhausted. Serious problems of industrial inertia for sunset (declining) industries, e.g. steel, textile, engineering. Major social, economic and environmental consequences of industrial decline, especially in 'one-industry' location, such as coal mining communities.	Zones of industrial transition. Urban conges lack of expansion space led to relocation to or to other urban centres. Containerisation water sites replaced labour-intensive indust dockland locations. Urban redevelopment s often reduced local labour pool. Governmer intervention.

Core/CBD	Industrial parks	Greenfield sites
ı administration and commercial businesses ıded in the CBD as residential population d to suburbs where land values were lower. In service land uses were segregated in multi- ɩ buildings. New office developments in 'brown- gap sites near CBD.	Originally developed at Trafford in Manchester in 1896, and Slough, west London, in 1920. With suburban spread and improved communications networks, many industrial parks were set up around cities after the Second World War.	Radical shift in location from cities to countryside, sunbelt or skibelt locations (previously unindustrialised) by high-tech 'sunrise' (young) industries or small businesses with electronic communications systems.
;ity'/West End of London, City of Paris, ne/Copenhagen, Ludwigstrasse/Munich, Place/Brussels, Old Town/Amsterdam	All large cities: Paris, Rome, Stuttgart, London, Brussels, Rotterdam; some inner city redevelopment locations	Scottish Highlands, Downs, Cevennes, Alps, Pyrenees, Cote d'Azure, Black Forest, Picardy
ce, commerce, newspapers and media, ›ort, entertainment, office HQs	Light engineering, components, office supplies, warehouse distribution, newspapers	Micro-electronics, bio-engineering, offices, software production

Economic development →

Late industrial — Post-industrial phase →

Motorway

City — Twentieth-century suburban sprawl — Countryside: mountains

City	Twentieth-century suburban sprawl	Countryside: mountains
ally developed as urban nucleus for istration or communication. Numerous ›ort systems common: railway, subway, urban way, heliport, coach, etc. Large workforce, and female, as commuters take advantage of ›ort systems.	Developed on rural–urban fringes close to major road networks and airports, especially suitable for transporting low-bulk, high-value products or services. Often small workforce, female orientated.	Necessary transport links are: road, motorway, electrified rail, and airports within 2 hours' journey time. More important are electronic communications facilities. Small workforce, male and female.
ɔort development (including subways, ɔters and cars) and high-rise technology ators, lifts) together with developments in ɔnics have contributed to the development of accessible core areas. Environment becomes rtificial: problems of air pollution, litter, noise.	Urban ring road together with computerised stock control and distribution systems facilitated the use of peripheral locations for light engineering, processing and distribution. Industrial parks have limited impact on the local environment because they are usually landscaped.	Electronic mailing, modem-linked computer systems, satellite technology, home banking, teleshopping, in-plant power generation, etc. have 'freed' industrial location in the late 20th century. Minimal environmental impact.
: CBD workforce lived nearby but, as transport ns developed, the workforce lived in the ɔs and commuted.	Suburban expansion in modern housing estates, both council and private. These provide a large pool of labour for industrial parks.	Counter-urbanisation to the thatched computer (rural residence with electronic communication) or factory unit. Village expansion.
levelopments include enclosed shopping s, car parks, and office complexes. ication (renovation and restoration by ier people) of older run-down properties on ge of the CBD reverses residential trend rds to suburbs. Private investment in modern development.	Peripheral urban expansion as more footloose industries move to city edges. Attractions include relocation incentives, good communications, cheap flat land with room for expansion, and little congestion. Outer urban ring road locations favoured, e.g. M25, London; Boulevard Périphérique, Paris.	Gradual regional shift to 'clean' environments for silicon engineering. Often there is a North/South dimension; e.g. in France movement south; in UK movement to Channel area. Often high amenity areas are associated with greenfield locations.

Industrial Europe

The employment structure of the member countries of the European Community (3.21) shows that the transition from early agrarian to today's post-industrial phase has taken place in all the countries (although the change is less marked in some). More varied energy sources, increased industrial efficiency, improved infrastructure, greater mobility, larger trade volumes, a wider variety of consumer goods, and the impact of microtechnology have all combined to create generally higher living standards and the emphasis on tertiary and quaternary, characteristic of the post-industrial phase. Industrial Europe, however, shows uneven growth and there is a marked contrast between its central and outlying regions.

The industrial and economic heartland of the Community – sometimes referred to as the **Euro-core** – can be identified as an area centred on Brussels with a radius of approximately 350 km (3.22). The area overlaps the most densely populated part of Europe (the population heartland: over 120 million people) and the Manchester–Milan industrial growth axis (see 3.22). The major decision-making economic growth centres of the Community (Brussels, Luxembourg, Strasbourg, Paris, Bonn and London) are located within the Euro-core. The area also includes the main concentration of manufacturing industry producing a very large proportion of the Community's coal (3.23), steel, petro-chemicals, engineering, textiles, vehicles, and food processing.

3.21 EC employment structure

Percentage employed, 1990

Member country: 0 10 20 30 40 50 60 70 80 90 100

U K
Belgium
Germany ★
France
Luxembourg
Denmark
Italy
Netherlands
Eire
Spain
Portugal
Greece

(★Estimate on National union)

Primary | Secondary | Tertiary and quaternary

In marked contrast are the areas farthest away from the economic core, sometimes referred to as the **Euro-periphery** (3.24). These include the less-well-developed areas such as Greece, southern Italy, Portugal, Eire and the Scottish Highlands. There have been considerable attempts to redirect new industrial developments to peripheral areas within the EC in order to narrow the gap between them and the Euro-core in terms of economic prosperity, varied employment and infrastructure (3.25). But the peripheral areas remain handicapped by distance and dependence on external investment. Despite industrial and employment growth in southern Italy, Spain and Portugal, the Euro-core maintains its dominant position because of its centrality, advanced economic structure, and large dynamic market centres.

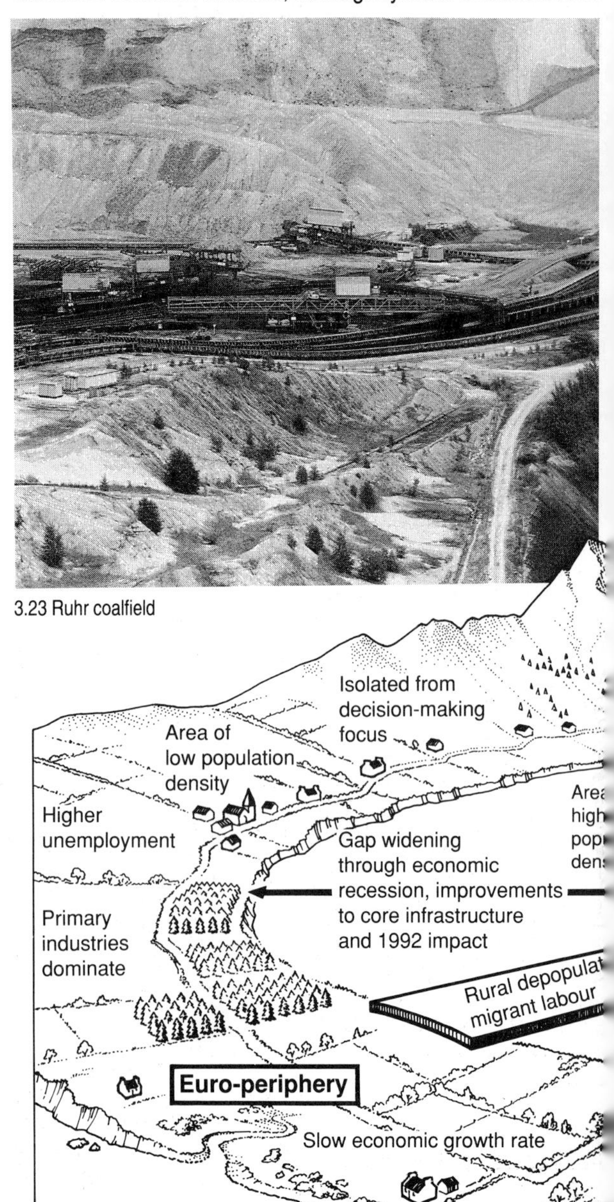

3.23 Ruhr coalfield

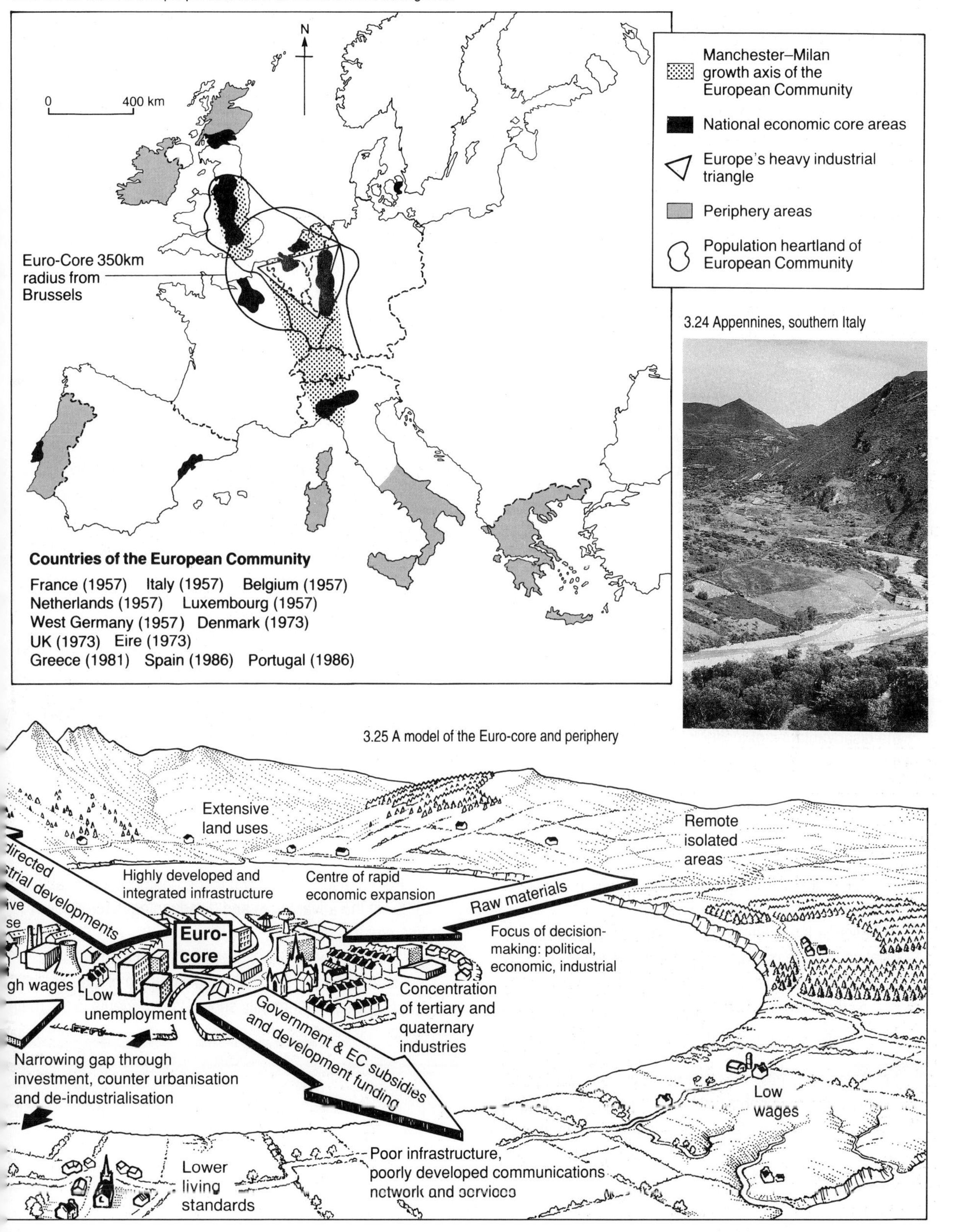

3.22 The EC's central and peripheral areas of economic and industrial growth

3.24 Appennines, southern Italy

3.25 A model of the Euro-core and periphery

Questions

Q THE INDUSTRIAL SYSTEM

1 (a) What is meant by 'industry'?
(b) In which ways can industry be regarded as a 'system'?
(c) Explain fully each of the following: primary industry, secondary industry, tertiary industry, quaternary industry.
(d) Name at least five examples of each type of industry.
(e) Make a copy of graph 3.2.
(f) Describe the process of industrialisation in a developed country.
(g) Define what is meant by deindustrialisation and the post-industrial society.

Q INDUSTRIAL LOCATION

2 (a) Classify the main influences on industrial location into those which are natural–physical and those which are human–economic.
(b) What are 'raw-material locations' and why have they been important factors in location of industry?
(c) Illustrate the influence of transport as a factor in industrial location.
(d) Why is the supply of labour an extremely influential factor in industrial location?
(e) Convert the data in diagram 3.7b into a suitable graph then comment on the importance of labour costs and productivity on the location of the European car assembly industry.
(f) Describe the impact of technology on industrial location then make two lists: one of the advantages and another of the disadvantages of technological improvements to the labour force.
(g) Define each of the following terms: inertia, footloose industries, break of bulk points, agglomeration, multinational companies.
(h) Compare the three main models of industrial location and comment on their relevance to modern industrial location.
(i) Describe the influence of industrial linkages on the location of large chemical companies such as ICI.
(j) What is an 'industrial park or estate'?
(k) List the main types of locations for industrial parks.
(l) What types of industry are located within industrial parks?
(m) A company from the inner city wishes to relocate to the area shown in photo 3.19. Write a set of proposals for presentation to its directors stressing the advantages of such a move.
(n) Are there any disadvantages of relocating to this area?
(o) Write an essay entitled 'The influence of government on changing patterns of industrial location and growth.'
(p) Discuss the statement that 'energy supplies remain one of the most important locational influences on industry, and their past effects are still strongly evident'.
(q) Study diagram 1 carefully. Describe how economic activity and population growth are linked together in a circular system.

Diagram 1 The industrial multiplier effect

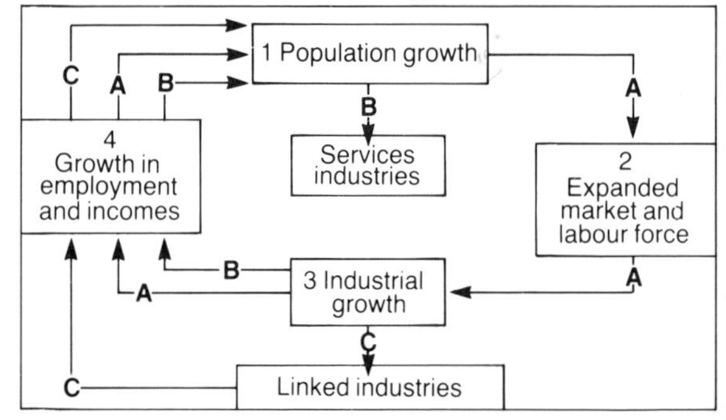

(r) For each location shown in the photographs in table 3.20 list the advantages and disadvantages for modern industry.
(s) Examine maps 3.4, 3.5 and 3.22 and then critically evaluate the assertion that the distribution of industry in the European Community suggests that inertia is the main locational influence.

INDUSTRIAL TRENDS

3 (a) What is the second Industrial Revolution?
(b) In which ways are industry's requirements changing?
(c) What have been the consequences of the rise in the tertiary and quaternary sectors of industry?
(d) How has the workforce evolved?
(e) Copy and complete a larger version of the table.
(f) Summarise the trends in the following influences on industry: transport, technology, quality of environment.
(g) What will be the important trends in future industrial development? (Try to think of some not in the text.)

Stage	Main industrial location	Main location factors	Example of industrial development	Associated urban development
Agrarian				
Industrialisation				
Post-Industrial				

INDUSTRIAL EUROPE

4 (a) Study diagram 2. Copy and complete the table.

Country	Primary %	Secondary %	Tertiary %
1 Belgium			
2 Netherlands	5	27	68
3 Eire			
4 Germany			
5 France			
6 Spain			
7 Portugal			
8 Denmark			
9 Luxembourg	4	32	64
10 Greece			
11 Italy			
12 UK			

(b) Describe and explain any patterns shown in the table.
(c) Make your own copy of map 3.22.
(d) Identify by name each national economic core area.

Diagram 2

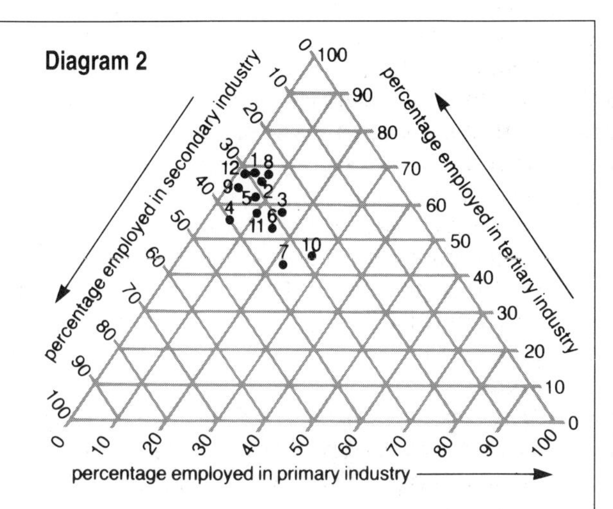

(e) What is meant by the 'Manchester–Milan' growth axis?
(f) Where is the Euro-core?
(g) Give at least four examples of peripheral EC areas.
(h) Make lists of Euro-core advantages, and Euro-periphery disadvantages.
(i) What steps should be taken to solve the major problems of the peripheral areas of the EC?

Research and Further Work

(a) Conduct an investigation into the industrial structure of your local area, and illustrate by statistical means sectorial employment within the area.
(b) Carry out an industrial study of one large local company.
(i) Investigate its industrial system and illustrate this using a flowchart.
(ii) Study the locational influences acting on the company and identify any problems.
(iii) Has the company a trading area? This is known as its **sphere of influence**. Show this area on a base map.
(c) Investigate a local industrial estate and produce an industrial study. This should include data and information on location factors, types of industry, employment, impact of technology, markets, and industrial linkages.

CHAPTER 3

Peripheral Industrial Landscapes

Introduction

Most of Western Europe's manufacturing and service industry is concentrated in regions of high **economic potential** (3.26). Regional economic potential may be defined as a given region's centrality in relation to the markets for its products.The map shows that economic potential declines with distance from the Euro-core (3.22). Privately owned companies, aiming to maximise profits, tend to locate in areas of high economic potential which offer cheap access to necessary resources: raw materials or components, energy, labour and markets. They make location decisions based on the continually changing modern economy of Western Europe. Where regions are abandoned or avoided for economic reasons by industry, there are consequent problems of unemployment and poverty for the people of the region. Government or public intervention in the post-war period has attempted to solve the problems in regions of low economic potential (the Euro-periphery) such as southern Italy, north-west Scotland and Spain.

The southern part of Italy, the land of the midday sun or Il Mezzogiorno, has been the focus for large-scale state intervention since the end of the Second World War. The Mezzogiorno, which lies on the Euro-periphery (3.22), comprises seven of Italy's nineteen administrative regions and has a population of 20 million people (36% of the total). The region accounts for only 25% of Italy's GDP (3.27) and has been plagued by persistent outmigration (since 1910 over 8 million southern Italians have left). Compared with wealthy northern Italy, the Mezzogiorno has been economically isolated and greatly lacking in industrial investment.

After the Second World War, the unity of the country was threatened by the fundamental division between the prosperous North and the disadvantaged South. The South had severe physical, social and economic problems which included a mountainous landscape, droughts, absentee landowners, low levels of economic activity, very low income levels (3.28), poor living conditions, isolation, a lack of raw materials, lack of infrastructure, and a high dependence on agriculture with resulting rural overpopulation (3.29).

The state introduced regional planning and investment schemes to combat some of these problems. The **Cassa per il Mezzogiorno** was established by the Italian parliament in March 1950 as a special fund for the improvement of the region and it

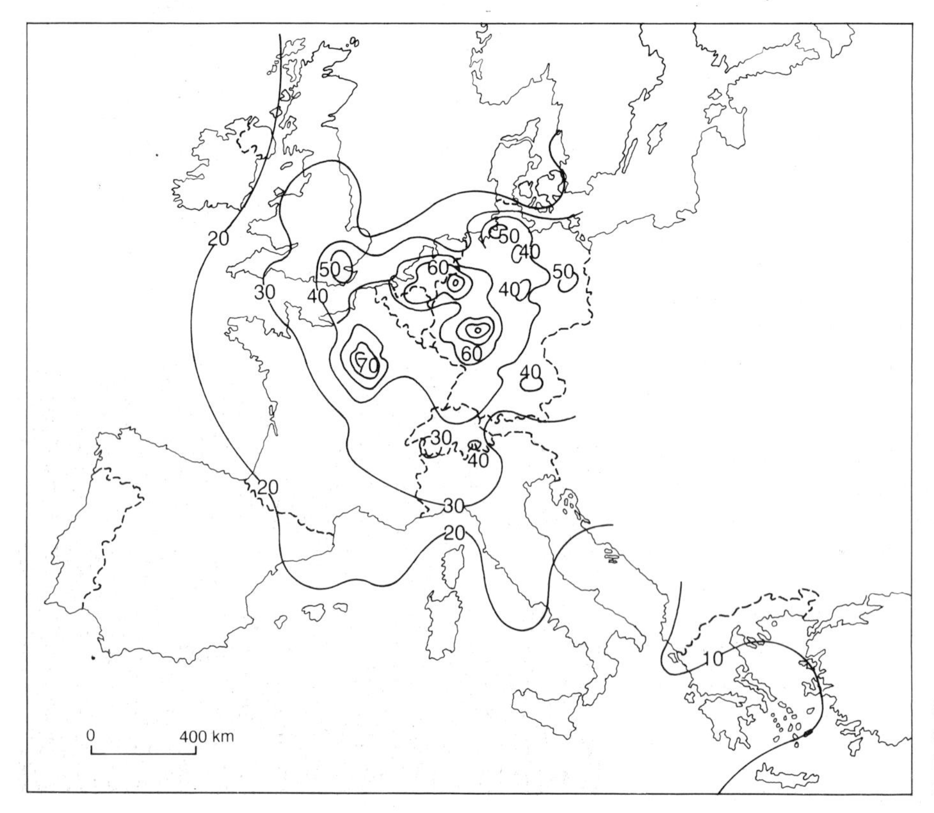

3.26 Economic potential values are shown as contour lines, each representing a percentage of the maximum economic potential

	Gross domestic product (thousand million lire)			GDP as a percentage of the overall EC GDP
	1960	1981	1988	1988
Italy	19 286	261 638	323 247	15.1
Lombardy	4 147	54 040	69 329	3.0
Apulia	823	12 744	15 667	0.8
Basilicata	111	2 035	2 611	0.1
Calabria	374	5 337	5 975	0.3
Abruzzi–Molise	370	5 626	6 125	0.3
Campania	1 225	16 735	19 813	1.1

3.27 Gross domestic product in selected Italian regions: a comparison

Per capita income index	1950	1970	1985	1988
Italy (average)	100	100	100	100
Lombardy	146	125	129	127
Liguria	151	130	126	125
Apulia	59	79	73	73
Basilicata	51	62	66	66
Campania	56	80	70	71
Calabria	42	61	64	63

3.28 Changes in the per capita index in selected Italian regions

initially concentrated on agricultural development. Land reform and better farming techniques were seen as the two principal methods of agricultural change. It was hoped that the much needed investment from the fund would stimulate demand and provide conditions favourable to the growth of industry. Large (*latifundia*) estates were taken over by the state from mainly absentee landowners, and split up into viable family holdings (*poderi*). In Apulia an area of over 200 000 hectares, once owned by 1500 landowners, was assigned to 31 000 families. The change to a much closer pattern of settlement necessitated the construction of roads, new power and water supplies, land reclamation by irrigation or drainage schemes, and new farm buildings and villages. A completely new infrastructure was developed and the original 'olive and wheat' farmscape was changed to one of industrial crops (oil seed, sugarbeet), citrus fruits and vegetables as well as livestock rearing (3.30). The subsequent establishment of processing, packing and refrigeration plants has contributed to the new rural infrastructure and because of the peripheral location of the region the Cassa had also to develop efficient transport networks, distribution and marketing facilities, and basic telecommunications.

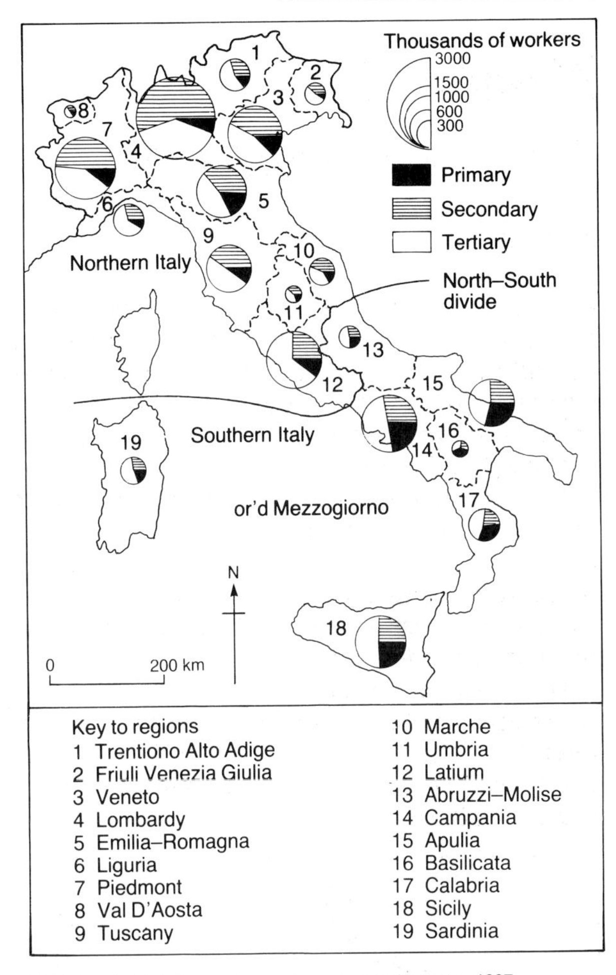

3.29 Italy: administrative regions and employment by sector, 1987

3.30 The 'new' landscape of the Mezzogiorno

However, it was realised that state intervention in the industrial sector would also be vital, to provide new employment. After 1965 there was a considerable shift of resources into the industrial sector (3.31). Many incentives were offered to industrialists, including capital for projects, grants for modernisation of existing plants, exemptions from local taxes, and duties on imported raw materials. The EIB (European Investment Bank) helped to establish many factories, and Italian state industries were directed to place 40% of their investment in the south.

	Expenditure (%) (thousand million lire)			**Estimated overall expenditure** (%)
	1950 (proposals)	1950–65	1966–69	1950–80
Agriculture	77.0	56.1	24.7	12.7
Infrastructure	20.5	22.4	19.6	20.2
Industry	–	6.9	36.0	49.9
Tourism and special projects	2.5	14.6	19.7	10.6

3.31 Expenditure of the Cassa per il Mezzogiorno

Much of the industrial development has been in large-scale industry including petro-chemicals, iron and steel, shipbuilding, heavy engineering, cement and oil refining because of the direction given by the state-owned industries. Large projects include steelworks at Taranto and Bagnoli, petro-chemical complexes at Brindisi and Siracusa–Augusta (Sicily), and the Alfa-Sud car plant near Naples. In addition 48 nuclei of industrial development have been designated, and three major industrial areas (**growth poles**) which have received considerable industrial investment (3.32).

Attempts to diversify the industrial base of the Mezzogiorno have centred more recently on tourism. The south has much to offer the tourist (3.33) with its beautiful beaches, mountain scenery, and historical legacy of ancient cities and architecture. The accessibility of the area has been greatly improved through

3.32 Industrial developments in the Mezzogiorno

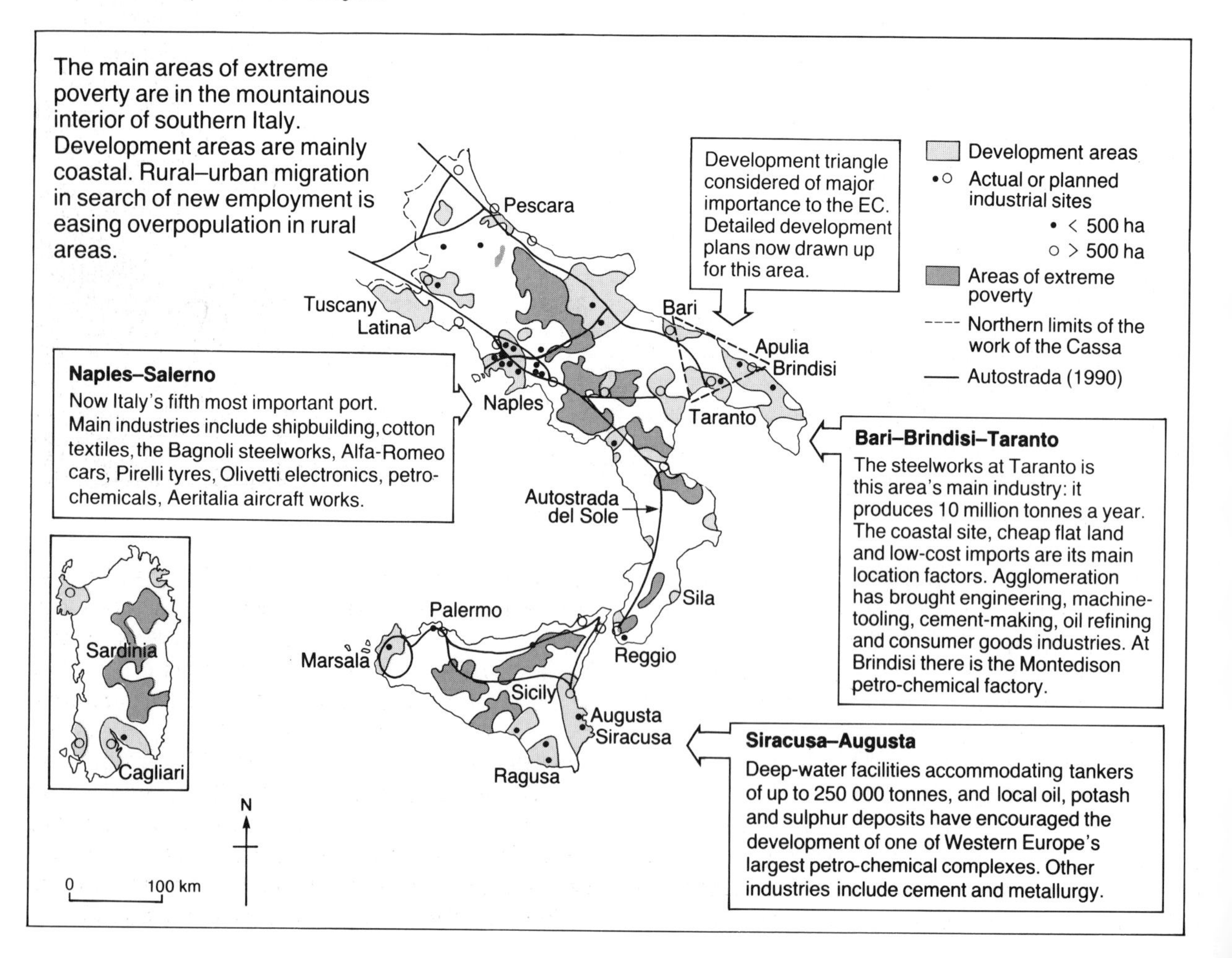

The main areas of extreme poverty are in the mountainous interior of southern Italy. Development areas are mainly coastal. Rural–urban migration in search of new employment is easing overpopulation in rural areas.
Development triangle considered of major importance to the EC. Detailed development plans now drawn up for this area.
Development areas
Actual or planned industrial sites
• < 500 ha
○ > 500 ha
Areas of extreme poverty
Northern limits of the work of the Cassa
Autostrada (1990)
Pescara
Tuscany
Latina
Bari
Apulia
Brindisi
Taranto
Naples
Autostrada del Sole
Sila
Reggio
Palermo
Marsala
Sicily
Augusta
Siracusa
Ragusa
Sardinia
Cagliari
N
0
100 km
Naples–Salerno
Now Italy's fifth most important port. Main industries include shipbuilding, cotton textiles, the Bagnoli steelworks, Alfa-Romeo cars, Pirelli tyres, Olivetti electronics, petro-chemicals, Aeritalia aircraft works.
Bari–Brindisi–Taranto
The steelworks at Taranto is this area's main industry: it produces 10 million tonnes a year. The coastal site, cheap flat land and low-cost imports are its main location factors. Agglomeration has brought engineering, machine-tooling, cement-making, oil refining and consumer goods industries. At Brindisi there is the Montedison petro-chemical factory.
Siracusa–Augusta
Deep-water facilities accommodating tankers of up to 250 000 tonnes, and local oil, potash and sulphur deposits have encouraged the development of one of Western Europe's largest petro-chemical complexes. Other industries include cement and metallurgy.

3.33 Tourist potential is based on the natural beauty and attractive climate of southern Italy

a road-building programme funded by the Cassa, which includes motorways (autostrada) linking Lombardy with Reggio Calabria, and local sight-seeing tourist roads. There have also been more funds allocated to the construction of hotels and other tourist amenities. The potential for tourism is massive and, given improvements such as the Autostrada Del Sole (motorway to the sun), the remoteness of the Mezzogiorno is now less of a problem for both the industrialist and tourist.

Criticisms of the regional development scheme have centred around the concentration of investment in growth poles often locally referred to as 'cathedrals in the desert'. Most of the 400 000 new jobs created during the lifetime of the Cassa have been in these areas. The main problem has been the over-concentration on large-scale capital-intensive projects such as the Taranto steelworks or the Alfa-Sud car plant near Naples. There have been relatively few labour-intensive or lighter consumer goods developments which are essential for a balanced industrial base. Despite the problems, the Mezzogiorno has experienced many fundamental changes (3.34) and the Cassa has achieved a limited economic miracle. The region will always be on the periphery of the EC but a modernised infrastructure should encourage closer, more efficient links with northern regions, and at the same time attract a wider industrial base, with tourism one of the main avenues for future growth (3.35).

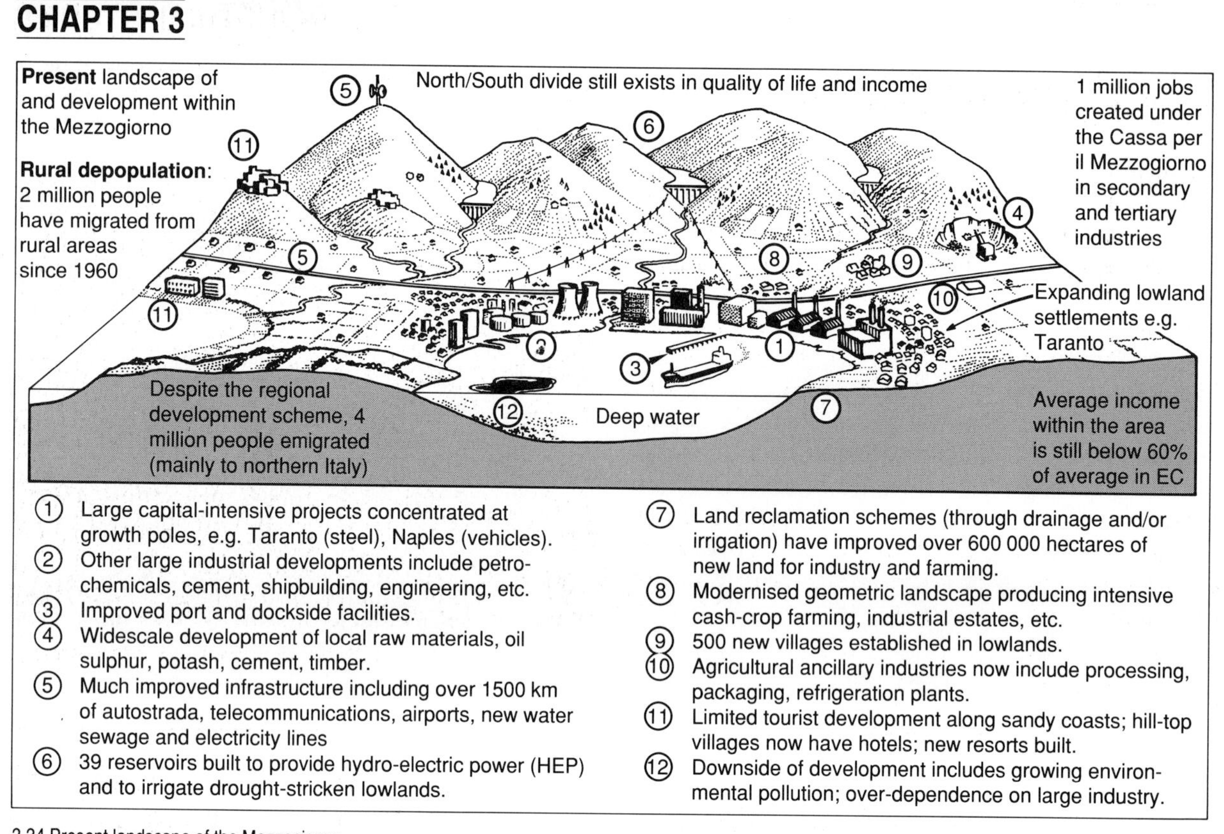

Present landscape of and development within the Mezzogiorno
Rural depopulation: 2 million people have migrated from rural areas since 1960
North/South divide still exists in quality of life and income
1 million jobs created under the Cassa per il Mezzogiorno in secondary and tertiary industries
Expanding lowland settlements e.g. Taranto
Despite the regional development scheme, 4 million people emigrated (mainly to northern Italy)
Deep water
Average income within the area is still below 60% of average in EC
① Large capital-intensive projects concentrated at growth poles, e.g. Taranto (steel), Naples (vehicles).
② Other large industrial developments include petro-chemicals, cement, shipbuilding, engineering, etc.
③ Improved port and dockside facilities.
④ Widescale development of local raw materials, oil sulphur, potash, cement, timber.
⑤ Much improved infrastructure including over 1500 km of autostrada, telecommunications, airports, new water sewage and electricity lines
⑥ 39 reservoirs built to provide hydro-electric power (HEP) and to irrigate drought-stricken lowlands.
⑦ Land reclamation schemes (through drainage and/or irrigation) have improved over 600 000 hectares of new land for industry and farming.
⑧ Modernised geometric landscape producing intensive cash-crop farming, industrial estates, etc.
⑨ 500 new villages established in lowlands.
⑩ Agricultural ancillary industries now include processing, packaging, refrigeration plants.
⑪ Limited tourist development along sandy coasts; hill-top villages now have hotels; new resorts built.
⑫ Downside of development includes growing environ-mental pollution; over-dependence on large industry.

3.34 Present landscape of the Mezzogiorno

3.35 Possible future landscape of the Mezzogiorno

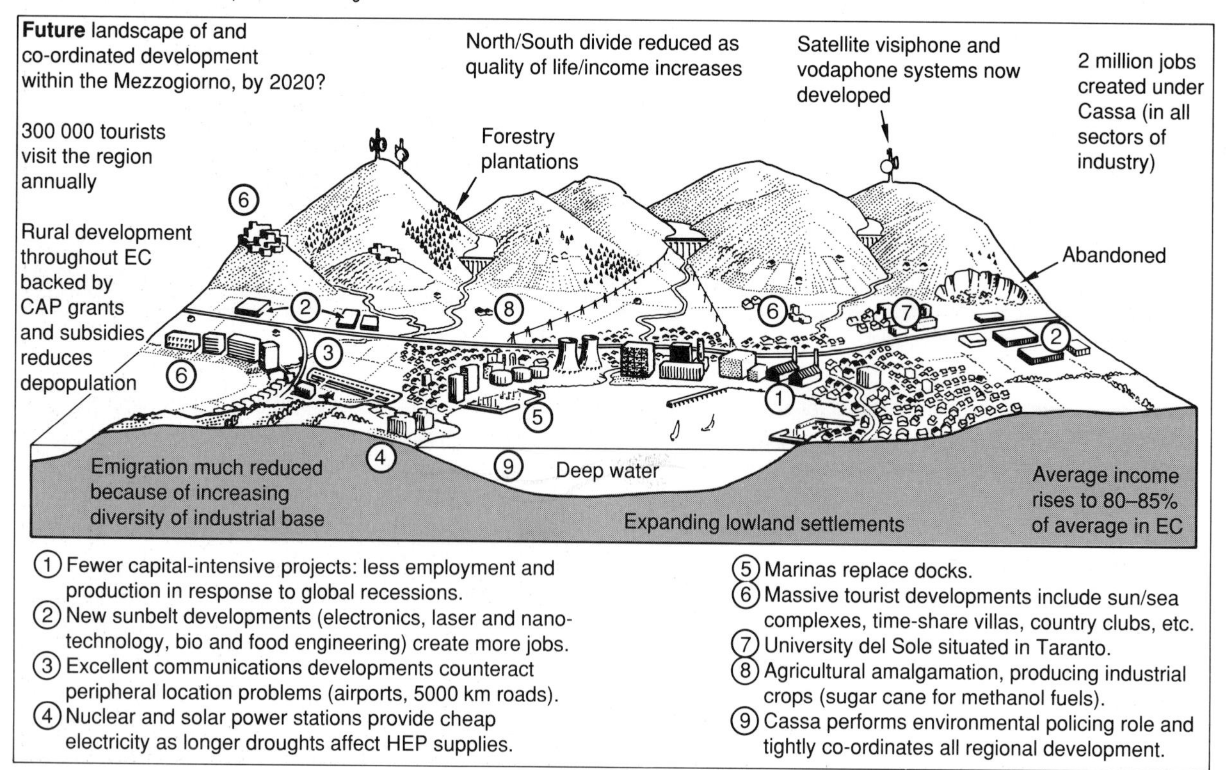

North & West Scotland

The north and west of Scotland is another of Western Europe's peripheral and mountainous regions (3.36). This area of high scenic value comprises all or parts of five Districts lying within Highland Region (3.37) and covers one-quarter of Scotland or one-twelfth of the UK. The difficulties of the natural environment combined with the area's lack of industrial investment and development have created many problems similar to those of the Mezzogiorno. The area, especially in the west, is one of the most inaccessible and undeveloped in Britain, taking the form of an extensive plateau heavily dissected by valley systems with thin, infertile soils. The north and west coasts have only limited areas of flat land and are mainly a mixture of uplands and coastal 'machair' (low sandy plains). Landforms created by both glacial and fluvioglacial erosion and deposition are prevalent throughout the area and add to its scenic appeal.

3.36 North-west Highlands: an isolated landscape

3.37 North and west Scotland

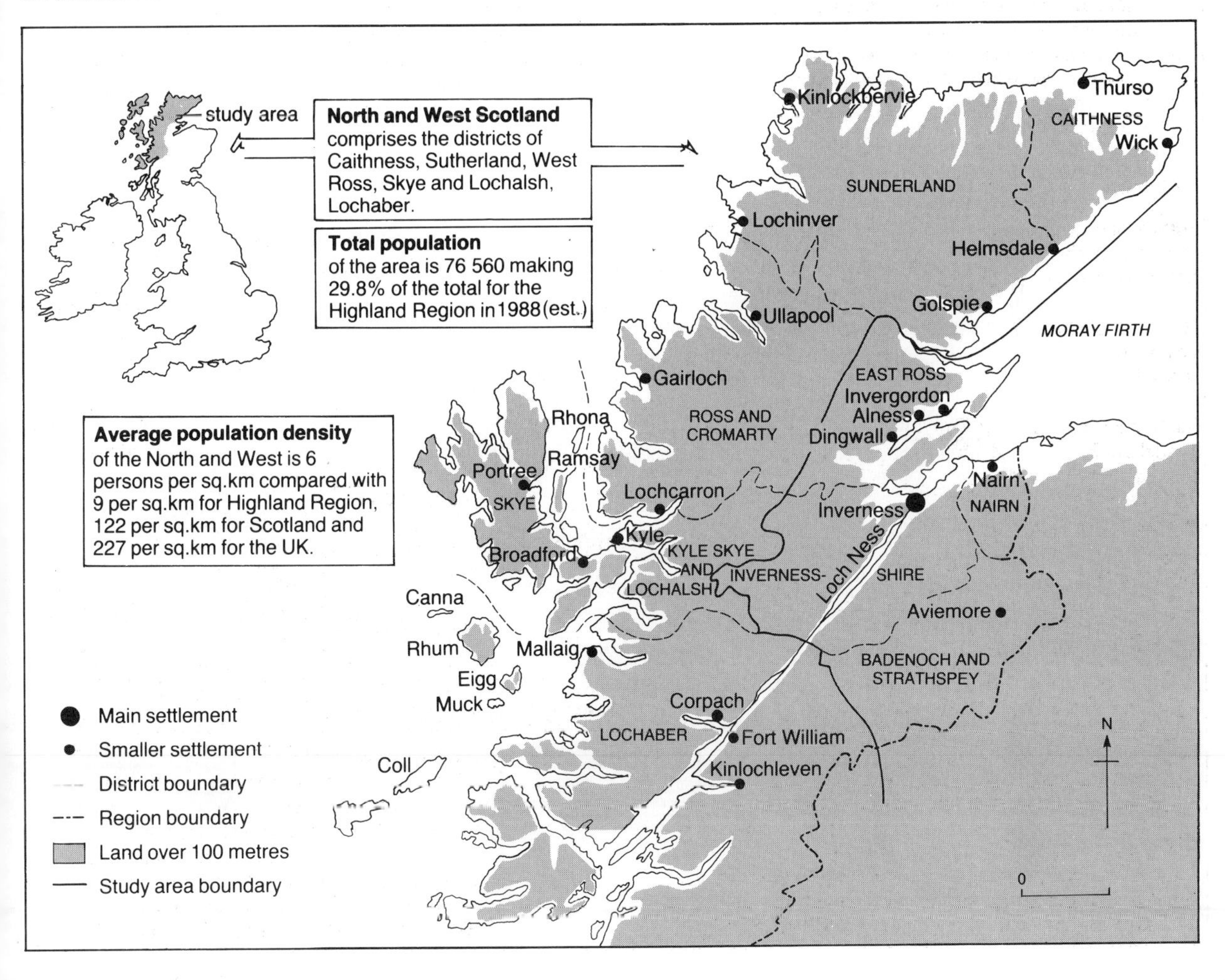

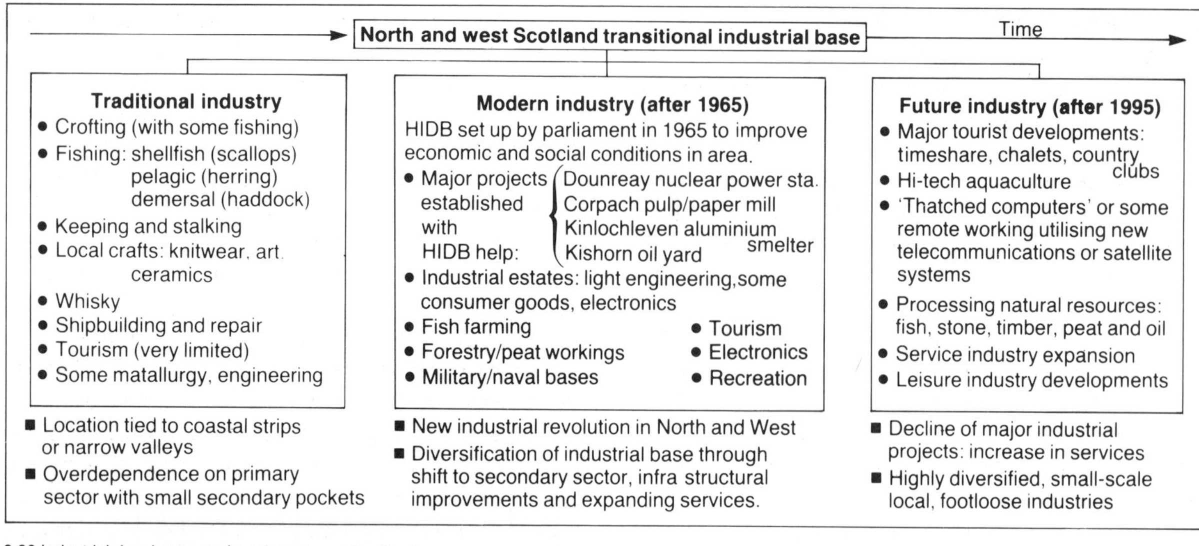

3.38 Industrial development of north and west Scotland

The climate is heavily influenced by the Atlantic which produces the 'wet belt' effects of often excessive precipitation and cloudiness. Throughout the uplands, acid soils predominate and on more gentle slopes peat deposits can be found. The associated moorland vegetation is generally dominated by heathers and poor grass species. Such areas are of low resource value in terms of agricultural development and are used extensively for grazing, forestry and recreational purposes. Good agricultural land is at a premium and its distribution within the area has always been a considerable influence on the location of settlement. The small population of the north and west is widely dispersed and there are few large urban centres. Although the area makes up 25% of Scotland's total land area it contains only 2.6% of the population. In regional development and planning terms, the area is regarded as both remote and rural.

Against this physical and climatic background the north and west has seen a gradual transition of its industrial structure (3.38) with consequent implications for the economic and social geography of the area. Until the late 1950s the industrial structure was largely dependent upon the primary sector. Limited Government encouragement for industries to move to the area was given some impetus through the decision to locate the Experimental Fast Reactor at Dounreay in the early 1950s. However, a new industrial revolution was instigated by the setting up of the Highlands & Islands Development Board (HIDB, now the Highlands and Islands Enterprise, HIE) in 1965. Its main task was to help improve the economic and social conditions of the Highlands. The Board set out to: increase employment opportunities and incomes; retain population; support business and industrial development, and improve the quality of life within the area. Through a variety of strategies including the provision of financial incentives, buildings, plant and equipment, advice and training, the HIDB have overseen the industrial development of the north and west of Scotland. Diversification of the industrial

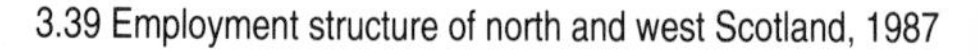
3.39 Employment structure of north and west Scotland, 1987

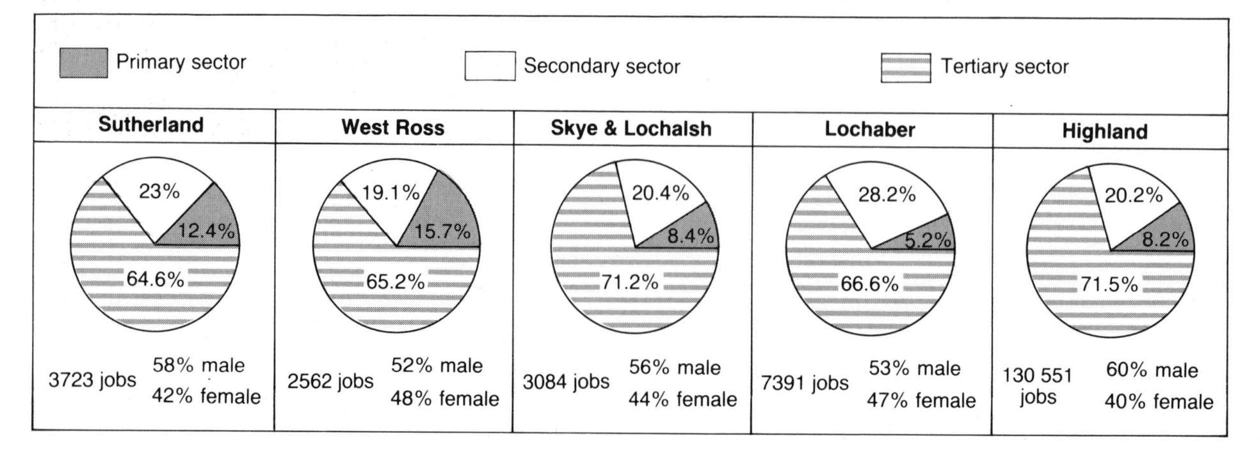

base was achieved in the 1970s by investing in and developing large secondary sector projects at growth poles such as Corpach and Kinlochleven. Many other smaller developments have also had financial help including the building of industrial estates, fish farms and tourist services.

Improvements to the infrastructure, including the upgrading of many roads, bridges, electricity, water and telecommunications systems, coupled with greater investment in facilities and amenities for visitors, contributed to a steady reversal of rural depopulation from the area, and gradual change to an employment structure dependent mainly on the tertiary sector (3.39). The increasing importance of the tertiary sector significantly cushioned the impact of industrial closures on the area in the early 1980s when large-scale industrial projects such as those at Corpach and Kishorn (see p.80) were affected by external competition and changing markets.

In the 1990s the north and west faces an uncertain industrial, economic and social future. The future strategy for industrial investment and development is likely to be one of highly diversified, small-scale and local projects in all industrial sectors. A successful pilot project, the Board's five-year Skye Development Programme 1983–88, was seen as a possible model for the future. Its main thrusts were the improvement of agricultural land, the establishment of small local industrial estates with advance units and the improvement of the island's infrastructure (3.40). The Skye DP also recognised that the increasing population (+13% 1971–88) required more services. A gradual expansion of the hotel and tourist trade and increasing employment in local services have combined to reduce the originally high unemployment rate. The bridge link to the mainland at Kyle of Lochalsh is now regarded as essential to the future prosperity of the island.

A series of similar, mainly land-based, projects are planned for the north and west for the rest of this century. Without a doubt improvements to the communications networks (roads, rail, airports and telecommunications) will encourage further tourist- and leisure-related expansion. High-tech aquaculture (oysters, lobsters, salmon farms, etc.), land improvement schemes and possible oil-related developments in the Minch and eastern Atlantic should also contribute to a more secure industrial base early next century. As a peripheral area of Western Europe, the north and west of Scotland, although still remote and rural, continues to experience industrial transition towards increasing tertiary sector dominance.

3.40 Skye Development Programme

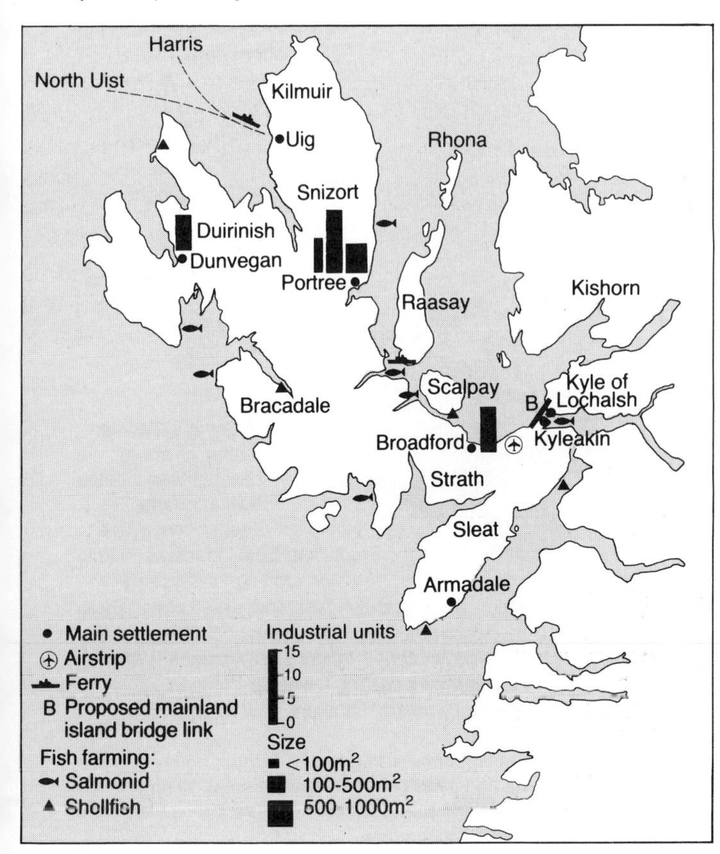

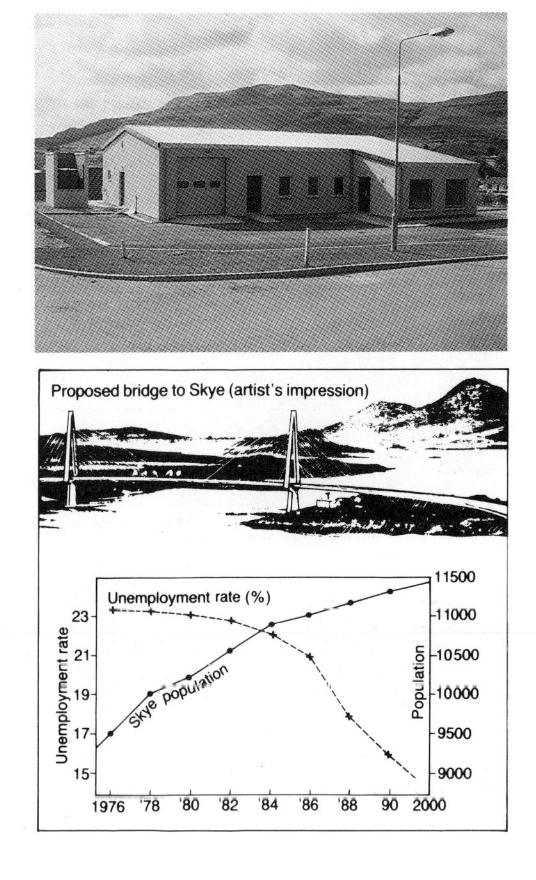

CHAPTER 3

Kishorn: case study

Kishorn was an area of restricted land-use potential with its population widely dispersed in crofting townships or in narrow valleys and dependent upon the primary sector (fishing, farming and forestry). The establishment of an oil platform construction site there (3.41) in 1975 brought many changes. The site was a £50 million investment by the Howard Doris company and created employment. Very large concrete and steel platforms (e.g. the Ninian Central Platform 1978) for the North Sea oil fields were constructed at the site.

During the first 'boom' years of the Kishorn site, there was a 12% increase in the local population and an injection of approximately £20 million into the local economy. The nearby villages of Lochcarron, Achintraid and Ardneaskan expanded as new housing was built to accommodate the rising numbers of people settling within the area, and roads, bridges and local services were all improved.

Changing technology and competition from construction yards on the east coast contributed to the closure of the site in 1985. The impact on the local population, economy, services, schools and landscape was considerable (3.42). Rural depopulation rose to its pre-oil-boom levels and unemployment peaked at 26%.

3.41 Loch Kishorn oil construction site

Further changes are expected within the area in the 1990s. Fish farming and tourism are set to be the main employers but many analysts now regard the recent explorative work in the Minch and eastern Atlantic as heralding another boom for the oil construction industry and the likely reopening of the now derelict Kishorn site.

3.42 Kishorn today

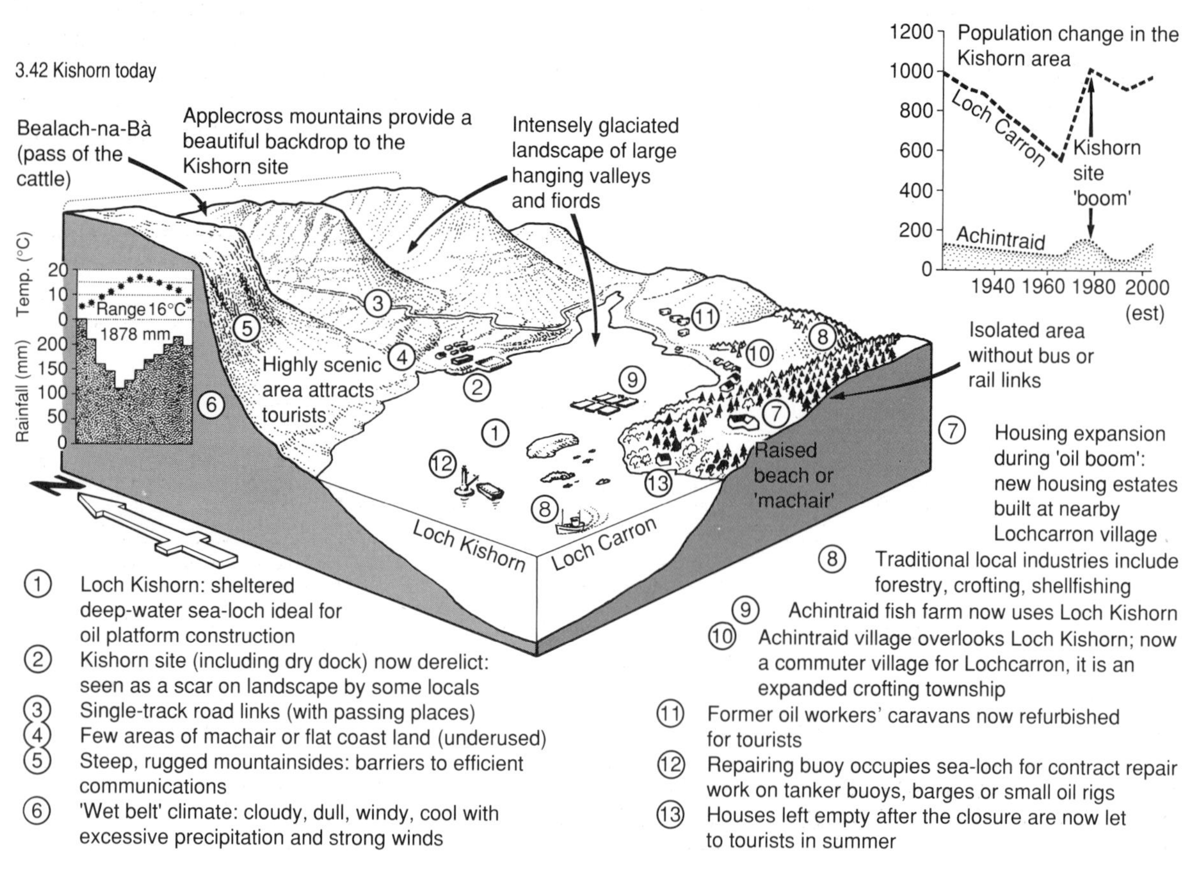

Diverse Industrial Landscapes: Spain

With 39 million people, Spain is a country of massive potential but one in which industrialisation is only a recent process. Since 1960 the country has undergone rapid industrial, economic and social change. Its original underdeveloped agricultural economy has been rapidly superseded by expanding and diversifying secondary (3.43) and tertiary sectors which have helped Spain become the world's tenth largest industrial country.

Spain is a mosaic of contrasting landscapes The maritime lowlands of the north and west coasts contrast with the hot and dry Mediterranean coastlines of the south and east. The parched and inhospitable Meseta (the high and deeply dissected interior) contrasts with the extensive fertile plains of Murcia and Valencia. Much of the agricultural landscape remains dominated by a system of large estates run by an absentee landowner, with fragmented farms and low productivity. Yet there are massive hydro-electric schemes, such as the one on the river Tagus, which not only provide irrigation and contribute to locally high agricultural productivity but also generate large-scale industrial activity.

3.43 The major industrial complex of Bilbao in northern Spain

Industrial and economic transformation (3.44) has occurred for several reasons. Since the death of the dictator General Franco in 1975, Spain has become a Western democracy and has encouraged Western influences and contact. The enormous influx of capital from the rapidly expanding tourist trade since the 1960s has helped to finance industrial development. The electrification of railways, construction of motorways and the

3.44 Transformation of the Spanish economy

Main elements	First industrial phase (until 1960 approx)	Second industrial phase (up to present day)	Future industrial phase (next century)
Main energy sources	Mainly coal or localised energy sources	Increasing diversity encouraged: electricity from HEP, solar, thermal and nuclear power stations	Diversity: electricty from HEP, wind, solar and nuclear sources
Employment	Manual labour Primary sector dominant	Skilled white-collar technical, administrative, professional Manufacturing Services	Tertiary/quaternary dominance, skilled labour urban-based
Transport	Limited rail, sea (+ human and animal-powered) transport	Improved roads, electrified railways, airports, lower costs per unit of distance	Highly developed networks: integrated road, rail, air services with rest of EC
Technology	Relatively simple technology Large, heavy technology	More complex, micro-electronic, control systems Light, miniature technology	Robotics, computer-aided systems, electronic linkages, new innovations, forefront technology
Products	Limited range: olive oil	Increasing range: textiles, steel, motor vehicles, chemicals, consumer goods, pharmaceuticals, souvenirs	Ultramodern consumer goods, lighter industrial goods, more research and development
Systems and organisation	Small farms, large estates. Family run, small-to-medium industries	Increasing size and complexity. Multi-plant, national and transnational companies	Large units of production. Rationalised locations and plants. Transnational companies important
Spatial Impact	Dispersed industrial production interlinked with agricultural locations. Localised markets	Concentration of industrial production around urban markets. Increasing large markets	Greater locational choice. Very large markets of EC

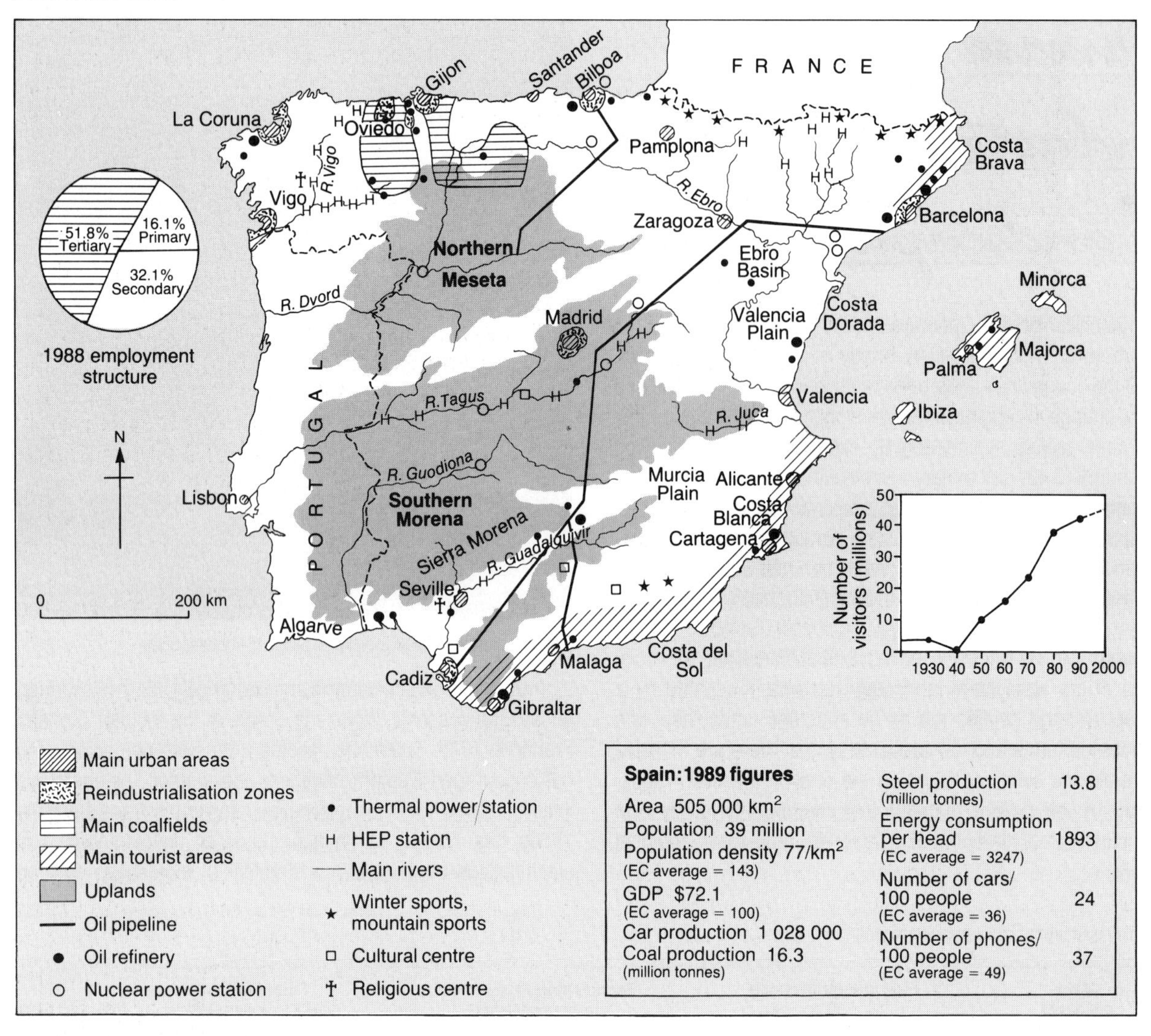

3.45 Spain's diverse industrial landscapes

modernisation of air and sea ports, together with an efficient national power grid, have given increased impetus to Spain's second industrial phase.

Agriculture accounts for 20% of exports and employs 16% of the workforce. State investments in modernising the rural areas helped increase the value of agricultural produce from 7% in 1970 to 12% in 1988. Spanish wines, vegetables, olive oil and fruit are exported all year round. There is an extensive internal market supporting the tourist industry and, with farm wages around 50% of the EC average, Spain produces food relatively cheaply.

Manufacturing industry in Spain accounts for 75% of all exports and employs 32% of the workforce. There is a comprehensive state aid system co-ordinated by the L'Instituto Nacional de Industria. Wide-ranging and generous incentives for industrial developments in the zones of reindustrialisation (3.45) are given for electricity production, oil refining, coal, steel, aluminium, vehicles, petro-chemicals, aviation and hotel construction. The energy consumed in Spain is the equivalent of 500 million tonnes of oil (TOE: tonnes oil equivalent) but only 185 million tonnes (TOE) are home produced (from hydro-electric, coal, nuclear and solar sources). Two-thirds of all energy is produced from imported oil.

Spain relies on its large ports, with their extensive areas of flat land, good communications, skilled labour force and massive state or foreign investment schemes, as the focus of its developing manufacturing sector. It is the fourth largest producer of EC steel, producing enough to supply its own expanding motor vehicle industry (SEAT) and to assemble Ford, Peugeot, Renault and GM cars, giving an annual total of over 1 million units. Barcelona

3.46 Ford's car plant at Valencia modern industrial complex

is the centre of the vehicle industry with branches and car plants at Valladolid, Vigo, Pamplona, Valencia (3.46) and Madrid. Steel is also used to build ships at Cadiz, Bilbao, Santander, Cartagena and Gijon. Oil refining, petro-chemicals and cheap pharmaceuticals are also of vital importance to Spain's economy. The modernity of Spain's manufacturing industry is reflected in the diversity of its exports: steel tubes, cars, refined oils and chemicals, electronics and fashion wear.

There are **three main industrial regions** in Spain (Madrid, Barcelona, and Oviedo–Gijon), with Madrid the political, administrative and financial centre. Its importance has increased with the development and integration of the national road and rail systems since Madrid is at the heart of the network. The city's population has doubled since 1960, to 4.30 million, as increasing numbers of people moved there from rural areas to find work. Madrid now manufactures electrical equipment, cars (Peugeots), chemicals and consumer goods, and processes foodstuffs.

The northern coast is Spain's manufacturing heartland and includes the Basque region of Bilbao and Navarre where iron-ores, coal and heavy industry are vital to the local and national economy. The region is Spain's most densely populated, with its own language and culture. The region capital is Bilbao, a very important steel-making centre. Other large employers here are shipbuilding, agricultural machinery, engineering (diesel engines), petro-chemicals and shoe making. To the west are the important ports of Santander and Gijon and the coal mining centre of Oviedo.

Barcelona is a financial, industrial and commercial city (population 3 million) centred in Catalonia. Its hinterland produces much of Spain's hydro-electricity and its main industries include textiles, vehicles, shipbuilding, railway engines, electronic components, chemicals, and food processing.

The Spanish economic 'miracle' has had several setbacks and had to face major competition and change, in particular during the global economic recessions of the 1970s and 1980s. The over production of steel, worldwide and in the EC, has caused the steelworks at Bilbao to cut its production and workforce by 12%. Industrial agriculture (olive oil, sugar beet, cotton) and textile industries have also suffered from cheap foreign competition.

Investments by transnational companies such as General Motors, Ford and IBM have, however, gradually increased, taking advantage of cheap labour costs (72% of EC average), enthusiasm and lack of industrial disputes among the workforce, and improving infrastructure.

Tourism has been **the most important economic and industrial development** since the early 1960s. Over 42 million people visited Spain in 1988 making it the most visited tourist destination in the world. The importance of tourism to the Spanish economy has been crucial since the income derived has been the main financing force behind the country's infrastructure and industrial development. The tertiary sector employs over 51% of the Spanish workforce, with tourism directly employing over 13%.

The physical advantages of most of the Mediterranean coastline: the hot sunny summers with up to 10 hours of sunshine daily, attractive coastline and scenery, warm sea, sheltered beaches, and very mild winters; and the (initial) low cost of living and cheap accommodation were major considerations in the development of Spain's most important industry. The construction of coastal airports and improved rail and road connections together with the increase in the number of cheap package holidays and charter flights all contributed to a rapid expansion of tourist resorts and amenities along the Mediterranean coast and on islands such as Majorca. The effects of tourist development have transformed small fishing villages into 'Manhattans on the Med' (3.47) with high-rise ribbon developments stretching along large sections of coastline. Paradoxically, however, the prosperity brought by tourism to the coastal economies of the Costas has also brought uncontrolled coastal sprawl, congestion, water supply and sewerage disposal problems, and environmental pollution so severe that the Spanish government has now implemented environmental protection schemes in many areas.

3.47 The Costa Blanca tourist landscape

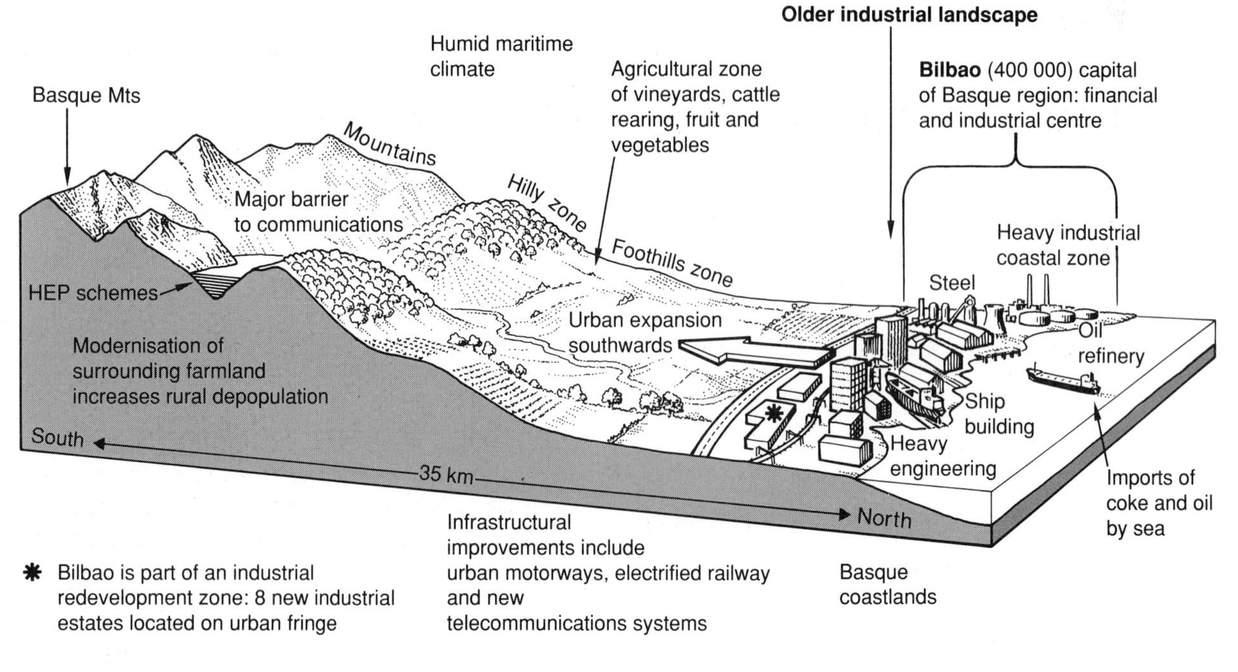

3.48 Spain's northern manufacturing area

The diversity of industrial landscapes within Spain (3.48 and 3.49) is well illustrated by the contrast between the northern coast and the south-eastern coast. Tourism has been predominantly coastal and of prime importance to Mediterranean areas. Manufacturing is centred in the north and west of the country. The future for the economy seems likely to be strongly influenced by both competition arising from membership of the EC and increasing international competition from NICs (newly industrialising countries of the South). Heavy demands are likely to be made upon the EC's regional development funds as Spain's labour costs rise and, as the EC imports more from Third World countries, the impact of competition will be severe on areas specialising in traditional manufacturing industries such as steel, textiles and shipbuilding. Job losses, increasing an already high unemployment rate of over 17%, will be an inevitable outcome if Spain cannot further diversify its industrial base.

3.49 Spain's south-eastern tourist area

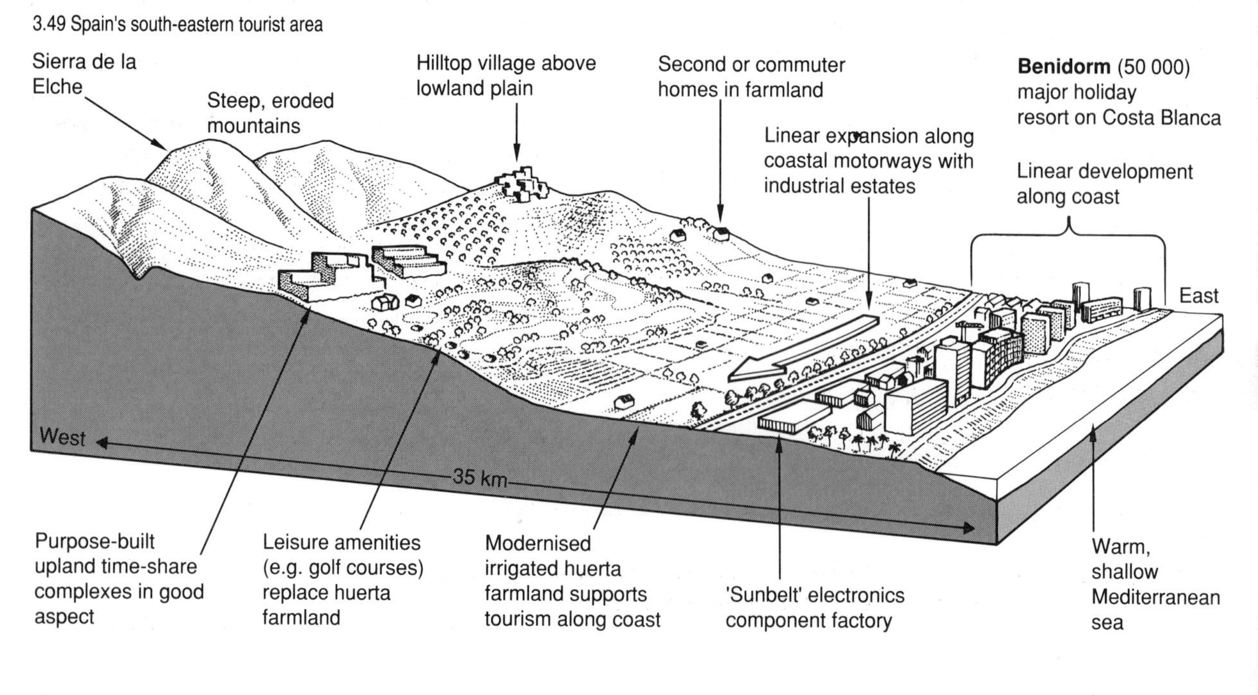

Questions

Q PERIPHERAL INDUSTRIAL LANDSCAPES

1 (a) Define economic potential.
(b) Why are southern Italy, north-west Scotland and Spain regarded as peripheral industrial areas?
(c) Using an atlas and map 3.26, make a list of the areas of highest economic potential in Europe.
(d) Why do private companies locate in areas of high economic potential?
(e) Make up a table to show the main characteristics of areas of high and low economic potential.

Q IL MEZZOGIORNO

2 (a) Draw a simple map to show the location of the area called 'Il Mezzogiorno', its regions and main settlements.
(b) What were the main physical and economic reasons for underdevelopment in southern Italy?
(c) Describe the role of state intervention in the development of the Mezzogiorno (i.e. the Cassa).
(d) Using the data in tables 3.27 and 3.28, draw graphs to show the main trends in GDP and income in Italy.
(e) Describe and account for these trends.
(f) Compare and contrast the employment structure of north and south Italy.
(g) In what ways did the agrarian reforms of the Cassa pave the way for industrial developments?
(h) Make a simple annotated sketch of photo 3.30.
(i) Use map 3.32 to comment on the type and distribution of industries introduced to the area.
(j) Prepare two arguments: one against industrial development in the Mezzogiorno, and one in favour. If you were an industrialist would you locate in the south?
(k) List the main attractions of the area for tourism.
(l) What is the likely future for the Mezzogiorno?

Q NORTH AND WEST SCOTLAND

3 (a) Make a simple annotated sketch of photo 3.36 to summarise the main difficulties of the environment.
(b) Explain why there has been such a lack of industrial investment in the north and west of Scotland.
(d) Make your own copy of chart 3.38, then explain the transition from traditional to modern industrialisation.
(e) Change to the industrial base of any area affects the social and environmental conditions operating within it. How far has north and west Scotland been affected?
(f) Why are small-scale development schemes now seen as more realistic than large-scale industrial projects?
(g) Which developments are likely to ensure a diversified industrial future for the north and west of Scotland?

Q DIVERSE INDUSTRIAL LANDSCAPES: SPAIN

4 (a) How is Spain a country of diverse industrial landscapes?
(b) Compare and contrast the land use along the north coast (3.43) with that of the south and east coasts (3.47). Suggest reasons for these differences.
(c) Why is Spain still regarded as a semi-developed industrial nation?
(d) What have been the main influences on the transformation of Spanish industry since 1960?
(e) Describe how the distribution of Spain's industry reflects the theory of optimum location.
(f) Why has water management been of vital importance to the development of Spain's modern economy?
(g) Why has the growth of the tourist industry had a paradoxical effect on Spain?
(h) Summarise both the advantages and disadvantages of Spain's membership of the European Community.
(i) Design a future industrial landscape for 3.48 or 3.49.

Research and Further Work

(a) Compare and contrast the industrial development, problems and future of southern Italy, north and west Scotland, and Spain.
(b) Why is it essential to improve the infrastructure before real industrial development can occur?
(c) Prepare a report on any other peripheral area in Western Europe discussing the problems of, and attempted solutions to, industrial development.

CHAPTER 3

The Inner Core

The most densely populated regions of the Euro-core, with their high accessibility to labour force, markets, finance, etc., have the major advantage of a communications network which efficiently interlinks the main industrial and urban centres (3.50).The integration of transport systems reinforces access to the core regions usually at the expense of the peripheral areas. Along the main corridors of communication, for example the Rhine corridor from Europoort to Basle, economic activity is stimulated. By contrast, peripheral areas tend to have localised communication networks, often unaffected by Euro-core networks.

Improvements to core communications, such as the Channel Tunnel, enhance the agglomeration effect within the core, increasing the isolation of industrial areas within Eire, Greece, southern Italy and Scotland.

As already discussed, regions on the Euro-periphery are more dependent than ever on developing an efficient infrastructure in the hope of shrinking their profitability gap with Euro-core regions. For new peripheral developments such as high-tech aquaculture, wholesale distribution centres or holiday complexes, the ability to communicate rapidly and efficiently with their markets is the key to economic success.

Though much of Europe has experienced substantial economic growth and prosperity, there is uneven growth with marked contrasts between core growth areas and peripheral regions. In the free markets within the European Community, industrial developments are mainly concentrated within an area centred on Brussels, of radius 350 km with a population of over 120 million people. However, it is now recognised that the free market trading principles operating in the EC need amendment to aid the less industrial or declining areas. State intervention through specialised agencies such as the Cassa or the HIDB have contributed positively to policy and decision making within the EC.

Within the Euro-core or economic heartland it is possible to delineate an inner area (3.51) at the hub of political, industrial and economic decision making.

Politically, Community decision making takes place between Brussels, Luxembourg and Strasbourg. The capital cities, Bonn, Paris, London and Amsterdam, of the key political and industrial nations are also within or close to the inner-core area.

Secondary industry is also concentrated within this area. Over 50% of the EC annual steel output and over 75% of the Community's textiles, chemicals, oils, and vehicles are manufactured in the Ruhr, eastern France and Belgium. This area, which also produces over 85% of the Community's coals, forms the **heavy industrial triangle** of the EC (3.51).

The inner core is also the **population heartland** of the

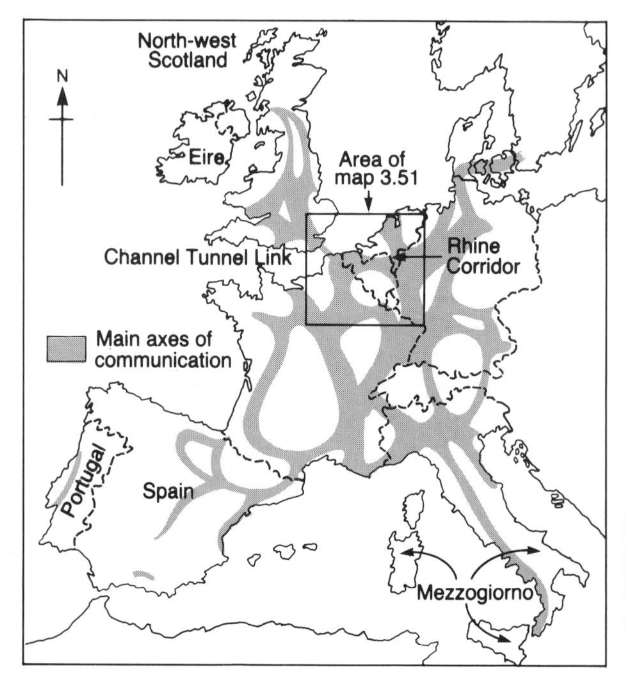

3.50 Major communications axes within the EC

Community. Although it covers only about 21% of the land area of the EC, it houses over 43% of its population. If **wealth** is measured as GDP (gross domestic product) per head, the average for the inner-core area is 40% higher than many peripheral regions such as southern Spain and Greece, and around 20% higher than core fringe areas (just outside the Euro-core), such as Brittany and Bavaria.

The Rhine water-route remains the central **communications** axis and routeway, containing the Community's major seaport, Europoort. **Mobility** is at its highest within the inner core both in terms of transport of materials and products, and also of population. With the introduction of the **Single European Market** (1992), easier professional and social mobility will be at its peak within 350 km of Brussels.

In addition the fertile landscape of the North West European Plain, with its loess, boulder clays and polder lands, has some of the Community's most **productive agricultural land**.

Many comparative studies have revealed the persistence of the core–periphery gap within the European Community. Despite recent industrial and economic growth in areas such as southern Spain and the Mezzogiorno, the Euro-core remains pre-eminent. Areas such as Randstad in the Netherlands (3.51 and 3.52) have the advantages of centrality, high economic potential, advanced economic structure and large urban areas with influential political and industrial institutions. However, industrial transition and economic weakness are not confined to peripheral areas within the EC. Severe problems within the traditional industrial centres of the Community have been created by the displacement of labour through the advance of technology.

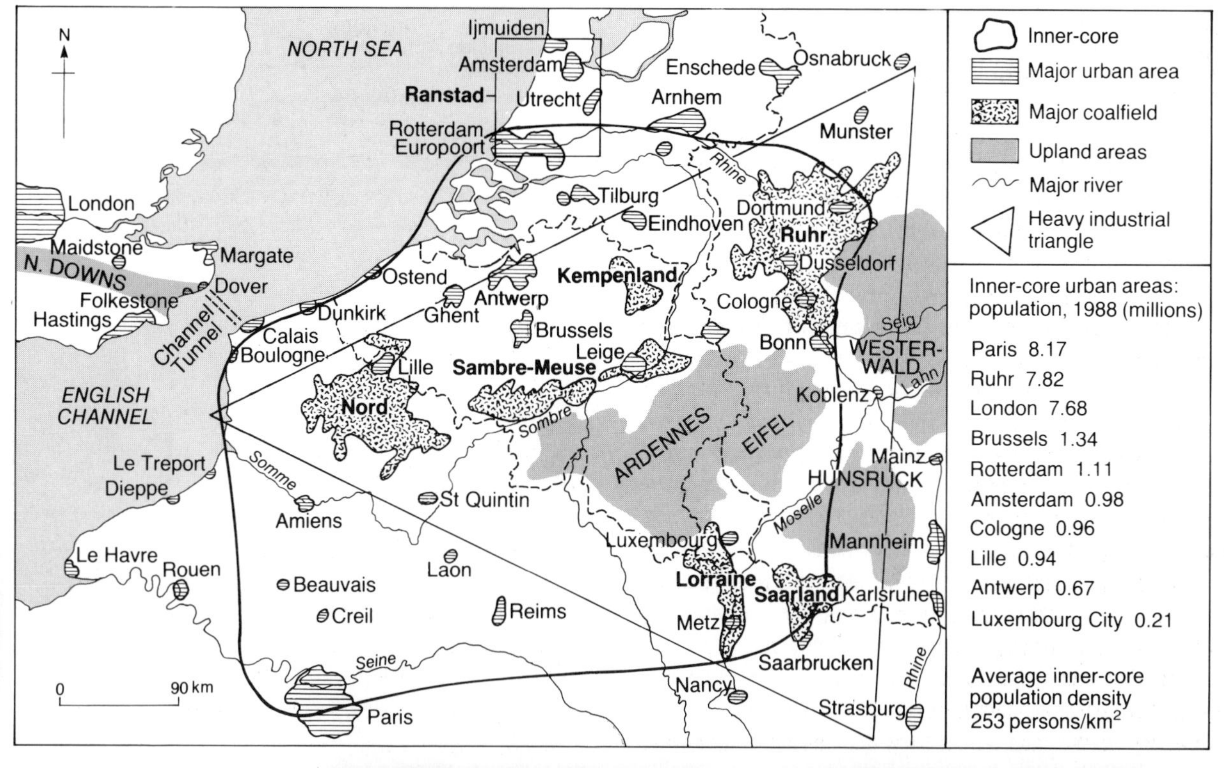

3.51 The inner core, centred on Brussels

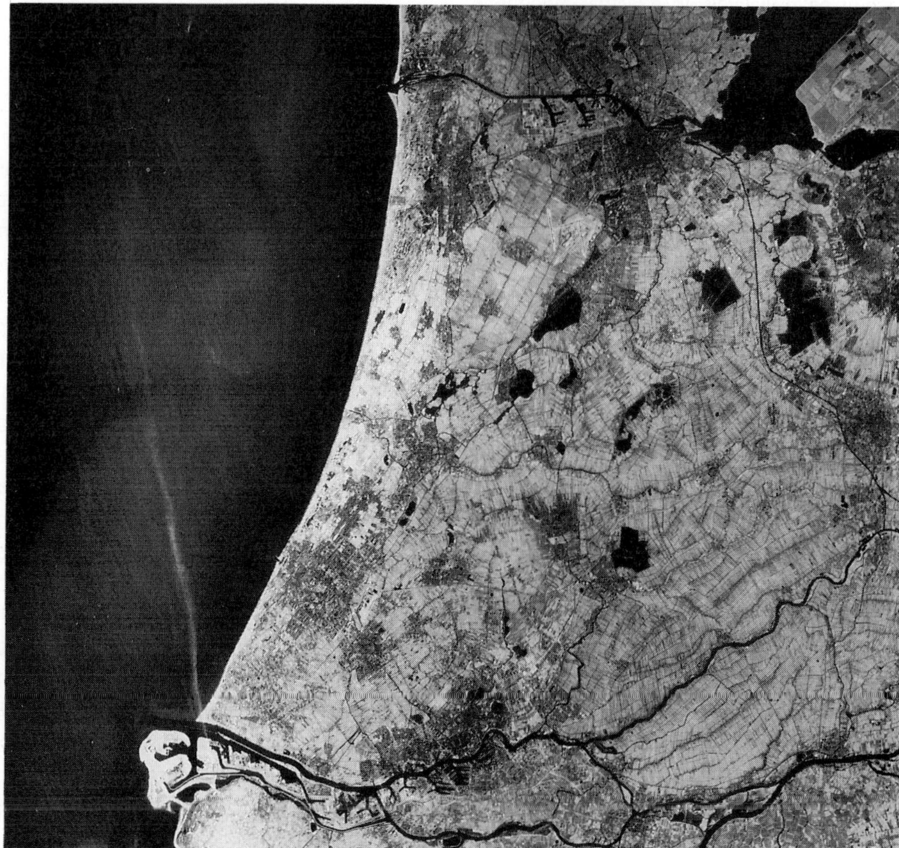

3.52 Satellite photo of Randstad

Ruhr in Transition

...pit heads and factories, miners black with coal and panting steel workers, slag-heaps and boggy industrial wastelands, smog and thunder, the sky full of the smoke of chimneys in the daytime, and at night the glowing red reflections of a thousand soot-belching fires - for decades such scenes have been the image of the Ruhr region.

(Ruhr,1938, *Geographical*, Oct. 1983)

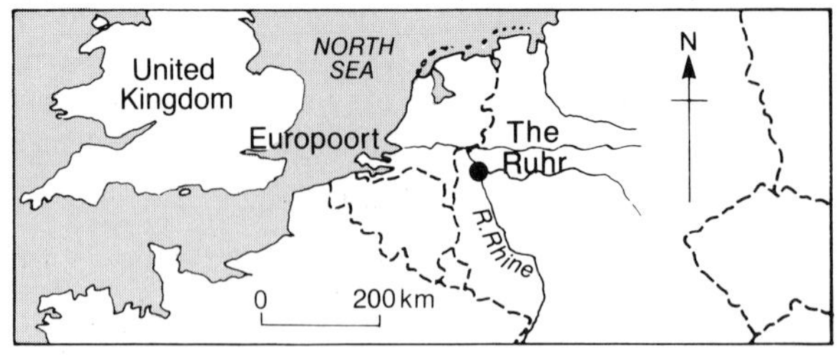

3.53 Location of the Ruhr

3.54 Run-down Ruhr industrial area

Descriptions such as this of one of the world's major industrial regions are now outdated, as the Ruhr has undergone considerable transition in recent years. Within the Euro-core there are great contrasts between regions that are thriving on their centrality and those that have reached an advanced state of economic decay. The Ruhr, which is Europe's largest and most important industrial region, shows signs of both industrial decline and growth: there is severe unemployment and some economic decay, but also great economic success. Although the Ruhr is a landlocked area, it has an excellent communications network which helps to maintain its industrial importance.

The Ruhr region is located around the confluences of the rivers Ruhr, Emscher and Lippe with the Rhine, approximately 230 km upstream from Europoort (3.53). For 70 km eastwards from the Rhine the view of an urban and industrial landscape is virtually unbroken by open spaces and countryside. Yet the apparent heavy industrial face of the region (3.54) disguises the degree of industrial transition affecting it. The Ruhr has been an industrial region for over 100 years and is one of the best examples of a heavy industrial area based upon a coalfield. The Ruhr still produces almost 22% of the EC's steel and over 31% of its coal, and is situated within its inner core or growth axis (3.51), with excellent access to large markets because of its central position.

High density of settlement closely associated with industrial development is an important feature of the area (3.55). Within the Ruhr Planning Region (SVR) there are over 6 million people and 20 towns and cities, stretching from Hamm to Duisburg (east to west) and from the river Lippe to the river Ruhr (north to south).

The coal industry

The Ruhr coalfield has been of vital importance in the development and concentration of industry on such a large scale. The coalfield dips to the north, with southern, exposed coal seams now exhausted (3.56). The slow and progressive relocation of coal mining northwards to deep-seat mines of an average depth of 1000 metres has left behind a scarred southern Ruhr landscape with economic and social problems. It has been estimated that there are over 60 000 million tonnes of reserves of 50 different varieties of Ruhr coals but costs of mining increase with depth.

Competition from cheaper energy sources (oil and gas) in the 1970s and 1980s caused coal production to drop from 125 million tonnes in 1956 to less than 65 million tonnes in 1988. At the same time the labour force fell from 500 000 in 1956 to less than 100 000 in 1988 as the number of collieries dropped from 140 in 1956 to 25 in 1988.

The development of robotics and other modern coal technology, associated with a massive increase in productivity as inefficient mines were closed and others amalgamated, helped the Ruhr maintain its position as the leading coalfield of the EC.

Most of the **pit closures** were south of the river Emscher. Towns such as Gelsenkirchen and Bottrop have been badly affected by unemployment as their economies were based almost solely on coal mining. South of the river Ruhr, coal mining has stopped altogether as the industry has relocated to fewer, modern deep mines in the area north of Recklinghausen and Dinslaken. The Ruhr, operating as one unit, is now a highly productive coalfield and poised to make the most of the continuing changes within the energy market of the 1990s. The uncertainties over supplies of oil are likely to protect the coal industry in the region: increases in the demand for coal are predicted until the end of the century.

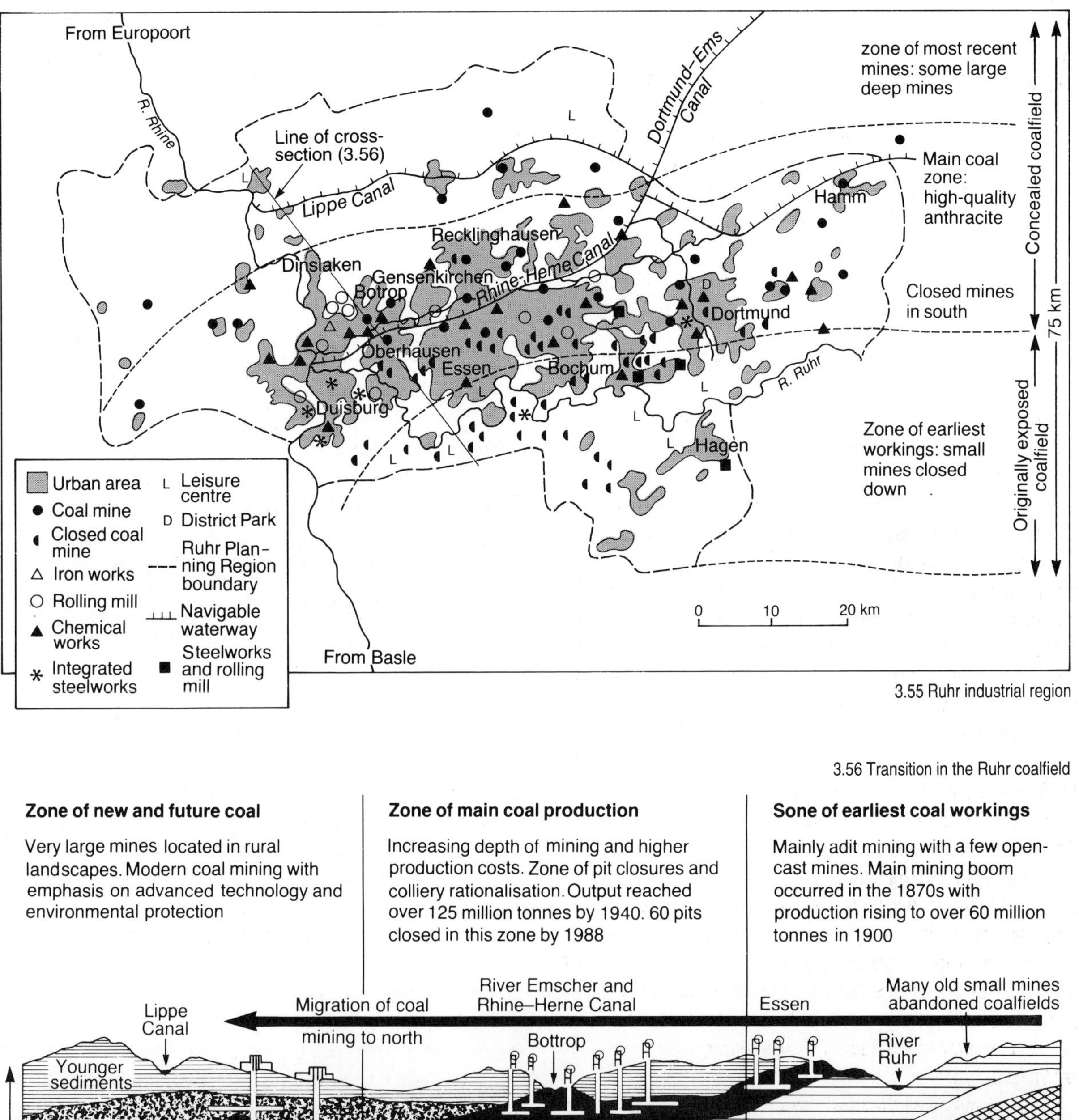

3.55 Ruhr industrial region

3.56 Transition in the Ruhr coalfield

Zone of new and future coal

Very large mines located in rural landscapes. Modern coal mining with emphasis on advanced technology and environmental protection

Zone of main coal production

Increasing depth of mining and higher production costs. Zone of pit closures and colliery rationalisation. Output reached over 125 million tonnes by 1940. 60 pits closed in this zone by 1988

Sone of earliest coal workings

Mainly adit mining with a few open-cast mines. Main mining boom occurred in the 1870s with production rising to over 60 million tonnes in 1900

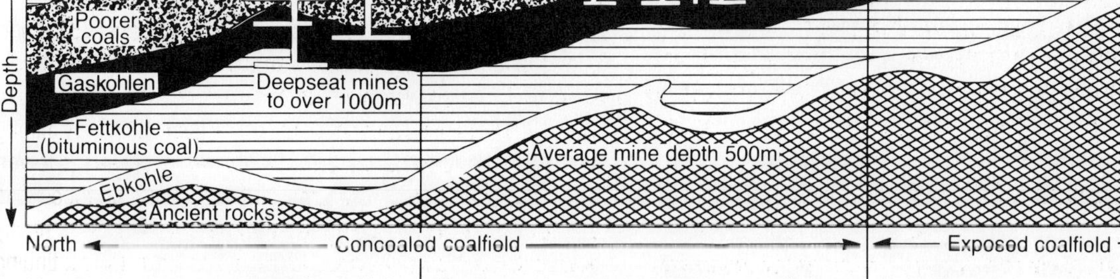

Very high investment, fewer jobs, in high-output, advanced mines. Restoration of areas contracted in licence for mining. 15 mines producing 30 million tonnes of coal annually

'Coal towns' experiencing high unemployment and consequent social problems. Redevelopment and reindustrialisation supported by national and local government in early 1990s

Scarred abandoned 'coalscape' seams now exhausted. Advanced industrial decay. SVR plans for rehabilitation of area with new industrial and leisure estates

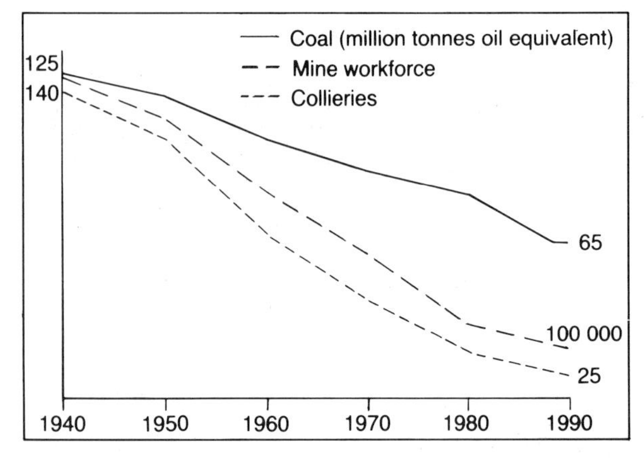

3.57 Decline in Ruhr coalfields

Iron and steel and other traditional industries

Industrial transition has not been confined to the coal industry. The iron and steel industry, traditionally the second industry of the Ruhr, has also declined. Competition from coastal steelworks and the increasing costs of Ruhr coals in the 1970s and 1980s caused steel production in the Ruhr to fall from 34 million tonnes in 1974 to 22 million tonnes in 1981 (the low point). The Ruhr produced 7% of world steel in 1960 but this had fallen to 2.9% by 1981. Throughout this period of transition, considerable rationalisation took place within the industry, with a concentration of production and investment around Duisburg and Dortmund. Steel making has relocated to waterfront locations (which allow greater cost-effectiveness) on the Dortmund–Ems canal and river Rhine at opposite ends of the Ruhr. Steel making has ceased in the central Ruhr, at Bochum and Essen, while specialised steels are manufactured at Krefeld and Remscheld. The advantages of waterfront locations, access to extensive imports of Swedish iron-ore via Europoort, and coals and limestones from the Rhine artery, led to substantial investment in steel plants and their reorganisation into larger integrated units, increasing production to over 24 million tonnes in 1988. The central area now uses steel for making Opel cars at Bochum and for engineering, machine tools, electro-technical and metallurgy industries in the Essen area.

Other traditional industries also suffered from industrial transition. Textiles and clothing lost over 200 000 jobs between 1965 and 1986. The chemical industry, stimulated by increasing oil imports via Europoort and the Rhine, and the expansion of the petro-chemicals and pharmaceuticals industries at Marl and Gelsenkirchen, increased employment within selected areas from 42 000 in 1975 to over 76 000 in 1988.

The wholescale industrial decline of the 1970s and 1980s in the coal and steel industries caused unemployment levels within the Ruhr to reach an average of over 13% in 1980 compared with a national average of around 7% (1970 figures: Ruhr 4.7%, national 6.7%). In an industrial area which had fewer than 21 000 people out of work in 1970, the situation by 1985 was serious with over 265 000 jobless. Areas along the Emscher valley suffered most with unemployment reaching 13%; lower unemployment is found along the Rhine and to the north and south of the Ruhr. The unemployment patterns within the Ruhr reflect the varying success or failure of settlements throughout the area to adapt to continuing economic changes.

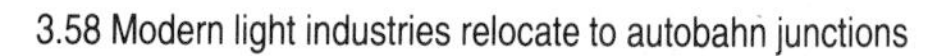

3.58 Modern light industries relocate to autobahn junctions

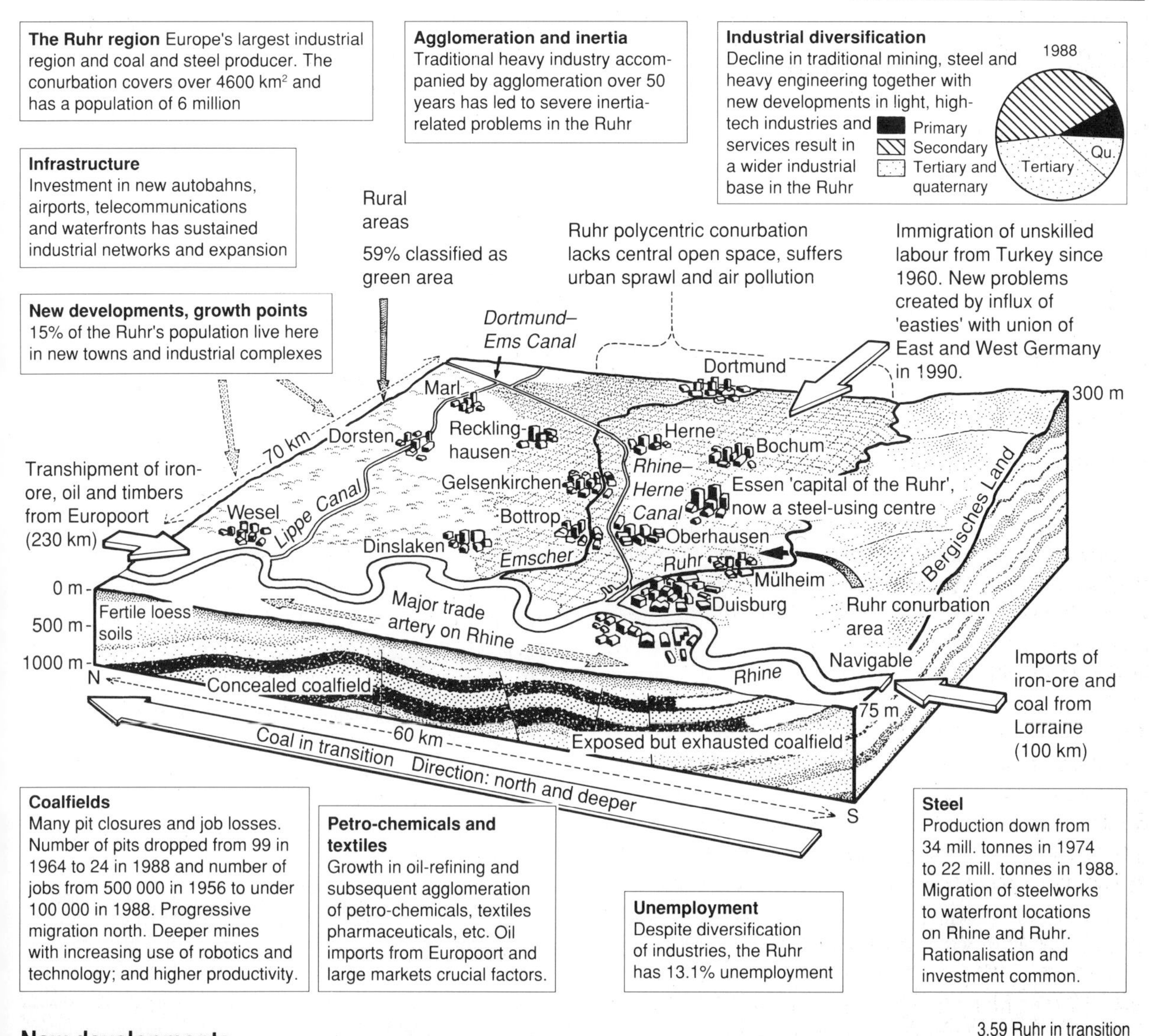

The Ruhr region Europe's largest industrial region and coal and steel producer. The conurbation covers over 4600 km² and has a population of 6 million
Agglomeration and inertia
Traditional heavy industry accompanied by agglomeration over 50 years has led to severe inertia-related problems in the Ruhr
Industrial diversification
Decline in traditional mining, steel and heavy engineering together with new developments in light, high-tech industries and services result in a wider industrial base in the Ruhr
1988
Primary
Secondary
Tertiary and quaternary
Qu.
Tertiary
Infrastructure
Investment in new autobahns, airports, telecommunications and waterfronts has sustained industrial networks and expansion
Rural areas
59% classified as green area
Ruhr polycentric conurbation lacks central open space, suffers urban sprawl and air pollution
Immigration of unskilled labour from Turkey since 1960. New problems created by influx of 'easties' with union of East and West Germany in 1990.
New developments, growth points
15% of the Ruhr's population live here in new towns and industrial complexes
Dortmund–Ems Canal
Dortmund
300 m
Marl
Recklinghausen
Herne
Bochum
70 km
Dorsten
Rhine–Herne Canal
Transhipment of iron-ore, oil and timbers from Europoort (230 km)
Lippe Canal
Gelsenkirchen
Essen 'capital of the Ruhr', now a steel-using centre
Bergisches Land
Wesel
Bottrop
Dinslaken
Oberhausen
Emscher
Ruhr
Mülheim
0 m
Major trade artery on Rhine
Duisburg
Ruhr conurbation area
500 m
Fertile loess soils
1000 m
Navigable
Imports of iron-ore and coal from Lorraine (100 km)
N
Concealed coalfield
Rhine
75 m
60 km
Exposed but exhausted coalfield
Coal in transition Direction: north and deeper
S
Coalfields
Many pit closures and job losses. Number of pits dropped from 99 in 1964 to 24 in 1988 and number of jobs from 500 000 in 1956 to under 100 000 in 1988. Progressive migration north. Deeper mines with increasing use of robotics and technology; and higher productivity.
Petro-chemicals and textiles
Growth in oil-refining and subsequent agglomeration of petro-chemicals, textiles pharmaceuticals, etc. Oil imports from Europoort and large markets crucial factors.
Unemployment
Despite diversification of industries, the Ruhr has 13.1% unemployment
Steel
Production down from 34 mill. tonnes in 1974 to 22 mill. tonnes in 1988. Migration of steelworks to waterfront locations on Rhine and Ruhr. Rationalisation and investment common.

3.59 Ruhr in transition

New developments

The industrial transition of the 1970s and 1980s has dramatically changed the industrial face of the Ruhr. Cities such as Bochum, Dortmund and Essen have been modernised into attractive, service-based centres with excellent office complexes and shopping precincts. There are many reclamation schemes which, in the wake of closures, have transformed derelict mining and manufacturing sites into industrial estates, shopping centres and business parks near to new autobahns and electrified rail networks (3.58). The transition from over-concentration on heavy industry to an economy based on tertiary and quaternary services has had other benefits for the Ruhr region. There has been a reduction in environmental pollution, with many areas now set aside as 'green wedges' for leisure and recreational purposes. Many of these areas have been reconstructed on waste heaps and former industrial sites. Waste recycling is now given region-wide priority and river pollution levels are currently at their lowest this century. Improvements to the Ruhr's communications network have been a vital element in the region's rehabilitation. Today there are over 500 km of autobahns and railways providing easy access by land or waterway through Europe's major growth axis. The interdependence of industry and communications within the region lies at the heart of the future economic success of the Ruhr.

Throughout a period of technological advance and intense external competition in industry, the Ruhr has managed to maintain its pre-eminent position in the EC. This is mainly due to increasing diversification of its industrial base and employment structure, massive investment in infrastructure, the rebuilding of its major settlements, and environmental improvements. Changed days from the coal and steel landscape of half a century ago.

CHAPTER 3

New Industrial Growth

Industrial location within the European Community has traditionally been affected most by the availability of capital, energy, raw materials, skilled labour, transport facilities and potential markets. Industrial decline or growth occurs through change in the relative importance of these factors. The concentration of heavy industrial areas within the Euro-core illustrates the importance of coal as the prime location factor, as in the Ruhr. Weber explained this in his theory of 'least-cost location' (page 61) where transport costs of low-value, high-bulk materials are minimised by locating the industry at their source. In large areas dominated by one heavy industry (**monotechnic**) the industry tends to remain in its coalfield location, and owes its survival to a variety of new factors, such as state aid, improved communications, technological innovation, etc., which help to preserve inertia.

Locational changes

Since the 1950s there has been a major shift in the distribution of economic activity within and on the fringes of the Euro-core (3.60). A number of factors have given rise to the development of **footloose industries**: modern, high-tech industries not restricted to a particular location, such as a coalfield or break-of-bulk point. The availability of cheap electricity; cheap and efficient transport of raw materials, products and labour by integrated transport systems; development of light and science-based industries with a greater emphasis on skilled labour than on raw materials; and technological advance have encouraged a flexible choice of location. Europe's modern growth industries – components, motor vehicles, electronics and telecommunications, retailing and banking – all have a flexible choice of location. The decentralisation of modern industry southwards has been spontaneous rather than state-guided and industrial expansion has occurred in greenfield sites around large urban areas such as Greater Paris or London and in the sunbelts and skibelts of southern and Alpine Europe. The dispersal of modern industry from the 'rustbelts' or older industrial areas reflects industrial development, product innovation, technological advance, improving infrastructure and increasing environmental awareness on the part of private companies whose products or services are often of high value or low bulk or both (e.g. car phones, satellites or advertising).

Even traditional retailing outlets are forsaking city centres and relocating to pleasant greenfield sites where excellent communications networks ease delivery problems and extend

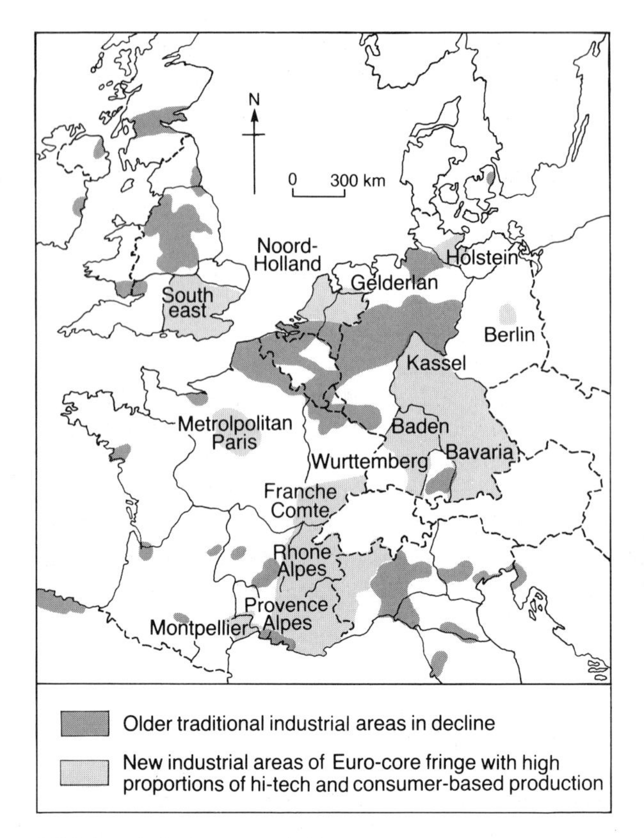

3.60 Industry in the Euro-core and fringe areas

the sphere of influence, thereby increasing profit margins considerably. In Britain there are numerous examples of 'greenspace' **out-of-town shopping centres and complexes**, such as Meadowhall in Sheffield (see p.95) and Foss Park (Leicester). Some shopping complexes (e.g. Retailworld, Rotherham) are built on former traditional industrial complexes. **Industrial estates** are found in almost every European urban area or around their rural–urban fringes, usually near major routeways for improved access. The increase in the number of industrial estates in the new industrial growth areas (3.60) from 120 in 1960 to over 2500 in 1987 confirms the growing pattern of industrial relocation from the Euro-core towards its fringes.

Modern high-tech manufacturing often requires sterile or dust-free operating environments (3.61) for the production of, for example, silicon-wafers, fibre-optics, lasers, nanotechnology (tiny mechanisms) or avionics. Greenfield sites are particularly suitable. Recent studies have shown that there are three main types of location favoured by high-tech manufacturing industries in Europe.

(a) **Previously unindustrialised sunbelt or skibelt regions** of high residential or environmental amenity, e.g. Grenoble, Toulouse, Côte d'Azur (France), Bavaria (southern Germany). These new industrial growth areas are regarded as both environmentally clean and residentially desirable. Recent improvements to communications networks, with upgrading of motorways and rail electrification, increase the attractiveness of these areas.

(b) **Outer regions of Europe's major urban areas**, e.g. Paris, London, Amsterdam and Stuttgart. Green Belt areas are very often ideal new locations for the production facilities of high-tech industries. Such urban fringe locations offer not only access to a skilled labour force and large varied markets but are also relatively 'clean' sites with excellent communication links via motorways and airports.

(c) **Selected 'assisted regions'**, including areas of rural decline, e.g. Brittany and western Eire, as well as rustbelt fringe areas such as Silicon Glen (Scotland) or Gwent (Wales). Governments often induce new high-tech development in Assisted Areas by offering a variety of incentive packages which can include the provision of purpose-built factories, relief on rates and taxes, relocation expenses for employees, and even free training initiatives in the first years of development.

Some experts are now suggesting that a process of **deglomeration** (dispersal, the reverse of agglomeration) may be affecting many sectors of the EC economy. As the EC moves from an industrial to a post-industrial society, the emphasis on service-based employment, high-tech industry and the domination of giant multinational companies in the economy will have major spatial implications for industrial growth. Analysts predict that further decentralisation of industry will strengthen the position of the new growth areas around the core fringe and lead to the development of 'satellite' production plants in former Eastern bloc countries such as Poland and Czechoslovakia. The reunification of Germany presents European industry with the possibility of locating research and development centres in high-amenity West German regions (e.g. Bavaria), and locating production centres for the same company around East German industrial areas (e.g. Dresden) where labour costs are lower. State intervention will continue to be necessary within the traditional industrial heartland of the EC to alleviate the severest side-effects of industrial decay and technological advance.

Future developments

Recent developments by Europe's leading computer manufacturer, IBM (International Business Machines), illustrate the dispersal and locational trends of high-tech manufacturing in Europe today (see p.94). Major plants have been built in southern France, at Montpellier (manufacturing) and La Gaude (research and development), in a sunbelt area well outside the Euro-core. Map 3.64 also shows the increasing importance of research and development to the manufacturing of computer hardware and software. IBM now has a wide network of plants, interlinked by efficient transport and communications networks, in environmentally clean, residentially and recreationally attractive locations, and producing highly skilled employment. This has set an example which planners and politicians are attempting to copy elsewhere in Europe.

Industry in the EC is not only controlled by giant corporations such as IBM, Ford, BASF or ICI. Small businesses make an important contribution to industry, and are being encouraged by governments in the 1990s. Giant corporations have great advantages of scale and technology but smaller companies are often more flexible and adaptable to innovation. They play an important role in the development and production of specialised products and components, and in providing new industrial growth in rural areas. Rural development agencies in fringe areas such as Franche Comte (see 3.60) actively encourage small businesses to build factories in rural areas and many of the electronics, data-processing and information technology industries are in small factories with a rural-based workforce.

3.61 High-tech manufacturing plant

CHAPTER 3

IBM in Europe: case study

The locational trends of high-technology industries are well illustrated by IBM, Europe's leading computer manufacturer. IBM is a large multinational company based in New York operating in 12 European countries and employing over 50 000 people in Europe. The company carries out high-tech manufacturing, research and development, and scientific applications (3.63) under the umbrella of computer technology in various locations including greenbelts, skibelts, sunbelts and assisted regions (3.64). For example, IBM have plants in greenfield sites at Essones and Boigny south of Paris; in areas of high residential or environmental amenity at La Gaude in the French Riviera (3.62) and Montpellier; and in assisted peripheral areas such as Santa Palomba (Italy), Greenock (Scotland) and West Berlin.

The company both manufacture and assemble a wide variety of over 750 products (3.63) using the goods and services of over 40 000 suppliers at a cost of over £1.5 billion (1990) annually. In over 40 years of operation there have been no redundancies, and plans for future European expansion include manufacturing plants in former Eastern bloc countries such as Czechoslovakia.

3.62 IBM plant at La Gaude, France

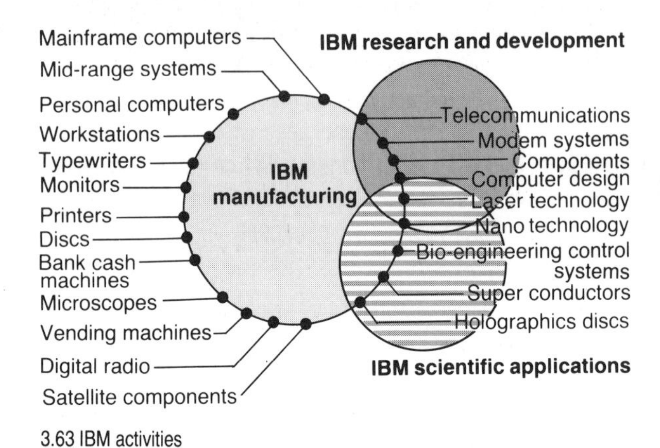

3.63 IBM activities

3.64 IBM in Europe

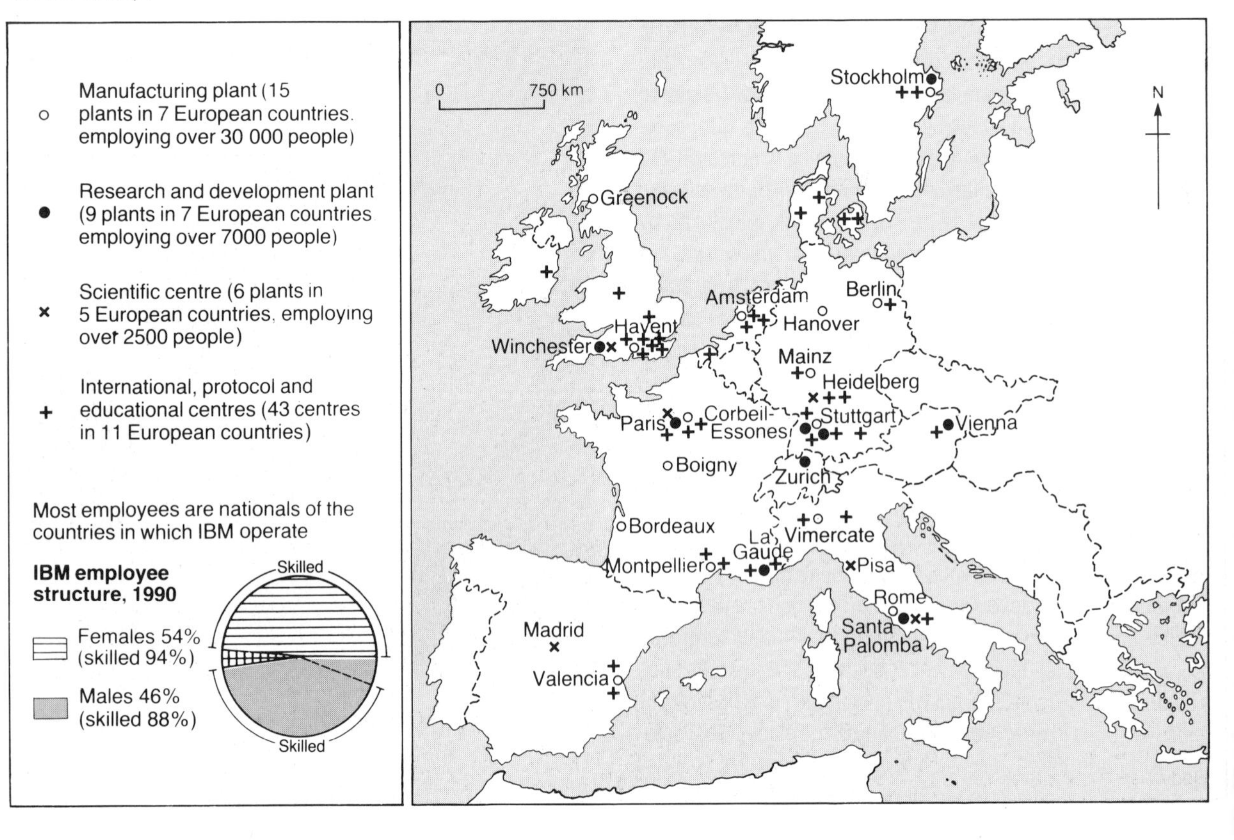

3.65 Meadowhall leisure shopping complex

To Leeds (North)
A6109
Meadowbank Rd.
Junction 34
River Don
M1 Motorway
Viaduct
Passenger interchange
A6178
To Rotherham
Meadowhall Rd
Junction 34
Vulcan Rd
Sheffield Rd
A6178
A6102
A631
Bawtry Rd
A6109
To Sheffield
To London (South)

3.66 Location of Meadowhall, Sheffield

Meadowhall, Sheffield: case study

Proclaimed as 'Europe's number one Leisure Shopping Complex', Meadowhall (3.65) opened in May 1990 as the latest in a series of out-of-town shopping centres under construction in the EC. The complex is located near junction 34 on the M1 motorway (3.66), about 11 km from the centre of Sheffield and is designed mainly for the car-shopper with free parking space for 12 000 cars. There is also one local railway station next to the centre, and bus links with all the surrounding settlements. At busy times over 100 buses an hour arrive at the complex. Meadowhall is estimated to have a sphere of influence of over 90 km and a **threshold population** of nearly 750 000 people.

The complex (or mall) houses 223 different stores, and the most modern facilities and amenities for shoppers (3.67). There is a deliberate European feel in the design and style of Meadowhall with continental restaurants, cafes, bars and entertainments on both storeys. The complex cost an estimated £25 million to build and was funded both by the City Council and retailers occupying space within it. Meadowhall is viewed as a model for future retailing location in the EC, in areas free from inner-city congestion.

3.67 Plan of Meadowhall, lower mall

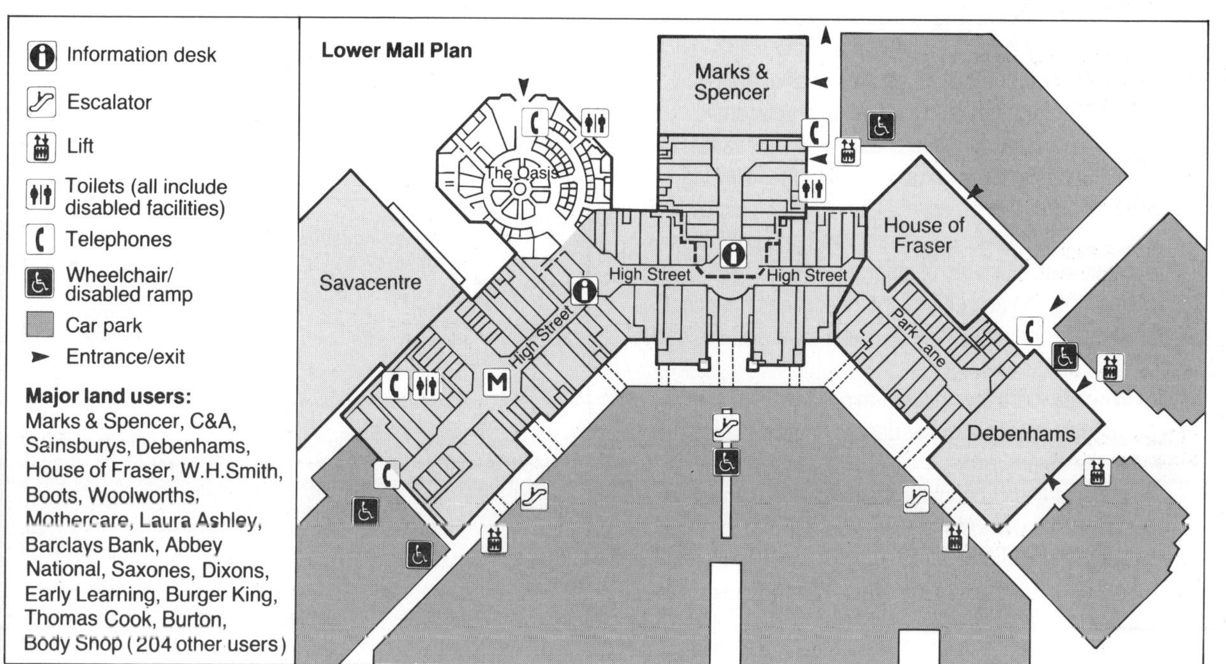

Questions

Q THE INNER CORE

Diagram 1 Euro-core

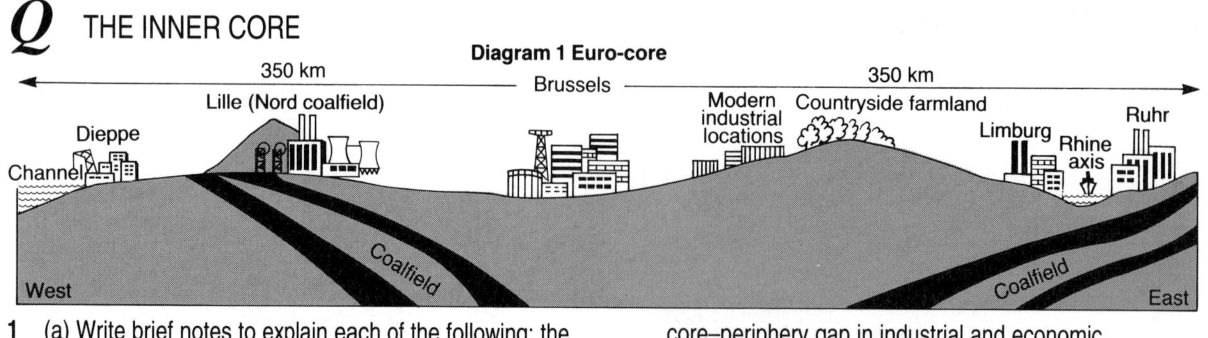

1 (a) Write brief notes to explain each of the following: the EC's inner core, heavy industrial triangle, mobility, communication axis, Single European Market.
(b) Copy diagram 1 neatly. Use it to define the Euro-core of the EC.
(c) Give examples of communication systems used within the EC and explain their vital importance to industrial development.
(d) Explain the main reasons for the existence of a core–periphery gap in industrial and economic development within the EC.
(e) Make a simple sketch map of photo 3.52. Use an atlas to identify the main urban and industrial complexes within the Randstad conurbation.
(f) What evidence is there to suggest that the area shown in photo 3.52 is typical of areas in the inner core?
(g) Design an advert stressing the major attractions of a location within the inner core (3.51) for a modern wholesale furniture distribution centre.

Q RUHR IN TRANSITION

2 (a) In which ways is the Ruhr an unusual industrial area within the Euro-core?
(b) Draw a base map of the Ruhr (see 3.55) and include the main waterways and settlements. Use information from the text to help you add labels to the map to show the importance of the Ruhr as an industrial area.
(c) Can the Ruhr be described as; (i) a polycentric conurbation; (ii) a declining coalscape? Give reasons.
(d) Write brief notes to explain each of the following: integrated steelworks, concealed coalfield, exposed coalfield, pharmaceuticals, green wedges, autobahns.
(e) Make a simple copy of diagram 3.56.
(f) Describe and account for the relocation of the coal mining industry in the Ruhr between 1870 and the early 1900s.
(g) Why are there few modern mines today?
(h) Suggest reasons for the decline in steel making within the central Ruhr.
(i) Describe and account for the relocation of modern steel plants to waterfronts within the Ruhr.
(j) Study diagram 2 carefully. Do you consider the Ruhr to be a good example of this type of development? Give reasons.

Diagram 2 Myrdal's model of the development of a region: sucess breeds sucess.

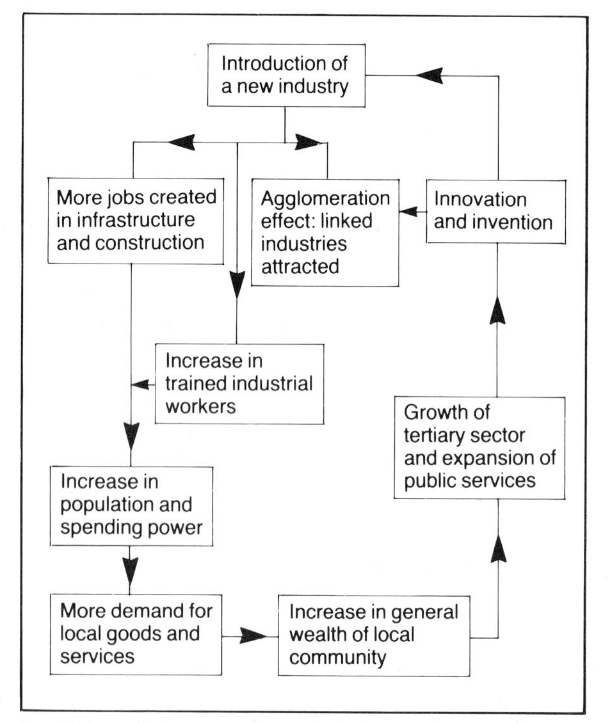

(k) Write a short essay summarising industrial transition in the Ruhr by expanding the labels on diagram 3.59.

Q NEW INDUSTRIAL GROWTH

Diagram 3

3 (a) Define each of the following terms: monotechnic, deglomeration, rustbelt, skibelt, sunbelt.
(b) Discuss the view that many industrial areas within the Euro-core owe their continuing importance to inertia rather than development.
(c) Make a list of areas of new industrial growth in the EC.
(d) Suggest reasons for the growing trend for industry to decentralise.
(e) For out-of-town retailing or shopping centres,
(i) describe their function,
(ii) identify their ideal location,
(iii) suggest both their advantages and disadvantages,
(iv) explain the opposition of city centre shops to this type of development.
(f) What is meant by high-tech industry?
(g) Design a simple map to show the main types of location of high-tech industry within the EC.
(h) Describe the main features of new industrial landscapes such as the IBM plant at La Gaude, southern France.
(i) In which ways does the development of the IBM plants at La Gaude and Montpellier indicate the post-industrial phase of industrialisation within the EC?
(j) Make a copy of diagram 3 and annotate it to describe the new industrial landscapes of the core fringe.
(k) Write a short essay explaining the main effects of technological advance on the social, economic and environmental geography of traditional industrial areas within the Euro-core.
(l) When new industry is established in semi-rural and rural areas of the core fringe there are advantages and disadvantages for the area being developed. Discuss these, using specific information to support your answer.
(m) Why will state intervention continue to be necessary within the EC?

Q COLOUR SECTION

Look carefully at the map extract on page 173. Identify a potential location for a modern industrial estate or a science park in the area.
Support your choice with map and other evidence.

Research and Further Work

(a) Examine the influence of government on the changing spatial patterns of industrial location and growth within the EC.
(b) Discuss the view that the location of tertiary industry is determined by accessibility.

Exam Style Questions

Production of crude steel, and associated employment

	Belgium	W. Germany	France	Italy	Luxembourg	Netherlands
			Production (thousand tonnes)			
1980	12 300	43 800	23 200	26 500	4600	5300
1987	9 800	36 300	17 400	22 900	3300	5100
			Employment (thousands)			
1980	47.4	201.0	113.6	100.6	26.0	21.0
1987	28.9	137.3	62.6	64.9	11.6	18.3

1 Study the table above carefully and then answer the following questions, illustrating your answer with maps and diagrams where appropriate.
With reference to specific examples,
(a) give reasons for the changes shown, (3)
(b) assess the impact of these changes on former, present and future steel-producing areas. (6)

2 Study map 3.4 which shows the major industrial regions of the European Community.
(a) Examine this map and critically evaluate the proposition that the distribution of industry suggests that inertia is the main locational factor. (9)

3 Describe the main changes in:
(a) industrial structure and employment within the EC, (3)
(b) industrial location within the EC, (3)
(c) Modern industry is seldom coalfield based in the 1990s. Referring to a specific example, explain why. (3)

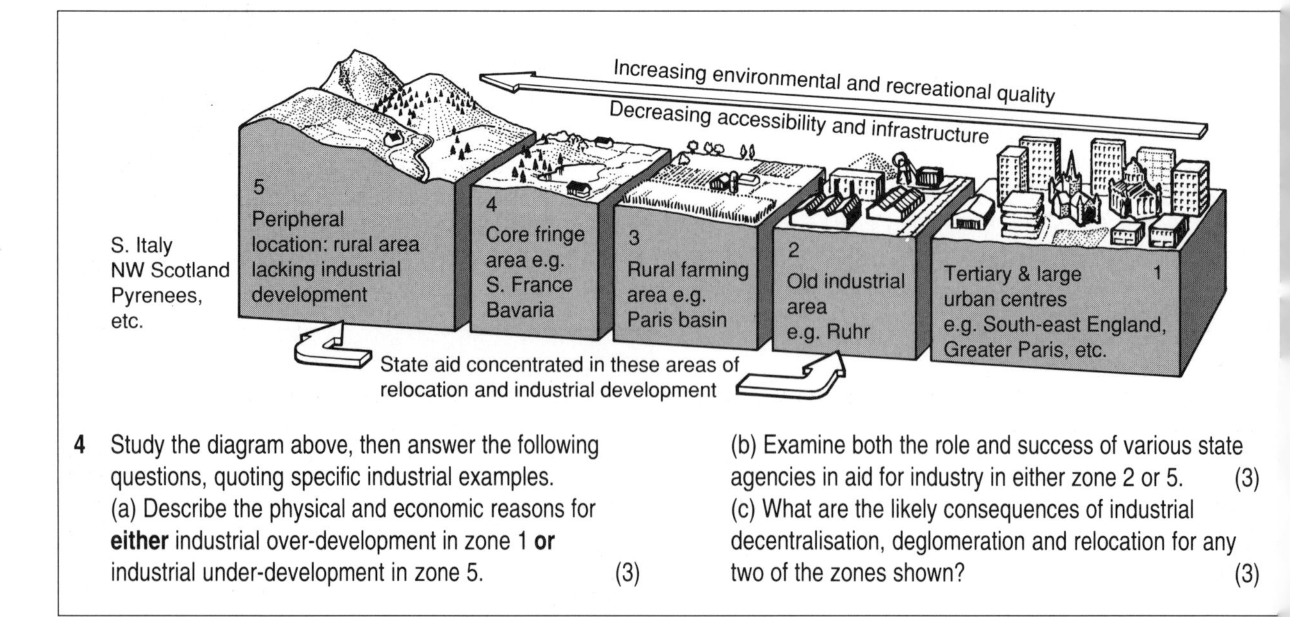

4 Study the diagram above, then answer the following questions, quoting specific industrial examples.
(a) Describe the physical and economic reasons for **either** industrial over-development in zone 1 **or** industrial under-development in zone 5. (3)
(b) Examine both the role and success of various state agencies in aid for industry in either zone 2 or 5. (3)
(c) What are the likely consequences of industrial decentralisation, deglomeration and relocation for any two of the zones shown? (3)

CHAPTER 4

URBAN STUDIES

Urbanisation

The greatest change in the pattern of human settlement this century has been the migration of people to cities. The pace of **urbanisation**, the process of becoming an urban society, has accelerated sharply during the twentieth century. In 1900, only 14 people in a hundred lived in an urban area. By 1960, the number of urban dwellers had risen to 34 in a hundred and, at the end of the century, it is estimated that over half of the world's population will be living in urban areas.

During the past 25 years, virtually all countries have experienced an increase in the proportion of the population living in urban centres. There are, however, considerable differences in the rates of urban growth from area to area (see 4.1) and also in the pattern and nature of urbanisation taking place.

In 1945, seven out of the world's ten largest cities were in the developed world. Only two of them, New York and London, had more than 10 million inhabitants. By 1985 the biggest ten cities were all in the developing world except for Tokyo and New York, and all of them had more than 10 million inhabitants. The world's biggest city, Mexico City, has an estimated population of over 20 million. The most rapid urban growth has been in the developing world where rates of urbanisation have grown from 10% in 1935 to over 30% today. It has been estimated that people are migrating to the cities of the developing world at the rate of over 80 000 each day.

While cities continue to attract larger and larger proportions of the population in most nations, the process of urbanisation is in decline in some developed countries. In places, urbanisation has given way to **counter-urbanisation** (and even ruralisation) as improvements in transport networks, standards of living, personal mobility and aspirations to the rural idyll have increased population growth in outlying rural areas.

4.1 Urbanisation in selected areas

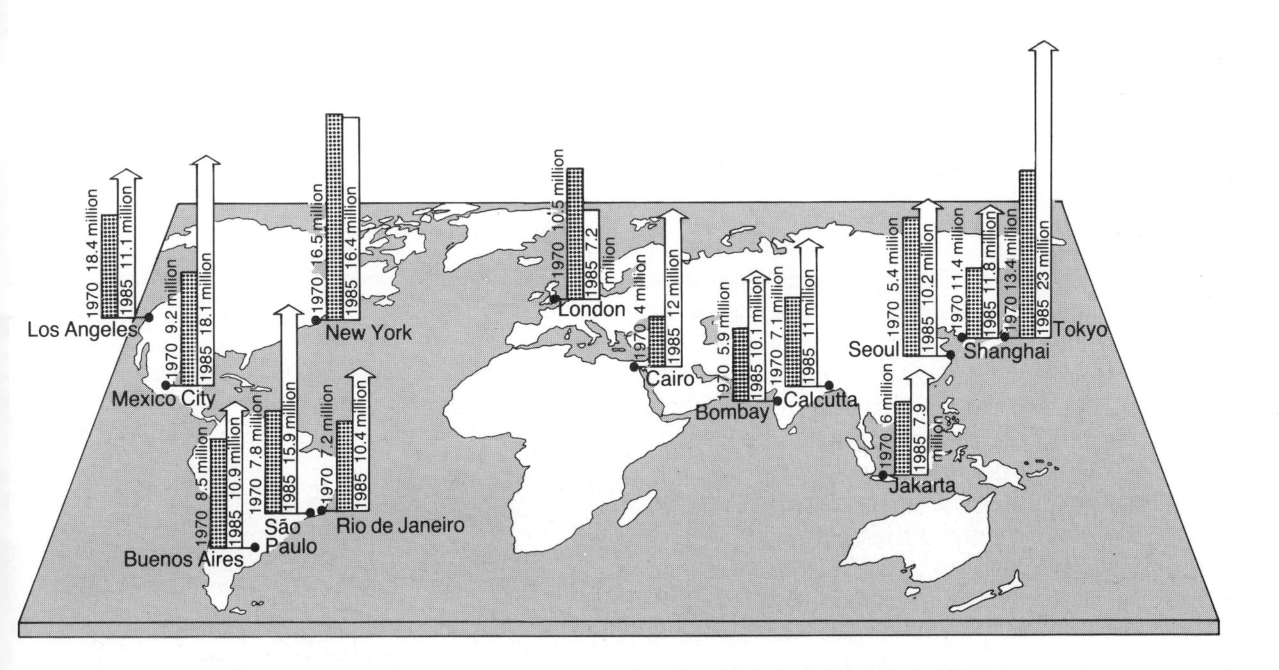

Urbanisation (percentage total population) by country, 1985

USA	77%	China	32%
UK	80%	India	27%
Brazil	70%	Ethiopia	17%
Mexico	71%	Australia	81%
Argentina	75%	Japan	52%
USSR	64%	Indonesia	28%

Urbanisation in AD 2000 (estimates in millions)

City	Millions	City	Millions
Mexico City	31.0	Cairo	14.1
São Paulo	26.1	Bombay	17.0
Buenos Aires	12.5	Calcutta	16.1
Rio de Janeiro	18.0	Shanghai	23.0
New York	21.0	Seoul	15.0
London	7.1	Jakarta	15.0
Los Angeles	15.0	Tokyo	24.0

CHAPTER 4

Rural to Urban

An urban area can be defined as an area in which most of the inhabitants work in activities other than the production of foodstuffs and raw materials (primary industries). They are engaged in manufacturing industry, trade, service, administration, research, development and entertainment. The urbanisation of developed countries has involved gradual change of the landscape over centuries from the climatic climax vegetation (usually mixed forest) to today's tarmac and concrete structures (4.2).

The original forest had to be cleared as the population increased and, with the development of efficient methods of agriculture, the natural landscape developed into a farmscape. It was not until the Industrial Revolution that urban centres really began to develop as rural people migrated in search of work in the new industries and factories. The cities of industrialised, developed countries grew very large and often merged to form urban agglomerations. Recent research has shown that the sequence or cycle of urban development (4.3) has now reached stage 3 and beyond in some countries of the developed world.

The gradual process of urbanisation that took place in developed countries in Europe is in contrast to that experienced in developing countries such as India and Brazil (4.4). The majority of people in developing countries lived in rural areas and were engaged in a wide variety of agricultural systems from nomadism to sedentary practices, mainly on a subsistence basis (see Chapter 2). But over the past few decades, the most striking feature of change in the 120 developing countries has been the rapid growth of urban areas. This growth began earlier in the twentieth century but has now accelerated to the position where some cities are growing at the rate of 20% every decade. While the centres of most cities in developing countries have a modern prosperous appearance their peripheral areas are undergoing a massive, less structured process of urbanisation. Up to 80 000 rural people migrate to developing cities each day in a bid to escape from a variety of serious rural problems (4.5), but often the living conditions in the cities are very poor.

The increasing concentration of people in urban centres has strained the capacity of most governments to provide basic services. Illegal settlements are common and estimated today to house over 1000 million people in developing countries. The perceived improvement in the quality of life in urban areas compared with the countryside is often nonexistent. The reality for most people involved in a rural-to-urban migration is unemployment, dire poverty, and overcrowded makeshift housing without clean water or sewage systems.

4.2 Generalised model of urbanisation in developed countries (based on Europe)

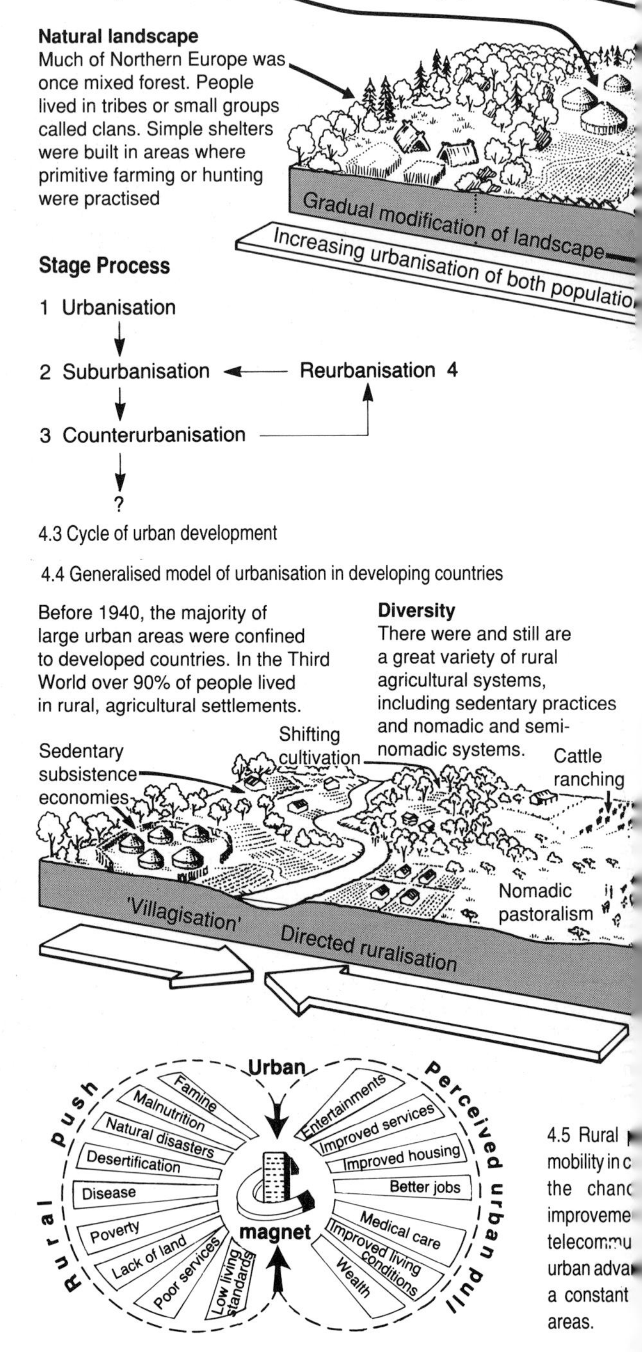

Pioneer fringe
The growing population necessitated a more sedentary lifestyle. Land was cleared as the fringes of cultivation were extended. Improved farming methods and an organised social system developed.
Farmscape
As the cleared land merged and the population increased, farming districts and villages developed. Marginal land was used for grazing and, like woodland, was common land belonging to the village
Natural landscape
Much of Northern Europe was once mixed forest. People lived in tribes or small groups called clans. Simple shelters were built in areas where primitive farming or hunting were practised
Gradual modification of landscape
Increasing urbanisation of both populatio
Stage Process
1 Urbanisation
2 Suburbanisation
Reurbanisation 4
3 Counterurbanisation
?
Before 1940, the majority of large urban areas were confined to developed countries. In the Third World over 90% of people lived in rural, agricultural settlements.
Diversity
There were and still are a great variety of rural agricultural systems, including sedentary practices and nomadic and semi-nomadic systems.
Shifting cultivation
Sedentary subsistence economies
Cattle ranching
Nomadic pastoralism
'Villagisation'
Directed ruralisation
Urban
magnet
Rural push
Perceived urban pull
Famine
Malnutrition
Natural disasters
Desertification
Disease
Poverty
Lack of land
Poor services
Low living standards
Entertainments
Improved services
Improved housing
Better jobs
Medical care
Improved living conditions
Wealth

4.3 Cycle of urban development

4.4 Generalised model of urbanisation in developing countries

4.5 Rural p… mobility in c… the chanc… improveme… telecommu… urban adva… a constant… areas.

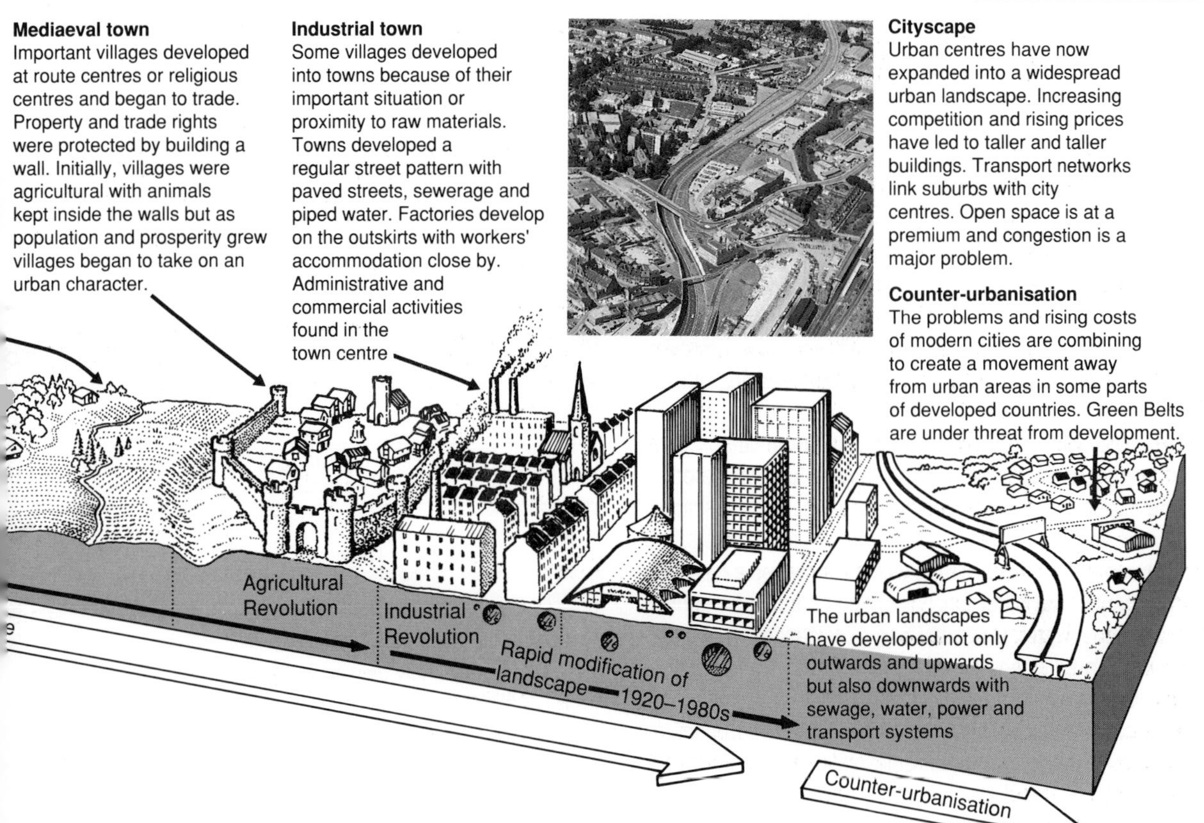
Mediaeval town
Important villages developed at route centres or religious centres and began to trade. Property and trade rights were protected by building a wall. Initially, villages were agricultural with animals kept inside the walls but as population and prosperity grew villages began to take on an urban character.
Industrial town
Some villages developed into towns because of their important situation or proximity to raw materials. Towns developed a regular street pattern with paved streets, sewerage and piped water. Factories develop on the outskirts with workers' accommodation close by. Administrative and commercial activities found in the town centre
Cityscape
Urban centres have now expanded into a widespread urban landscape. Increasing competition and rising prices have led to taller and taller buildings. Transport networks link suburbs with city centres. Open space is at a premium and congestion is a major problem.
Counter-urbanisation
The problems and rising costs of modern cities are combining to create a movement away from urban areas in some parts of developed countries. Green Belts are under threat from development.
Agricultural Revolution
Industrial Revolution
Rapid modification of landscape 1920–1980s
The urban landscapes have developed not only outwards and upwards but also downwards with sewage, water, power and transport systems
Counter-urbanisation

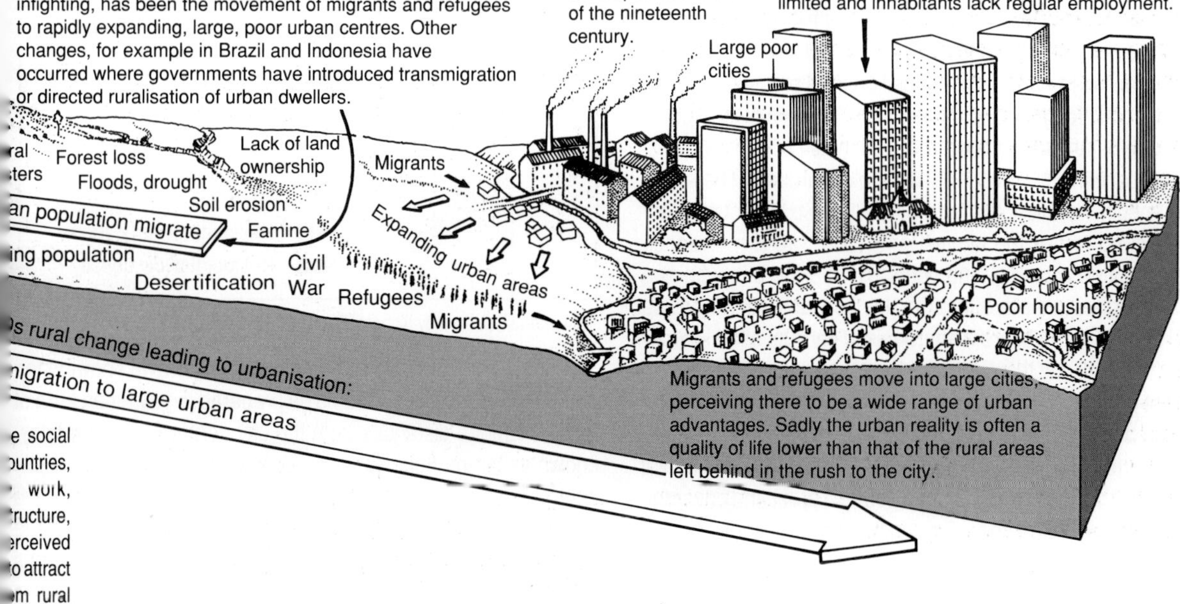
Rural change
Over the last three decades, several changes have occurred in many developing countries' rural areas. The biggest change, brought on by increasing population, civil war and political infighting, has been the movement of migrants and refugees to rapidly expanding, large, poor urban centres. Other changes, for example in Brazil and Indonesia have occurred where governments have introduced transmigration or directed ruralisation of urban dwellers.
Existing important administration centres developed at the end of the nineteenth century.
Megacities
The centres of big urban areas in the developing world have a superficially modern, prosperous appearance though their productive systems are limited and inhabitants lack regular employment.
Large poor cities
Forest loss
Lack of land ownership
Floods, drought
Soil erosion
Famine
Desertification
Civil War
Refugees
Migrants
Expanding urban areas
Migrants
Poor housing
rural change leading to urbanisation:
to large urban areas
Migrants and refugees move into large cities, perceiving there to be a wide range of urban advantages. Sadly the urban reality is often a quality of life lower than that of the rural areas left behind in the rush to the city.

CHAPTER 4

Factors Influencing Urban Land Use

When we examine any large urban area in the developed world, such as London (4.6), the first impression is one of a very complex structure of land uses linked by various levels and types of communications networks. Careful study suggests, however, that identifiable zones of land use, such as shops and offices, industry, residences, and greenspace, exist and that their distribution can be traced in time, height, and distance from sites of central importance. Some functional zones are dominated by one land use, for example expensive housing. Other functional zones involve several associated land uses: for example, the **central business district** (**CBD**), which mainly contains shops and offices, also has other functions such as transport termini, public buildings, warehouses and some residences.

Competition between the many different land uses, whose location within the urban structure is of vital importance to economic success, is almost uninhibited in a free market economy such as the UK. Some land uses require special sites, such as flat land, and businesses will be prepared to pay well for them. More commonly, some (e.g. supermarkets and shops) need accessible situations in order to attract customers if they are to survive. Different land users will be attracted by particular site qualities, and this results in zones of similar land uses in which there is economic competition between users. Not all land users face the same pressures to obtain particular sites and hence there are differences in the intensity of competition within different zones. It may also not be possible to obtain a desired location because of cost, planning problems or opposition from pressure groups.

If economic forces alone influence the location of land uses, the pattern of land use in a large city such as London will result from competition between the various potential users. Therefore, at any specific location, the land will be used by the competitor who is willing to pay the highest price. The site is in essence auctioned; all competing land users bid and the one who can afford the highest price acquires the site. For each urban land use there will be a maximum rent affordable at each location in order to make a profit, and there will be a location at which it can make the most profit. A site in the heart of the city at the centre of the transport network is important for major shops since it gives the best opportunity to attract the necessary number of potential customers (threshold population) to make a profit and cover the cost of running a large shop. The cost of such sites is very high because they are in very short supply. Within a few hundred metres there are fewer transport routes and consequently less accessibility to customers, so these sites are cheaper.

4.6 Central London

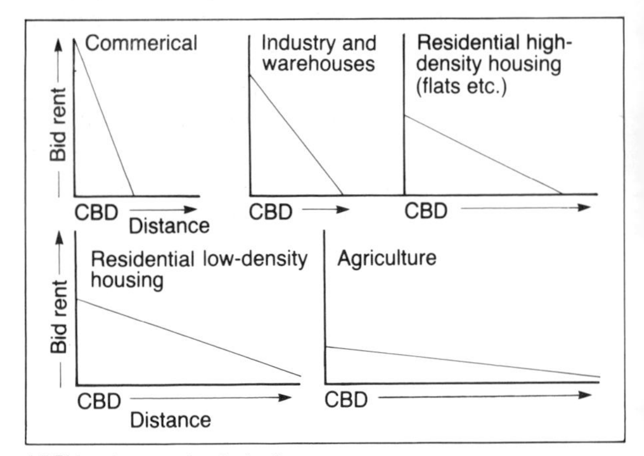

4.7 Bid-rent curves of major land uses

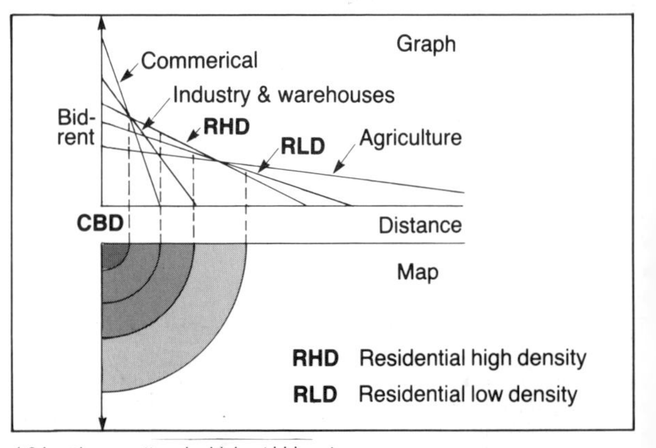

4.8 Land-use pattern by highest bid-rent

For each type of land use a graph can be drawn showing the price (rent) the land user would be prepared to pay for an area of land at various distances from the city centre (4.7). The lines, known as bid-rent curves, slope downwards away from the city centre. Businesses that can afford high prices in the centre have a steep graph; those that are less affected by location will have a graph with a gentler slope. If we combine the bid-rent graphs for all city land uses, then a concentric series of functional zones emerges (4.8).

Large urban areas have a land value peak at the centre and much smaller peaks at other desirable locations where accessibility is above average, for example at major crossroads or suburban shopping centres. The simple pattern illustrated in diagram 4.8 is complicated by the inclusion of the smaller centres to produce the mosaic of bid-rent peaks shown in diagram 4.9.

The economic gradient of the bid-rent relation operates vertically as well as horizontally from the centre (4.10). It is, for example, common to find shops occupying the ground floor in a CBD site with offices and other functions occupying the upper floors. Other factors influencing the patterns of land use in a large urban area are those of peripheral development and building age. Much of the newer development of an urban area occurs at the periphery. As buildings age they can become very costly to repair or rehabilitate to meet current demands, for example installation of computer networks, lifts, etc. These factors may encourage their owners to move to more modern facilities elsewhere. Older but centrally located office blocks, warehouses or factories may have a highly desirable site and existing owners may decide to sell the site for demolition and rebuilding and take the profits with them to peripheral locations. Alternatively, older premises may be subdivided and re-let to a range of smaller companies and, in this way, there is continual change of land and building use, and therefore of bid-rents.

A large urban area has a complex structure and shape that is said to be in a state of **dynamic equilibrium** caused by the balance between two contrasting sets of influences on land use patterns: the **centrifugal** and **centripetal** forces (4.11).

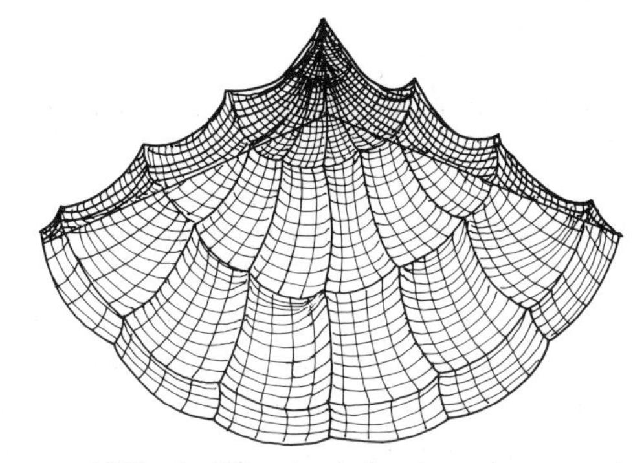

4.9 Mosaic of bid-rent peaks for a large urban area

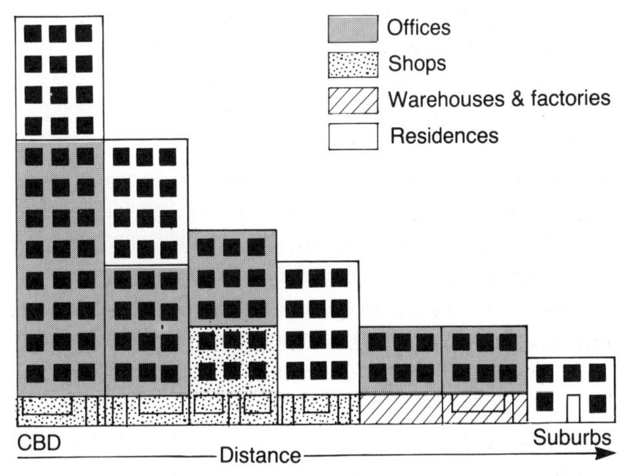

4.10 Vertical land-use structure

4.11 Urban dynamic equilibrium

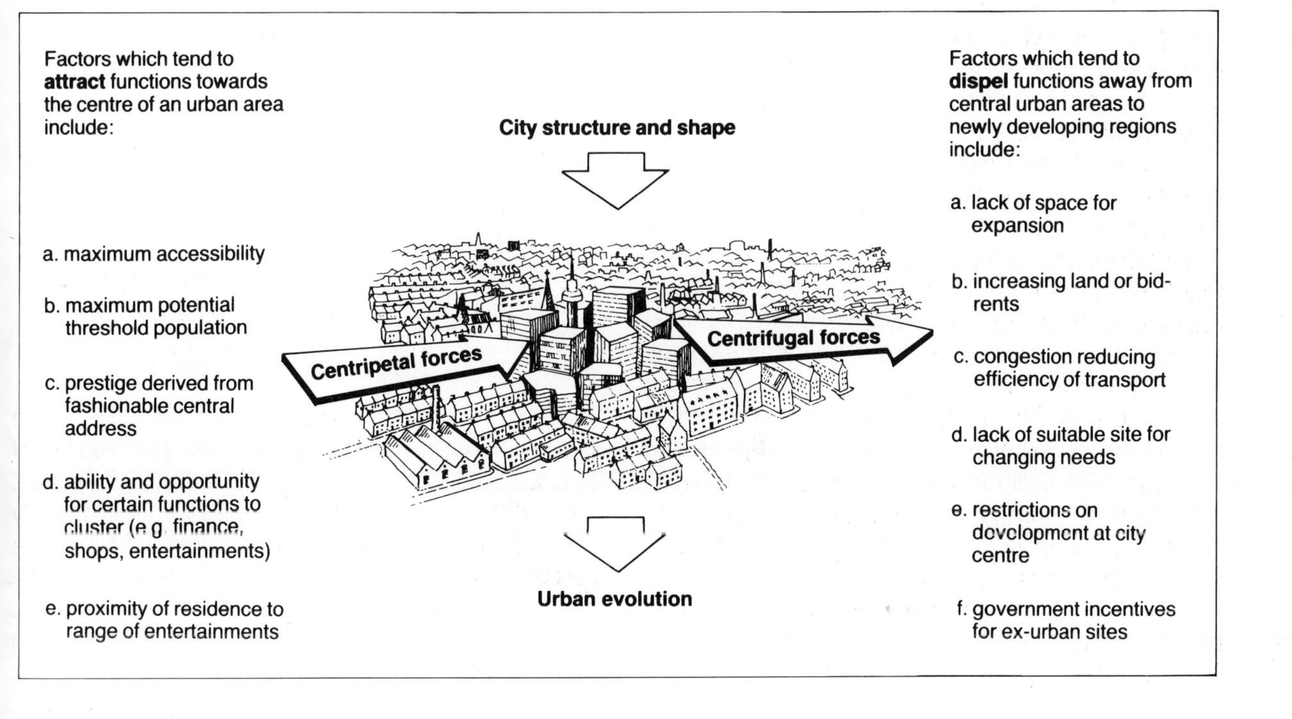

Factors which tend to **attract** functions towards the centre of an urban area include:
a. maximum accessibility
b. maximum potential threshold population
c. prestige derived from fashionable central address
d. ability and opportunity for certain functions to cluster (e.g. finance, shops, entertainments)
e. proximity of residence to range of entertainments
City structure and shape
Centripetal forces
Centrifugal forces
Urban evolution
Factors which tend to **dispel** functions away from central urban areas to newly developing regions include:
a. lack of space for expansion
b. increasing land or bid-rents
c. congestion reducing efficiency of transport
d. lack of suitable site for changing needs
e. restrictions on development at city centre
f. government incentives for ex-urban sites

Models of Urban Structure

The factors described on pages 102–3 influence the choice of location within the urban landscape. Accessibility, market forces, communications networks, and the ability to pay for a desired site all influence the final decision on urban location. What results is a pattern of land uses within an urban area which is difficult to summarise. There have been several attempts to do so simply, the most important of which are described in 4.12–4.15.

The **concentric** model of urban structure (4.12) is based only on the bid-rents for a homogeneous area (similar throughout). It does not consider the physical characteristics of the city site or changes which may take place over time. It also pays little heed to the complex mixture of land uses which can develop as a result of the reluctance of people to relocate. In reality, each zone has a mixture of functions all of which can afford the same bid-rent. Another difficulty with the concentric model is that it does not recognise the effects of transport networks. The location of land use is dependent on both travel time as well as pure distance within an urban area.

The **sector** model (4.13) is based on lines of communication and tries to link these with bid-rent analysis. There are similarities between the concentric and sector models since the pattern remains roughly concentric.

Both these models describe some aspects of urban land use. Few cities, however, conform to any geometric plan and show a structure more complex than in either model. In addition, some functions, such as shipbuilding, will be independent of any formal structure as they are tied to specific urban sites.

The **multiple-nuclei** model (4.14) develops the idea of a cell-like pattern to urban land use, in which related functions tend to cluster. Given current trends in urban planning, where functions are segregated within urban areas, the multiple-nuclei model is perhaps more relevant today than the other remaining model, Mann's model of a British city (4.15). Any city comprises many different parts each with its own pattern. Murdie (4.16) suggested that housing patterns may be distributed concentrically, industry may be distributed sectorally, and ethnic status may occur in cells or groups, and, if viewed collectively, urban areas in developed world countries in reality display an almost random cellular pattern.

4.12 Concentric zone model

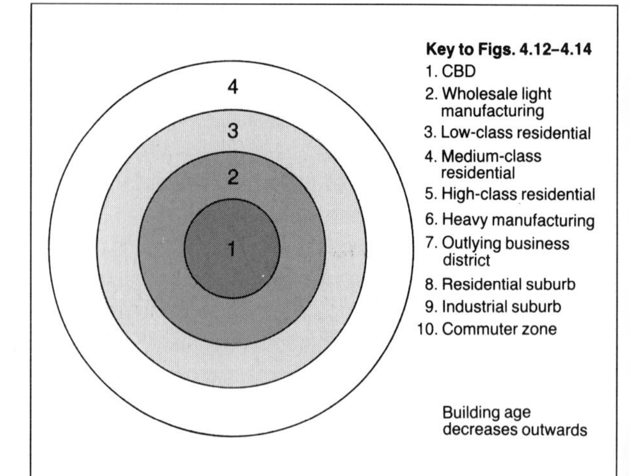

The **concentric zone model** (Burgess, 1925) was based on the ideas developed by the Chicago School of Urban Sociology and is the earliest structure model. The Burgess model is based on a particular period of North American history and is a development of the bid-rent analysis. The ability of commercial and industrial functions to pay rent segregates them into concentric zones. This idea can also be extended to include residential and agricultural land uses. Segregation based on the ability to pay rent influences the development of the urban area: commercial land uses will be able to afford the highest rents and therefore dominate the CBD. Agricultural land uses take over only where all urban land use competition has ceased.

Burgess was the starting point and his model generated intense discussion over recognisable patterns of urban structure.

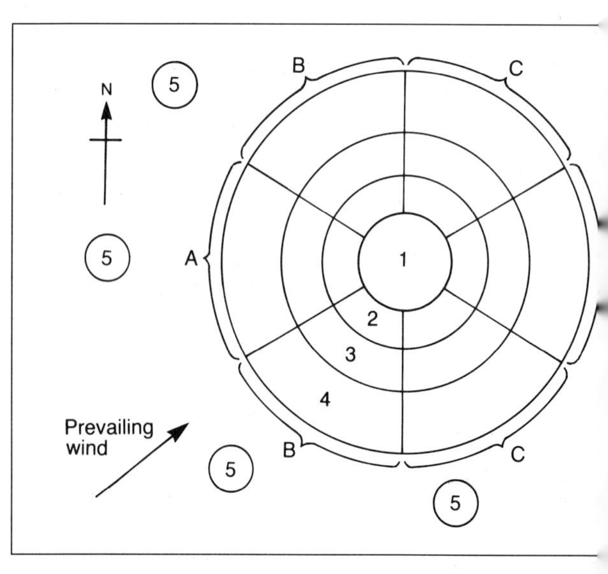

4.13 Sector model

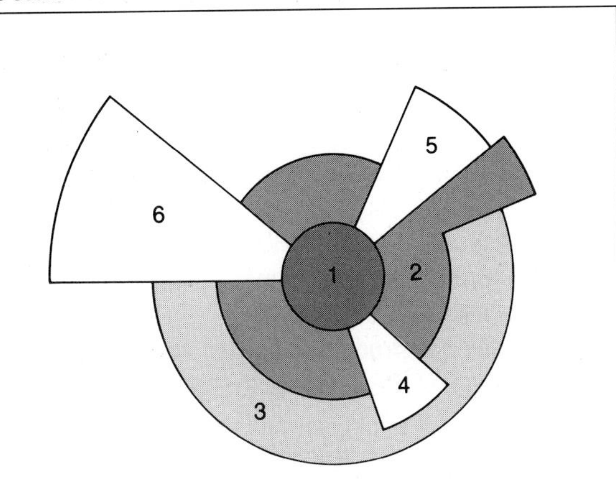

The **Hoyt sector model** (1939) takes into account rent data and the influence of transport routes on economic activity, as well as the distribution of socio-economic groups within an urban area. It too was based on North America. Since it takes less time to travel by major roads than by side-roads, zones tend to distort from circles to form star-shapes, with extensions occurring along main roads and railways. This is of vital importance to industry. Factories are located close to main lines of communication rather than in the relatively inaccessible areas inbetween. A pattern of **sectors** then forms with industries occupying positions near routeways. Agglomeration of industries occurs in sectors or wedges as each grows outwards by developing ancillary or related functions. In this way, urban areas are not static but grow as functions segregate into outwardly expanding sectors.

4.14 Multiple-nuclei model

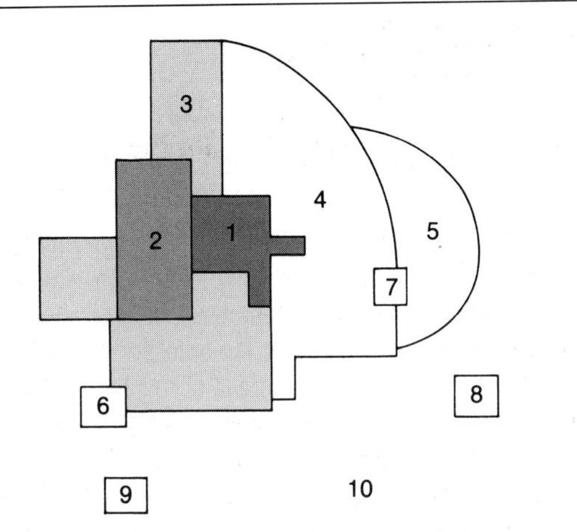

The **Harris/Ullman multiple-nuclei model** (1945) recognised the complexities of the development of modern North American cities. Harris and Ullman suggested that the development occurred around pre-existing foci (villages). Each of these would often develop a particular set of economic activities or a unique social attractiveness, leading to distinctiveness, i.e. becoming a nucleus. The number of such nuclei depends on the size of the city and on its range of old and developing functions. Many cities are too large and complex to be organised around one single centre and have developed a cellular structure with distinctive types of land use arranged around a number of growth points or nuclei. In a large city, there may be no single most accessible point and therefore there may be more than one CBD; for example, London has two and Tokyo has ten places of central importance.

4.15 British city model

The **Mann model of the British city** (1965) is a composite model which includes concentric zones and sectors. Mann further shaped the pattern by introducing the influence of the direction of the prevailing wind. Mann argued that high-value housing would be built in areas away from the outfall zones of wind-borne pollution. The model reflects more accurately the the periods of growth and land use of cities and is more useful in the British context, although it is already dated.

1 City centre
2 Transitional zone
3 zone of small terraced houses in sectors C and D, larger by-law houses in sector B; large old houses in sector A
4 Post-1918 residential areas, with post-1945 development mainly on the periphery
5 Commuting-distance 'village'

A Middle class sector
B Low-middle-class sector
C Working-class sector (and main municipal housing areas)
D Industry and lowest working-class areas

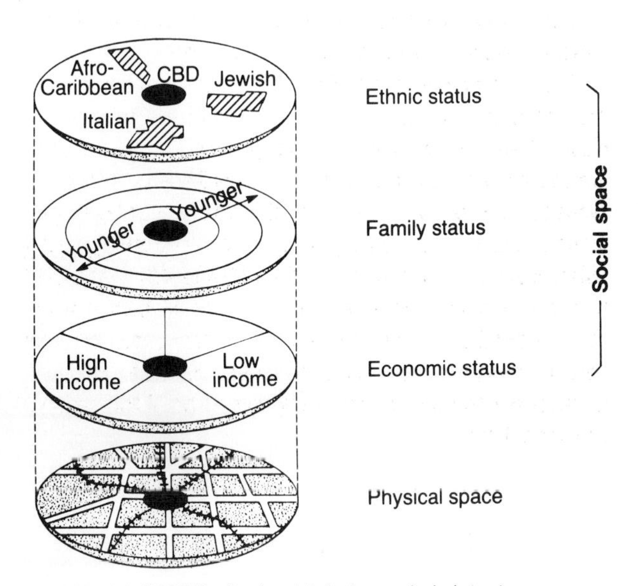

4.16 Murdie's (1969) idealised model of urban ecological structure

CHAPTER 4

Central Business District

All models of urban structure recognise the importance of the CBD or central business district. It is generally the heart of the city and the focus for the urban transport system. The importance of such areas is due to their having the greatest accessibility from all areas within the city. Land here is of limited availability and, with intense competition for space in the CBD, already high land values will increase even further. Developments are usually multi-storey in order to accommodate as many different land uses as possible at this prime site within the urban system. The resident population is often very low because of the high land values, which are more affordable to large businesses.

The central business district can be delineated in several ways.

1 **Mapping land uses** and noting areas of changing land use. Uses change around the edge of the CBD.
2 Finding the **central business intensity index**: the area of floor space used for business activities as a percentage of the total area of floor space. (The CBD has over 50%.)
3 Using the **central business floor space index**, obtained by dividing the total business floor space in a block by the total **ground** floor space. (The CBD index is over 1.)
4 Using the **rateable value per metre of street frontage** (CBD has highest values in £/metre).
5 **Artificially constructed obstacles** which limit the growth and spread of CBD areas: for example, railway lines, motorways or parks.
6 **Historic districts conserved** by Parliament which can only be adapted for certain specific functions.

Central business districts display many common characteristics (4.17) and contain a mixture of retailing, commercial and professional offices, city administration and entertainment districts. The larger the urban area, the more distinct each area is within

4.17 Characteristics of the CBD

1 Intensive competition for space in the CBD increases land values to the highest in the city.
2 Multi-storey buildings common. Building height increases towards the centre of CBD.
3 CBDs have a great scarcity of open space and have a very high density of buildings and road networks.
4 Only big businesses can afford to pay the high rates and bid-rents required for a site in the centre of the CBD. These include commercial and financial land uses.
5 Large department stores, e.g. Marks & Spencer plc, and nationwide supermarkets occupy CBD sites in order to achieve a rapid stock turnover.
6 CBDs also have a very large variety of shops, with many different goods for sale and large volumes of stock.
7 Offices are commonly found in the CBD, especially those involved in finance, law or administration, e.g. banks, building societies, solicitors, etc.
8 Transport termini are located in CBD: rail, bus, metro, heliport stations.
9 High traffic and pedestrian flows especially at commuter rush-hours and on Saturday (for shoppers).

10 Because of high land values, CBDs have a low residential population density.
11 On the fringe of the CBD are often found less profitable or non-profit-making land uses including universities, museums, libraries, football grounds, etc.
12 CBDs house the main areas of entertainment including cinemas, theatres, discos, etc.
13 Modern developments in the CBDs include shopping centres, pedestrian precincts, etc.
14 Specialist shops, selling high-order goods including jewellery, electrical and furniture goods, etc. are found around the CBD.
15 Ancillary industries are common in the CBD area, e.g. stationery, computer services, fast food, etc.
16 Common problems in CBD areas are:
   i increasing atmospheric pollution
   ii increasing traffic flow
   iii competition from rural–urban fringe for land for shopping centres, cinemas, etc.
   iv increasing numbers of homeless people.

the CBD. In some large cities, such as Edinburgh or London, it is possible to recognise **segregated areas** where associated land uses dominate districts within the CBD. Financial land uses (banks, building societies), chain stores (e.g. Marks and Spencer, British Home Stores, Littlewoods), specialist shops (jewellers, ladies fashions), etc. are often found in distinct districts or **functional areas** such as St Andrew Square or Princes Street in Edinburgh; The City, Oxford Street, or Saville Row in London. This segregation of distinct land uses is due to the **external economies** to be gained by locating close to similar land uses.

The **core–frame concept** (4.18) develops the simple idea of the CBD to take account of the city's rapid dynamism. The **core** is the traditional CBD outlined above. The **frame** is the zone around the CBD, characterised by the land uses shown in diagram 4.18. The model accepts the fact that most CBD areas are undergoing change and that there is a strong interlinkage between the core and the frame. Very often the CBD will undergo expansion into one part of the frame. Redevelopment of surrounding areas into new hotel or business complexes creates a **zone of assimilation** necessitating reclassification as CBD. Elsewhere CBD land uses are being abandoned as a **zone of discard**, where sites are being redeployed as parking lots, indoor markets or warehouses.

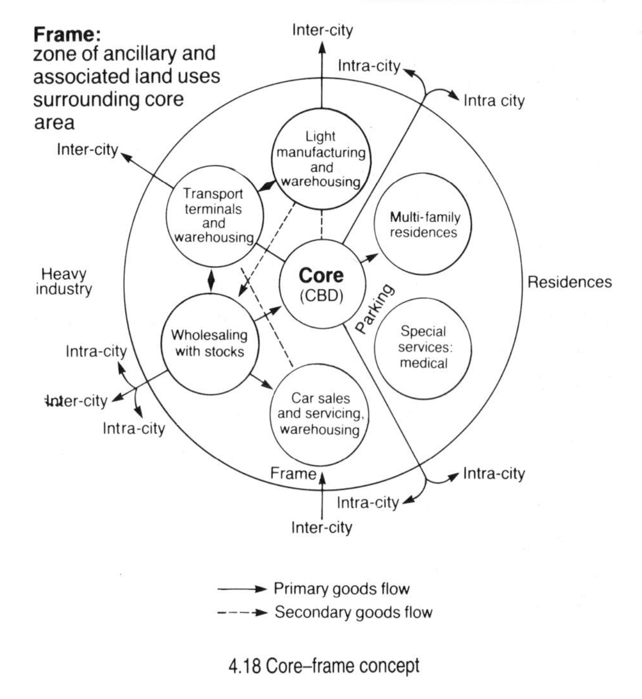

4.18 Core–frame concept

There are also many processes at work within the core itself (4.19) which lead to conflict between interested groups, mainly 'developers', residents and councils. There are a growing number of problems within CBDs including congestion, strain on commuter transport systems, pollution, and increasing numbers of homeless people sleeping rough. As a result, there have been plans to restrict development and relocate CBD land uses to the urban periphery. In London, CBD land uses have already relocated near to motorway intersections on the M25 leaving the central areas deprived of the employment they once enjoyed.

4.19 Urban core processes

Comprehensive redevelopment
Clearance of sites for complete rebuilding, including new street layouts, often leads to conflict between residents, developers and councils

Tourism
More hotels built to meet growing demands of conference tourism, business or luxury tourism

Gentrification
The movement of higher socio-economic groups into an area, which results in rehabilitation of buildings and services

Decentralisation of functions
Redeployment of: offices to suburbs or to greenfield sites; wholesale to more accessible sites near motorways; retailing to peripheral shopping centres

Pedestrianisation
Improvements to urban traffic management are increasing number of pedestrianised CBD areas

Conservation schemes
Opposite of redevelopment where historic sites are often protected by Acts of Parliament

CHAPTER 4

Patterns of Urban Functions

Any study into the spatial distribution of the main urban functions – offices, retailing, industry, and housing – reveals a constant pattern of change, and therefore conflict over redevelopment and relocation.

Offices

Increasing demands for all types of office space in the CBD has led to ever-increasing bid-rents and the assimilation of older, peripheral housing areas into the CBD. These have been replaced by modern office blocks or converted to office complexes (4.20). This in turn increases the size of the CBD area as agglomeration factors encourage yet more development.

Today's offices cluster mainly in city centres thereby taking advantage of available information, personal contacts and highest accessibility to the whole urban area. The quality of available information is also of vital importance to office location: a site in the CBD offers access to a wide range of ancillary, quaternary services including computer services, advertising and financial advice. Mutual dependence for information and services is self-reinforcing: more office development requires more quaternary servicing which in turn attracts more office development to take advantage of the increasing range of available services.

Better electronic and spatial communications, both within and between cities, also generate a pattern of sustained growth with dispersal of selected office sector functions (4.21). The growth of office business has led to the segregation of those functions

4.21 Diversity of office locations

4.20 Wharf buildings being converted into offices and flats

which require a CBD location from those which require fewer external contacts or quaternary services. These internal changes lead to dispersal of office functions to accessible sites outwith the CBD, in office parks or greenfield sites close to good communication links such as ring roads, motorways or airports. Change in internal office functions reduces employment within the CBD and leads to conflict over the expansion of urban areas, as routine office functions are relocated to cheaper sites on the urban periphery.

Retailing

The pattern of retailing across an urban area (4.22) strongly reflects the uneven distribution of local factors including population, wealth and communications.The shape of each retailing area is closely related to its location and function within the city and, in general, the quality of shopping centre increases with its accessibility and size.The shops of the CBD can be subdivided into distinct nodes of high-quality, specialist shops in the centre and lower-quality shops towards the edges.Suburban centres provide for less specialised, multi-purpose shopping trips whereas the shops of the inner city (core 'frame' area surrounding the CBD), often located in linear arrangements along main roads, provide for mainly everyday needs.The most recent changes in urban retailing functions have reflected the problems of congestion and high bid-rents in the centre. Hypermarkets and out-of-town shopping centres are being located in peripheral sites with high accessibility, low bid-rents and room for expansion and parking. This development will clearly Influence the pattern of retailing in the future.

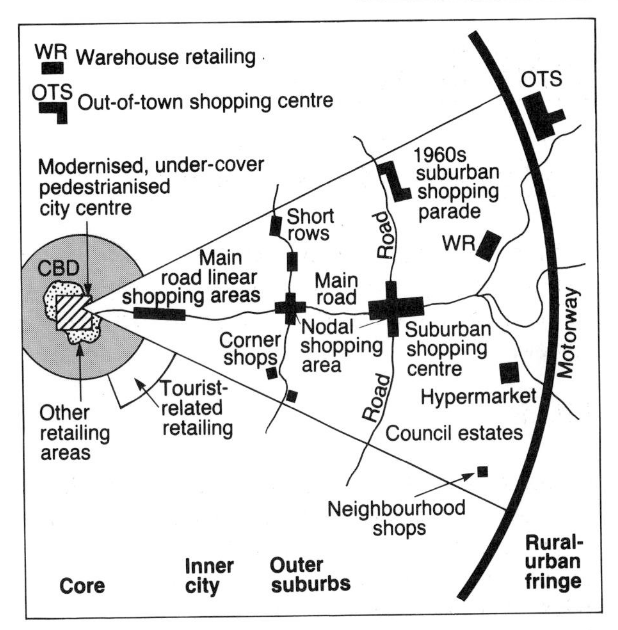

4.22 Different retail locations in a city

Industry

Industries, like offices and retailing, have undergone both spatial and internal change in urban areas with consequent increases in unemployment in inner city areas.

Improvements to communications, new technology and the greater influence of urban planning have contributed to changes in industrial locations (4.23). In the past, when urban areas were small and transport was based on canals, ports and railways, a central location was essential for access to raw materials, markets and labour. With developments in road networks, industries began to relocate along arterial routes where cheaper land was available for expansion. As urban areas expanded and competition for land in the centre increased, local government planning policies of segregating industry from housing began to influence the pattern of industrial land uses. Industrial estates were developed along major routeways in suburban areas, encouraging relocation from central areas and continuity of agglomeration, which meant industries could move but remain clustered.

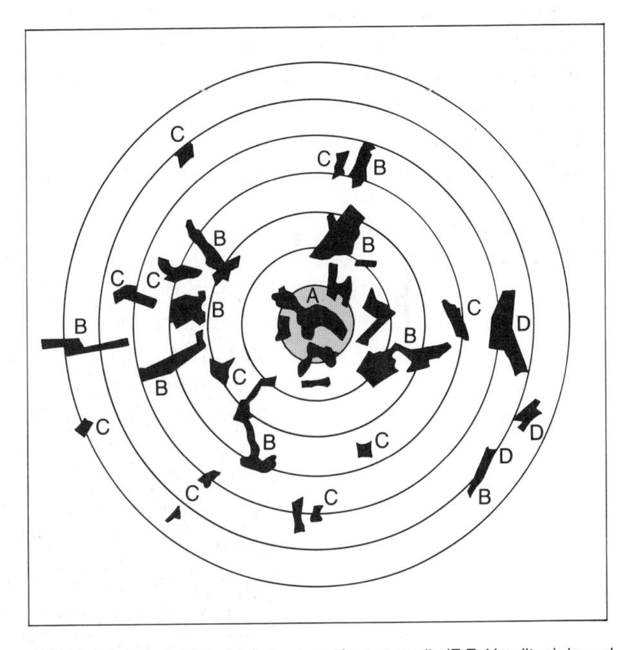

4.23 Model of spatial industrial structure of a metropolis (F.E. Hamilton), based on industrial areas within London. The four locations shown are:

A central
B port
C radial or ring transport artery
D suburban.

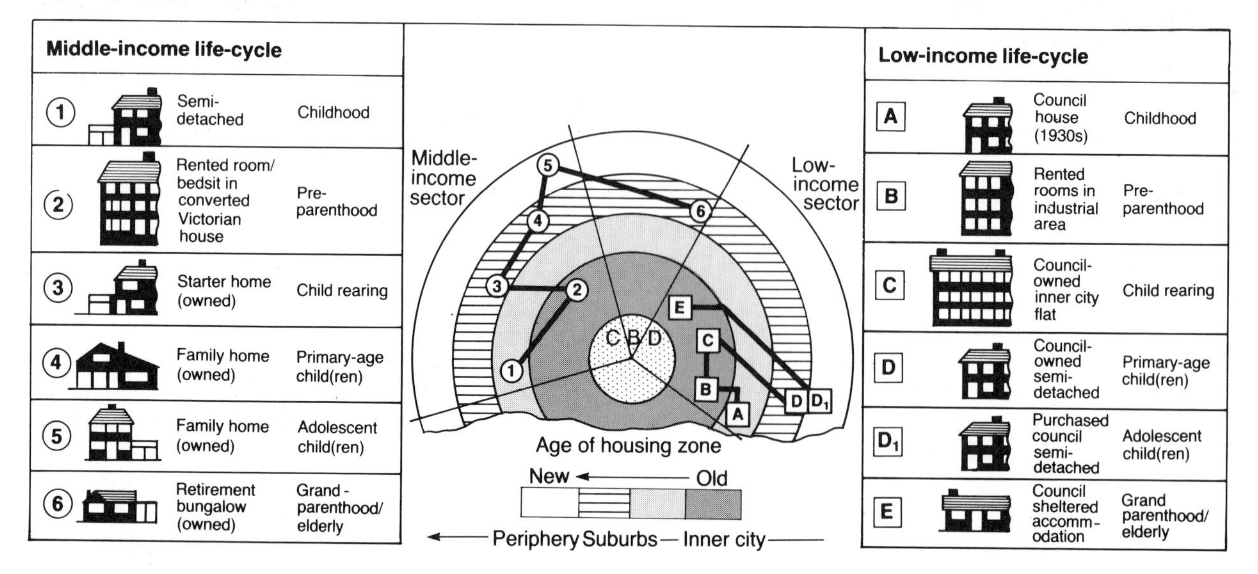

4.24 Contrasting life-cycle and social housing moves in a British city

Housing

Housing is the largest land user in urban areas and in any large urban area there are many different types of housing on offer. The choice of housing is controlled by various institutions such as building societies, landowners, housing and planning departments of local authorities. The pattern of housing, from older inner-city to newer suburban dwellings (4.24) reflects the location, age and bid-rent of any particular site within large urban areas. The pattern of housing choice (or even non-choice) is based upon inhabitants' life-cycle and income (4.24). Super-imposing both patterns reveals a complex distribution of housing types as well as the gradual evolution of housing functions. Housing patterns are also subject to **filtering** (4.25) in which, as housing deteriorates with time, it tends to move downwards through social groups. This process is reversed in some areas by **gentrification**, when middle-income groups upgrade older city properties by renovating them.

The most complex area of the city is the zone between the CBD and the suburbs: the inner city. Most of the housing stock in this area was built in the nineteenth century for workers without private transport. It usually follows a grid-like layout, with housing often intermixed with factories. Decay, the ravages of the Second World War, the relocation of larger industries to the suburbs, and the attempts of planners to rebuild the inner city as a place of residence have left behind an urban 'minestrone'. Today's inner city encompasses a great mixture of housing stock, ranging from high-rise blocks to penthouse accommodation in converted warehouses, from rehabilitated Victorian tenements to new semi-detached housing estates built on brown-earth gap sites close to docks or inner ring roads.

The suburbs, now the largest sector of the urban landscape, are mainly residential areas that have grown and dispersed throughout the twentieth century. As transport systems improved, the physical limits to the development of the suburbs were relaxed. Cheaper more accessible public transport networks made living in suburban areas a reality for the lower-income groups. With the relocation of offices, retailing and industries outwards to the suburban periphery of cities, there was also a movement of the labour force into residential areas previously designated as rural.

4.25 Filtering and gentrification

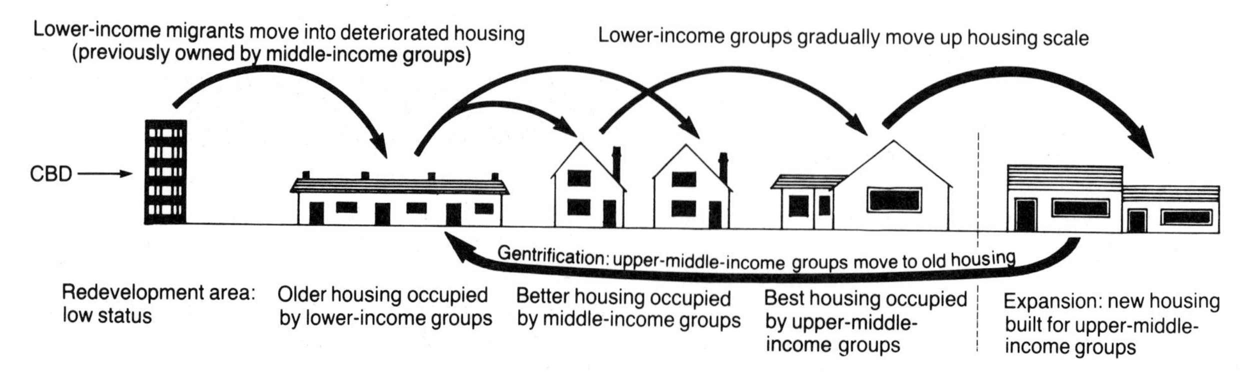

Q URBANISATION

1 (a) Write brief notes to explain: urban area, urbanisation.

(b) Compare the pattern of urbanisation in 1945 and 1985.
(c) Graph selected statistics to illustrate the growth of the following urban areas: New York, Mexico City, London, São Paulo, Jakarta, Tokyo, Cairo.
(d) What is meant by counter-urbanisation?
(e) Contrast the pattern and nature of urbanisation in developed and developing areas.

Q RURAL TO URBAN

2 (a) Write brief notes to describe each of the following: natural landscape, pioneer fringe, farmscape, medieval town, industrial town, cityscape, suburbanisation.
(b) At which stage did rapid urbanisation occur in developed countries? Explain why.
(c) Explain the cycle of urban development.
(d) Describe and explain the factors, both rural and urban, which have encouraged rapid urbanisation in many developing countries.

Q FACTORS INFLUENCING URBAN LAND USE

3 (a) Which are the most important factors influencing the development of different functional zones within cities?
(b) Define the following terms: commercial, residential low density, residential high density.
(c) What are bid-rent curves?
(d) Why do land values decline with increasing distance from the CBD?
(e) What are centripetal forces?
(f) What are centrifugal forces?
(g) In which ways do these forces interact in urban evolution?

Q MODELS OF URBAN STRUCTURE

4 (a) List the main models of urban structure.
(b) List the main elements of each model of urban structure.
(c) Which model may be most relevant to today's urban areas? Why?

Q CENTRAL BUSINESS DISTRICT

5 (a) Define the term central business district.
(b) Why are CBDs so important?
(c) Which land uses are found in the CBD?
(d) Which other characteristics are commonly found in the CBD?
(e) Explain why there are few industries and a low residential population within the CBD.
(f) Explain why segregated nodes of land use develop in CBD areas.
(g) Describe the main changes experienced in and around the CBD of a large urban area.
(h) What problems are CBDs suffering from today?

Q PATTERNS OF URBAN FUNCTIONS

6 (a) Describe the pattern of office location in urban areas.
(b) Why do offices cluster in the CBD?
(c) What are quaternary services?
(d) How has segregation of office functions influenced their location?
(e) Describe the pattern of retailing in urban areas.
(f) Which factors influence this pattern?
(g) Where are new developments taking place and why?
(h) Describe the pattern of industrial land uses within an urban area.
(i) What changes are occurring in urban industrial location?
(j) Why do industries no longer require a central location within an urban area?
(k) What advantages do peripheral areas offer modern industries?
(l) Describe the pattern of housing age in an urban area.
(m) Illustrate the process of filtering.
(n) What is gentrification?
(o) Compare and contrast the life-cycle and social housing moves within a British city.

Research and Further Work

(a) Research examples of re-urbanisation where once-abandoned urban areas are being reused.
(b) Delineate the CBD/centre of any urban area you are familiar with.
(c) For the settlement in which you live identify and account for recent peripheral development and expansion.

CHAPTER 4

London: Growth and Diversity

4.26 The growth of London, 1851–1951

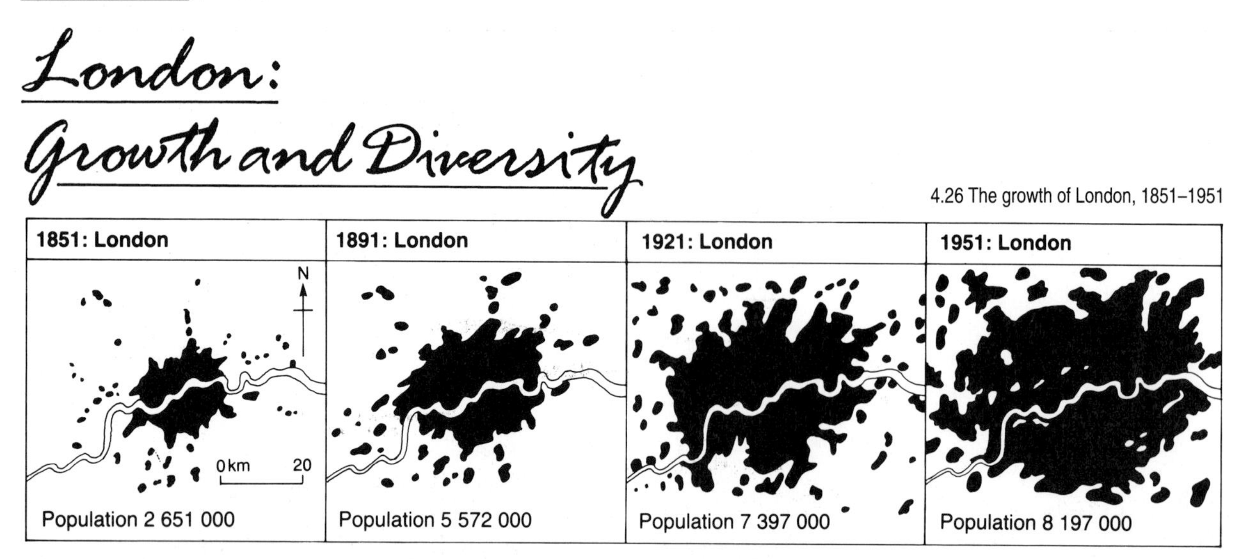

London is by far the largest urban area within the British Isles. It is number one in the hierarchy of settlement (**primate city**) being at the same time the largest settlement (6.87 million people), largest port and industrial centre, capital, major international communications centre, and largest conurbation within the country.

The growth patterns shown in diagram 4.26 reveal accelerating urbanisation of the landscape both north and south of the River Thames, from 1851 onwards: a process involving both industrial and commercial competition whose influence still dominates the structure of the city today. This huge urban complex (4.27), rated as the fifteenth largest in the world, grew from a small settlement that has its origins in pre-Roman times.

Even then, 2500 years ago, London was a nodal centre as routeways from the chalk uplands of the North and South Downs converged on the marshy lowlands along the margins of the Thames to afford a crossing of the river. The first major urban expansion occurred when the Romans built their defensive settlement of Londinium on the low river terraces to the north of the Thames. Londinium was the settlement at the heart of the Roman route network and was the principal town. In the eight troubled centuries following the departure of the Romans, the urban expansion of London stagnated but in the Middle Ages the seeds of fundamental change in the interpretation of the landscape were germinating. In the fertile landscape of the south-east, agricultural improvements and innovations combined to produce a surplus of farm products which was directly responsible for a rise in commercial activity, the development of new products for sale, and the innovation of new types of manufacturing systems. The Industrial Revolution had begun and London began to attract a rapidly increasing number of rural people in search of work.

During this time, political power and administrative organisation were concentrated in London. There was also a focusing of

4.27 London's administrative divisions

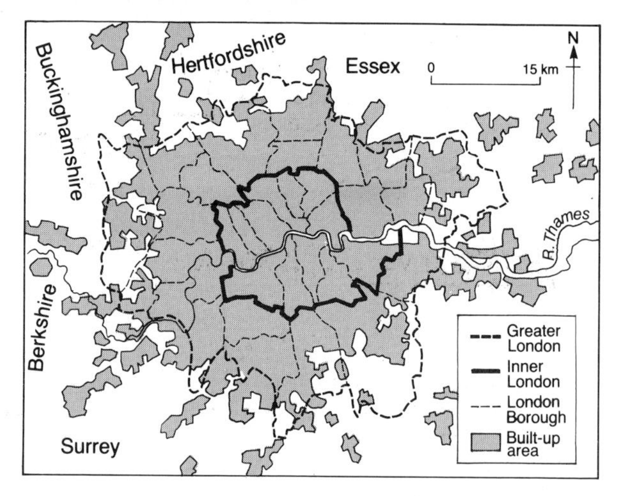

4.28 Two-way flow of information and innovation produces urban growth

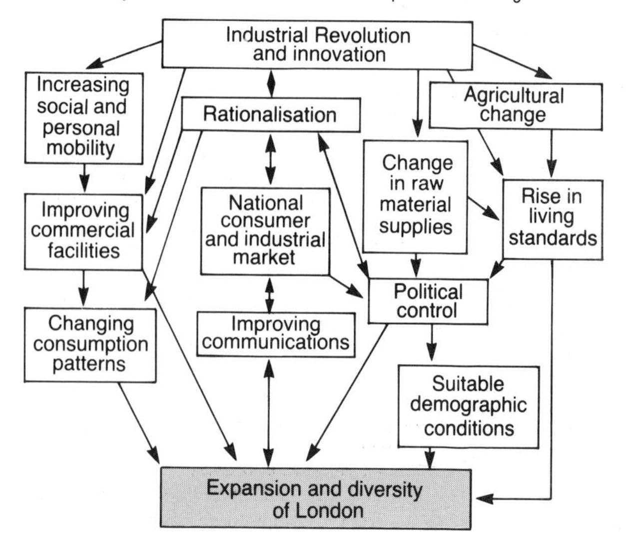

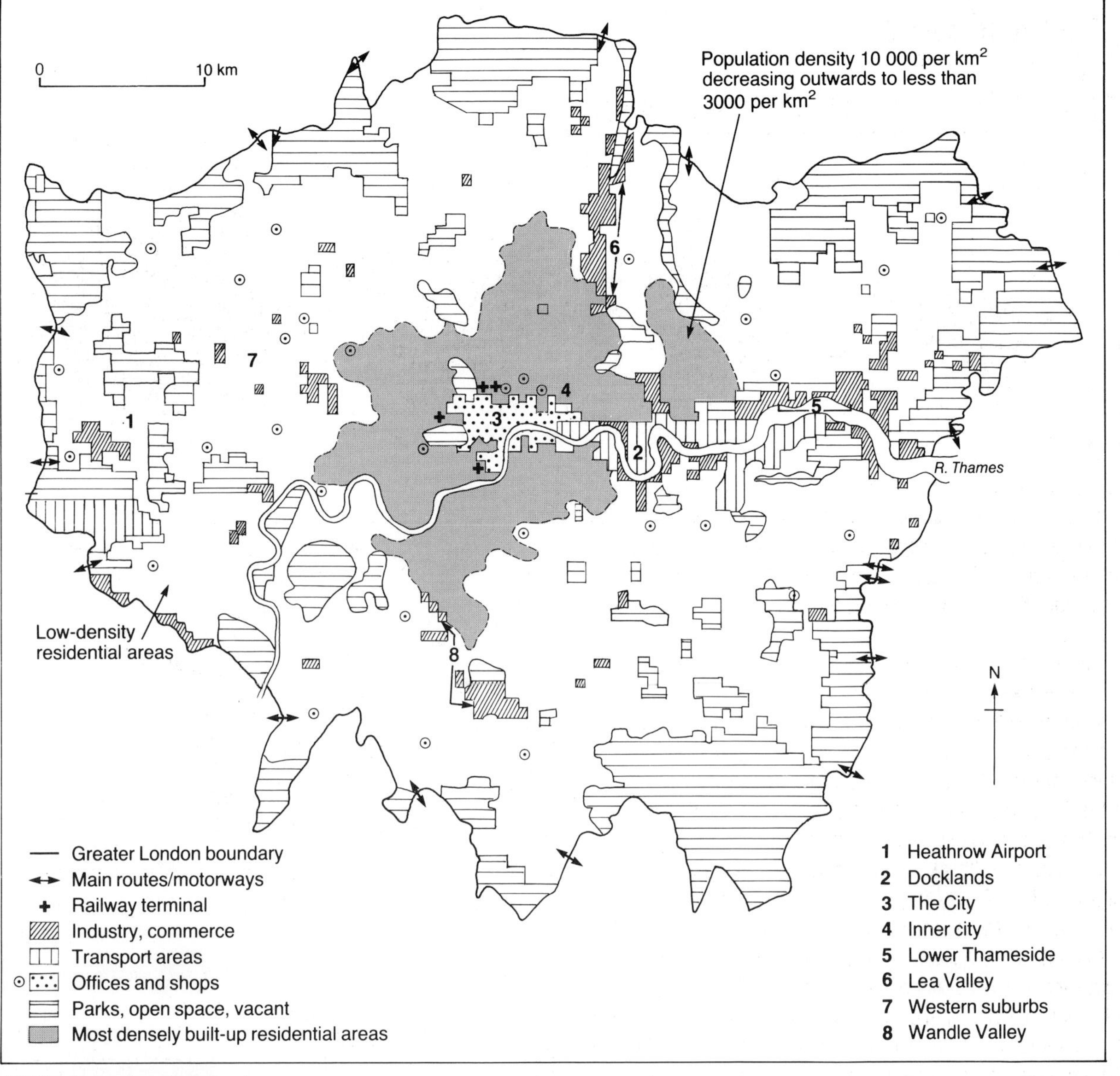

4.29 Greater London: selected land uses

wealth which attracted an even greater influx of rural migrants as London continued to expand and became the **primate city**. Meanwhile industry and commerce developed apace with new technology and foreign trade. London was well placed to take advantage of trade links with Europe, North America and Africa. London, with its embryo commercial structures, provided finance, excellent distribution and a large local market for traded goods. London was therefore able to grow rapidly as industrialisation proceeded and eventually a self-reinforcing growth structure developed (4.28).

Throughout the growth of London, as in any major urban area, a natural conflict arose between potential land users for city sites. As the population grew, this competition was further increased by the need to house the labour force near their workplace. Changes in technology, improvements to communication links and the general rise in living standards have also influenced the pattern of diverse land uses within the area known today as Greater London (4.29). It is still possible to locate the mediaeval city of London which occupied a site approximately the size of the present City of London. It should be noted too that this urban nucleus lies at the heart of the area of Greater London today. During the growth and diversification of London, the prospects for continuous economic success have also brought problems including congestion, spiralling land costs, and urban sprawl.

CHAPTER 4

London: Some Facts

London spread

The influence of the nation's primate city is one which is felt far beyond the limits of the Greater London boundary. Planners have now recognised that London has leapfrogged its Green Belt. An area defined as Metropolitan London or the Outer Metropolitan Area (OMA) covers over 2500 km^2 in the south-east of Britain (4.30). Greater London exceeds 1500km^2 and houses a population of 6.87 million people.

4.30

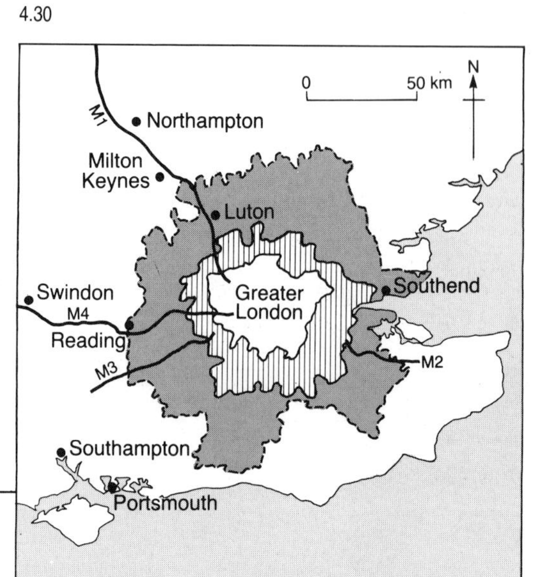

Population change

As graph 4.31 shows, the population of Inner London has been in decline since 1901. The growth of Outer London's population reached its peak in 1961 and is now also in decline. During this time, population densities have also undergone much change. Residential densities are lowest in the City (at 21 people/ha). The highest densities recorded are those recorded in the inner city (at 78 people/ha). As London's population has increased and its suburbs expanded, the peak densities are to be found about 14 km from the city centre (see 4.32). Population structures are reflected in the age/sex pyramids of people living in both Inner and Outer London (see 4.32). Selected population pyramids show that, in some parts of Inner London, there are high proportions of young people, but in most outer parts the population is predominantly middle-aged.

4.31 Population growth

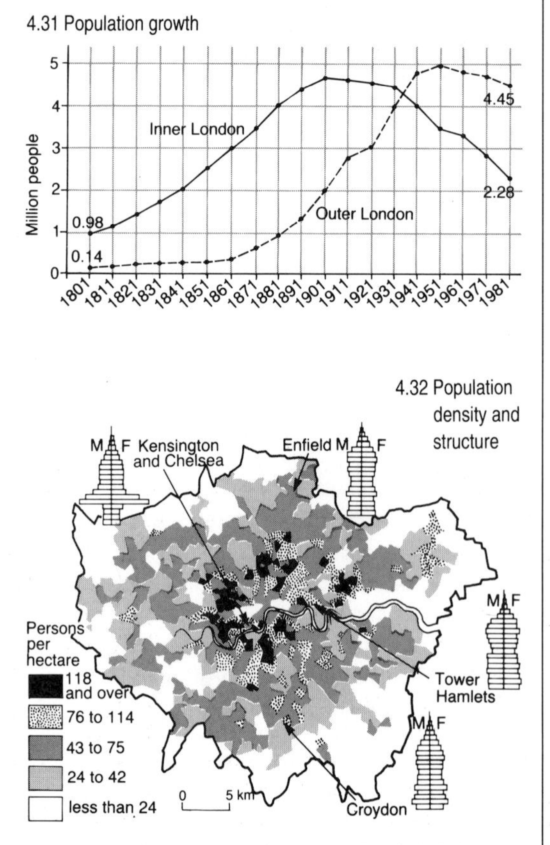

4.32 Population density and structure

4.33

Comings and goings

Inner London has experienced ma changes. The deindustrialisation of central area meant the loss of 2.2 mill manufacturing jobs between 1973 a 1983. However, there has been a ma expansion in office and service jo with 1.5 million new jobs created in same period. Of all offices in the U over 14% are located within cen London (4.33), where there is now massive 117.9 million square feet (1

Cardboard city

In London one in four houses are unfi live in. There is a serious shortage o least 120 000 homes. 200 000 sin people live in unsatisfact accommodation or sleep rough. In West End alone, there are over 50 homeless sleeping rough or 'skipper

Developed City

ion square metres) of office space
ailable. With bid-rent values of £60
square foot (£645 per m^2), Central
ndon has the most expensive real
ate in the country. Daily, 1103000
nmuters make the journey to work in
ntral London, creating major
gestion and environmental pollution.
rism also contributes over 8.9 million
tors and £3.55 billion to central
don.

4.34

ardboard boxes for warmth (4.34)
ough this area (3km^2) has the richest
estate in Britain. A wide cross-
tion of Londoners experience the
blem of homelessness, including the
rly, infirm and ethnic minorities.

Administrative regions

One in every eight people in the UK live in London. The city is bigger than the combined total of the next 15 largest cities. It houses more people than Scotland and the value of its property is the equivalent of 25% of the total for the UK. Greater London comprises 32 boroughs (4.35), with Croydon (319 000) and Kingston (133 000) having the largest and smallest residential populations, respectively.

4.35

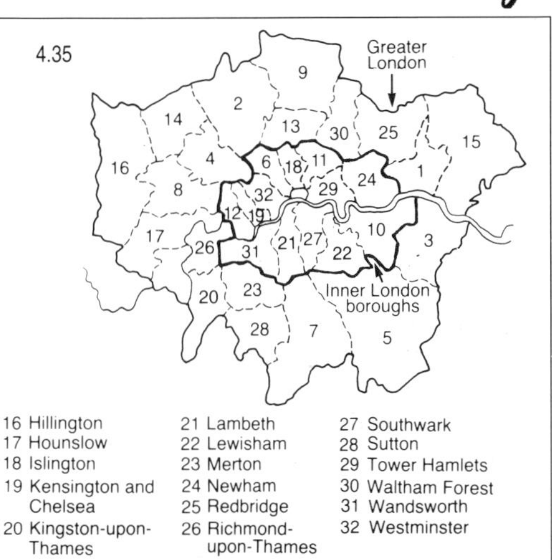

1 Barking
2 Barnet
3 Bexley
4 Brent
5 Bromley
6 Camden
7 Croydon
8 Ealing
9 Enfield
10 Greenwich
11 Hackney
12 Hammersmith
13 Haringey
14 Harrow
15 Havering
16 Hillington
17 Hounslow
18 Islington
19 Kensington and Chelsea
20 Kingston-upon-Thames
21 Lambeth
22 Lewisham
23 Merton
24 Newham
25 Redbridge
26 Richmond-upon-Thames
27 Southwark
28 Sutton
29 Tower Hamlets
30 Waltham Forest
31 Wandsworth
32 Westminster

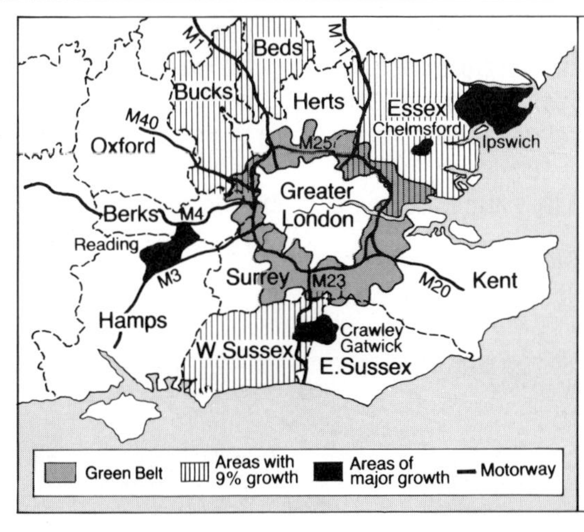

Moving out

The decline of population and employment in the City has contributed to the overdevelopment of the South-East. People and companies are moving into the 'Home Counties' (4.36), encouraged by improved communications, but this is threatening Green Belt areas. Growth poles are emerging with Buckinghamshire achieving over 18% growth in population and areas such as Ipswich and Reading developing into major centres of growth.

4.36

Gentrification

The combination of a shortage of good housing in central London and the 1969 Housing Act which made home improvement grants available has encouraged a reversal of the outward trend of residential population. **Gentrification** has taken place (4.37) where upper-middle-income groups have moved into inner-city areas such as Clapham, Fulham and Camberwell, and renovated run-down housing. The areas were originally middle-class Victorian suburbs, now rehabilitated with a concomitant rise in property values.

4.37

Core London

Behind the facade of obvious wealth, success and thriving city life of some of London's central areas (4.38), the core, including the central business district, is in the midst of great change (4.39).

The daily commuting of over 1 million people is evidence of the fact that over the last 30 years there has been a slow haemorrhaging of over 1 million residents to Outer London and beyond. Some of the relocation has been planned: large schemes for redevelopment in areas such as Hackney and the Isle of Dogs dispelled people to the suburbs. However, an increasing number of problems in central London (4.40) caused concern that the area had lost its locational attractiveness to business, industry and resident population.

In a series of attempts to reverse the dominance of centrifugal over centripetal forces, more rebuilding and redevelopment schemes (e.g. new office, riverside and expensive residential developments) were introduced in the 1960s to 1980s. The principal direction of growth has been westwards, increasing the area of discard in the east and south. The core areas of the City and the West End (sometimes regarded as London's twin CBDs) remain surrounded by a frame of expensive real estate but areas such as Lambeth, Spitalfields and the Docklands have until recently suffered urban decay and multiple deprivation on a grand scale.

4.38

Solutions to core problems?

- Planned **comprehensive redevelopment eastwards** of the Docklands and riverside areas.
- **Inner-city aid schemes** tackling the problems of multiple deprivation within central London. **Partnership Authorities**: for example, Lambeth now receives 75% of the cost of approved redevelopment schemes from the government.
- Undirected, free market developments including gentrification of business and residential properties.

Even some of the solutions, however, have resulted in conflict and controversy.

4.39 Core London

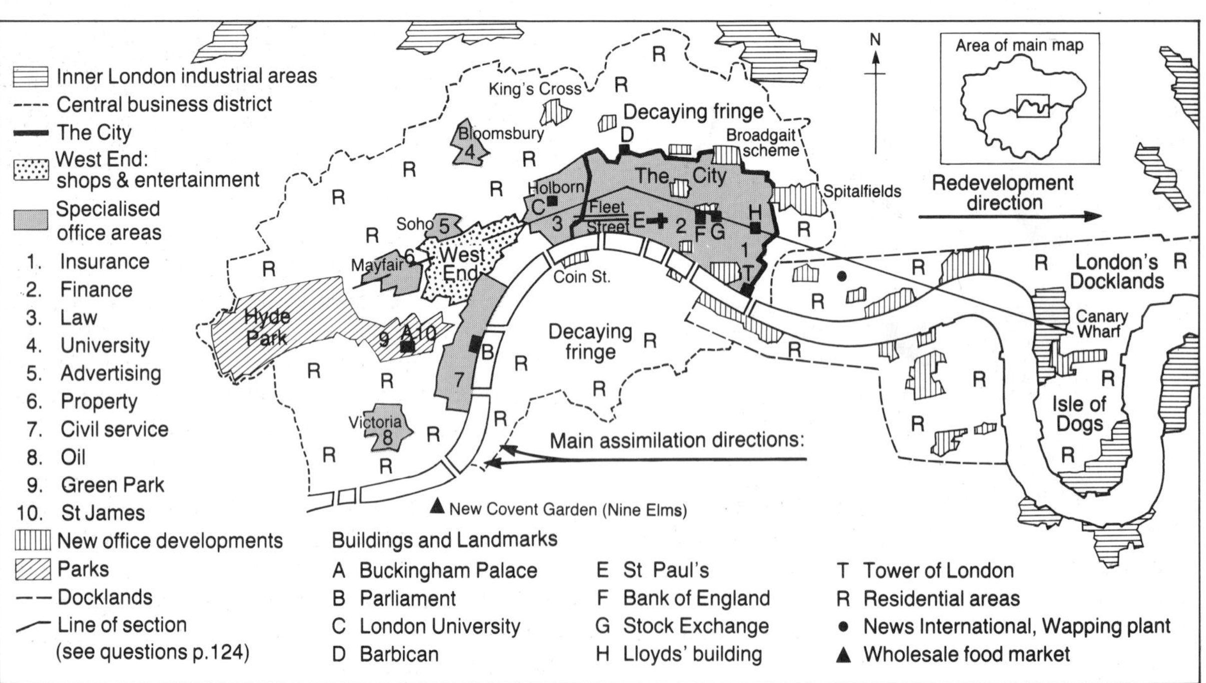

4.40 Problems of Core London

Outmigration Between 1963 and 1983 the population of core London dropped from 3.4 to 2.2 million. Outmigration has reduced population densities in core London, increased densities in the suburbs, and at the same time increased the area of London.

High land values Intense competition for space in the CBD has created very expensive land values, at over £60 per square foot of office floor, and multi-storey developments. Pressure of demand has also generated large numbers of office developments in the City fringes, for example at Spitalfields (4.39). Core London has lost over 300 000 jobs as companies have relocated to cheaper sites in less congested and cleaner suburban environments.

Competition from the periphery The **Location of Offices Bureau** mounted an advertisng campaign stressing the disadvantages of core London and emphasing the advantages of suburban locations. Other forces have also been at work to encourage **decentralisation**: the high proportion of old outmoded buildings, spiralling commuting costs, and the growing need for businesses to be near to airports and Channel Tunnel links.

Increasing costs of services With increasing movement of people to the suburbs, there are major problems in funding the public services for those remaining in the centre, who often require extra services. Higher than average local taxes are seen by some as necessary to provide these services.

Traffic congestion is increased by the narrow, grid iron street layout and is worst at morning and evening rush hours where over 700 000 vehicles generate gridlock jams and increasing air and noise pollution. Each year between 700 and 900 people are killed on the roads.

Rising unemployment The **deindustrialisation** of core London's manufacturing base – textiles, food processing, metallurgy and engineering – has inevitably brought high unemployment. The employment structure is now dominated by administrative and service sectors which outweigh manufacturing jobs by 5 to 1. Even with the creation of over 150 000 new jobs, there was an annual net loss of 31 000 jobs between 1970 and 1990.

Housing and urban decay Despite a falling population, there is still a shortage of good housing in core London. In 1984, 175 000 houses were deemed unsuitable for human habitation and 215 000 were in a state of serious disrepair. In addition, 104 500 houses were fit but lacked basic amenities. The combined problems of ageing and decaying buildings; lack of amenities; substandard high-rise blocks; the poor quality of the environment (and a lack of gardens); intermixture of residence, industry and wasteland; together with increasing localised unemployment have contributed to the **multiple deprivation** of parts of core London.

The combination of these and other **negative points** led to building societies red-lining districts of core London as unsuitable for loans because of their high crime rate, poor environmental quality, or problems of social unrest. Other more favoured core areas were, however, green-lined as suitable for loans because of factors such as gentrification, future potential, or possession of the 'right' address.

Development schemes in themselves have also created problems especially where development is viewed by locals as a threat to their existing community, as happened in the Docklands areas. The high incidence of public enquiries over proposed new schemes has inhibited new businesses from locating within such areas.

CHAPTER 4

London's Third City?

4.42 Canary Wharf development

In an area larger than Leicester, with a population greater than present-day Edinburgh, the former Port of London Docklands, which stretch downstream from Tower Bridge (4.41), are undergoing dramatic regeneration. With the completion of the gigantic Canary Wharf development (4.42) in the mid 1990s, Docklands in effect will join the twin cores of the City of London and the City of Westminster to become London's third City.

There is however vehement disagreement over the comprehensive redevelopment of the 24 km² of Dockland area. One group, pro-business, aligns itself to the view that this is an oustanding example of economic transformation and creation of wealth, where a totally derelict area apparently without prospects is being transformed into a new-town-in-town, with new jobs, new houses and a new urban landscape. Masterminded since 1981 by the **London Docklands Development Corporation** (LDDC), the redevelopment of the entire area has been handled and planned independently of the four Dockland boroughs. The scheme has so far attracted over £4000 million of private investment, and work on improving the infrastructure (its communications and services) has brought public investment over £440 million (4.43). This has also brought increased rates revenues to the Docklands boroughs and so far over 10 000 new jobs to the area. For some, this is proof that the private sector is successfully regenerating the Docklands.

Another group, pro-local, finds the redevelopment scheme unacceptable, viewing it as financially speculative, totally disregarding of the existing community's needs for new affordable housing and local jobs, creating a yuppie and dinky (dual income, no kids yet) paradise for wealthy outsiders who do not wish to contribute to the local community.

Developers and residents seem continuously to be deadlocked in debate over current and future plans (4.44). Locals say that the LDDC have steamrollered physical regeneration of communications and buildings without regard to the social infrastructure of the Docklands. Their further criticism of the LDDC's work focuses on the developing differences between the Docklands and the rest of London. Unlike most of the rest of London, the Docklands are developing into a series of homogeneous cells of segregated land uses. Locals say that the results of current and future developments will be to segregate areas socially on the basis of demand, high bid-rents and occupation.

There have undoubtedly been both successes and failures in the Docklands regeneration scheme. It can be argued that the local authorities, facing major financial problems after the great deindustrialisation of the Docklands in the 1960s and 1970s, could never have realistically led an economic revival. Existing

4.41 Docklands: recent developments

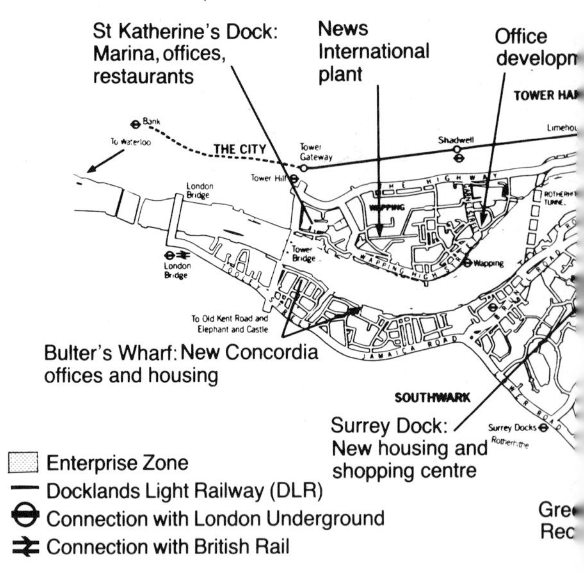

and planned development schemes will, it is hoped, create over 100 000 new jobs by the end of the century. There is a virtual new town being created in Beckton with a large area of land used for low-cost starter housing. The Docklands are now on the London tourist circuit and there are new communications links, shopping centres, pubs and entertainment facilities. And the Dockland area of Inner London is not the only potential development site. The redevelopment of the King's Cross/St Pancras area (4.38) seems destined to generate equal controversy, albeit without the jewel of riverside potential.

WHY MOVE TO THE MIDDLE OF NOWHERE, WHEN YOU CAN MOVE TO THE MIDDLE OF LONDON?

LDDC started in 1981 and faced the challenges of:
- large areas of derelict land
- no private investment
- creating private/public partnership
- 95% housing stock rented and in need of repair
- outdated infrastructure (roads, railways, drainage, electricity and communications) in need of major investment

Docklands today are recognised as an area of major opportunity for business and residence in the heart of London. The comprehensive redevelopment of the Docklands by private/ public partnership includes:
- plans for 2.3 million square metres of new commercial space and 2.4 million square metres of industrial space. Canary Wharf alone will cost £3 billion and account for 1.1 million square metres of space.
- plans for 30 000 new houses
- new Docklands Light Railway and London City airport now open
- new multi-million pound road-building, sewerage and drainage schemes.
- plans for the creation of up to 150 000 jobs by year 2000
- New recreational, entertainment and shopping complexes.

Can *you* afford not to be here?

4.43

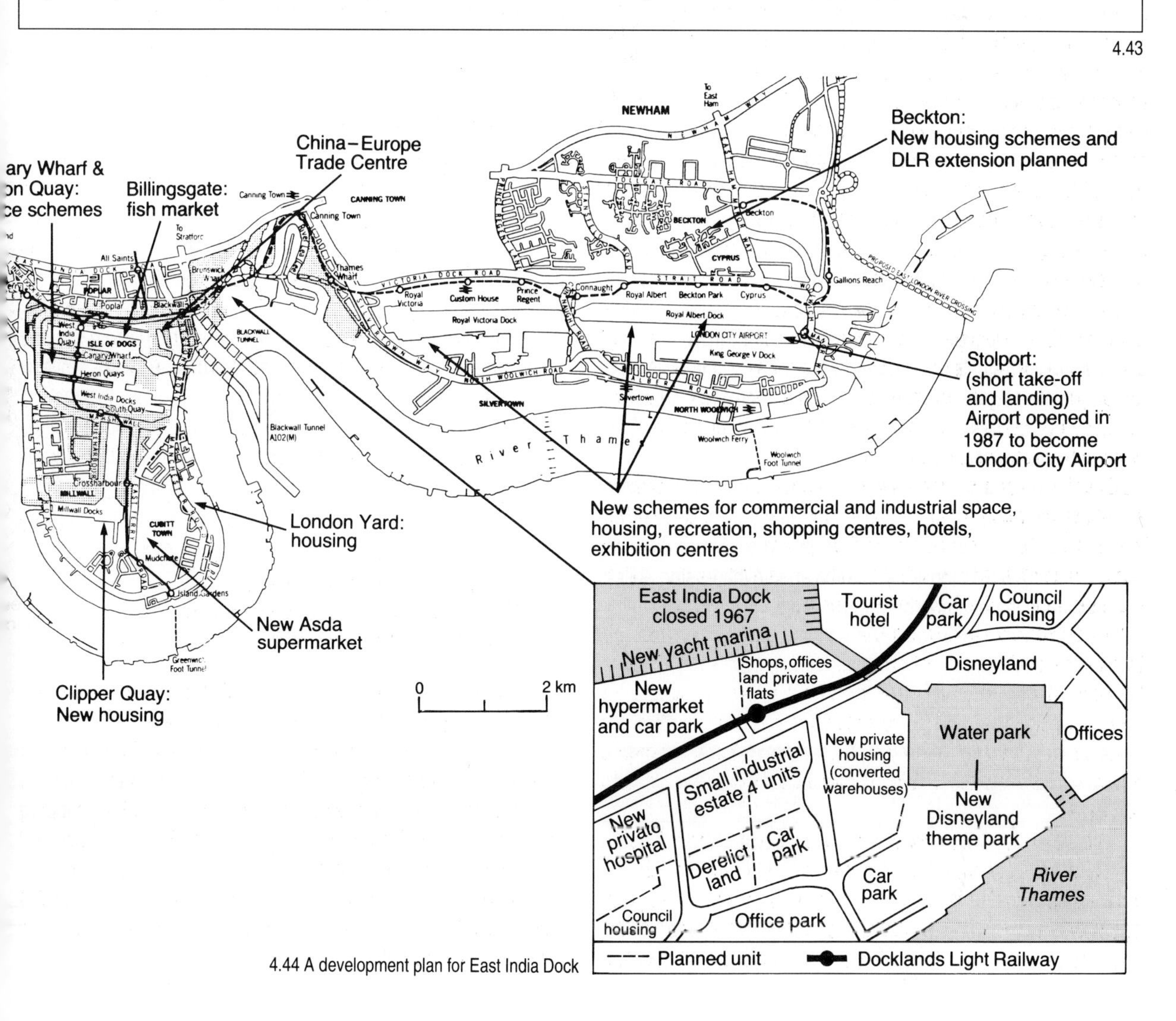

4.44 A development plan for East India Dock

CHAPTER 4

'Suburbopolis'

> Today's well-to-do have moved out of town, to a cramped and joyless Arcadia of Wendy houses, which announce on signboards of simulated rough-hewn wood 'Polperro' or 'Ischia', the destination of a honeymoon. Each house is dutifully decorated with the trappings of rural mythology manufactured by a garden centre industry for town dwellers. The centre of the town is left increasingly to the poor, the old and the immigrants.
>
> P. Hall, *London 2001*, Unwin/Hyman

So wrote J.Seaburn in 1969 revealing his disenchantment with suburban sprawl. In the case of London, this movement to the suburbs has been a process which has taken most of this century and has had the effect of ripples of growth followed by troughs of decline. This can be traced by the redefining of administrative boundaries sometimes referred to as the 'suburbopolis' of the South-East (4.45).

By the end of First World War, London's rural–urban fringe was already 11 km from the city centre. The inital expansion, fuelled by cheap, accessible railways, was then superseded by the tremendous suburbanisation that took place between the wars when the urban area of London almost doubled and Outer London was created. Expansion tended to occur in bursts, at first mainly directed by existing railways, and later extended ones. Suburbs were built around what were then villages in the country: for example, Wimbledon or Sidcup. The engulfing of the villages, making them part of London and turning them into suburbia occurred later when motor transport allowed more flexibility of movement away from rail links. Backfilling of the remaining gaps between villages and the unplanned sprawl of London during the interwar period was also fuelled by the location of 80% of all London's new factories there at that time. There was a corresponding expansion of population and an increasing ability to afford new, improved suburban housing.

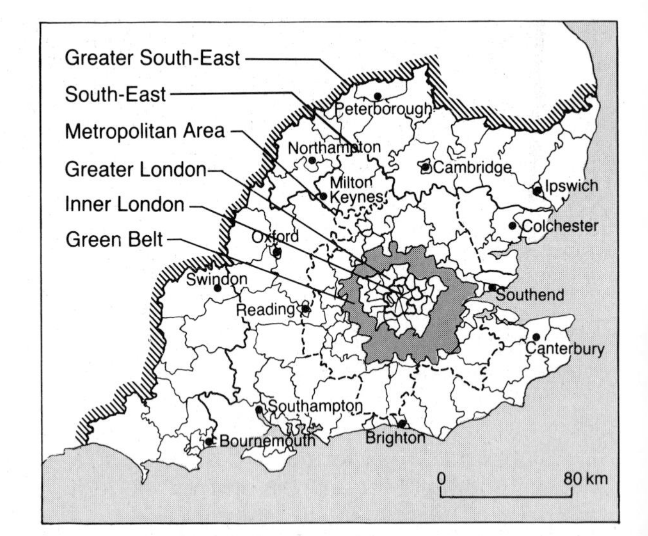

4.45 The expanding South-East

About 25 km on average from London's CBD, suburbia gives way to countryside. The suburban expansion of the 1930s declined when the Second World War, and then the enforcement of the 8–25 km wide Green Belt, acted as effective stoppers to the spread of the metropolis. By 1963, the administrative boundary of Greater London no longer adequately defined the area affected by urban change in the South-East. Continued improvements to the communications network (rail electrification/road construction), increased car ownership, increasing inner-city land values, and the attractions of greenfield locations for new industrial complexes led to counter-urbanisation. From around 1950, Greater London began losing population (4.46) while a ring around it – up to 80 km from the CBD – was the fastest growing part of Britain. Today's Greater South-East houses over 35% of the British people and is seen by some as the natural product of the cycle of urban development (4.3) where containment of the expanding suburbs (4.47) encourages counter-urbanisation.

4.46 Decline in population in the South-East

	Population				
	1961 Census	1971 Census	1981 Census	1981 Estimate	1986 Estimate
'Greater South-East'	18 217 529	19 484 079	19 615 233	19 859 800	20 266 300
South-East	15 993 116	16 930 630	16 795 756	17 010 400	17 264 600
Greater London	7 992 443	7 452 346	6 713 165	6 805 700	6 775 200
Inner London	3 492 879	3 031 935	2 497 978	2 550 200	2 511 700
Outer London	4 499 564	4 420 411	4 215 187	4 255 500	4 263 500
Outer Metropolitan Area	4 390 087	5 206 831	5 461 918	5 513 600	5 581 000
Outer South-East	3 610 586	4 271 453	4 620 673	4 691 100	4 908 600

4.47 London: suburbia

The above photograph shows part of the interwar outer suburban area of north-west London. Rapid outward growth was encouraged by the introduction of public transport which was then accelerated by the increase in the popularity of the private car. This expansion led to the construction of vast tracts of private suburbs such as the one shown above.

Outer suburbia is characterised by:

1. original linear development along rail or road links;
2. backfilled residential areas usually with crescent/avenue street layouts;
3. low-density, semi-detached/detached, two-storey housing often with bay windows;
4. front and back gardens;
5. shopping parades clustered around rail/tube stations (4.22);
6. large areas of open spaces as playing fields, parks and schools;
7. mature, tree-lined areas.

The highest proportion of **owner-occupied housing** is found in these areas (1981 61.9% compared with 27.3% in Inner London), reflecting the predominantly middle-income family-with-children character of outer areas (4.24).

Outer suburbia offers **many advantages** for living:

- pleasant environment;
- more modern housing with amenities,
- cheaper bid-rents;
- less environmental pollution;
- better equipped schools;
- safe play areas, parks and gardens.

But there are **disadvantages and growing problems** within the outer suburbs which are experiencing a trough both in development and in population.

- increasing commuting problems including congestion, rising costs;
- distance from, and lack of, shopping provision and car parking;
- increasing maintenance costs of houses now 50–70 years old;
- lack of entertainment provision;
- increasing cost of houses;
- competition from exurban areas with fewer planning restrictions and more advanced communications.

CHAPTER 4

South-east Sprawl

4.48 Green Belt and the M25

The process of urban growth and suburbanisation in the London area has now been superseded by counter-urbanisation initiated by the development of the **Green Belt** (4.48). This is a zone, up to 25 km wide, created to restrict the uncontrolled urban sprawl of London and to prevent the agglomeration of neighbouring settlements within it. The **1938 Green Belt Act** was later reinforced by the 1947 Town & Country Planning Act which required landowners to obtain permission from their local authority to change the use of their land. Local authorities could then restrict building in the designated Green Belt.

London was becoming too large to administer at the time between the wars. Fertile farmland was being lost and towns and villages were being engulfed by rapid development. At the same time proposals following the Abercrombie Plan for the South-East (1944) led to the New Towns Act (1946). This was an attempt to regulate the population movement by creating newly planned settlements which would relieve overcrowding and urban decay within the London area now hemmed in by Green Belt developments (4.49).

To some extent, London's designated Green Belt has been a success. Urban sprawl has been restricted and urban development schemes such as Docklands have been confined to inner-city locations. In 1984, a Commons Select Committee Report (**Green Belt and Land for Housing**) confirmed the value of the belt and even recommended its more positive enforcement. But the pressures on London's rural–urban fringe are increasing. It has been estimated that over 1 million new houses will be required in the South-East by the year 2000, most of which will need to be built outside Greater London. Major improvements to the communications networks around London are also pressurising the belt. The construction of the M25 (see colour map, page 173) has used much Green Belt land and is likely to become a magnet for office, factory and shopping centre developments. In addition, the upgrading of roads and the electrification of railway networks (4.50) has greatly increased the commuting sphere of influence of the South-East.

As London house prices spiralled during the 1970s and 1980s, many peopled sold up and moved into semi-rural areas in the South-East. Commuting is now a way of life and the resultant congestion and insatiable demand for more and better communications encourages more counter-urbanisation. It is clear that the Green Belt has been **leapfrogged** by developers and commuters. In recent years organisations such as the CPRE (Council for the Protection of Rural England) have been involved in the Great Green Belt Battle in an attempt to protect what some critics regard as mere buffer zones between settlements. They now argue that the green belt is detrimental to the countryside of the south-east of Britian since it is the areas outside the belt which are now under most threat. Some say that the belt is now not worth fighting for as it has been diluted and spoilt by open-cast gravel sites, motorways and reservoirs.

4.50 London's commuting sphere of influence

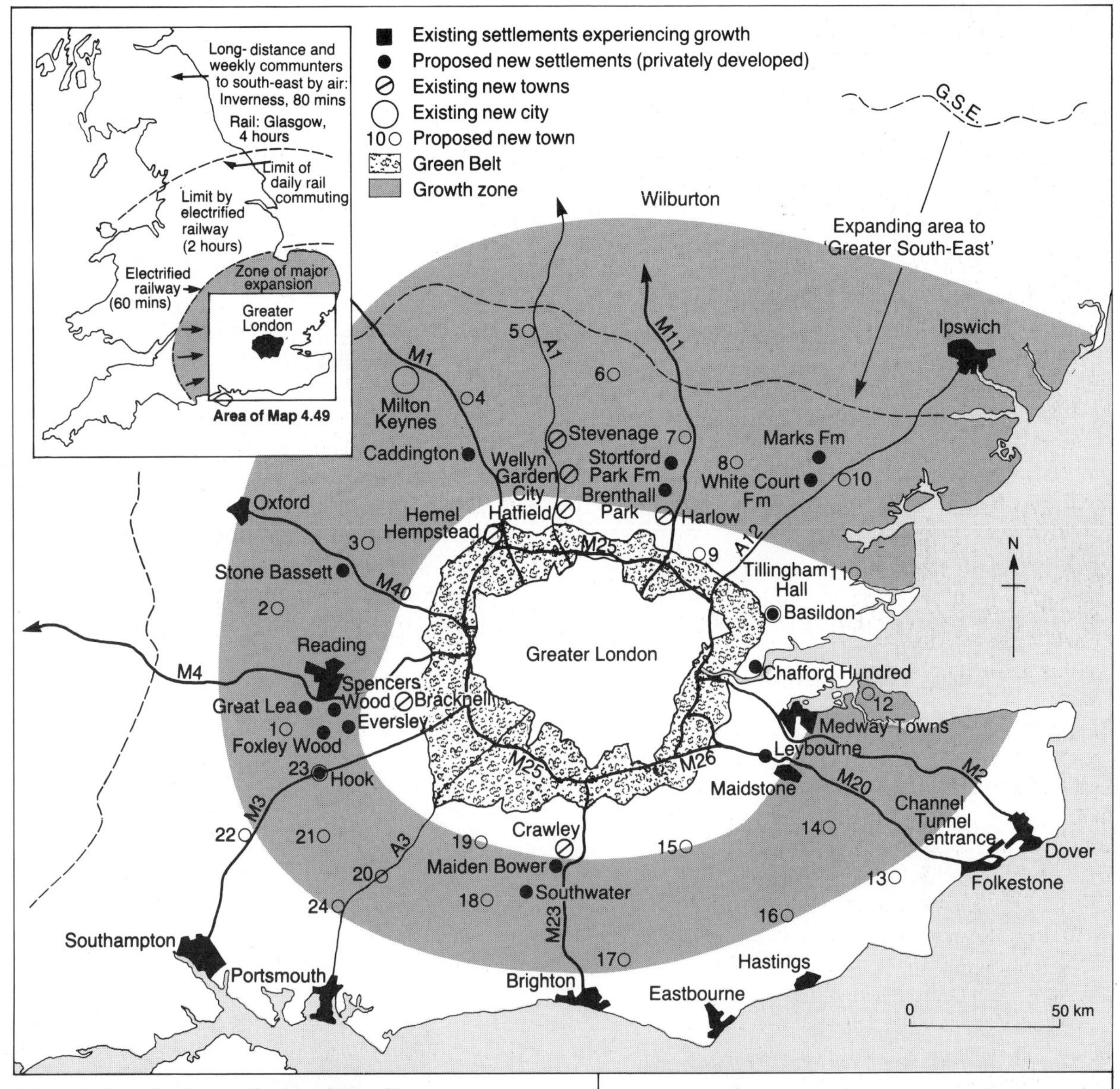

4.49 Greater South-East (towards Randstad, England?)

The anticipated demand for future housing could necessitate the development of 25 new towns (4.49) in a zone of development around London. Many experts now predict that London will become the Randstad (ring city) of England early next century (similiar to Ranstad in the Netherlands, which has become a massive ring of unbroken settlement). In Britain, a central city, London, would be surrounded by a ring of satellite settlements connected by excellent communications in a polycentric urban development. Opponents of the Green Belt argue that its continued strict enforcement will lead to the overdevelopment of the South-East (exacerbated by the Channel Tunnel), and the eventual obliteration of much of its green and pleasant countryside.

25 Proposed new towns for London

1 Silchester
2 Wallingford
3 Princes Risborough
4 Flitwick
5 Sandy
6 Royston
7 Quendon
8 Great Dunmon
9 Ongar
10 Kelvedon
11 Woodham Ferrers
12 Queenborough Minster
13 Hamstreet
14 Headcorn
15 Ashurst
16 Robertsbridge
17 Plumpton
18 Billinghurst
19 Cranleigh
20 Liphook
21 Alton
22 Micheldelver
23 Hook
24 Petersfield

Q LONDON: GROWTH AND DIVERSITY

1 (a) Briefly describe the growth of London.
(b) What was the distance across London from east to west in 1851 and 1951?
(c) In which ways did the surrounding villages and towns change over this period?
(d) Which factors contributed to London's rapid growth?
(e) Write brief notes on: primate city, settlement hierarchy.
(f) Compare and contrast the pattern of selected land uses (4.29) with any urban land-use model you know.
(g) Which problems have been generated by the continuous economic success of London?

Q CORE LONDON

3 (a) Copy and complete the simple cross-section (diagram 1) through core London identifying the main physical features, types of land use and buildings (the cross-section is taken from map 4.39).
(b) List the main CBD functions found in this area.
(c) Where are new office developments located in core London?
(d) Do you agree with the statement that London has twin CBDs? Give reasons.
(e) List the main advantages and disadvantages of core London for: *(i)* new office location; *(ii)* living.
(f) Describe the main changes which have occurred in Core London.
(g) Which has been the principal direction of expansion and growth in London's core?
(h) List the main centrifugal forces at work in core London.
(i) Write brief notes to explain multiple deprivation, quaternary services, decentralisation.
(j) Which schemes have been introduced to increase the centripetal forces of Core London?
(k) Study diagram 2 below. Describe the pattern of, and main reasons for, office developments around London.

Diagram 1

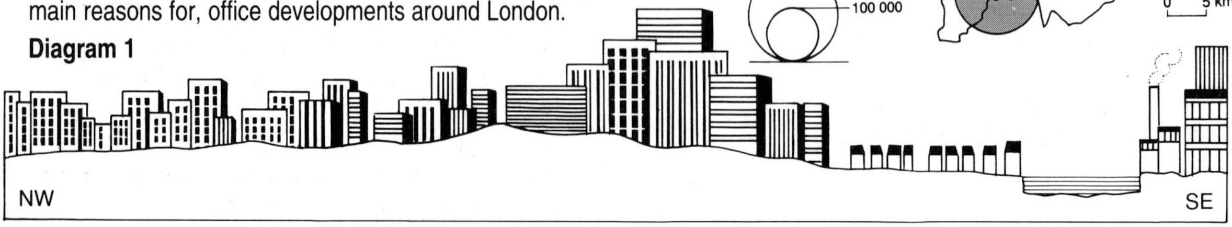

NW

SE

Q LONDON: SOME FACTS

2 (a) What is the population of London?
(b) Copy graph 4.31 carefully.
(c) Describe and then explain the changes revealed by graph 4.31.
(d) Has population decline been advantageous to London? Why?
(e) Using map 4.32, describe the population structure of each of the four selected Boroughs (use the population pyramids).
(f) Where are population densities in London *(i)* lowest; *(ii)* highest? Explain why this is the case.
(g) Make a simple outline fieldsketch of photo 4.33. Identify any famous London landmarks and characteristics of the central business district.
(h) Which major changes have occurred in the industrial functions, and therefore employment, in Inner London?
(i) What is 'cardboard city'?
(j) List the main ways in which London is the most important British City.
(k) Why do tourist developments often result in conflicts over land use?
(l) Where are the main growth poles in the south-east of England? Explain why this is the case.
(m) What is gentrification?

Diagram 2 Office developments 1984–5, outside the City of London

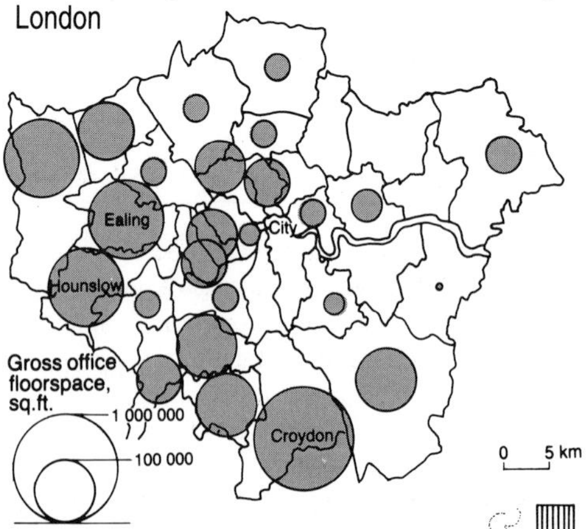

Q LONDON'S THIRD CITY?

4 (a) Study all the information given on pages118–19.
(b) Now study map 4.44 which is a plan for the redevelopment of East India dock.
(c) Divide into groups of 9 or 10, each member adopting one of the roles outlined below.
(d) Your task is to consider very carefully your role, how you would relate to the proposals and to take part in the final planning meeting.
(e) You may need to carry out detailed research and the following contact list provides some useful addresses.

LDDC Schools' Liaison Officer, Great Eastern Enterprise, Millharbour, London, E14 9TJ (071 515 3000)
Newham Voluntary Agencies Council, Durning Hall, Earlham Grove, London, E7 9AB (071 555 8254)
Docklands Consultative Committee, Unit 4, Stratford Office Village, 4 Romford Road, London, E15 4EA (071 519 5485)

(f) When research is complete, your next task is to attend a simulated planning meeting at which the proposals and any alternative plans for redevelopment are to be considered then decided upon.
(g) A final report and redevelopment plan must be drawn up after final decisions have been reached. The report must give the main reasons for the final decisions, listing the ways in which they were arrived at.
(h) Once this has been completed, evaluate the agreed redevelopment scheme from the point of view of local residents, developers, LDDC, tourist related businesses, traffic management, etc.

Interested parties for East India Dock redevelopment scheme

1. Chairperson of planning committee.
2. Developers: Mackay Consultants, Ltd.
3. LDDC investment representative.
4. Local residents' representative.
5. Local councillor for East India area.
6. Local estate agents' representative.
7. Local school leaver.
8. Waterfront Society (boatbuilders and repairers) chairperson.
9. Local publicans' and hoteliers' representative.
10. Traffic management committee representative.

Q SUBURBOPOLIS

5 (a) Define suburbia.
(b) Explain why administration boundaries have had to be redefined in the area around London.
(c) List the main characteristics of London's outer suburbia.
(d) Design and complete a table showing the main advantages and disadvantages of living in outer suburbia.
(e) Write brief notes to explain Green Belt, counter-urbanisation, exurbia, Greater South-East.
(f) Why does the containment of the suburban expansion encourage counter-urbanisation around London?

Q SOUTH-EAST SPRAWL

6 (a) When was the Green Belt policy enacted?
(b) What were, and still are, the main aims of the Green Belt policy?
(c) Design then complete a table to summarise the advantages and disadvantages of London's Green Belt.
(d) What is the relationship between the Green Belt and: *(i)* house prices in London *(ii)* the expansion in Greater South-East?
(e) Outline the case for relaxing the strict enforcement of the Green Belt around London.
(f) Why are some experts predicting the development of a Randstad, England, in the south-east of Britain?

LONDON: COLOUR SECTION MAPWORK

(a) Design and draw a sketch map and key to identify the main types of land-use zone (rural, Green Belt, rural–urban fringe, suburbs, M25, etc.) shown on the colour map on page 173.
(b) A development plan for the area includes new private housing around Pratt's Grove (4862) and an out of town shopping centre and business park around Hewitts (488633). Write two sets of reports evaluating both the advantages and disadvantages of each development scheme, incorporating map evidence. Which scheme should be given the go-ahead? Why?

CHAPTER 4

Urbanisation in Brazil

4.51 Urbanisation in Brazil

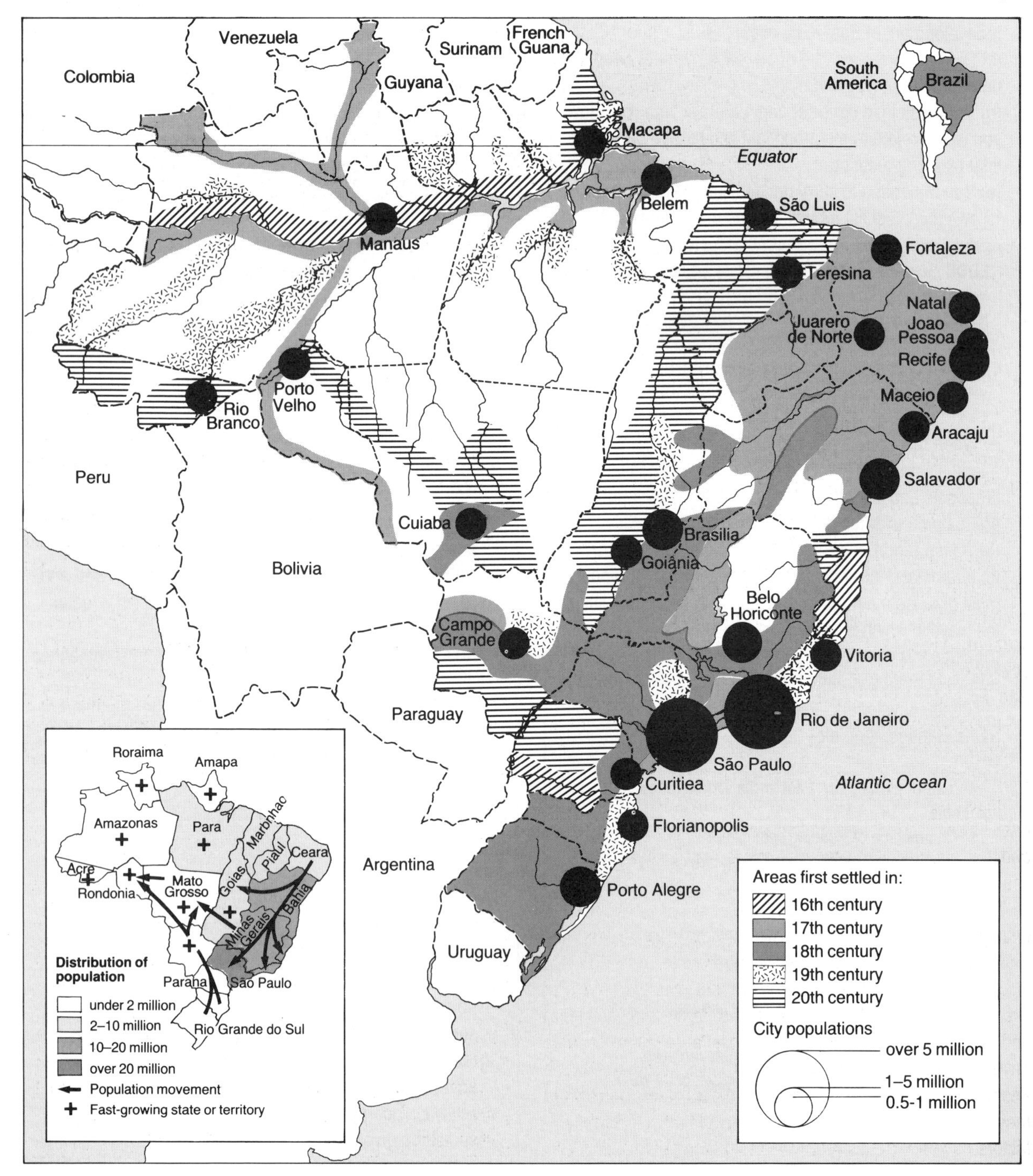

4.53 Shop windows in São Paulo. Contrasting life styles: homeless poor, and shop window advertising consumerism

The urbanisation process in the countries of the South is a source of growing concern. More than half of the world's urban dwellers live in the South and by the end of the present century this proportion will have grown to two-thirds. Brazil, the world's sixth largest country, with a population of 145 million, has witnessed a dramatic shift in the proportion its population that lives in cities, from 34% in 1950 to over 71% in 1990.

The pattern of urbanisation in Brazil can be seen by considering early development of settlement and then the present phase of rapidly expanding urban areas. Until the mid-1950s, Brazil was a mainly agrarian society. Indeed the development of settlement for the last four centuries was closely interlinked with the spread of agriculture. The arrival of the Portuguese in 1500 began the **colonial phase** of settlement of the country that was later to become Brazil (4.51). Until then indigenous Indians had lived in scattered tribes for over 3000 years. The earliest European settlers followed the courses of Brazil's major rivers, the Amazon, São Francisco and Patanaiba, spreading settlement to the interior in search of agricultural land and minerals. By the time of **independence** in 1822 only a small proportion of the vast country had been settled. Immigrants from Italy, Japan and Africa extended the spread of settlement into Amazonia and the south-east. Laws to restrict immigration were established in the 1930s and the colonisation of interior areas was confined mainly to the coast north of Rio de Janeiro.

The latter half of the twentieth century has seen a major change from a static agrarian to a rapidly urbanising society, with urban values, employment and living conditions (4.53). So vigorous has this transformation been that massive growth of Brazil's major cities (4.54), such as São Paulo, Rio de Janeiro and Belo Horizonte, has occurred. These large urban magnets have attracted millions from rural areas, away from their villages and rural occupations (4.52). **Rural migration** is one of the main reasons for the fast urbanisation in Brazil. Other contributory factors have been the steadily increasing population of urban areas, immigration and industrialisation, along with the many urban improvement schemes which serve to attract even more rural migrants in search of a higher quality of life. In contrast to Britain, Brazil does not have a **primate city**: São Paulo and Rio de Janeiro are the two largest cities, Rio de Janeiro being not much smaller than São Paulo. The distribution of urban areas in the country is very uneven. Most large urban areas are located in the south-east and along the coast. This area is the most densely populated and highly developed region of Brazil. Some experts believe that the three cities of the 'golden triangle', São Paulo, Rio de Janeiro and Belo Horizonte, could spread to become a solid mass of urban development (like Randstad in the Netherlands). Few large urban areas have developed in the interior, apart from riverport cities such as Manãus.

The construction of planned settlements, such as the capital Brasilia (1960) and Goiânia (1937) within the interior, and countless new settlements within Amazonia and Rondonia herald a change in the pattern of urban growth in Brazil. Government policy is attempting to influence the distribution of settlement and reverse the rural-to-urban trend which has led to the development of huge megacities such as São Paulo in the late 1900s.

4.54 Brazil's growing cities

	Population (thousands)			
City	1950	1970	1980	2000 (est.)
Belo Horizonte	409	1505	2279	5110
Brasilia	0	538	1082	2614
Curitiba	157	647	1093	2013
Fortaleza	251	864	1340	2111
Porto Alegre	464	1409	2133	4020
Recife	647	1630	2307	3411
Rio de Janeiro	3044	6847	9619	18000
Salvador (Bahia)	396	1067	1563	2167
São Paulo	2336	7838	12273	26100

CHAPTER 4

Megacity, Brazil

São Paulo is the largest and richest city in South America and in Brazil. It has been described as a 'paradise, scarred by ulcers of shanty towns' and a megacity. Like most cities of the developing world, São Paulo is expanding rapidly and now occupies an area the equivalent of the island of Skye. Each year, the city grows by 65 km^2 and the population increases by over 550 000. São Paulo is approximately twice the size of London both in terms of area and population and is experiencing rapid urbanisation at a time when cities such as London are undergoing counter-urbanisation. It is both the rate and the sheer scale of the urbanisation that is placing severe stress on the city. The result is a quite different city structure (4.55) from that found in the cities of developed countries, such as London.

The city occupies a site consisting of a plateau dissected by numerous valleys, such as those of the rivers Tietê, Pinheiros and Tamanduatei (see colour section map, page 178). São Paulo sits at an altitude of over 760 metres above sea level and is bounded to the south by the Serra do Mar and two major reservoirs, Billings and Guarapiranga. There are ten major communications routeways which have either followed existing river courses or have been constructed across the massive lake-reservoirs surrounding the city. City development and land-use patterns have been directly influenced by both the plateau site and its communications sectors.

São Paulo's central business district, known as the Triangulo (see 4.58), is located on the plateau above the valley of the river Tietê, to the north of the city (4.56). This site stands at the intersection of the main routeways east–west and north–south and was first developed by a colonialist administration as a central plaza surrounded by a grid-iron street pattern. As the city developed into a commercial and administrative centre, the CBD gradually extended southwards along the Via Anchieta and Rodovia dos Imigrantes as a zone of modern high-rise blocks housing offices, shops and apartments for the wealthy.

After the Second World War, São Paulo was restructured to take advantage of a boom in manufacturing industry. The city's main industrial districts are located along routeways in the Santo Andre and São Bernado do Campo districts in the north–south spine, and in the Guarulhos and Osasco districts on the east–west spine. Most factory workers have had to live close to their workplace in a city such as São Paulo and, for this reason, housing and industry are located next to each other within the city, causing problems of pollution for residents.

In contrast to the wealthy suburban development of cities such as London, there are huge areas of *periferia* and shanty housing on the edges of São Paulo. With very limited financial resources there is a major problem in providing basic housing

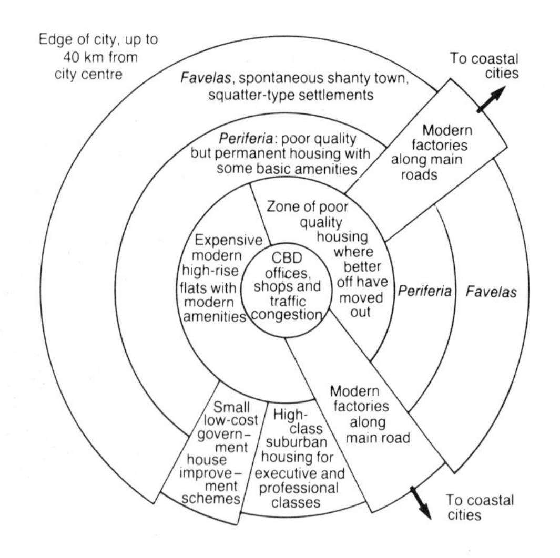

4.55 Land-use model of a Latin American city. Unique to the culture and economic development of the continent, the Latin American city displays elements of both the concentric and sector land-use models where industrial sectors develop along important natural routeways.

amenities, refuse collection and public transport systems. The demand for planned and serviced housing has long since outstripped supply and has led to the growth of many **spontaneous settlements** (shanty towns or slum colonies) on the fringe of São Paulo or along the steeply sided valleys of the main rivers.

Latin American cities such as São Paulo display a marked contrast between a wealthy minority and a poverty-stricken majority. The elite continue to occupy a grossly disproportionate amount of land in relation to their number: it has been estimated that less than 5% of São Paulo's population occupy over 25% of the land. The city's pavement dwelling population is now as high as 4%.

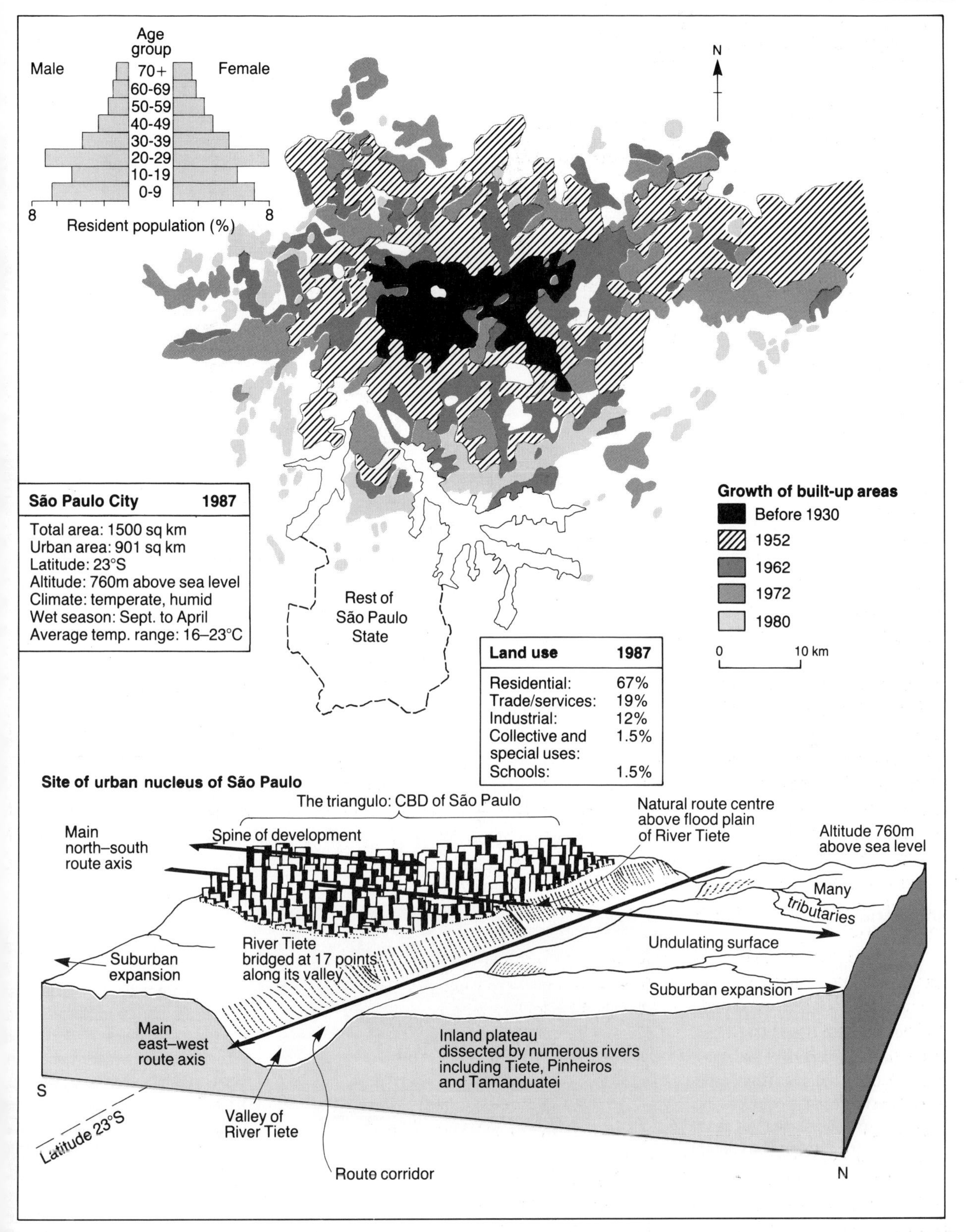

Age group
Male
Female
70+
60-69
50-59
40-49
30-39
20-29
10-19
0-9
8
8
Resident population (%)
N
São Paulo City 1987
Total area: 1500 sq km
Urban area: 901 sq km
Latitude: 23°S
Altitude: 760m above sea level
Climate: temperate, humid
Wet season: Sept. to April
Average temp. range: 16–23°C
Rest of São Paulo State
Land use 1987
Residential: 67%
Trade/services: 19%
Industrial: 12%
Collective and special uses: 1.5%
Schools: 1.5%
Growth of built-up areas
Before 1930
1952
1962
1972
1980
0
10 km
Site of urban nucleus of São Paulo
The triangulo: CBD of São Paulo
Main north–south route axis
Spine of development
Natural route centre above flood plain of River Tiete
Altitude 760m above sea level
Many tributaries
Undulating surface
Suburban expansion
River Tiete bridged at 17 points along its valley
Suburban expansion
Main east–west route axis
Inland plateau dissected by numerous rivers including Tiete, Pinheiros and Tamanduatei
S
Latitude 23°S
Valley of River Tiete
Route corridor
N

4.56 São Paulo profile

São Paulo: Some Facts

São Paulo spread

The largest city in Brazil is situated 100 km inland and at an altitude of 850 m. The city has now spread to cover over 1500 km² and each year expands a further 65 km² around the confluence of the rivers Tietê and Tamanduatei (4.57). There are 11 main commuter corridors leading to an 8-km wide, CBD known as the Triangulo (4.58). São Paulo has now spread south to Billings reservoir and expansion is also planned along the east–west axis of the Tietê river.

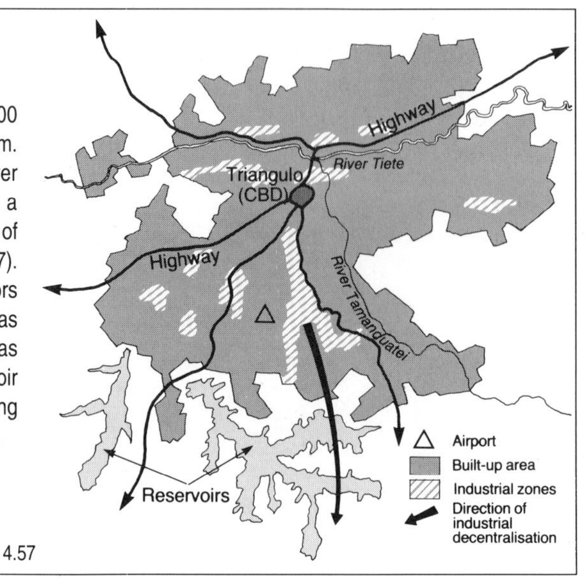

4.57

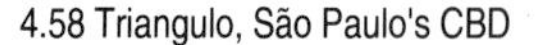
4.58 Triangulo, São Paulo's CBD

Population change

In the period between 1950 and 1980 the population of São Paulo trebled as rural to urban migration dramatically increased the official city population, and the proportion of people living in the many spontaneous shanty settlements (known as *favelas*) rose to 40% (4.59).

Million people
0
2
4
6
8
10
12
14
16
18
1870
1880
1890
1900
1910
1920
1930
1940
1950
1960
1970
1980
1990
2000
São Paulo
Favelas (est.)

4.59 Population growth

Facts and figures

The population of São Paulo was c
16 million in 1990. The city houses 1
of the Brazilian people and produ
49% of the net industrial produc
Brazil. The city metro, opened in 1
carries 800000 Paulistanos daily (4
and the city's major problems
congestion and growing air pollu
seem insoluble at present.

Industrial giant

4.60 Industrial park

São Paulo is the industrial heart and magnet of Brazil. There are 11 major industrial districts encompassing over 25 000 industrial units. The city's industrial base includes the coffee industry, steel, cars, oil and petrochemicals, textiles and food processing. São Paulo's advantages of cheap hydro-electric power, excellent communications network, ready workforce, and government investment in high-technology industry have led to 16% of the country's factories being located in the city, employing 34% of the labour force. The recession of the 1980s however has seen the loss of 750 000 jobs and a policy of decentralising industrial developments is also contributing to increasing job losses.

Residential inequalities

São Paulo is a growing city of contra
(4.64 and 4.65): affluence and
poverty are to be found side by s
Near the city centre there are la
areas of high-rise blocks provid
homes for the wealthy who make
only 10% of the city's population.
there is great inequality in hous
provision within the city. With ove
million poor inhabitants and a daily in
of 1300 poor migrants, there is
increasing polarity of wealth and pove
The poor and the migrants, who acco
for over 45% of the population, liv

Developing City

Administrative regions

The municipality of São Paulo is divided into 17 Administrative Regions (ARs) as shown on map 4.62. These are responsible for garbage collection, street cleaning, small-scale public works, and overseeing any building work done in the area.

1	Pirituba	10	Centro
2	Freguesia	11	Lapa
3	Santana	12	Butanta
4	Maria	13	Pinheiros
5	Penha	14	Mariana
6	San Miguel	15	Ipiranga
7	Guaianases	16	Santo Amara
8	Prudente	17	Campo Limpo
9	Mooca		

4.62

Moving in

It is estimated that São Paulo is growing at the rate of over 550 000 people annually and that it receives 1300 migrants each day (4.63). The city's population growth rate reached a peak of 6.1% in the 1970s and slowed to 4.5% in 1989. The city houses 2 million migrants from the poverty stricken North-East region alone.

4.63

4.65

favelas (4.65) usually located along main routeways or on the city periphery, on wasteland, in river valleys and on steep hillsides. These shanty towns of makeshift houses have few or no services, and conditions are often unsanitary. The situation is exacerbated by Brazil's inflationary economy; even those in well-paid jobs cannot afford other than *favela* housing. The uncontrolled development of peripheral housing is seen as the most pressing problem for São Paulo as the demand outstrips supply and leads to the creation of 200 temporary houses every day.

CHAPTER 4

Core São Paulo

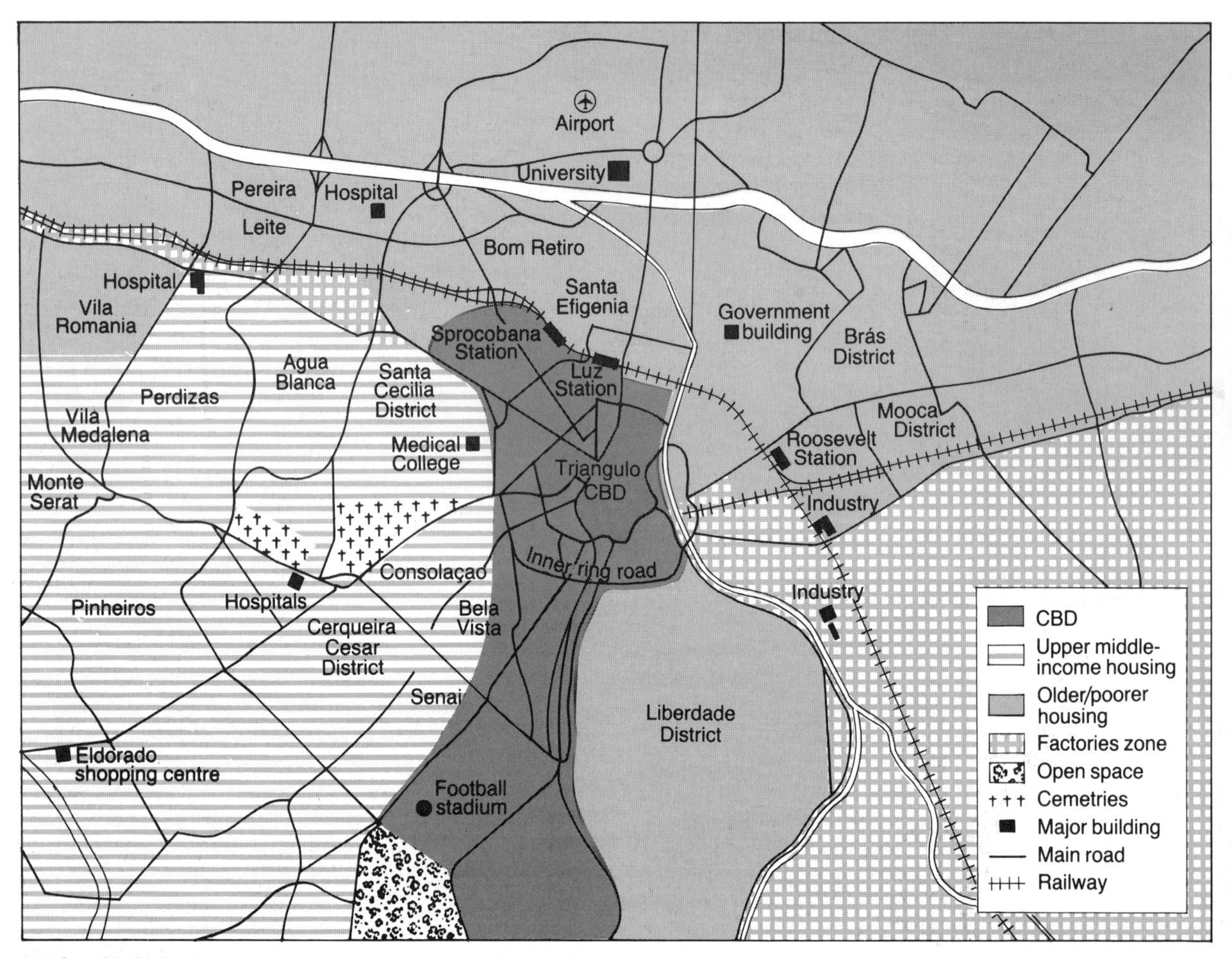

4.66 Core São Paulo

The central area or core of São Paulo occupies an area of over 100 km^2 on a site originally established in 1554. The original settlement developed as a small but important route centre. The real stimulus to its development was the nineteenth-century coffee industry. The growth, processing, storage and export of the product were overseen in São Paulo, and the need for finance, transport and administrative structure brought about 400% urban growth between 1890 and 1900 alone.

By the time of the worldwide economic recession in the 1930s, São Paulo had developed a good infrastructure and had become the social, economic and political centre of the country. In 1934 the population of the city reached 1 million and the historic core or urban nucleus remained the city's central area. In addition to the tree-lined boulevards of expensive housing in the Consolação and Santa Cecilia districts, more upper- and middle-income residences were constructed on increasingly valuable land in the city centre. Along the main highways and railways new factories and zones of workers' houses were rapidly constructed.

After the Second World War, the city grew at a fast rate, as industrialisation attracted migrants from rural areas in search of work in factories or the construction business. The expansion in manufacturing led to the development of the tertiary sector which in turn led to many new developments within the core area (4.66).

Today São Paulo has a modern centre of high-rise buildings: very few old buildings remain. The pace of redevelopment has contributed to the dominance of the core area where over 170 000 students are educated annually, and most of the city's elite live. The Triangulo (4.67) is a vast central business district

4.67 The Triangulo

4.68 The S-shaped Copan housing complex is in the centre of the CBD

with dense, complex road networks, shopping areas, banks (33% of all Brazilian cash is deposited here) entertainment districts and administration areas. The core has twelve times as many hospital beds per person as the rest of the megacity and there are 770 hypermarkets within the area.

São Paulo is the commercial, retail and cultural centre of Brazil. Its core area is affluent and crowded. There is a shortage of open space, and land values are extremely high. Traffic congestion, litter, street crime and growing air pollution (at an altitude of 760 metres vehicle exhaust emissions cause dense smog problems) are common problems, as in most megacities.

But in contrast to many cities of developed countries, core São Paulo has a high resident population of over 3 million, who live in upper- and middle-income housing districts close to the CBD (4.68).The facades of the Western-style high-rise city centre apartment blocks conceal major urban problems and inequalities. The wealthy residential districts to the west of the Triangulo can be thought of as elite islands within a sea of urban poverty.

> São Paulo, more than any other city reflects the social and economic contradictions being experienced by the whole of Brazil. The space between the city centre and the periphery is best measured not in kilometres but in terms of social distance.
>
> Mario Covas, Mayor of São Paulo

Favelas

São Paulo has been called a megacity of slums and skyscrapers. Like many cities in developing countries, it has an inner-city elite area fairly close to the CBD and several enclaves of higher-class residences within a relatively short distance of the centre. But the outer areas of the city contain vast settlements of poor quality housing.

The major urban expansion of São Paulo has been associated with the large-scale influx of rural migrants from the 1960s onwards. Many experts have suggested that the rate of rural–urban migration is indicative of the severity of problems in rural areas rather than the level of attraction of large urban agglomerations. Among Brazil's rural problems are natural disasters such as severe drought in the north-east, overpopulation, soil erosion, inefficient agricultural practices, limited food production, and lack of rural services (schools, hospitals). Rural people are attracted to megacities such as São Paulo in anticipation of a higher quality of life, better-paid jobs in factories, improved social services and housing, more reliable sources of food, and a wide range of accessible entertainments.

With rates of rural–urban migration in excess of 1300 each day, São Paulo has little chance of providing sufficient housing to meet the demand. As a result the majority of migrants must find or make their own accommodation, and the reality of city life is very different from their original perceptions. Studies of migration to a megacity (4.69) have revealed a complex system of intra-city movement. Most migrants move into the spontaneous settlements known as ***favelas*** on the outskirts of São Paulo (4.70, 4.71). Some *favelas* are the size of towns but, because they develop spontaneously as more shanty houses are built, they lack basic services (4.72). Many *favelas* have an informal structure based around a grid network of roads with housing blocks arranged on a 'village' basis. Some *favelas* have gradually developed their own internal structure and are viewed positively by their inhabitants. Many favelas have been upgraded both by their residents and the city government into suburbs or *periferia*.

4.69 Migration to a megacity

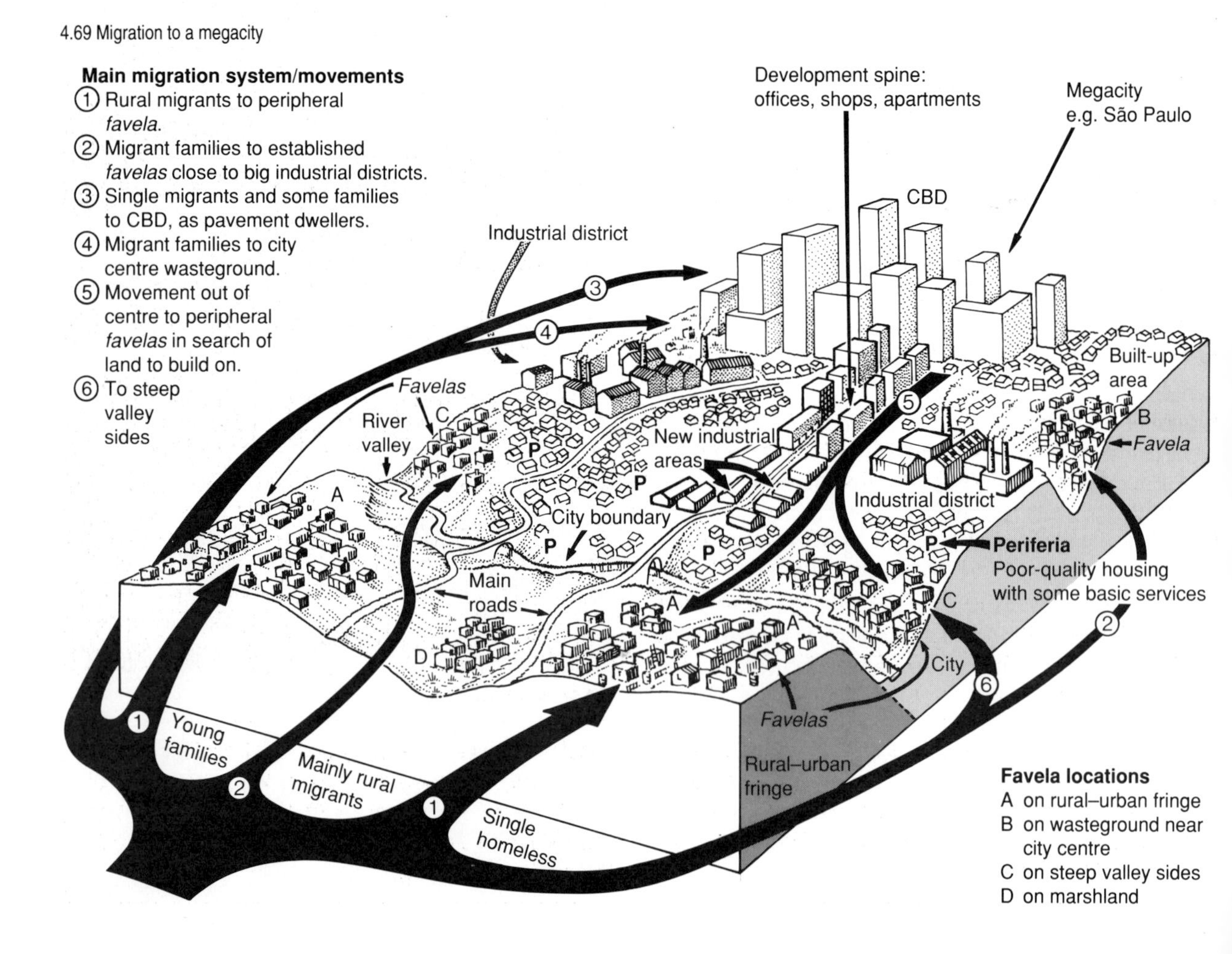

Positive aspects of *favelas*
- Provide homes for rural migrants.
- Cheap homes for people on low incomes
- Easy to construct or rebuild
- Large pool of labour for city
- Community spirit develops in otherwise large, anonymous megacity

Negative aspects of *favelas*
- Built on illegal sites
- Unhealthy living conditions
- Unsafe houses
- Urban eyesores
- High unemployment levels within resident population
- Often centres of crime, vice and violence
- Centres of mass poverty

4.71 Hillside *favela*

Characteristics of *favelas*
- Develop on a **variety of sites**, such as steep, unstable hillsides, marshland, wasteground, rubbish tips, or areas liable to flood, most of which are **illegal**.
- Inhabited by **low socio-economic groups** within a megacity such as São Paulo.
- **Population density is usually high** with families living, eating and sleeping in one room.
- **Accommodation** mainly comprises one-roomed **makeshift shacks** constructed of corrugated iron, cardboard, sackcloth and plywood.
- **Lack of basic services** such as running water, sewerage, electricity and gas, and street lighting.
- Lack of sewage disposal and refuse collection leads to **spread of epidemic diseases** such as diarrhoea, typhoid and cholera. *Favelas* often have large foetid rubbish dumps colonised by vermin, another source of disease.
- Many inhabitants are in **poor health**. Diseases spread quickly as drinking water and sewage are inadequately separated and water taps are comunally used, sometimes by thousands each day.
- **Communications are often poor**, with few bus services to the city shops or to work, and only dirt roads. There are no postal deliveries, phones, or private cars.
- The **unemployment rate is high**. Those *favelas* located close to factories may have a higher proportion of permanent wage earners but, because of the inflationary economy of the country, these workers are unable to afford to move to permanent housing.

4.72 Characteristics of *favelas*

- **Social services are mostly non-existent**. Education is very limited. There are few doctors, nurses, mid-wives or dentists, and life expectancy within the *favelas* is often less than two-thirds the life expectancy of higher socio-economic groups in the same city.

CHAPTER 4

Urban Planning

In contrast to the cities of developed countries which grew up as independent centres for the manufacture, exchange and consumption of goods and services, megacities such as São Paulo are geared to production and exchange of goods, not to their consumption. Most people live on a subsistence level or by informal (non-tax-paying) means within the city economy. The high levels of consumption are confined to the rich elite who live on a formal (tax-paying) level. This results in a polarisation of lifestyles revealed in housing inequalities (pp.132–135) common to many developing world cities. It also means there is a lack of finance to pay for city planning since so many of the residents do not pay taxes. The uncontrolled development of peripheral shanty settlements, and their associated problems (see p.135), is a major concern in most megacities. Development plans to bring about social/environmental improvements have been portrayed as the best solution to these problems. But these plans take many different forms, and are open to criticism (4.73).

Criticisms of developing megacities

- Planning lacks co-ordination and organisation across the city.
- Priorities are unclear in most development plans.
- Urban planning fails to take into account rural planning.
- Planning is based on 'Western' models.
- Much planning is thwarted by rich elites in order to maintain the status quo.
- Land ownership is in the hands of the rich minority who are unwilling to give it up.
- Schemes for *favelas* take little account of local opinion or needs.
- 'Showpiece' development is considered more important than the needs of the poor *favela* population

4.73 Criticisms of development plans for megacities

Some experts believe that megacities interact with their rural hinterlands in a positive way, providing processed goods, services and information in return for raw materials, such as coffee, and labour. They think that better planning and improvements to megacities will help to spread progress to rural areas. Others argue that megacities such as São Paulo exploit rural areas, buying raw materials as cheaply as possible and selling back expensive processed goods. Proponents of the negative view of megacities believe that the rural hinterland is destabilised by urban growth. They say that urban development plans and improvement schemes act merely to attract even more rural migrants, especially the young, leaving poverty-stricken rural areas.

In recent times, urban improvement schemes and development planning have included the following approaches.

Trickle-down development focuses on wealth creation which it is hoped will eventually be passed on (trickle down) to poorer inhabitants. It concentrates on development of a high-rise CBD with large hotels, office blocks and prestige apartments. Critics state that wealth remains concentrated within the elite minority who hold political and economic power.

4.74 Community housing project in São Paulo.

BRAZIL

People power

São Paulo, South America's largest city, is also one of the fastest growing in the world. Like Mexico City and Tokyo, the only two cities on earth that are bigger, it is on a scale which is truly staggering for those of us from 'normal cities'. São Paulo is driven ever outward and upwards by the engine of economic growth that throbs at its centre.

The badges of the mega-city are everywhere. The air is saturated with ethanol gasoline pollution. The main streets are clogged with a perpetual traffic jam. High-rise buildings shoot upwards like the mercury in a thermometer on a hot Brazilian summer afternoon. But it's the scale of it all that overwhelms. In São Paulo there is not one high-rise area but several, punctuated every so often by plush low-density areas like Jardim where the mansions of the wealthy crouch behind the thick masonry of security walls.

Paulista, the city's principal financial avenue, is a canyon through which a stream of near stagnant traffic inches its way between precipitous walls of 30-storey Brazilian banks. Here you find the motor and the contradictions of the world's eighth-largest economy. The modernity of the financial centre is dramatically set off against some of the worst slums on the continent – home to more than 10 per cent of São Paulo's people.

Over 50 per cent of the city's 12.5 million people have migrated from the impoverished north-east of Brazil. It's an old story: poor people either squeezed out by the expansion of large-scale agriculture or fleeing poverty and starvation. They squeezed their way into the cracks of the city through settling in the backyards of family members already there, illegally subdividing already minute plots or simply invading land and squatting there.

Not surprisingly these poor areas or *favelas* have been largely ignored by all levels of government. During the long night of military dictatorship that stretched from the 1960s to the 1980s any protest by *favela* residents was met by police batons and the arrest of 'subversives'. As a result one of the world's wealthiest cities provides services for the poor that barely enable them to survive.

But there is a chink of light. These marginalized people have campaigned for a better and fairer design to their city through a political party, the Partido do Trabalhadores (PT). And to the surprise of many, perhaps even the party itself, the PT swept to victory in the municipal elections of November 1988. The new Mayor, Luiza Erundina de Souza, is an immigrant from the North-East. She is also a militant of the *favelas*.

The PT views urban design as a battle over the allocation of resources. On one side are the residents of the *favelas*, organized into over 1,000 base groups. On the other side is the old guard of real-estate developers and transportation monopolies whose interests have always shaped the physical fabric of São Paulo.

They key to addressing the inequalities built into the design of São Paulo is the decentralization of power, the PT believes. They are breaking the city down into 20 regions and are proposing that these should be further subdivided into neighbourhoods. Local public assemblies could soon be making decisions about parks and recreation centres.

If the PT is successful this could be a major breakthrough for locally controlled community development in Latin America. Other elements of the PT program are no less ambitious – a 'war' on land speculation, more money for poor areas, and support for self-help housing. The stakes are high: the redesign of one of the biggest cities in the world.

New Internationalist, December 1989

4.75

Community housing: self-help schemes (4.74) encourage local *favela* communities to plan and then self-build basic, serviced housing in an attempt to increase their inhabitants' commitment to the city and its improvement. Some critics describe this approach as 'taking aspirins for cancer', because it addresses the symptoms and not the cause of the urban problems.

Basic social and political change (4.75). This approach is based on the belief that urban inequalities are the result of the control of wealth and power by a minority of rich elites, and that improvement will only happen with political change.

With its change in power structure from regional government to local decision-making (see 4.74), São Paulo has proceeded along the path of urban improvement and at the same time has adopted a policy of decentralisation of industry and new residential development to its rural hinterland.

Many experts argue that the only real answer to rapid urbanisation and all its associated misery is the introduction of a long-term rural development programme. They say that the megacities of the developing world, such as São Paulo, are approaching an urban apocalypse and that economic and environmental disaster is inevitable without clear and fair strategies to improve the quality of life for all their people and not just their rapidly expanding urban population.

Questions

Q URBANISATION IN BRAZIL

1 (a) Why is urbanisation a growing concern in Brazil?
(b) Describe the pattern of urbanisation in Brazil.
(c) Describe the distribution of cities in Brazil.
(d) Write brief notes to explain each of the following: static agrarian society, rapidly urbanised society, rural migration.
(e) Name Brazil's three largest cities.
(f) Explain why there has been a rapid rural to urban movement in Brazil.
(g) What effect has government policy had on Brazil's urban development?
(h) Draw combined line graphs to illustrate the data given in table 4.54.
(i) Where is Brazil's Randstad?

Q MEGACITY, BRAZIL

2 (a) Annotate your own simple copy of the block diagram in 4.56 with details of São Paulo's site and location.
(b) Contrast the layout of a Latin American city such as São Paulo with that of a Western city such as London.
(c) Study diagram 1. Explain the distribution of wealth in São Paulo.
(d) Describe and account for the distribution of industrial districts within São Paulo (see map 4.57).
(e) Explain why spontaneous settlements are necessary within developing cities such as São Paulo.

Diagram 1 Distribution of wealth in a developing city

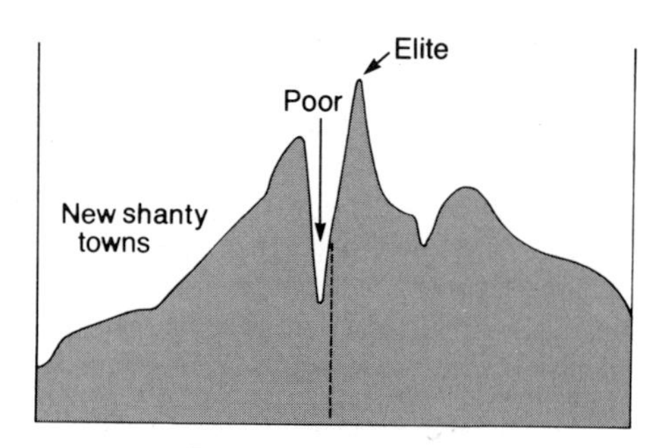

Q SÃO PAULO: SOME FACTS

3 (a) Make a simple copy of map 4.57, including the key.
(b) Find evidence in the information on pages 128–9 to support each of the following statements.
São Paulo is
- Brazil's largest city
- a city of greatly contrasting wealth
- a highly diversified industrial centre.

(c) Make a 'Did you know' information leaflet on São Paulo using the information on pages 130–1.
(d) Describe residential inequalities within São Paulo.
(e) Make a simple sketch of photo 4.58. Annotate your sketch to show at least six pieces of evidence supporting the view that this is São Paulo's CBD.
(f) Describe the change in population of São Paulo between 1950 and 1980.

Q CORE SÃO PAULO

4 (a) Describe the urban landscape shown in photo 4.67.
(b) What is the population of the CBD?
(c) Make your own copy of map 4.66 then describe the layout of São Paulo's CBD.
(d) List the main centrifugal and centripetal forces acting upon the CBD.
(e) What influence has the past had on the Triangulo?
(f) Compare the problems of São Paulo's CBD with those of London's CBD.
(g) To what extent do you agree with the statement that the wealthy residential districts of the Triangulo are elite islands in a sea of urban poverty.
(h) Use diagram 2 as the base for a summary diagram of the characteristics of the CBD of São Paulo.

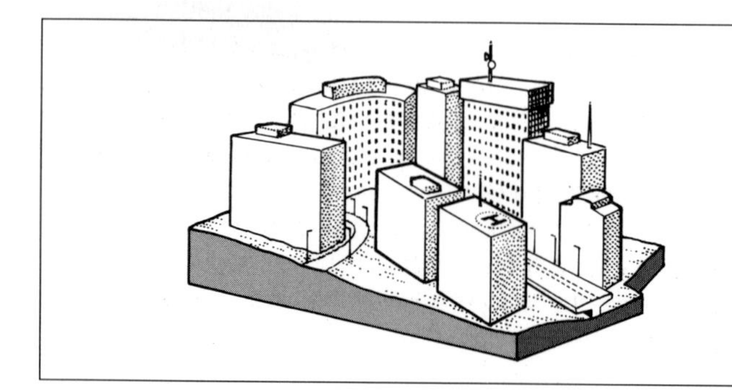

Diagram 2 São Paulo's CBD

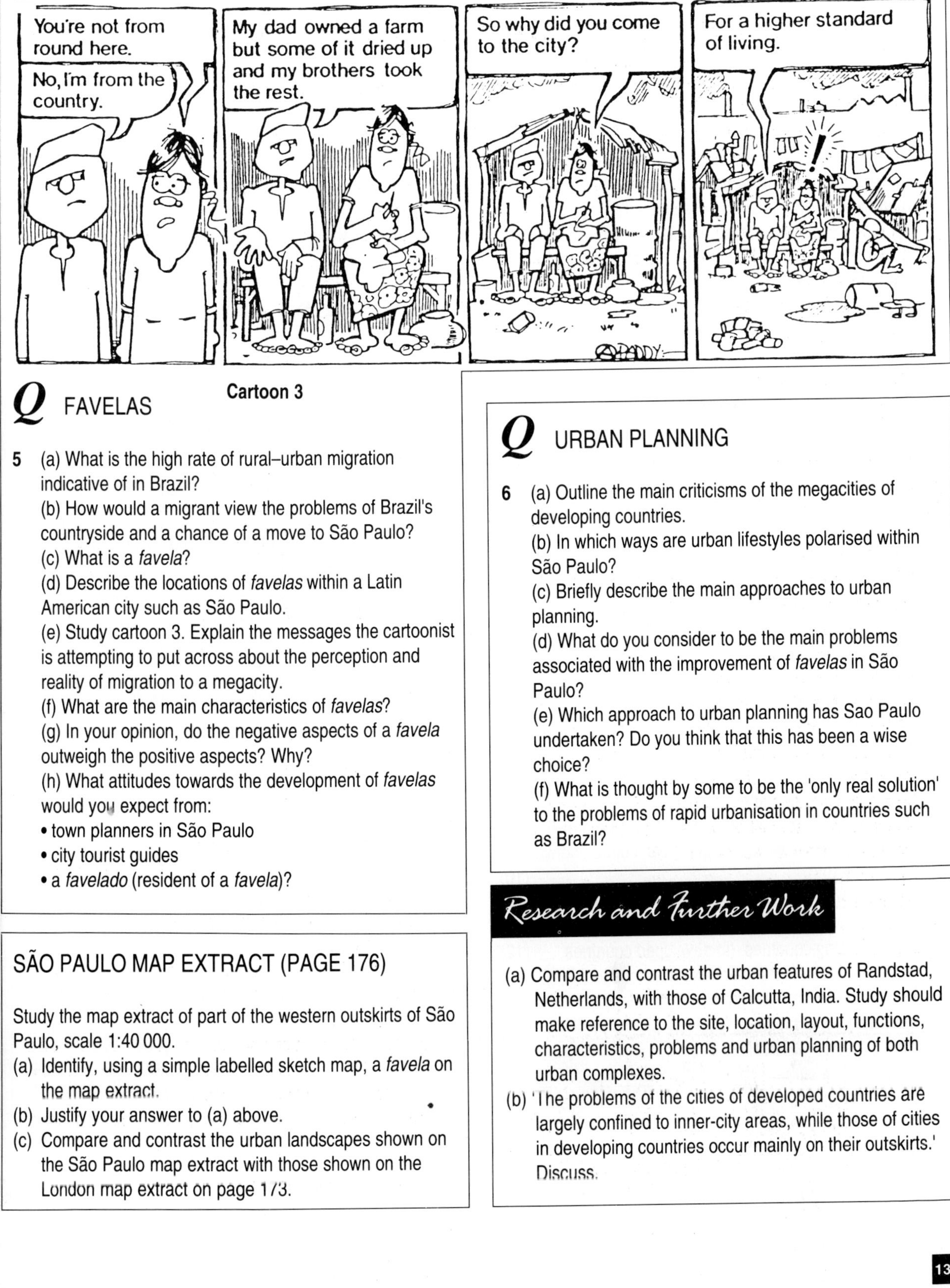

Cartoon 3

Q FAVELAS

5 (a) What is the high rate of rural–urban migration indicative of in Brazil?
(b) How would a migrant view the problems of Brazil's countryside and a chance of a move to São Paulo?
(c) What is a *favela*?
(d) Describe the locations of *favelas* within a Latin American city such as São Paulo.
(e) Study cartoon 3. Explain the messages the cartoonist is attempting to put across about the perception and reality of migration to a megacity.
(f) What are the main characteristics of *favelas*?
(g) In your opinion, do the negative aspects of a *favela* outweigh the positive aspects? Why?
(h) What attitudes towards the development of *favelas* would you expect from:
- town planners in São Paulo
- city tourist guides
- a *favelado* (resident of a *favela*)?

SÃO PAULO MAP EXTRACT (PAGE 176)

Study the map extract of part of the western outskirts of São Paulo, scale 1:40 000.
(a) Identify, using a simple labelled sketch map, a *favela* on the map extract.
(b) Justify your answer to (a) above.
(c) Compare and contrast the urban landscapes shown on the São Paulo map extract with those shown on the London map extract on page 173.

Q URBAN PLANNING

6 (a) Outline the main criticisms of the megacities of developing countries.
(b) In which ways are urban lifestyles polarised within São Paulo?
(c) Briefly describe the main approaches to urban planning.
(d) What do you consider to be the main problems associated with the improvement of *favelas* in São Paulo?
(e) Which approach to urban planning has Sao Paulo undertaken? Do you think that this has been a wise choice?
(f) What is thought by some to be the 'only real solution' to the problems of rapid urbanisation in countries such as Brazil?

Research and Further Work

(a) Compare and contrast the urban features of Randstad, Netherlands, with those of Calcutta, India. Study should make reference to the site, location, layout, functions, characteristics, problems and urban planning of both urban complexes.
(b) 'The problems of the cities of developed countries are largely confined to inner-city areas, while those of cities in developing countries occur mainly on their outskirts.' Discuss.

Exam Style Questions

Answer either question 1 or question 2.

1 Study map 1 carefully.
(a) Describe and account for the layout and land uses shown on this model of a city in the developing world. (6)
(b) To what extent is the model an accurate representation of the layout of a named city of the developing world that you have studied? (4)
(c) With the aid of a sketch population pyramid, describe the population structure of a city in the developing world which has been affected by large-scale migration from its rural hinterland. (5)
(d) Referring to any two named cities, one from the developing world and one from the developed world:
(i) contrast their urbanisation processes,
(ii) compare their urban problems,
(iii) evaluate the effectiveness of the planning approaches adopted to deal with their respective problems. (15)

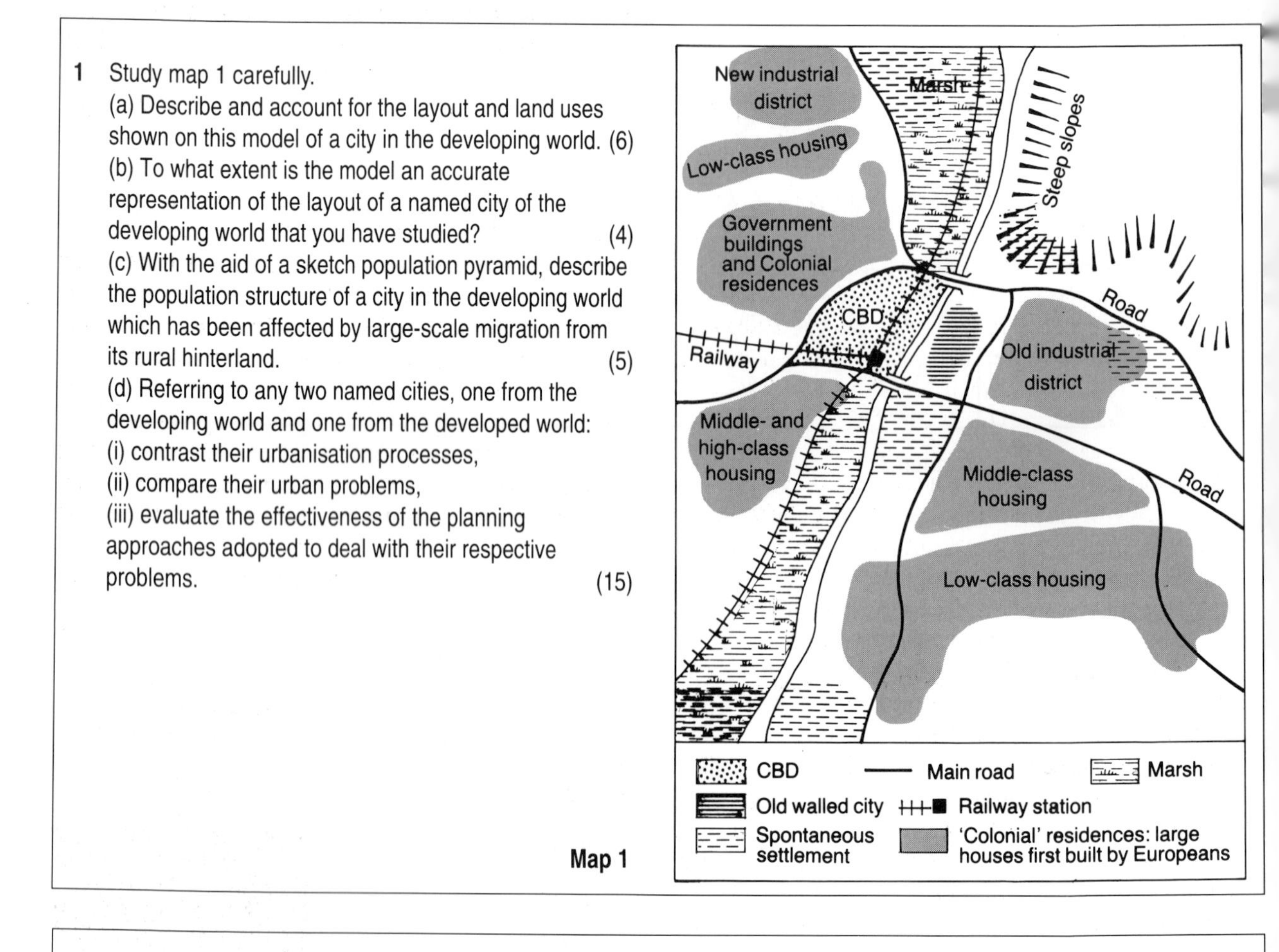

Map 1

2 Study the table on the right carefully.
(a) Describe and account for changes in the growth and distribution of the world's major urban centres between 1950 and 1987. (10)
(b) Identify and discuss the main problems arising from urban growth in
(i) developing countries, (ii) developed countries. (12)
(c) Contrast attempts to achieve solutions to the problems of urban growth in both developing and developed countries. (8)

Table The world's major urban areas, 1950 and 1987

	Population (millions)		
	1950		1987
New York	12.3	Mexico City	19.3
Tokyo/Yokohama	8.6	Tokyo/Yokohama	17.1
London	8.2	São Paulo	16.1
Shanghai	6.1	New York	16.3
Chicago	4.9	Shanghai	11.9
Paris	4.7	Calcutta	11.3
Calcutta	4.6	Los Angeles	11.1
Moscow	4.4	Buenos Aires	10.9
Los Angeles	4.0	Rio de Janeiro	10.5
Buenos Aires	3.7	Seoul	10.3
Leningrad	3.0	Bombay	10.2
Philadelphia	2.9	London	7.2

DEVELOPMENT AND HEALTH

What is Development?

The world is divided by levels of wealth and poverty with the richest 10% ('the haves') controlling 60% of the world's wealth and the remainder ('the have nots') economically tied to the rich countries. The Agricultural and Industrial Revolutions of the eighteenth and nineteenth centuries effectively divided the world into those countries which were involved and those which were not involved. Countries which industrialised later have been trying to catch up with wealthy countries. But the contrast between the rich and poor is greater now than it has ever been as the wealth accumulates in the industrialised countries. In the middle of the last century the difference in per capita income between developed and developing countries was in the order of about 2 to 1. In 1986 it was in the order of 17 to 1 ($10 700 average GNP per capita in developed countries; $640 average GNP per capita in developing countries); see 5.1.

The poorer countries of the world are undeveloped in terms of technological application and economic organisation. The development process is about changing economies and social organisation to reduce the gap between rich and poor nations. These poor countries have been given a number of labels such as **Third World** and **least developed countries** but since this chapter is concerned with development and health the term **developing countries** is a more appropriate label.

Measurement of development usually involves examination of a range of economic and demographic characteristics. This form of measurement shows that, although very poor countries are near the bottom of the scale for most factors, some countries may be high on one scale and low on another. This confirms that there isn't a clear divide between developed and developing countries and that throughout this century some countries have progressed to higher levels of **economic development.** The different levels of wealth suggest that there is a 'ladder of development' up which nations can climb. Some nations have further to climb than others and some have more difficulties to overcome than others. Although some nations have made substantial progress, notably the newly industrialised countries (NICs) of South-east Asia and Latin America, many are falling further behind and the number of people in poverty is increasing.

In 1971 the United Nations drew up a list of 24 countries which it called LDCs (least developed countries). These LDCs were identified on the basis of three criteria: **GNP (gross national product)** per capita of less than $100; manufacturing share of GNP less than 10%; and an adult literacy rate of 20% or less. (GNP per capita is the total value of goods and services provided by the economy of a country in one year divided by the number of people in the country.) By 1981 the criteria had been slightly modified and the list of these poorest countries was extended to 31 (5.2).These poorest nations of the world are largely, though not exclusively, tropical. Most of the world's poor live in two **poverty belts,** one stretching from the Sahara to Malawi and the other from Ethiopia to East Asia (5.4).

In order to develop and increase wealth the developing countries need access to advanced technologies which come from the industrialised nations. The transfer of this technology which can create wealth is controlled by multinational companies (also known as transnational corporations) who concentrate their attention on relatively few developing countries: those which offer them advantageous economic conditions. Other countries have to rely on assistance from aid packages, unless they are fortunate enough to have valuable natural resources, such as oil, to exploit. Without the technology to develop industry, many developing countries will be unable to climb the development ladder. Even those countries that have attracted outside investment don't always have control over the decision making and can't spread the benefits throughout the economy.

5.1 Rich world, poor world

Poor World
3931 million people
Average GNP per capita
$640

Rich World
1198 million people
Average GNP per capita
$10 700

5.2 The 30 least developed countries

Afghanistan	Comoros	Nepal
Bangladesh	Ethiopia	Niger
Benin	The Gambia	Rwanda
Bhutan	Guinea	Somalia
Botswana	Guinea-Bissau	Sudan
Burkina Faso	Haiti	Tanzania
Burundi	Laos	Uganda
Cape Verde	Lesotho	Western Samoa
Central African Republic	Malawi	Yemen (Republic of)*
Chad	Maldives	
	Mali	

*the Yemen Arab Republic and People's Democratic Republic of Yemen unified in 1990

CHAPTER 5

Measuring Development

Before development can be measured, the characteristics which separate the developed and developing countries have to be agreed on. The following list of characteristics are good indicators of developing countries:

- most people work in agriculture, largely subsistence farming;
- most people are very poor and don't have all of life's basic necessities – sanitation, clean water, decent housing, access to medical facilities and education;
- high incidence of disease, with high infant mortality;
- high levels of illiteracy;
- rapid population growth, large percentage of population under 15 years of age.

Development is a relative term since a country is only developed or developing by comparison with others. A number of measures may be used to compare countries: **GNP per capita** is one of the most common measures (5.3). However GNP per capita is not without faults as a measure of development. In many poor countries a large proportion of the population is engaged in subsistence agriculture and GNP takes no account of this production. GNP per capita is also an average measure which conceals differences in wealth distribution. GNP per capita could be rising without benefiting the bulk of the population because in many developing countries, as in some developed countries, much of the wealth is held by a small proportion of the population. This inequality can be measured by comparing the share of nation's income earned by the rich and poor. In Peru, for example, 70% of the country's wealth is held by 20% of the population compared with 38% of the wealth in the USA held by the wealthiest 20%. A number of other measures can be used as alternatives to GNP per capita.

Alternative measures of development

The following list of alternative measures of development is not exhaustive. Each factor reflects in some way the characteristics of developing countries mentioned earlier.

Diet The quality and quantity of food intake in developing countries tends to be lower than in developed countries. Daily food supply is usually measured as the energy value (in calories) of an average diet in a country. An average person needs around

5.3 World population and per capita GNP. This map shows relative population size, as represented by area, and the shading used indicates the GNP per capita

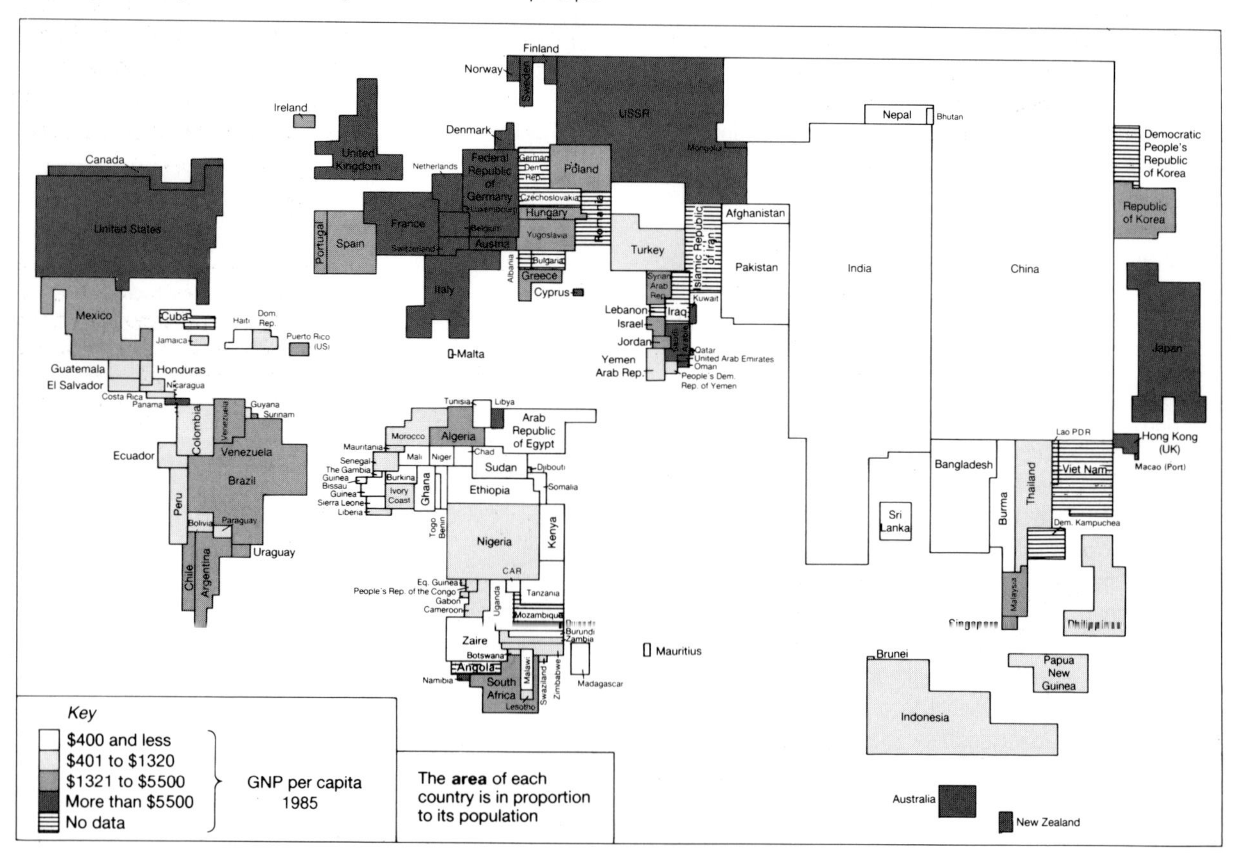

2450 calories per day to maintain good health. In developing countries the average intake is around 2000 calories as opposed to 3600 in the developed world. Sometimes, average protein intake is used as a measure because some diets in developing countries are both monotonous and lacking in protein. Average intake of animal protein in developing countries is around 50 grams per day while it is around 110 grams per day in developed countries.

Demographic characteristics Developing countries generally have high birth rates and high population growth rates. The average crude birth rate for developed countries is around 15 per thousand inhabitants while for developing countries the average is around 31 per thousand. The average population growth rate for developed countries is around 0.6% while for developing countries it is around 2.1%.

Medical facilities tend to be poorer in developing countries and this is often revealed by high infant mortality rates (the number of infant deaths per 1000 births). Infant mortality figures tend to have a significant effect on life expectancy figures which are also influenced by availability of medical care. The number of hospital beds or doctors per 1000 people are also used as measures of medical care but these measures do not give an indication of the distribution of services and in many developing countries hospitals and doctors are concentrated in urban areas.

Energy consumption per person in developing countries tends to be much lower than in developed countries because of lower levels of mechanisation, lower car ownership and limited industrial development. Energy consumption is usually measured in kilograms of coal equivalent (the amount of power that can be derived from a kilogram of coal regardless of the fuel that is actually used).

Agricultural labour force When expressed as a percentage of the country's total labour force the agricultural labour force is a useful guide to the country's level of development. The mechanisation of farming in developed countries has reduced the need for agricultural labour while traditional labour-intensive methods still predominate in developing countries.

Literacy rates The adult literacy rate indicates the percentage of adults who can read and write; this is a useful indication of education provision in a country.

To avoid the failings of one measure of development a number of measures can be combined into one index. A quality of life index that combines information on life expectancy, calorie intake and literacy can illustrate the failings of single measures such as GNP per capita.

For example, Costa Rica has a GNP per capita of around $1420, a relatively low to middle income level. However life expectancy at birth is 74 years, higher than the average for developed countries, and calorie intake per person per day is 2766 calories which is well above the average for developing countries. The literacy rate is also high at 90% which again is equivalent to many developed nations. These figures illustrate that although Costa Rica is a developing country when judged by its GNP it has been able to promote development in health, food supply and education.

The **physical quality of life index** (PQLI) is one example of a combined measurement. It combines infant mortality, literacy and life expectancy information and then rates countries on a 0 to 100 scale. The most developed countries like the United Kingdom have PQLIs of over 90 while the least developed countries such as Ethiopia have PQLIs of less than 30 (5.4).

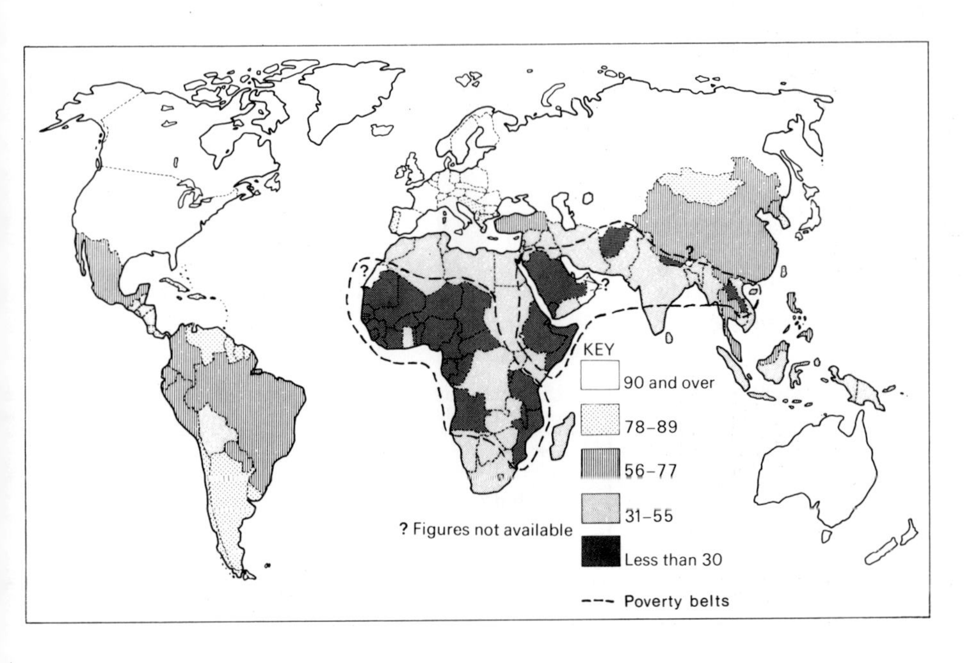

5.4 World physical quality of life map. Countries with a high PQLI are developed whilst countries with a low PQLI are developing. Two belts of poverty can be picked out from this map. The poorest countries have a PQLI of less than 30.

Patterns of Development

Since the Second World War many of the factors that are used as indicators of development, such as life expectancy, have improved in developing countries. Average life expectancy in developing countries is now 60 years, a figure that wasn't achieved by Western European countries until after the First World War. Much of the improvement is due to falling infant mortality brought about by improvements in living conditions.

The development of the world's poorer nations has also become a more important political issue and many of the United Nations' agencies play an active part in promoting development. The impact of the World Health Organisation (WHO) in co-ordinating programmes to control major communicable diseases such as smallpox and bubonic plague has been significant. Both of these diseases have been almost eliminated. Malaria and cholera have also been targeted by WHO and deaths from these diseases have been significantly reduced.

Education has also seen significant progress in developing countries: in 1950 pupils in primary schools numbered around 70 million; by 1970 200 million; by 1985 350 million. To maintain the 1985 enrolment rate to the end of the century, educational facilities and teachers need to increase by around 50%. The higher investment and enrolement rates in education in developed countries ensure that they maintain a lead over developing countries (5.5 and 5.6).

However, food intake per person has not increased markedly since the Second World War. This is not due to a straightforward lack of food in the world, because more food is produced than is required to feed all the world's population. The poor go hungry because they cannot afford the food or it cannot be easily distributed to scattered rural settlements. Each year around 40 million people die from hunger-related diseases and on current projections around 600 million people are likely to be severely undernourished by 2000.

The most developed countries of the world lie in the temperate zones and this tends to suggest that there is a climatic factor which influences development. Certainly aspects of tropical climates can create problems for agriculture but it would be wrong to assume that the conditions in the Tropics are responsible for the lack of development.

Many parts of the developed world have had to overcome serious environmental difficulties, which although different from tropical conditions are just as likely to impede development. Winters in the continental interiors of North America and Eurasia are very severe and drought can be a problem in summer. Technology has enabled unpromising soils, such as those on reclaimed marshes, to become highly productive.

In the past Europe was plagued by many major endemic diseases, such as cholera, smallpox, bubonic plague and malaria, which only began to diminish as Europe developed.

The correlation between developed countries and the temperate zones is not perfect, as many tropical countries such as Singapore, Venezuela and Taiwan have developed rapidly in recent years. Some non-tropical countries such as Albania, North Korea and Mongolia on the other hand have not made significant progress.

Environmental difficulties are more difficult to cope with when a country is not developed, which is different from saying that development is dependent on certain environmental conditions.

5.5 Literacy. This diagram illustrates the scale of illiteracy in developing countries

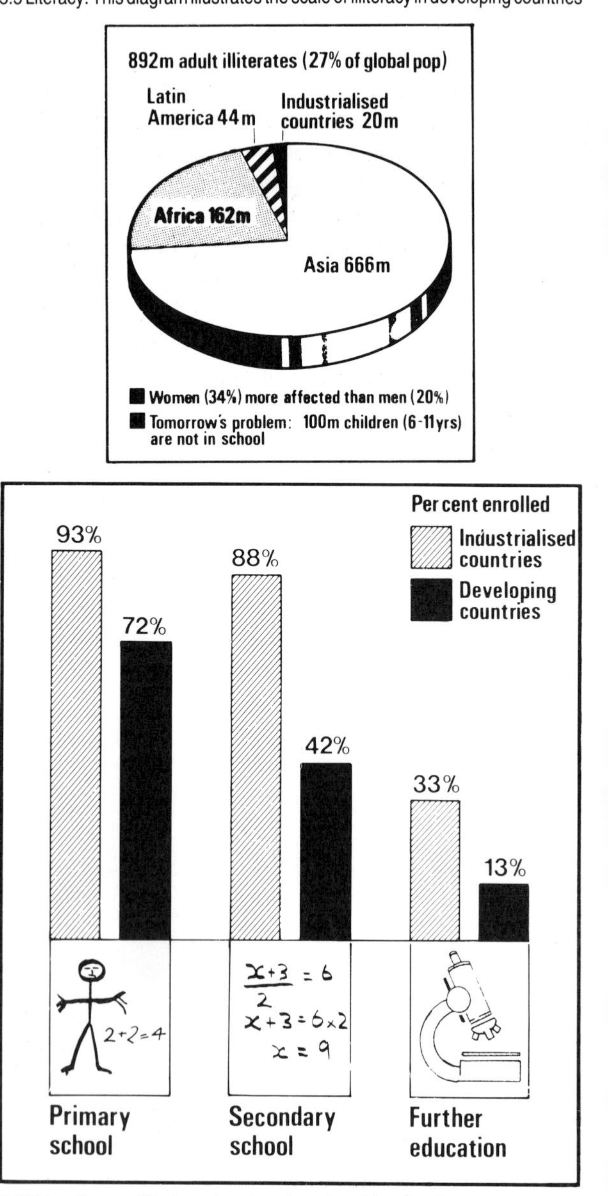

5.6 Education gap. The investment and enrolment in education reinforces the developed countries' advantages over developing countries

Stages in Development

Rostow's model

The idea that economic growth and hence development occurred in a series of stages has been suggested by a number of economic historians. However, the five-stage model which reflects the process of development in Europe has become most closely associated with Walt Whitman Rostow. Rostow formulated his model of development in a number of works between 1952 and 1963. The five stages of development proposed by Rostow are: traditional society; preconditions for take-off; take-off; drive to maturity; and age of mass consumption (5.7).

Traditional society has limited technology and makes decisions on the basis of custom rather than scientific knowledge. This sort of society is economically and socially static.

The preconditions for take-off stage occurs when there is some form of investment possibly in infrastructure (roads, railways, canals, etc.) and some form of social and/or political advance (emergence of merchant class or development of some political institutions). The economic surplus for the investment may arise because of some form of manufacturing emerging or agricultural surpluses from developments in farming.

Take-off occurs when there is sufficient investment in manufacturing and extractive industries to create a faster rate of growth in GNP than in population. The wealth created is reinvested to sustain economic growth and further increases in GNP. This stage is characterised by some redistribution of wealth and rising standards of living.

The **drive to maturity** is the stage when economic growth takes place throughout all parts of the economy and is a period of self-sustaining growth. The **age of mass consumption** is characterised by the movement in manufacturing toward the production of consumer durables (televisions, cars, washing machines, etc.).

Rostow considered the first three stages particularly relevant to developing countries. He didn't believe that developing countries would achieve take-off unless the increased economic growth was also accompanied by a change in the economy and society which would sustain the economic growth.

Rostow's ideas on development were based on the experience of Britain which achieved take-off between 1780 and 1800, reaching maturity about 1850 and the age of high mass consumption after the Second World War. Other Western European countries which started this development process later were able to learn from Britain's mistakes and passed through the stages in a shorter time.

5.7 Rostow's stages of development

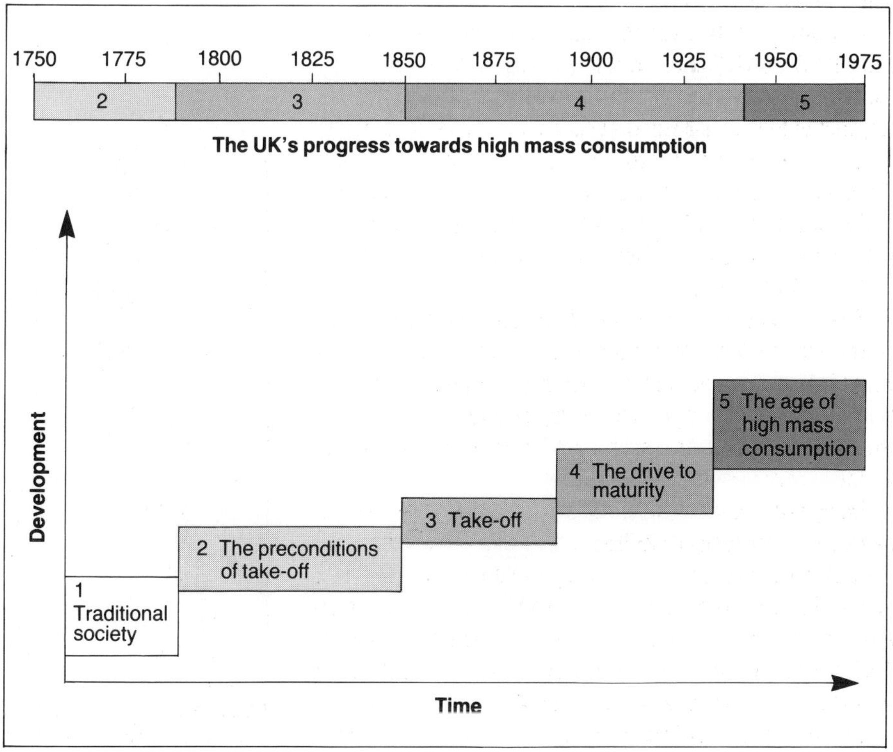

CHAPTER 5

Weaknesses of Rostow's model

Although a number of newly industrialised countries, such as Japan, Mexico, Singapore, Korea and Brazil, have increased GNP and established a broad-based economy it seems that it will be very difficult for many others to follow. Already the richest countries use and control a disproportionate share of the world's resources (food, energy, minerals, etc.). This uneven sharing of the world's resources (5.8) makes it very difficult for developing countries to acquire sufficient resources to pass through all five stages of development. This does not mean that development cannot take place but that the different conditions of the present day may require different routes to development.

Developing countries will not be able to repeat the experience of Britain and other countries that went through the development process earlier because economic competition now is much stronger and the wealthier countries exert considerable control over the world economy. The countries which developed first had no such competition and markets were large and expanding. Any attempts to compete in present-day export markets meet with strong competition from the developed nations.

Some industries can develop by adopting an **import substitution** strategy (producing goods which will replace imports). However home markets may be limited in buying power and eventually industries will need to export in order to expand.

The limited nature of the world's natural resources means it is unlikely that developing countries will ever achieve the standard of living enjoyed in developed countries. Already the developed countries have control of many of the world's natural resources and with increasing population these resources are likely to become scarcer.

Developing countries have also had to cope with fast-growing populations at the same time as trying to develop economically. Better disease control and health care, which has been made possible by advances in developed countries, has had the effect of stimulating population growth before industrial development can create the jobs or wealth necessary to support the increasing population. Until early this century, people from the developed nations were able to migrate in their millions, to North and South America, Australia and other relatively 'empty lands'; the surplus population from the developing countries has no such opportunity to exploit.

5.8 Unequal resources. This map shows the per capita resources of different regions. Many developing countries have few natural resources and those that do have some have difficulty in developing them. The developed countries often exert considerable control of resources in the developing countries because of their economic power.

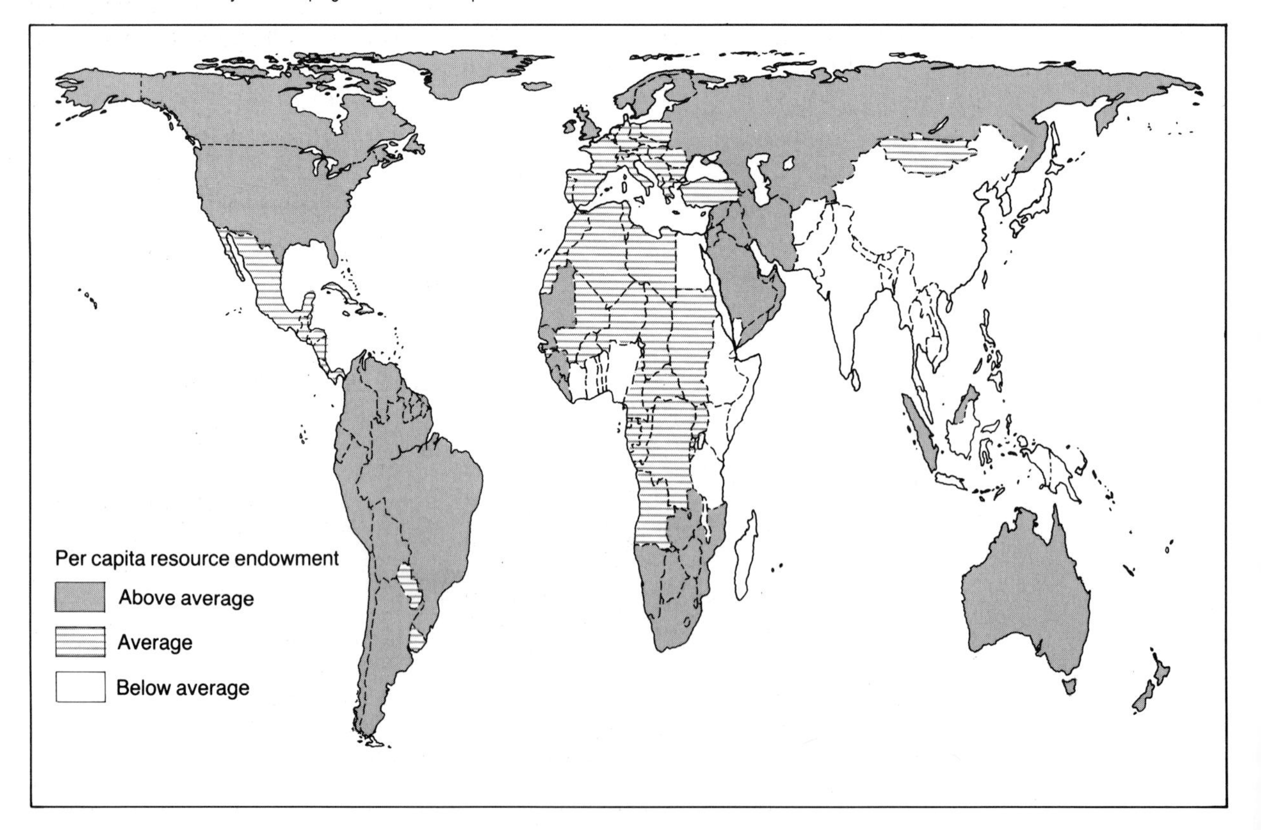

Core and Periphery

It has already been mentioned that developing countries find it difficult to achieve 'take-off' because they are competing with the developed nations in a world market. This market was established, and to a large degree is controlled, by developed countries. Although developing countries are relatively 'low-cost' producers, because wage levels are low, they are unable to compete successfully. This is because markets are either closed by protective tariffs or they cannot achieve a scale of production large enough to benefit significantly from their lower costs. It is like a corner shop trying to compete with a supermarket.

The idea of a world-scale **core and periphery** comes from the distribution of developed and developing countries on a world map. The developed countries of North America and Europe form the **core** or **heartland**. Japan, Australia, New Zealand, South Africa and Argentina are outlier (detached) secondary core areas. The rest of the world is the **periphery** of developing countries (5.9). The peripheral regions are economically linked to the core and dependent on it. The developing countries of the periphery have suffered because developed countries have tended to be interested in exploiting their mineral and agricultural resources without this leading to a diversification of their economies.

Peripheral regions tend to be disadvantaged as they are seen to be less attractive locations for developing industry. The economic pull of the core attracts the bulk of investment in manufacturing industry as success breeds success. The peripheral regions are most likely to be dominated by primary industries (agriculture, mining, forestry, etc.). This disparity in economic activity is not the result of a deliberate conspiracy but is brought about by private investment seeking out the opportunities that offer the highest and usually quickest returns.

The core areas are successful because they are able to generate innovations while the peripheral areas are to some extent dependent on the core. This economic model can be used at a number of scales: national, regional and world.

The attractions of core areas also create problems for the periphery as many of the most skilled and energetic members of the population are likely to migrate to the core if possible. The contrast between core and periphery is showing no sign of diminishing: if anything the gap is widening.

The inequality between core and periphery is largely attributed to differing levels of industrial development. A Swedish economist Myrdal outlined three stages of economic development in his model of cumulative causation.

1. Pre industrial stage, largely an agrarian society
2. Industrial stage, development of industry next to raw materials, energy, harbours and markets etc. The successes of early industries sets up a 'snowball' effect with more industries attracted and increased wealth. As the industrial areas grow the disparity between the wealthy and less favoured non-industrial areas becomes more marked. This encourages rural–urban migration.
3. Post-industrial stage. The wealth created by industry spreads out from the industrialised regions to the poorer areas, lessening the regional disparities.

Myrdal's model goes some way to explaining the existence of industrial cores and their less favoured peripheries.

5.9 Core and periphery model

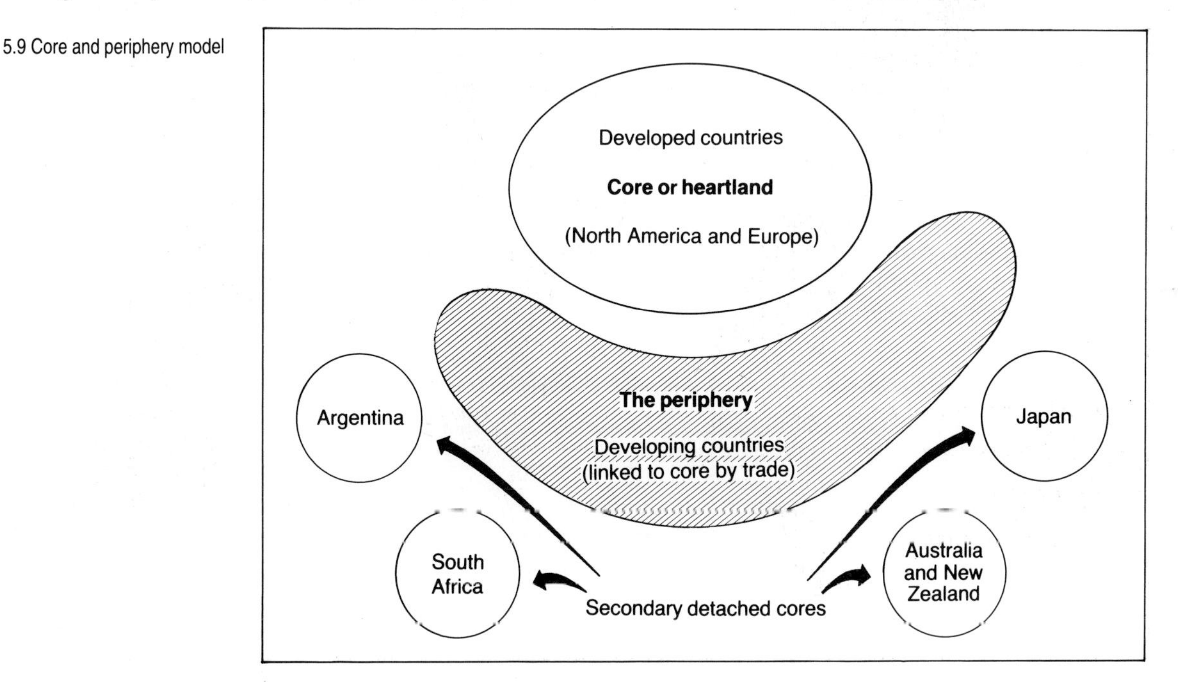

Route to Development

Most people and governments recognise the need to improve living standards in the poorest countries. However a number of different routes or strategies to development have been proposed and attempted.

Rostow's stages of development model has been influential in shaping some of these strategies. The development of an industrial sector which provides jobs has been seen as an important element of many **development strategies**. Industrialisation has been promoted since it is believed that developed countries built their wealth on the Industrial Revolution.

The same development strategy in two countries might have very different results and there is therefore a need to adopt a strategy which suits the environment and society it is designed to change. For example, Singapore has made significant progress with a strategy based on **export reliance** while Ghana has not been as successful.

Table 5.10 outlines five possible development routes and indicates the advantages and drawbacks of each.

Development plans which have relied largely on government funding have tended to be clearly directed if not always entirely successful. Some countries have tried to encourage private sector investment within their development strategies which has tended to achieve some economic growth but often without other social benefits. After gaining independence many developing countries adopted development plans based on the Soviet **five-year plans.** India was one of the first developing countries to plan its development in this way (5.12).The early plans were aimed at turning India into a major industrial country as well as developing the rural economy.

5.11 Small-scale, low technology: textile industry in India

5.10 Routes to development

Development route	Advantages	Drawbacks
Small-scale, low technology based on local resources and manpower. Labour intensive (5.12).	Not reliant on imports, encourages community co-operation, can be maintained locally, benefits the poor.	Relies on research to provide new techniques/technology which is low cost.
Large-scale, high technology e.g. large dams with HEP, irrigation schemes, disease control schemes.	Clear national strategy, large scale is efficient. Significant impact on area affected.	Local opinion often in conflict with government plan, benefits not spread to all, expensive, may increase imports.
Large-scale, intermediate technology for industrial development. Using technology which may be 10 to 30 years old to build up industry.	Cheap equipment, often second hand, relatively labour intensive. No innovation required.	Industry may pollute the environment, rural development ignored.
Large-scale, high technology, run by multinationals.	Fast, efficient economic growth.	Exploitive development, controlled by others. Wealth not spread. Uneven development, environmental damage.
Small-scale, high technology. The technology adapted to village needs.	Aimed at improving living standards e.g. solar cookers, high-yielding variety crops. Direction from government but rural communities benefit.	Costly, relies on some aid. Depends on technology being adapted. Little increase in local industry.

Development Planning in India

5.12 India's five-year plans. The data show progress being made particularly since 1974, despite a rapidly growing population.

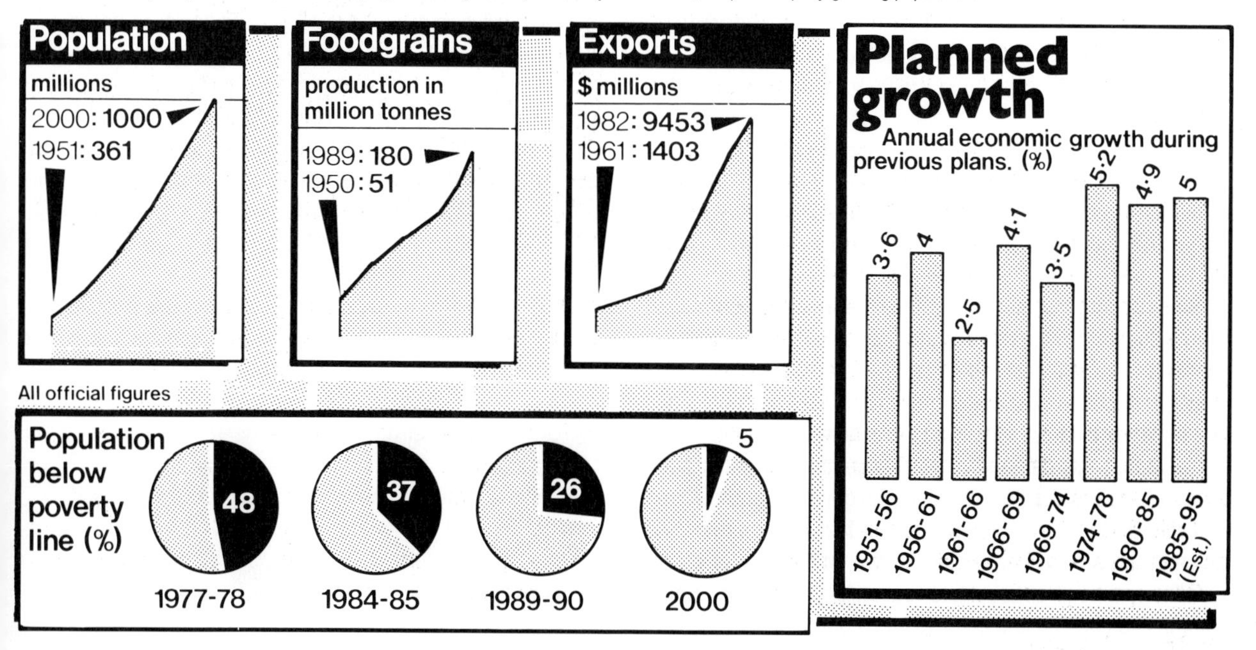

India is the second most populous country in the world, with around 73% of its 817 million people living in rural areas. This proportion has only declined from 82% over the last fifty years, despite the growth of India's cities, 36 of which are over half a million in size. Even with an estimated growth rate of only 1.9% the population of India grew by 17 million in 1990. The majority of the working population (69%) work in agriculture.

India's GNP was around $270 in 1988, a modest increase from $240 in 1980. The rate of growth in GNP was only around 1.4% above population growth until the late 1970s which suggests a very slow improvement in living conditions. Current growth is around 3% above population growth. The level of GNP is well below the average for developing countries, of $640.

India's five-year plans

After India gained independence in 1947 the government set about planning for social and economic development. The first five-year plan appeared in 1951 and it had four main aims:

- a high national industrial growth rate to create wealth for reinvestment
- to be as self-sufficient as possible, over a wide front
- to provide employment for all
- to reduce economic inequalities in the population.

India has had many difficulties to overcome since independence, and its development plans have had their successes and failures. Planned growth rates of 5% were not reached until the late 1970s and this has meant that industry has not produced the wealth for reinvestment or redistribution that had been hoped for. Insufficient extra jobs have been created to provide an alternative to farming. Agricultural productivity has increased since 1950, more than trebling by 1989. This increase in production has provided enough food for India to withstand poor harvests in drought years, without having to import food. The advances of the 'Green Revolution', such as improved seed and better farming practices, have enabled India to feed its rapidly growing population but increase in food production has not been much more than population growth.

During the years of British colonisation, India's economy had been developed as an exporter of commodities such as jute, cotton and tea. Development of cotton mills and iron and steel plants began early this century but they catered only for the domestic market. By the time of India's independence, industry still employed only a small proportion of the labour force.

In striving for self-sufficiency India has emphasised building up its heavy industries and those producing intermediate goods, i.e. those industries which process raw materials. Concentration on **capital goods** rather than **consumer goods** has characterised India's five-year plans and, with restrictions on imports until the 1980s, consumer demand has been held in check by government policy. Indian industrial policy is described in an extract from the Indian Planning Commission (1966).

> A special feature of industrial development, especially since the commencement of the Second Plan in 1956–57, has been the growth of capacities in steel, aluminium, engineering, chemicals, fertilizers and petroleum products. Apart from these, large investments have been made in industries producing heavy electrical equipment, heavy foundry forge, heavy engineering machinery, heavy plates and vessels etc. – all of which will become available in increasing quantities from now on.

Since the late 1970s India has attempted some diversification of its industries: petrochemical industries have grown with the development of oil and gas fields, and there has been some growth in electronics. Industrial growth has been hampered by a lack of demand for capital goods; the very industries that would have created this demand (light engineering) have not been encouraged. This imbalance in industrial development has been criticised by some economists. Another factor which restricted industrial growth until recently was the unreliability of power supplies and poor infrastructure (particularly transport). Some progress has been made in these areas during the 1980s.

Industrial development has not been spread evenly throughout the country with about half of the production in the three states of Maharashtra, West Bengal and Gujerat.

Exports have risen significantly since the 1960s but imports have also risen and India has a balance of trade deficit (imports are greater than exports). Raw materials and intermediate goods (clothing) still comprise the bulk of India's exports, while fuel and machinery are the main imports.

Population pressure, with an increasing proportion of children, has forced India to divert investment into education and social services that would otherwise have been used to develop agriculture and industry. Despite the many obstacles facing development, during the 1980s there was a reduction in the proportion of India's population living below the poverty line (Indian government estimates). The wealth created has not, however, been distributed evenly; the wealthy minority gaining most.

Employment opportunities have not kept pace with population increase and there is significant overmanning in many industries. The development of capital-intensive heavy industries does little to provide extra jobs. The rural sector is still very labour intensive although mechanisation is jeopardising jobs. However, some additional labour may be needed to work on land where two or three crops can now be grown, where only one grew before.

India's five-year plans have not yet fulfilled their original aims but there has been progress through the 1980s. The still rapidly growing population is a constant drain on national resources.

Alternative strategies

India's development could be helped if future development plans took alternative routes toward its ultimate goals. To achieve full employment, industrialisation could be focused on labour-intensive industries which provide jobs and create demand, as well as develop products for export. Manufacturing could also be spead more evenly, to small towns throughout the country, providing jobs for displaced agricultural workers. The agricultural sector, which has already made progress, could be further developed to provide a secure and productive agricultural base which retains its workforce.

Progress will be slow unless population growth diminishes and this will require further family-planning programmes which stress the desirability of smaller families.

5.13

Average annual population growth rate:
1960–1970 2.3%
1970–1980 2.1%
1980–1990 1.9%

Birth rates
1950 44 per thousand
1960 42
1970 38
1980 32
1990 28 (estimate)

Population totals
1950 350 million
1960 431 million
1970 551 million
1980 688 million
1990 847 million (estimate)

Death rates (per thousand)
1950 25
1960 22
1970 18
1980 14
1990 12 (estimate)

Projected population
2000 1013 million
2020 1309 million

Life expectancy
1950 38 years
1990 58 years (estimate)

Infant mortality (per 1000 live births)
1950 190
1990 100 (estimate)

Population per doctor
1950 5125
1984 2500 (estimate)

Calories per person per day
1950 1700
1990 2280 (estimate)

Tractors in use
1950 8100
1970 111000
1986 649000

Rice production (million tonnes)
1950 33
1970 63
1988 102

Steel production (thousand tonnes)
1950 1300
1970 6286
1988 14196

Energy production capacity (million kWh)
1970 16
1986 55

Questions

Q MEASURING DEVELOPMENT

1 (a) Give a definition of development in your own words.
(b) Describe how the rich countries get richer, and the gap between rich and poor widens.
(c) Draw a map of the world showing the two main poverty belts (5.4).
(d) Why is GNP per capita, on its own, not without faults as a measure of development?
(e) Describe some common measures of development.
(f) How can the failings of one measure of development be avoided?

Q ROUTES TO DEVELOPMENT / DEVELOPMENT PLANNING IN INDIA

3 (a) Make a copy of table 5.11 describing the advantages and disadvantages of different development strategies.
(b) List the aims of India's five-year development plans.
(c) What have been the main obstacles to India's economic development?
(d) Briefly state the main successes and failures of India's five-year plans.
(e) Examine table 5.13 showing economic and social indicators for India. Describe the main trends in your own words.
(f) What possible alternative strategies could India explore in an attempt to promote development?

Q PATTERNS OF DEVELOPMENT / STAGES IN DEVELOPMENT / CORE AND PERIPHERY

2 (a) Why have many of the indicators of development improved in developing countries over the last 40 years?
(b) Explain why there is hunger and malnutrition in the world when more food is produced than is required.
(c) Why is it tempting to link development to climatic factors? Why may this link be suspect?
(d) Describe the pattern of literacy and educational enrolment shown in 5.5 and 5.6.
(e) Make a copy of the diagram illustrating Rostow's stages of development (5.7).
(f) List Rostow's five stages of development, giving the dates that the UK reached these levels.
(g) Make a list of the main weaknesses of Rostow's theory.
(h) Explain why developing countries find it difficult to compete in world markets even though their costs are low.
(i) In your own words describe the core and periphery model.
(j) What does the diagram 'The queue in the waiting room' indicate about the different levels of development? Why might this one measure be an inadequate measure of development?

The queue in the waiting room

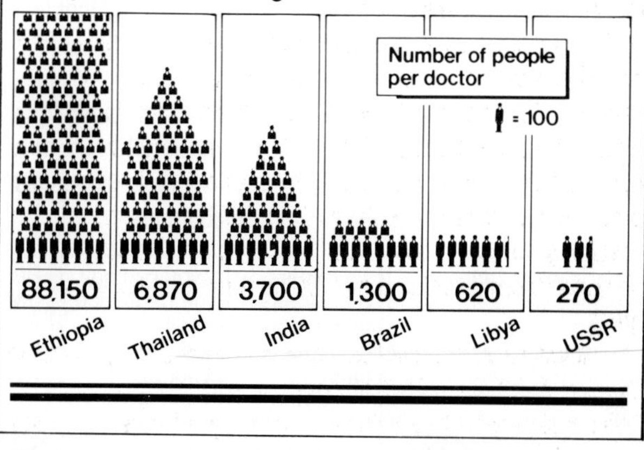

Research and Further Work

(a) Find out about the development strategies of a developing country other than India.
(b) Describe the development strategies pursued in developed countries such as the UK.
(c) Find out which British banks have begun to write off international debts owed by developing countries.
(d) Which countries benefit from British aid and how is this aid money spent?
(e) Why is the role of women in the development process so important in the poorest countries?
(f) Availability of energy is crucial for development. Examine the energy choices that have to be made in developing countries and suggest the energy sources which would be most beneficial to people in rural areas.

CHAPTER 5

International Debt

An additional burden for many developing countries is increasing debt. This debt crisis can be traced back to the oil price increases in 1973–4, when developing countries had to borrow to pay for their growing oil bills. Some of the oil-producing countries invested their oil wealth in banks and other financial institutions which were eager to relend this money to developing countries, particularly those with growing economies.

The oil price rises of 1974–5 were followed by further significant increases in 1979 and 1990. At the same time commodity prices worldwide were falling so these poor countries were earning less from their exports of copper, coffee, tea, sugar, etc.

Interest rates rose steadily throughout the 1980s resulting in markedly increased repayments. These changes have been outwith the control of the developing countries and are often the result of monetary policies in the richest countries. It has been calculated that the poor countries are now repaying more to the rich countries than they currently receive in aid and new loans. So, contrary to most people's expectations, money flows from poor countries to rich countries as a result of international debt (5.14).

Who lent the money?

Western commercial banks, including many British high street banks, provided large loans to developing countries that had growing economies with an expanding manufacturing sector. Brazil has the largest debt at around $114.5 billion in 1987. Mexico too has large debts and it was Mexico in 1982 that first drew world attention to **international debt** when it said it couldn't repay its debt.

The poorest countries have tended to obtain loans from international institutions such as the **International Monetary Fund** (IMF) and the **World Bank**. These institutions are controlled by the governments of the world's richest countries.

What does the debt mean for the debtor countries?

Brazil is currently due to pay around $20 billion each year to its creditors. This figure is around 75% of Brazil's annual earnings from exports. Sudan and some other African countries are even worse off, owing nearly as much as they earn each year through exports.

African countries have been particularly hard hit by the current debt crisis (5.15). On one hand they have had to pay more for oil imports and on the other they are being paid less for the export commodities they produce. Zambia relies on copper exports for over 90% of its earnings, but the price of copper has dropped to around only 75% of its 1973 value (in real terms). The fall in value of exports from developing countries is to some degree due to increased production. This has been encouraged in an effort to produce economic growth and wealth for development. However the result has been to flood the markets and reduce world prices.

Robert Mugabe, Prime Minister of Zimbabwe, said in July 1987 'Few scourges in human history can claim so many victims as today's debt crisis'. This statement reflects the serious human and economic crisis facing Africa as resources are being drained to pay debts instead of funding development. Austerity measures introduced by some governments in an attempt to clear their debts have caused considerable suffering. Inevitably it is the poorest people who suffer most.

A United Nations survey in 1987 of the poorest countries that are saddled with crippling debts showed that malnutrition and infant mortality had increased throughout the previous decade. Health and education services had been starved of funds and some diseases which were thought to have been eliminated had reappeared. As well as cuts in basic services, many developing countries have increased the price of basic necessities such as food. Wage freezes and job losses have also been common. This increased poverty has led to discontent and riots in a number of poor countries.

Us bankers are here to help you poor folks. Here, take this.
As this is a business relationship, I'll charge you interest. If you have trouble with repayments...
...you can pay me for advice or I'll reschedule your debt (for a small fee).
But now I'm giving you more money than you lent me!
Yeah!
© NEWS-SCAN INTERNATIONAL LTD
PADDY

5.14 International debt

Is suffering an inevitable result of debt?

Rich and poor countries can do much to reduce the impact of the debt crisis on the poorest in society. The poor countries themselves could make financial cutbacks in defence expenditure, instead of health and education which affect peoples lives directly. Military spending accounts for a high proportion of earnings in many developing countries and is often the last area to be cut.

Scarce resources could be directly targeted towards increasing food production, providing jobs and primary health care which would benefit the poorest most. The government of Ghana introduced one such programme of reforms to mollify the effects of the debt crisis. The Programme of Action to Mitigate the Social Costs of Adjustment (PAMSCAD) aims to provide: employment projects; credit for small farmers; food for the malnourished; and some basic health services. This programme is not the answer to the debt crisis but it does attempt to provide some protection for the people who are most vulnerable.

The rich countries can also help by putting the interests of the poor first. The international financial institutions have tended to treat the debt crisis as a financial problem with little regard for the human misery it creates. The present situation of the poor paying more in debt repayments than they receive in aid has to be seriously questioned. Some debts will need to be written off, particularly those from the poorest countries. US banks relaxed debt repayments from 39 debtor nations in 1989 but the countries that benefited were those of political and strategic significance to the USA, such as Brazil and Mexico.

By 1987 only five countries had achieved a UN goal of giving 0.7% of their GNP in aid. Netherlands, Norway and Sweden had achieved this by the end of the 1970s and have since been joined by Denmark and France. Some of the wealthiest countries give only a small fraction of the recommended target (1986–7: USA 0.21% of GNP; Japan 0.30 % of GNP; UK 0.29% of GNP). In the long term the debt crisis will only subside if the rich countries help to:

- stabilise commodity prices
- lower interest rates
- remove protective trade tariffs
- encourage economic growth in developing countries

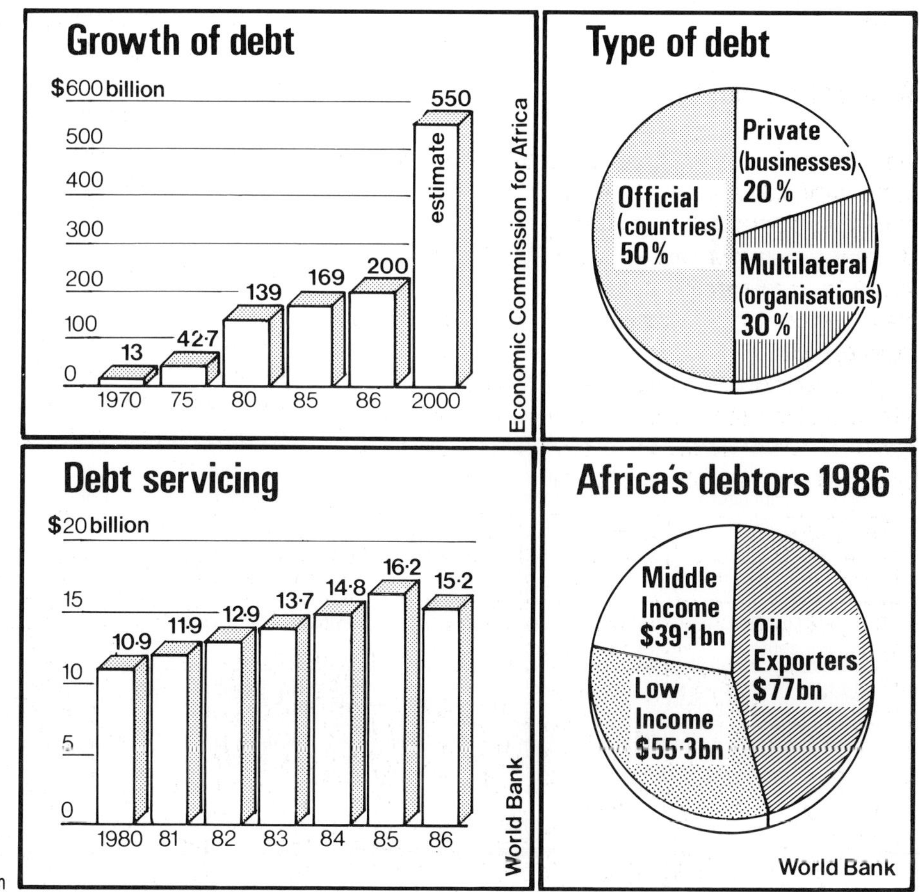

5.15 Africa's debt problem

Exam Style Questions

1 (a) Examine the data in table 1 on life expectancies for selected countries. Describe the changes between 1950 and 1988. Suggest reasons for any patterns in the data. (5)
(b) Examine the health data in table 1. Explain the differences in levels of health with reference to the data in the table. (10)
(c) The model in diagram 1 shows some possible strategies for economic development. For an area you have studied explain the strategies which have been adopted to achieve economic development. Discuss the successes and/or failures of these strategies. (15)

Table 1

Country	Life expectancy 1950	1988	Population per doctor	Infant mortality	Calories per capita per day
Ethiopia	33	50	88150	118	N/A
India	39	54	3700	104	2204
Brazil	51	65	1300	63	2643
USSR	64	69	270	25	3394
Sweden	72	77	390	5.9	3049

Diagram 1

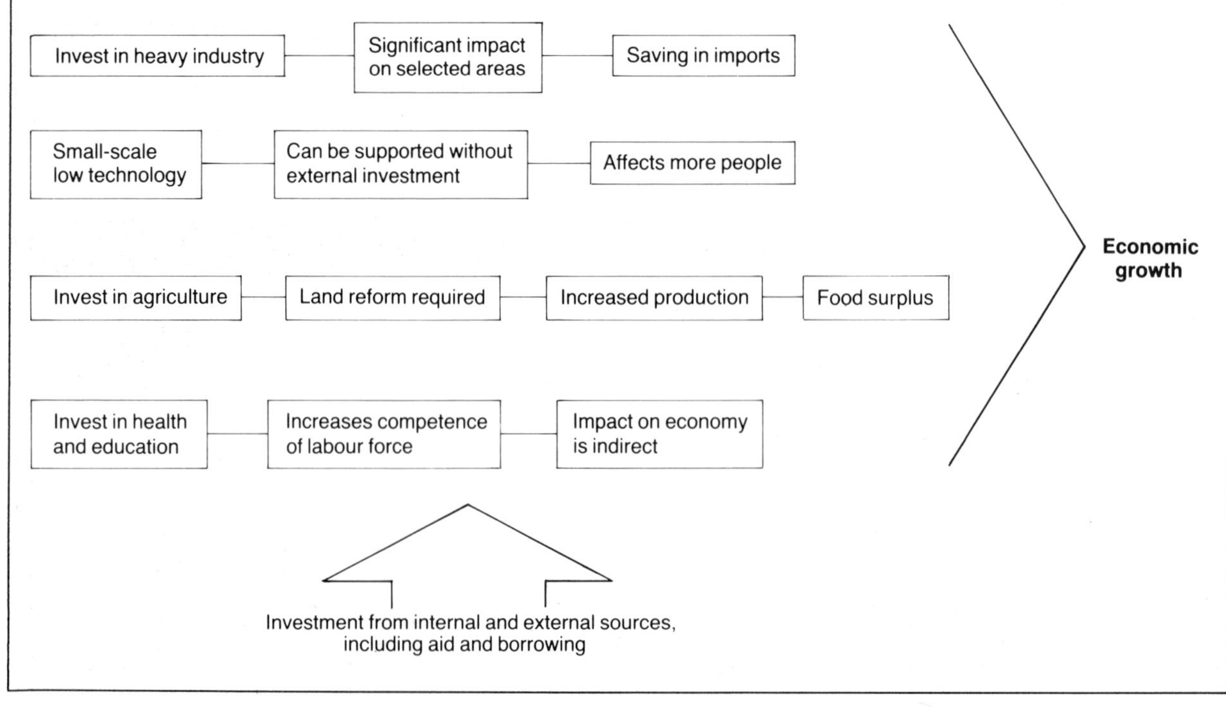

2 (a) Many newly independent developing countries at first concentrated on industrialising to achieve economic growth but more recently agriculture has received more attention. Why has there been a switch of attention toward agricultural development? (10)

(b) Describe the problems facing developing countries that seek to industrialise. (8)

(c) Trade barriers are one way in which the rich countries control the world economy. Examine the flowchart (diagram 2) which illustrates the effect of trade barriers. Explain why trade barriers tend to work against developing countries and restrict economic development. (12)

Diagram 2 The effect of trade barriers

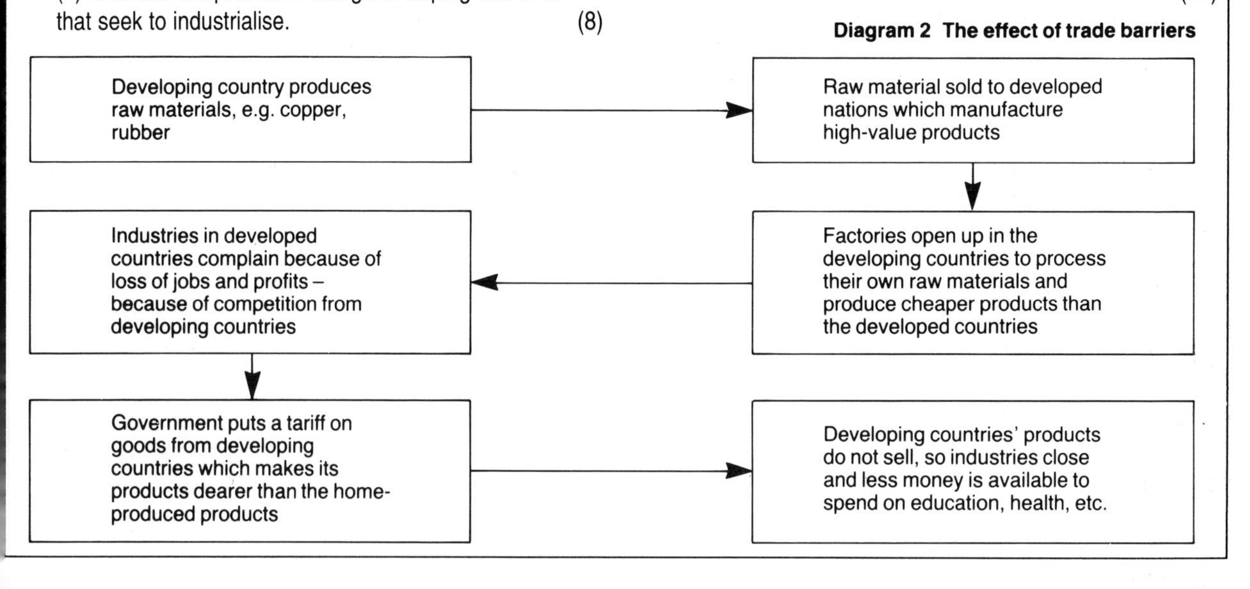

3 (a) Examine diagrams 3 and 4 on the debt crisis. Describe the impact of the debt crisis on developing countries. (6)

(b) Explain how the debt crisis arose and what can be done to protect the poorest people. (10)

(c) Describe the role of foreign aid in the economic development of any developing country you have studied. (6)

(d) Explain how a country you have studied is trying to improve its health care and control disease. (8)

Diagram 3

Diagram 4

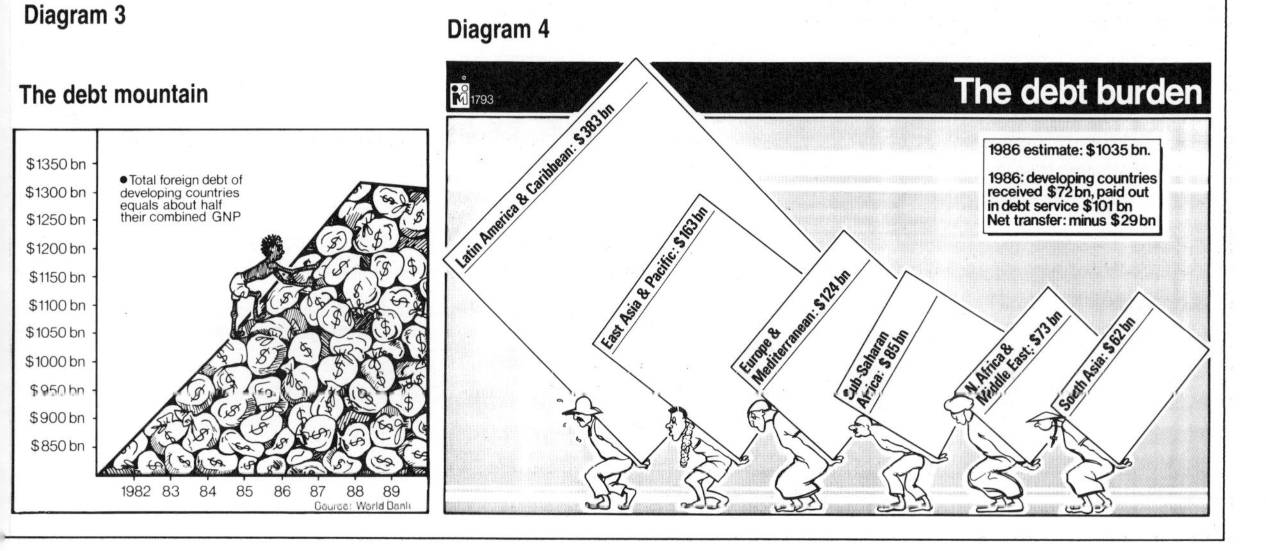

CHAPTER 5

Levels of Health

Everyone has the right to good health but not everyone has equal access to the basic diet and medical care necessary to give them a healthy life. Illness and disease exist all over the world but people in developing countries suffer much more from ill health than those in developed countries.

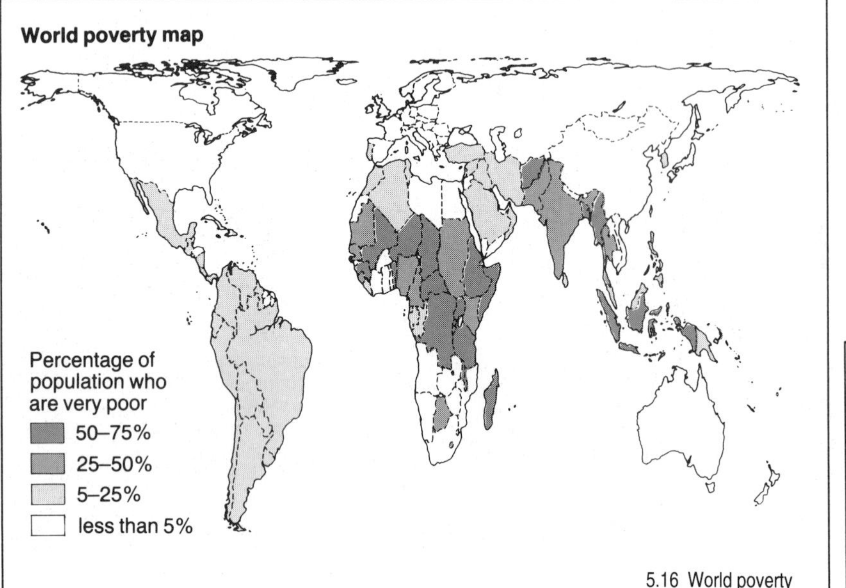

5.16 World poverty

Poverty trapped

For over 40% of the population of developing countries, life at a subsistence level is a matter of survival. These people live on a knife-edge between constant hunger and starvation, in great poverty and hardship. The global pattern of poverty (5.16) reveals stark inequality between wealthy and poor nations. In the least developed countries, such as Ethiopia, Chad and Bangladesh, whose average GNP per capita is less than $200 a year, the majority of people live below subsistence level, without access to medical services, adequate food or safe water supplies. Trapped by poverty in a vicious circle of despair, they suffer varying degrees of malnutrition, illness and high death rates. The poverty trap and associated ill health are perhaps the biggest factors retarding development within developing countries.

Infants and children

Infants and children account for many more of the deaths in developing countries than in developed countries. In diagram 5.19 all the deaths in both sets of countries are grouped into three main age groups. In 1988 children under 5 accounted for 28.5% of deaths in developing countries and 1.3% of those in developed countries. The main cause of child death in developing countries in 1988 was diarrhoea.

The long and the short

Life expectancy in years	1975	1988	Percentage increase
Japan	73	78	7
Canada	72	77	7
Netherlands	74	77	4
Norway	75	77	3
Spain	72	77	7
Sweden	73	77	5
Switzerland	72	77	7
Australia	72	76	6
UK	72	76	6
USA	71	76	7

Life expectancy in years	1975	1988	Percentage increase
Afghan.	35	42	20
Ethiopia	38	42	10
Sierra Leone	44	42	-5
Guinea	41	43	5
Angola	39	45	15
Mali	38	45	18
Niger	39	45	15
CAR	41	46	12
Chad	39	46	18
Somalia	41	46	12

5.17 Contrasts in life expectancy

Starved of funds

The majority of illnesses in the developing world could be prevented or treated by **primary health care** workers, who are trained and supervised by more qualified personnel. Serious health problems could be referred to better qualified staff in hospitals. But primary health care is often starved of funds while hospitals in urban centres, usually serving only a very small proportion of a country's population, consume on average 75% of their country's health budget.

The long march for survival: the average life-span of these Ethiopians may be as low as 28 years

5.18

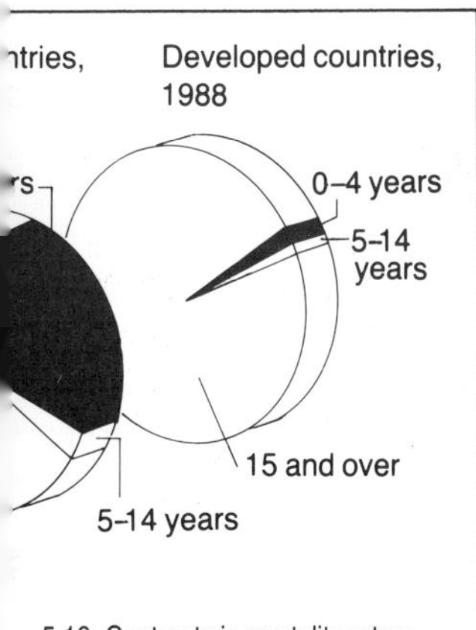

5.19 Contrasts in mortality rates: percentage of total deaths, by age group

.20

Percentage of government expenditure on health allocated to hospitals, 1987

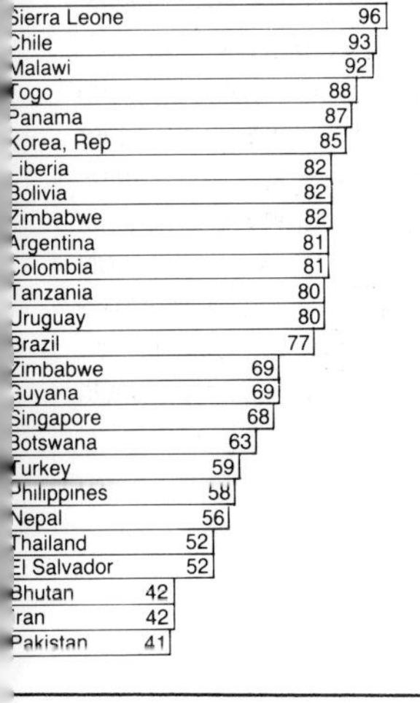

Parasites persist

Over 700 million people suffer from diseases caused by four of the world's worst parasites (5.21). These parasites persist in humid tropical regions of developing countries and are described as the great neglected diseases of humankind: great, because they debilitate and kill millions of people; and neglected because for most of this century they have been ignored by governments, scientists and drug companies.

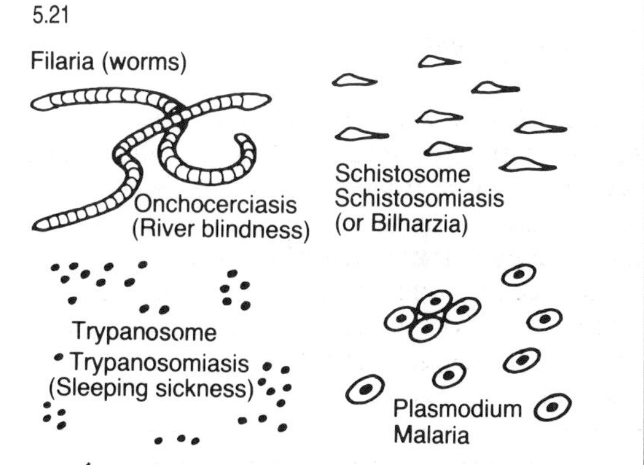

Cancer by region

Cancer in general is increasingly slowly worldwide, and in certain regions lung cancer is increasing at quite a fast rate. The global mortality rate for cancers is 4.4 million annually, of which nearly 2.35 million occur in the South.

5.22 Types of cancer: top three killers in various regions, 1988

	Latin America	Africa	China	India and other Asia	UK
Men	**Stomach** (28 000)	**Liver** (43 000)	**Stomach** (128 000)	**Mouth** (97 000)	**Lung** (30 000)
	Lung (25 000)	Lymphatic (20 000)	Esophagus (109 000)	Lung (62 000)	Prostate (10 000)
	Prostate (19 000)	Mouth (13 000)	Liver (81 000)	Stomach (43 000)	Bladder (7000)
Women	**Breast** (49 000)	**Cervix** (37 000)	**Cervix** (137 000)	**Cervix** (141 000)	**Breast** (24 000)
	Cervix (44 000)	Breast (27 000)	Stomach (68 000)	Breast (95 000)	Lung (11 000)
	Stomach (17 000)	Lymphatic (12 000)	Esophagus (59 000)	Mouth (48 000)	Colon (9000)

CHAPTER 5

Matters of Life and Death

Recent information released by the **World Health Organisation** (WHO) states:

- 20% of the world's population, or about one billion people, are malnourished, in ill health or diseased.
- The greatest health problems are to be found in sub-Saharan Africa where 160 million or 30% of people are ill or undernourished.
- In Central and South America, 25% of people (90 million) are ill.
- Health spending in the least developed or poorest countries averages less than $5 per head per year. This compares poorly with an average of over $400 per head per year in most developed countries.
- About 3 million children die annually from vaccine-preventable diseases such as polio, tetanus, measles, diphtheria and tuberculosis. At current prices, it costs about $10 per child to vaccinate against these five diseases.

Among the questions any thinking individual may ask are 'why do the peoples of the countries of the South suffer proportionately more from ill health?' The answer is not a simple one and requires a great deal of integrated thinking not only about the physical environment of many developing areas but also about the social factors contributing to the levels of health and high incidence of disease occurring there. These in turn have direct effects upon the mortality rate and life expectancy of the population of many countries of the South. Indeed, many experts regard a low provision of health care as an indicator of lack of development and unlikely economic growth. Comparisons of the major causes of ill health in developed and developing countries reveal significant differences. For example, the major causes of ill health in countries such as Japan, Britain and Italy (5.23) are those of the **endogenous** type, whereas **exogenous** diseases are mainly found in developing countries (5.24). Exogenous diseases include all the **infectious diseases**, both epidemic and endemic. **Epidemic diseases**, such as cholera or influenza, are defined as diseases common to a great many people over large areas, spread by the direct actions of people and not usually confined to specific geographical areas. From time to time an epidemic may flare up into a **pandemic** – affecting a huge area at one time, for example the worldwide occurrence of El Tor cholera of the 1970s. International air travel and tourism has had the effect of extending the spread of various epidemics over the world. **Endemic diseases**, such as malaria or schistosomiasis, are diseases habitually present in an area because of permanent local environmental and social factors. For example, endemic diseases such as river blindness are confined to the habitat of the female blackfly whereas

Country	Year	Causes of death
Japan	1988	Cancers, cerebrovascular attacks, old age, influenza
Britain	1988	Heart disease, cancers, cerebro vascular attacks, accidents
Italy	1987	Cancers, heart disease, influenza
Canada	1988	Heart disease, cancers, influenza
Scotland	1988	Heart disease, cancers, cerebro vascular attacks, bronchitis
Ethiopia	1988	Birth problems, diseases of infancy, pneumonia,undernourishment
Sri Lanka	1988	Diseases of infancy, gastroenteritis, old age
Nigeria	1987	Birth problems, diseases of infancy, pneumonia, gastroenteritis.

5.23 Major causes of ill health in selected countries

5.24 Major causes of ill health in developing countries

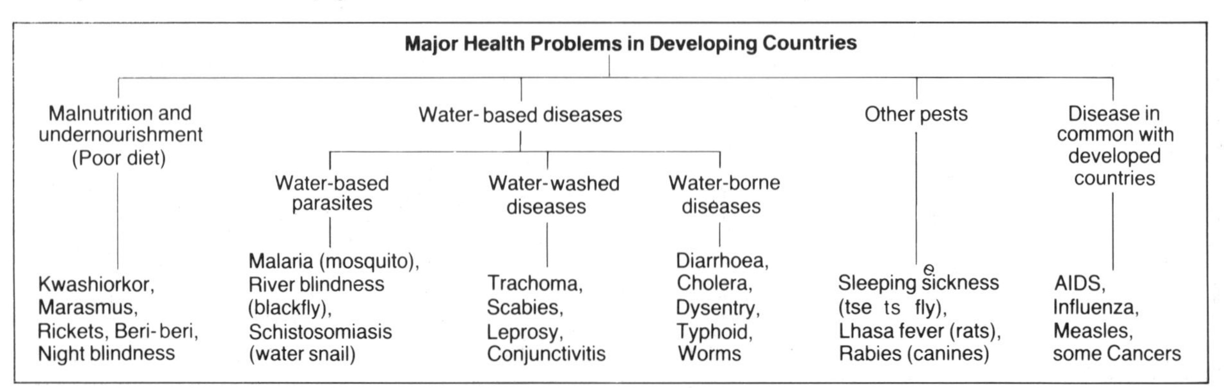

hookworm (5.25) is found in areas where there is inadequate provision of safe water and sanitation facilities (5.26).

According to the WHO, there are direct links between ill health and the lack of clean safe water. In fact over 80% of the leading diseases in developing countries depend on water for their impact. All too often there is not enough water in developing communities for basic domestic needs. Precious water, often carried for many kilometres by women, tends to be used over and over again and ends up as very dirty water, an ideal habitat for various diseases. Well over half the people of many developing countries have no access to clean water supplies (5.27) and, worse, three out of every four people have no acceptable form of sanitation. In rural areas, lack of water and sanitation is the norm. Rivers, lakes and ponds are both the main sources of water and the main sites for make-shift toilets. Dirty water is thought to be the principal transmission agent for eight out ten developing world diseases. Of these (5.28), diarrhoea in its many forms is the most serious: every hour over 1000 children die from diarrhoeal diseases. In one way or another, water-related diseases are estimated to account for over 25 million deaths annually, three-fifths of these being children. In addition to water-related deaths, millions more sufferers are debilitated and often left unable to work properly: 73 million working days are lost to water-related diseases and the annual costs to production are over $1 billion.

Clean water, adequate sanitation and food and health service provision are among the most basic needs in any society. Most inhabitants of developed countries take these for granted. But in many developing nations, despite attempts at improving their provision, such basic needs are assured to only a relatively small proportion of the population. Shortages of food and inadequate diets lead to the two main groups of food-related diseases: starvation and malnutrition.

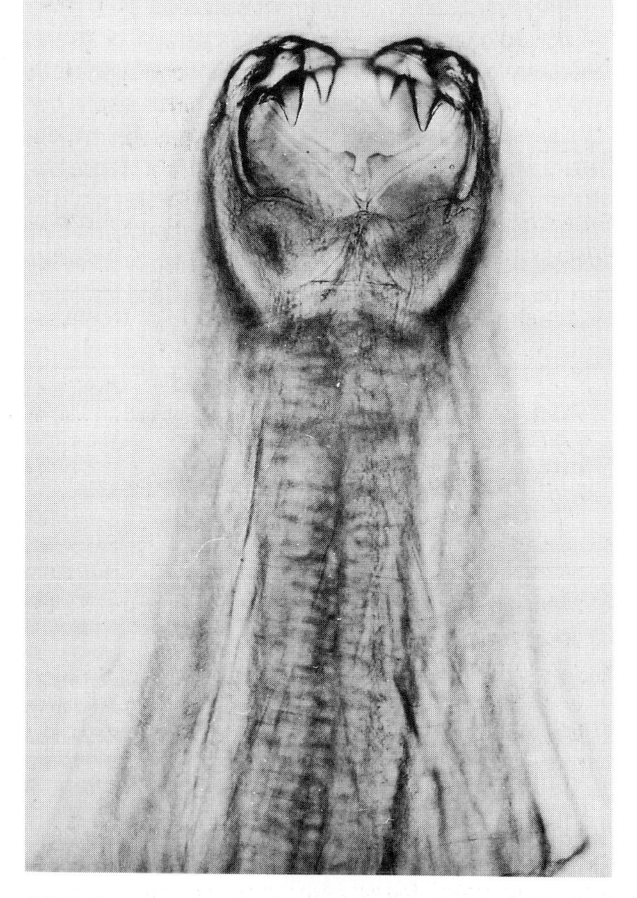

5.25 Hookworm larvae usually enter humans by burrowing through the soles of their feet. Heavy infestation can cause death in children.

5.26 Safe water and sanitation – for whom?

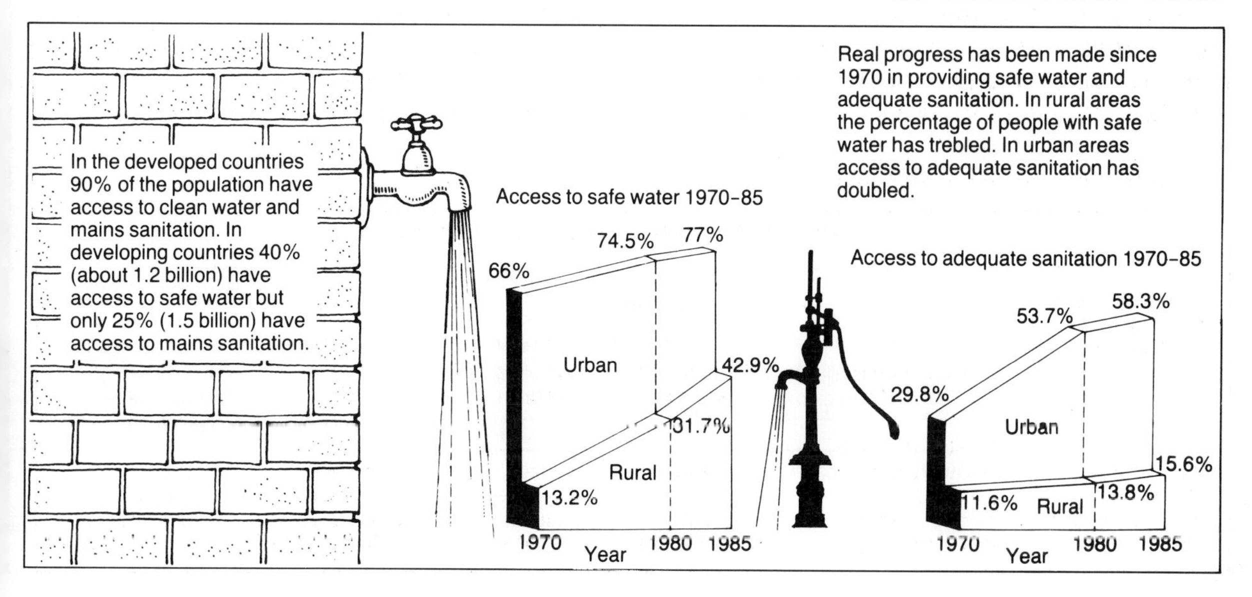
In the developed countries 90% of the population have access to clean water and mains sanitation. In developing countries 40% (about 1.2 billion) have access to safe water but only 25% (1.5 billion) have access to mains sanitation.
Access to safe water 1970–85
66%
74.5%
77%
Urban
42.9%
31.7%
Rural
13.2%
1970
Year
1980
1985
Real progress has been made since 1970 in providing safe water and adequate sanitation. In rural areas the percentage of people with safe water has trebled. In urban areas access to adequate sanitation has doubled.
Access to adequate sanitation 1970–85
53.7%
58.3%
29.8%
Urban
15.6%
11.6%
Rural
13.8%
1970
Year
1980
1985

Starvation or **undernourishment** is the result of not having enough **calories** to eat. The minimum number of calories necessary for healthy living is 2400. The Ethiopian famine of the 1980s accounted for the deaths of over 2 million people from starvation and related food deficiency diseases. **Malnutrition** results when there is an inadequate diet and lack of necessary vitamins and minerals (5.29). Night blindness, for example, is the result of severe vitamin A deficiency leading to kidney failure and corneal ulcers. Food-related diseases are generally linked with low income, limited educational opportunities and insufficient resources. They debilitate and are often fatal, especially to children.

The environment of many developing countries is also often plagued by various pests which can either directly or indirectly contribute to health problems. The tse-tse fly spreads the trypansome parasite responsible for sleeping sickness which affects both people and animals, especially cattle, over vast areas of Africa. This disease indirectly adds to Africa's food problems and malnutrition diseases since the continent could be a massive meat producer were it not for the effects of the tse-tse.

5.28 Dirty, wet and dangerous? Water-related diseases

Class	Type	Disease	Symptoms/result	Distribution	Treatment
Water-based diseases	**Hand to mouth (faecal–oral diseases)** Sick person transmits diseases in faeces. Wormeggs, amdebic cysts, viruses, bacteria, etc. pass into water or onto hands and food, then eaten or drunk by uninfected people.	Diarrhoea	Victims often die from loss of body fluids and salts, vomiting and severe cramp.	Worldwide. 300 million affected. 18 million deaths/year.	Rehydration through replacement of weak sugar, salt solution.
		Cholera	Severe diarrhoea, vomitting and cramps. 60% mortality rate in many poor areas.	Developing nations. 500 million affected. 10 million deaths/year.	Massive rehydration by saline drips, hospital-based.
		Dysentry	Severe diarrhoea with mucus and blood caused by tiny animals called ameba.	Worldwide. 400 million affected. 50 000 deaths/year.	Modern drugs effective: improved hygiene, education.
		Typoid	Salmonella bacteria produces sever diarrhoea, weakness and purple rash on the stomach.	Worldwide. 70 million affected. 1 million deaths/year.	Antibiotics effective. Improved hygiene.
		Polio	Acute disease spread by viruses in faeces. Can affect brain/spine.	Worldwide. 80 million affected. 20 000 deaths/year.	Lack of effective treatment.
		Roundworm	Tiny worms swallowed in water grow into 30cm adults in body.	Worldwide. 500 million affected. 1 million deaths/year.	Minor surgery and modern drugs.
Water-washed diseases	**Skin to skin** Unwashed skin and clothes encourage disease (transmitted by touch or by flies).	Trachoma	Virus infection of outer parts of the eye – causes build up of scar tissue and blindness.	Developing nations. 500 million affected. 30 000 deaths/year.	Modern drugs; surgery; clean safe water for washing in.
		Leprosy	A bacterial disease leading to blindness, crippled muscles, etc.	Worldwide. 500 million affected. 1 million deaths/year.	Modern drugs and surgery.
Water-borne diseases	**Walking in the water** Disease passes from faeces, urine or sick person into water-dwelling snail. Spreads in water.	Schistosomiasis	Watersnails release tiny worms which burrow into skin. Worms cause blood loss, bladder and kidney infections, and death.	Tropical areas. 500 million people affected. 3 million deaths/year.	Effective modern drugs but must be used on entire population to work.
		Guinea worm	Worms, swallowed in dirty water, grow to 100cm in body and break through skin as sores.	Tropical areas. 500 million affected. 3 million deaths/year.	Minor surgery; clean, safe water.
	Bitten in the water Water breeding insects bite humans for blood and pass on parasites in saliva.	Malaria	Plasmodium parasite enters into blood, destroys red blood cells – fevers, lethargy, coma and death.	Tropical areas. 400 million affected. 3 million deaths/year.	Mass drug treatment to kill parasites in humans.
		River blindness (Onchocerciasis)	Tiny worms live in human blood, cause itching, debilitation and eventual blindness.	Tropical areas. 350 million affected. 500 000 deaths/year.	Almost no real treatment: drugs kill worms in humans.
	Stepping into danger People step into infected faeces.	Hookworm	Eggs in faeces enter bare feet, pass into lungs, coughed up and swallowed into gut. Severe bleeding and anemia result.	Developing areas. 600 million affected. 50 000 deaths/year.	Modern drugs and surgery. Clean, safe water and footwear.

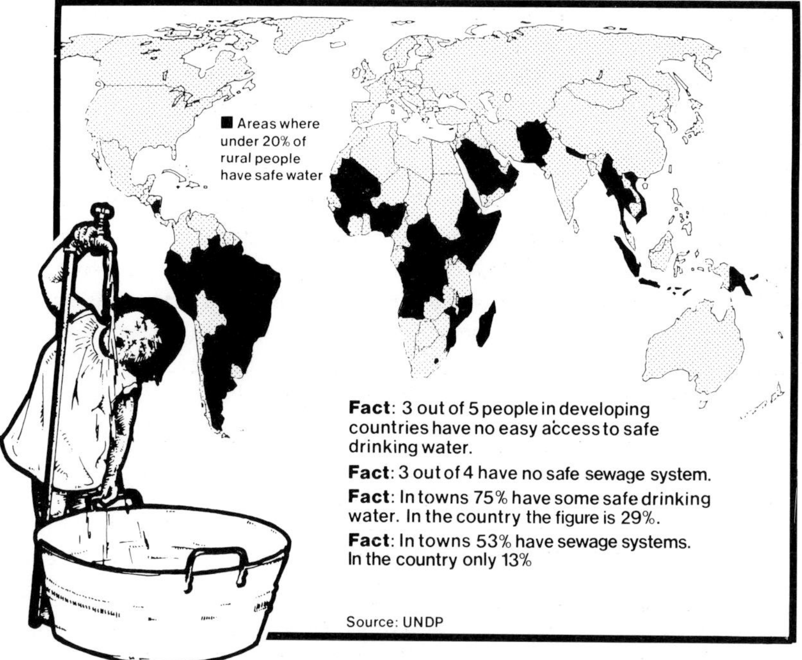

■ Areas where under 20% of rural people have safe water
Fact: 3 out of 5 people in developing countries have no easy access to safe drinking water.
Fact: 3 out of 4 have no safe sewage system.
Fact: In towns 75% have some safe drinking water. In the country the figure is 29%.
Fact: In towns 53% have sewage systems. In the country only 13%
Source: UNDP

5.27 Water facts

Other pests also spread diseases directly, varying from Weils disease and Lhasa fever transmitted by rats to rabies carried by canine animals such as wild dogs, foxes or hyenas. Locusts and quelea birds indirectly influence the patterns of ill health by destroying food crops: plagues and swarms can devour an entire region's growing food crops overnight thus increasing the already serious food shortage, and diet-deficiency diseases.

There are also diseases which are common to both developing and developed countries (5.24). These include AIDS, measles, hepatitis and some cancers (see 5.22).

There are enormous costs to developing countries from the high incidence of exogenous diseases. If inadequate nutrition, or unsafe water or sanitation causes child deaths on a vast scale, high infant mortality rates will then stimulate high birth rates, which in turn help perpetuate high population growth, malnutrition and poverty.

5.29 Major diet-deficiency diseases common in developing countries

Type	Disease	Symptoms	Distribution	Treatment
Protein deficiency	Kwashiorkor	Retarded growth, apathy and swollen stomach, skin rashes. Deadly if untreated.	Africa, S.E. Asia	High-protein fluids; well-balanced diet.
	Marasmus	Severe starvation in combination with lack of proteins. Wasting of tissues.	Africa, S.E. Asia	Breast-milk, cereals, fats, oils; immediate treatment.
Vitamin deficiency	Night blindness	Severe vitamin A deficiency, dry skin, kidney infection, corneal ulcers, inability to see in dark/shade.	S. America, W. Africa, S.E. Asia	Vitamin A-rich foods, e.g. green vegetables, milk, eggs, fruits.
	Beri-beri	Vitamin B deficiency, wasting of limbs, nervous disorders, skin sores, heart failure.	S.E. Asia	Vitamin B-rich foods, well-balanced diet.
	Peliagra	Lack of niacin (vitamin B defic.). Skin inflam-mation, diarrhoea, dementia, dermatitis.	Maize eating areas, Italy, S. Africa	Well-balanced diet with meat and green vegs.
	Anaemia	Iron deficiency, lack of energy and appetite, breathlessness. Child killer at birth.	S. America, S.E. Asia, Africa	Meat, liver, iron-rich foods, fruit and green vegs.
	Rickets	Vitamin D deficiency, bone deformity of legs, pelvis and spine.	S.E. Asia	Diet of calcium-rich food and Vitamin D.
	Scurvy	Victamin C deficiency, hair, teeth fall out, internal bleeding, skin sores.	Africa	Diet of fresh fruit, vegetables and fish.

CHAPTER 5

Million Killer

Malaria

Malaria is one of the world's biggest killers: two billion people are at risk. The World Health Organisation (WHO) estimates that each year over 100 million people are affected by the disease and some 8 million die as a result. Malaria is endemic in sub-Saharan Africa (5.31) where most of the population is regularly infected and some resistance develops, with the result that those over five years old are usually able to survive an attack. Very young children, however, are most susceptible to malaria and, in Africa, the disease kills a million children annually. In Tanzania, malaria affects over 70% of the population.

Malaria remains one of the world's most widespread diseases. The disease occurs in areas which provide **habitats** (breeding sites) for the female of the anopheles species of mosquito. The mosquito requires temperatures between 15 and 40 °C, human (blood reservoir) settlement, areas of shade in which to digest human blood and a stagnant water surface in which to lay its larvae. Water surfaces can be lakes, tank wells or water barrels, irrigation channels, paddy fields, or even puddles. Spread of malaria is also encouraged by bad sanitation, and poor irrigation or drainage.

The disease is caused by **protozoa** (single-cell) parasites called **Plasmodium** (5.33). There are four types which cause malaria in humans. The most dangerous is *Plasmodium falciparum* which is found in Africa, India and South-east Asia. The female anopheles (5.33) requires human blood, full of proteins and vitamins, for her larvae. A female mosquito becomes infected with parasites after ingesting them from an infected person. The malarial parasites are then injected into an unifected person's bloodstream during another bloodmeal. Once in a

5.30 Flooded farmland provides breeding grounds for mosquitoes

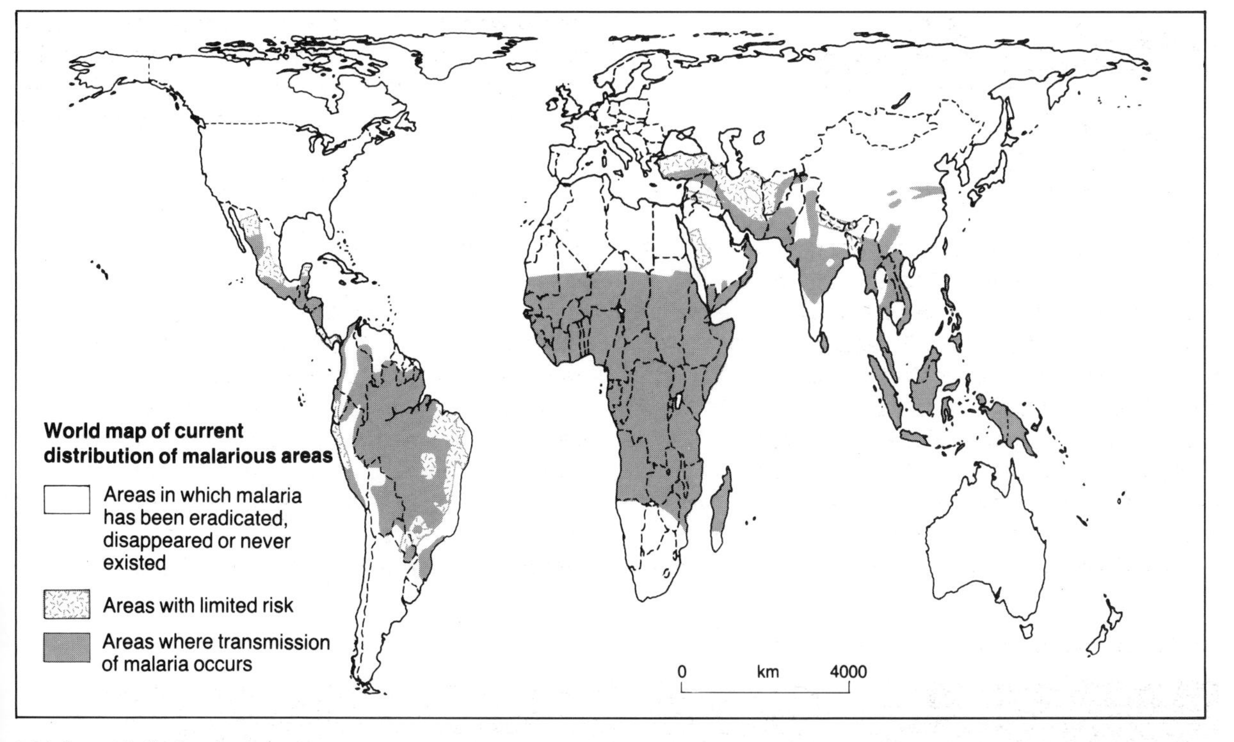

5.31 Current distribution of malarious areas

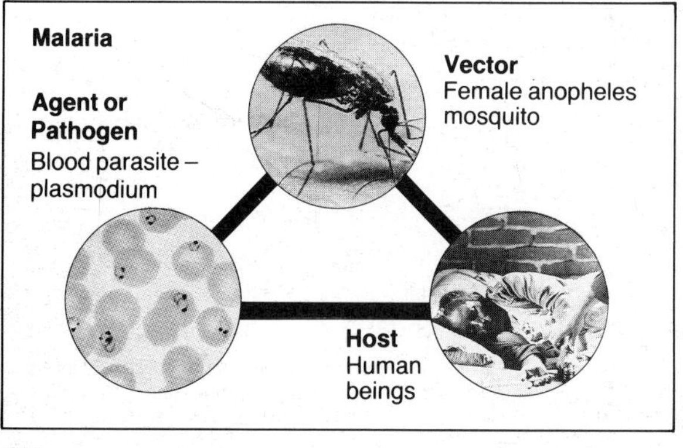

5.32

5.33 Transmission of malaria

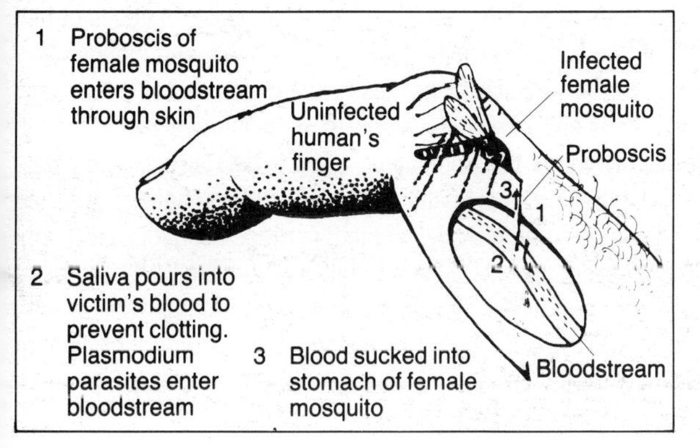

person's bloodstream the parasites make for the liver where they grow and multiply. After two weeks, thousands of mature parasites break out of the liver and invade the red blood cells. Here they multiply, burst the blood cells and invade other blood cells. The effect is fever accompanied by headache, nausea and stomach pains. With falciparum malaria over 80% of the red blood cells are attacked. Those people without immunity or early treatment become very ill and often die. Falciparum malaria can cause anaemia, kidney failure and affect the brain (blood capillaries become obstructed by infected red blood cells and this results in convulsions and coma). Other types of malaria, though debilitating, rarely kill. Some parasites may lie dormant in the liver for many years and cause recurrent attacks or relapses.

Recently many areas of Africa, Asia and South America have been facing a resurgence of previously controlled malaria. Significant progress in malaria control was achieved in the 1960s and 1970s in several malarious areas of developing countries. At that time the World Health Organisation co-ordinated a two-pronged attack on the disease. Primarily, the transmission of malaria was tackled by attacking infected mosquitoes with insecticides such as DDT. Secondly, the blood parasites were treated with various anti-malarial drugs such as chloroquine. In much of South America, Malagasy and Sri Lanka, for example, during this period the administration of both insecticide programmes and anti-malarial drugs led to the disappearance of anopheles mosquitoes, and malaria was virtually eliminated.

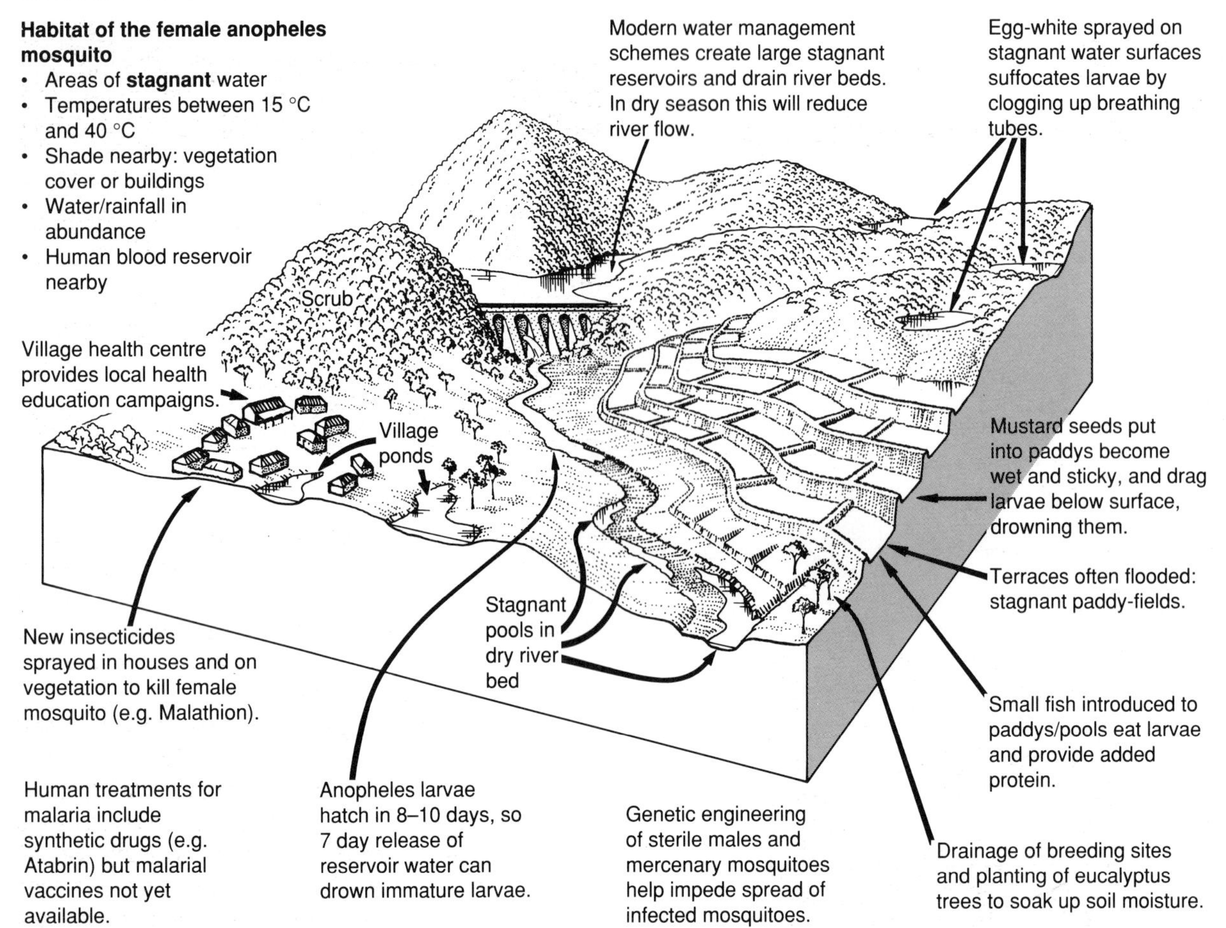

Habitat of the female anopheles mosquito
• Areas of **stagnant** water
• Temperatures between 15 °C and 40 °C
• Shade nearby: vegetation cover or buildings
• Water/rainfall in abundance
• Human blood reservoir nearby
Modern water management schemes create large stagnant reservoirs and drain river beds. In dry season this will reduce river flow.
Egg-white sprayed on stagnant water surfaces suffocates larvae by clogging up breathing tubes.
Scrub
Village health centre provides local health education campaigns.
Village ponds
Mustard seeds put into paddys become wet and sticky, and drag larvae below surface, drowning them.
Terraces often flooded: stagnant paddy-fields.
Stagnant pools in dry river bed
New insecticides sprayed in houses and on vegetation to kill female mosquito (e.g. Malathion).
Small fish introduced to paddys/pools eat larvae and provide added protein.
Human treatments for malaria include synthetic drugs (e.g. Atabrin) but malarial vaccines not yet available.
Anopheles larvae hatch in 8–10 days, so 7 day release of reservoir water can drown immature larvae.
Genetic engineering of sterile males and mercenary mosquitoes help impede spread of infected mosquitoes.
Drainage of breeding sites and planting of eucalyptus trees to soak up soil moisture.

5.34 Some modern control methods for malaria

Unfortunately these achievements did not endure and malaria returned with increased ferocity to Sri Lanka and Malagasy in the late 1980s. The WHO, which had declared in 1974 that global eradication of malaria was possible, accepted that such claims were unrealistic for many reasons. Without continued aid from multi-lateral organisations such as the WHO and Red Cross, many developing nations could not afford to consolidate earlier results. Many mosquitoes gradually began to become resistant to various insecticides. The number one killer, *P.falciparum*, developed resistance to all anti-malarial drugs in over 50 countries. Large-scale implementation of agricultural and industrial projects, including the construction of hydro-electric power schemes, have encouraged the re-infestation of mosquitoes to many areas which were malaria-free. Large-scale and widespread migration has led to the development of many spontaneous settlements often constructed on marshland, in areas without paved roads, sewage or garbage collection. Lack of public investment in health, sanitation and education in poor countries has also encouraged the re-advance of the disease.

With eradication now thought impossible, the emphasis is on control of malaria which takes the form of a concerted and combined attack using modern chemicals, biological controls, new drugs and environmental measures (5.34). In South America for example, the Pan American Health Organisation (PAHO/WHO) is promoting an integrated approach involving the application of residual insecticides (e.g. Malathion) acting upon the adult mosquitoes, together with the use of varieties of fish that feed on mosquito larvae in paddies and ponds, and environmental measures such as regular dam flushing and drainage of swamps. Similarly, to prevent mortality and reduce morbity within the population, PAHO/WHO also recommends strengthening local health services, improving health education campaigns, and distributing modern drugs used for prevention.

Yet according to the latest statistics from the WHO, there are at least 400 million people still suffering from the disease, with over 230 million of the cases due to *P. falciparum*. Many experts now agree that malaria remains a major public health problem and a continuing obstacle to development.

AIDS – The Deadly Epidemic

AIDS: the basics

AIDS, Acquired Immune Deficiency Syndrome, is a fatal disease caused by the human immunodeficiency virus (HIV). Scientists are convinced that the virus is new. Tests on stored blood show that AIDS first infected people during the late 1970s. There are uncertainties about its origins. It could be a mutation of a similar virus which causes immune deficiency in some African monkey species. But it also resembles genetically the sheep-killing virus visna. Like both other viruses, HIV is often slow-acting and may lie dormant in the body for long periods.

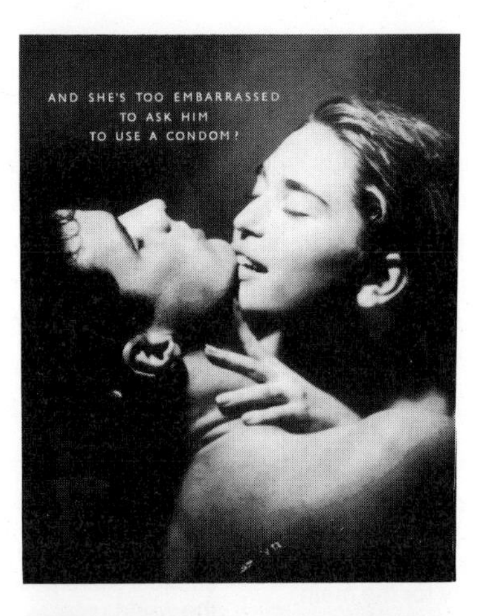

5.35

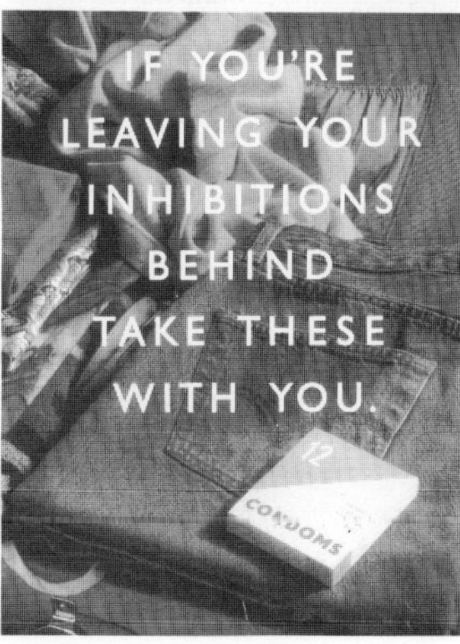

5.36 Government anti-AIDS campaigns concentrate heavily on advertising in various countries

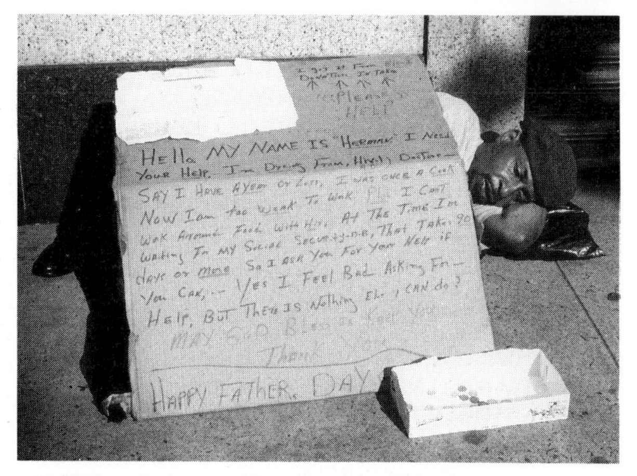

5.37 WHO predict that 10 million will die from AIDS by 2000

Though exact figures are difficult to obtain, the World Health Organisation estimates that over 100 000 people around the world have so far died as a result of AIDS (5.35), with a further 100 000 terminally ill. This sounds a lot but other diseases have killed far more people. For example, malnutrition-based diseases annually kill over 5 million children in Africa.

Set in this context, many have questioned the international outcry that AIDS has provoked and the effectiveness of its expensive advertising and education campaigns (5.36). But in 1990 the WHO predicted that by the end of the century there could be as many as 10 million deaths worldwide and over 100 million people affected by AIDS. And from recent research it can be stated that for every case of full-blown AIDS (5.37) there are at least 100 carriers of the infection who have not as yet developed the disease. If we accept these figures then at present there are over 10 million people carrying the virus.

There is currently a very widespread epidemic of AIDS around all parts of the world (5.38). The rate of spread of the epidemic is fairly uniform (5.39). Initially the number of cases doubles every six months. A country with 600 cases of AIDS today will therefore have more than 500 000 cases in ten years and over a million in eleven years. The USA currently has about 43 000 cases giving an estimated carrier population of 4.3 million.

AIDS is caused by a virus, HIV viruses are the smallest of all disease-causing organisms: about 1000 can fit into a red blood cell and about 300 red blood cells can fit on the nib of a ball point pen. Viral diseases such as the common cold or influenza, have so far defied scientific efforts to find a cure. The disease caused by HIV, AIDS, is always fatal once it develops. The virus remains in the body for life.

By inserting itself into human cells, the HIV virus uses its genetic reproductive mechanisms to manufacture more viruses. These kill the host cells and then invade adjacent cells. In turn, these are transformed into virus factories and killed. HIV targets

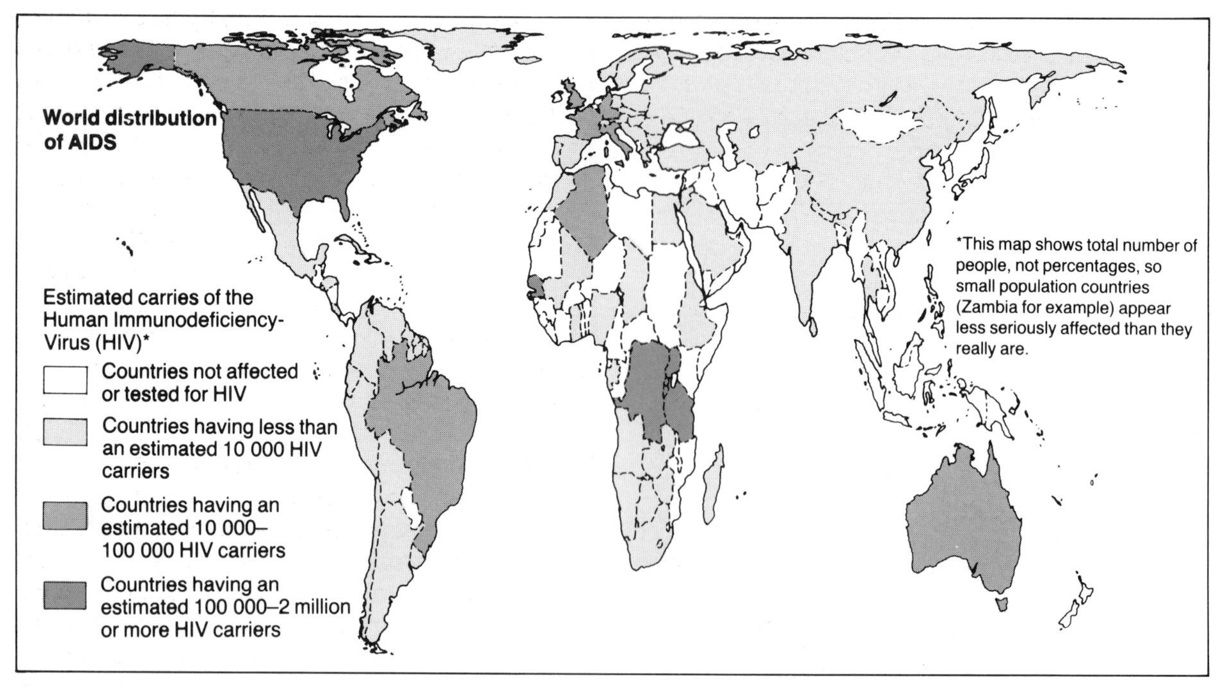

5.38 World distribution of AIDS

the body's T-cells which are the main line of defence against all other infections. People with AIDS thus have drastically weakened immune systems (hence the name Acquired Immune Deficiency Syndrome) and are unable to combat common diseases which uninfected people can fight off without difficulty. AIDS sufferers are prone to what are known as opportunistic infections: killer diseases that become established only because of severe immune deficiency. These include PCP (respitory failure), CMV (gut, brain and retina failure), catastrophic diarrhoea (loss of up to 12 litres per day) and various fungal infections (such as Cryptococcus neoformans). HIV also directly affects the brain because it targets and destroys brain cells as well as T-cells. The resulting condition, called 'AIDS dementia' is caused by slow withering of the cortical tissue, leading to brain death.

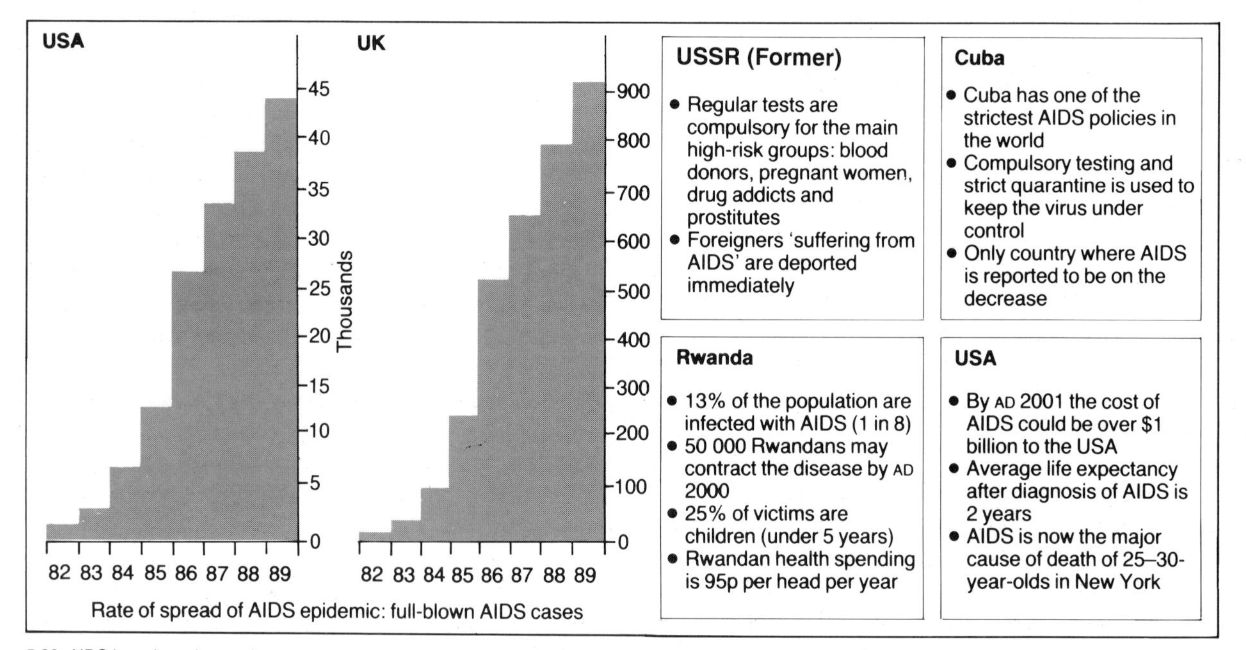

5.39 AIDS by selected countries

AIDS is transmitted through contact with infected blood or blood products and through sexual contact involving the exchange of bodily fluids. Congenital transmission also occurs both in the uterus and in breast milk. About 50% of children born to mothers with AIDS develop the disease shortly after birth. In developed countries, blood screening has removed almost all danger of acquiring the virus through transfusions, but the sharing of needles by intravenous drug users continues to put at risk the life of many addicts. Few developing countries are able to afford effective screening programmes and the risk of infection remains high, especially in Africa (5.40) where 21% of donated blood was infected in 1988. Sexual intercourse remains the main carrier of the epidemic in all parts of the world. In developed areas, homosexuals remain the worst-affected group although this is changing as more and more heterosexuals become infected. In Africa, heterosexual intercourse has long been established as the primary transmission route – with equal numbers of men and women infected. More sexually active groups such as prostitutes and their clients are much more prone to infection than those with fewer sexual partners. There have been no cases of transmission through routine social contacts.

5.40 The South: an urgent need to screen the blood supply as AIDS spreads

There is no cure for AIDS yet. All the opportunistic infections respond to treatment, but when the treatment is withdrawn they recur, usually more severely. In the end they will always kill the sufferer. Scientists are therefore researching to find a drug that will attack the HIV virus and the suppression of the immune system it causes. After a decade of research no such drug has been found. Even the best drug available, AZT (azidothymadine) blocks the virus in some (not all) people but does not alleviate the suppression of the immune system. Possibly more promising is the search for a vaccine which according to the WHO is at least a decade away. Governments have therefore concentrated the attack on HIV and AIDS through education campaigns aimed at 'safer sex' and thus at prevention. These include the promotion of limited sexual contacts, an increase in the use of condoms during intercourse and free blood testing. For the present, education remains the best 'vaccine' against AIDS.

The devastating potential of AIDS in the years ahead calls for urgent worldwide action. Because it transmits itself mainly through sex, because it kills, and because it is at present incurable, AIDS represents a major threat to humankind. Already there are predictions of serious economic impact. HIV singles out the most productive and sexually active age group: those between 15 and 50, on whom national economies depend for wealth generation and income. Some experts now believe that AIDS will precipitate a worldwide economic disaster. But AIDS affects the poor much more than the wealthy (5.41). In underfunded African hospitals and clinics the virus continues to be spread by the practice of reusing needles and syringes which, in better economic circumstances, would be disposed of after each injection.

Unless control of the deadly epidemic is treated as a priority, we may face an ineradicable reservoir of a lethal virus which will pose a major threat to the future of human life on Earth.

But it is in Africa that the AIDS epidemic finds its most virulent and life-threatening expression. Even if a maximum effort were made – both by countries immediately concerned and by the international community – hundreds of thousands, possibly millions, of Africans would still die.

All evidence suggests that the disease is out of control and that Africa is now irrevocably set on course for a health disaster of biblical proportions. Added to existing mass killers like schistosomiasis, bilharzia, malaria and dysentery; added to malnutrition-linked diseases like kwashiorkor and marasmus; added to the poverty, war and famine that stalk from country to country and from region to region, AIDS represents an intolerable extra burden. This is particularly so because, in the insanitary conditions and depressed economic circumstances of the world's poorest continent, amongst people who are badly fed, sapped by ill-health and consequently already severely immuno-suppressed, the concept of specific 'risk groups' like drug takers is absurd: the 'risk group' in sub-Saharan Africa is the entire population.

5.41 From 'AIDS and the countries of the South' (source: *New Internationalist*, March 1987)

CHAPTER 5

Improving Health: A Basic Human Right

Absolute poverty has been described by Robert McNamara, former president of the World Bank, as 'a condition of life so characterised by malnutrition, illiteracy, disease, high infant mortality and low life expectancy as to be beneath any reasonable definition of human dignity'.

Of the world's almost 1 billion absolute poor, 90% live in rural areas, more than half are small farmers, and one quarter are landless labourers. In the countries of the South where the absolutely poor form the majority, such as Bangladesh (75%) or Indonesia (53%), poverty is self-sustaining and self-generating (5.42). Every three seconds a child in the developing countries dies and, despite this and the fact that over 1000 million people have no access to medical services, we spend 25% more each year on war than on health. The developing countries have a double burden to bear. Their main fight lies with infectious diseases but they also have to provide the infrastructure for health care. Even simple, readily countered threats such as the micro-organisms that cause diarrhoeal diseases (page 161) kill millions of children in the South.

According to the **Brandt Commission** (1980) the prime objective of every nation should be to utilise its human potential to the full and thereby increase not only the quality of life for its people but also its national development (5.43). Both the WHO and the FAO believe that development should be considered in terms of provision for the basic needs of human beings and not solely in terms of economic and industrial development.

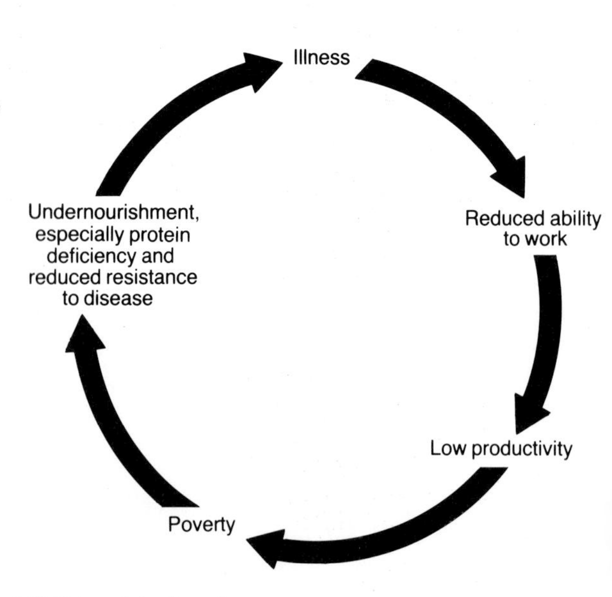

5.42 Vicious circle of poverty

5.43 Model of development

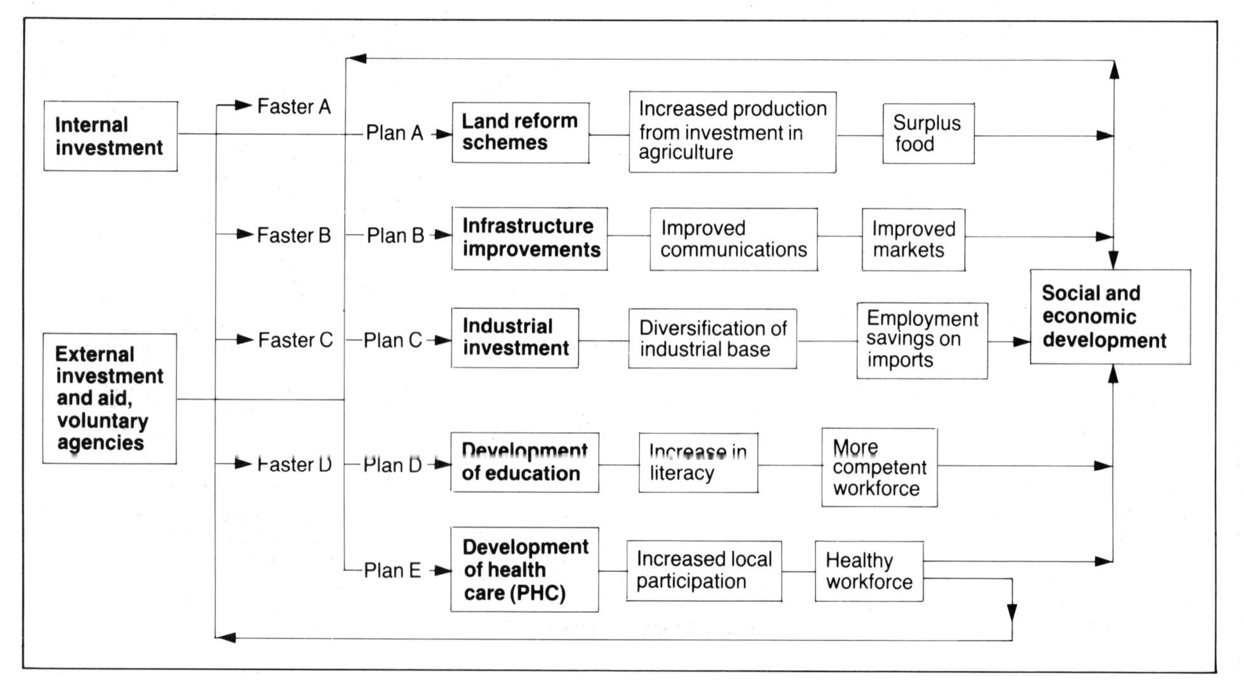

5.44 Choices for the future and PHC

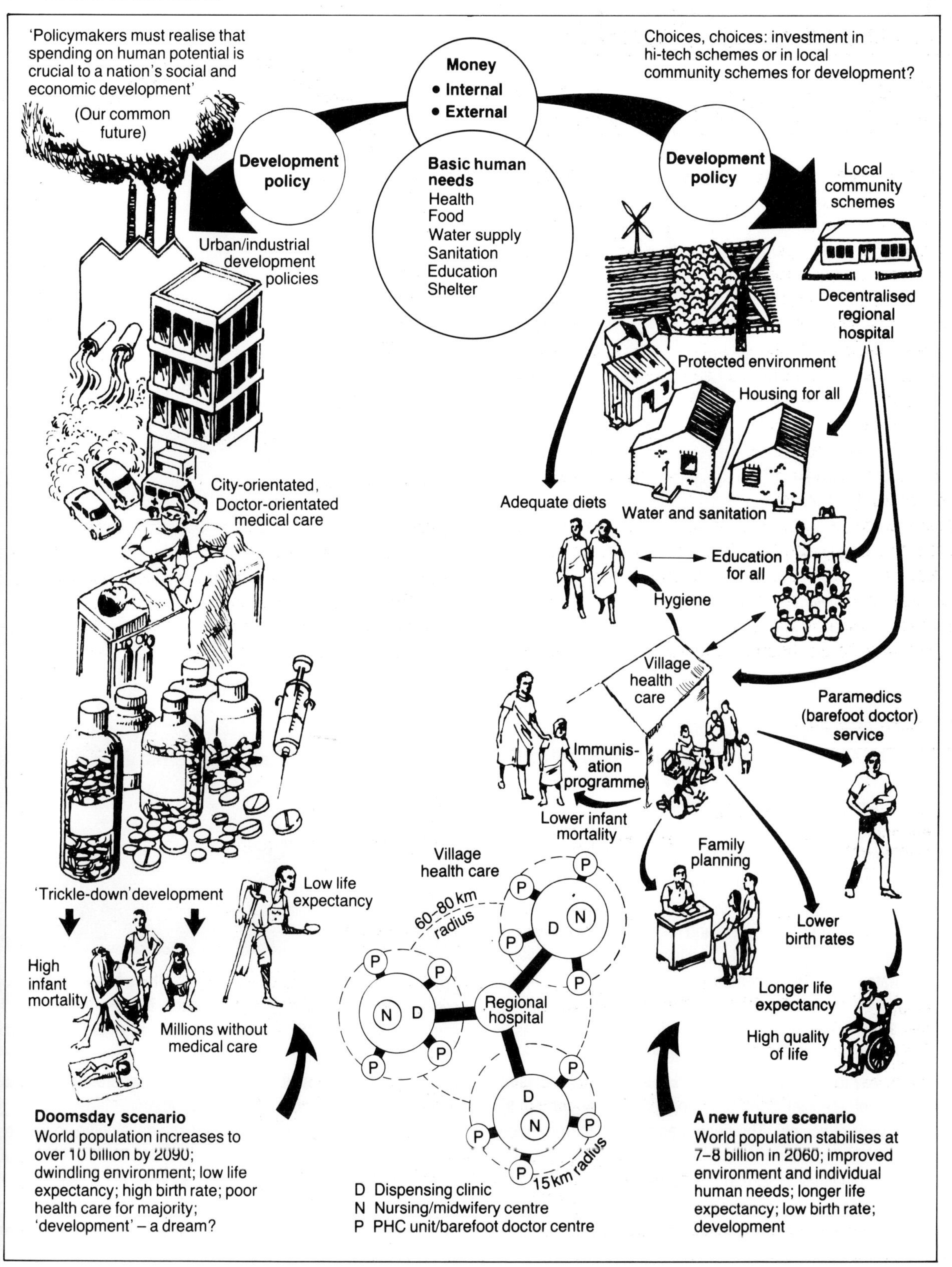
'Policymakers must realise that spending on human potential is crucial to a nation's social and economic development'
(Our common future)
Money
• Internal
• External
Choices, choices: investment in hi-tech schemes or in local community schemes for development?
Development policy
Basic human needs
Health
Food
Water supply
Sanitation
Education
Shelter
Development policy
Local community schemes
Urban/industrial development policies
Decentralised regional hospital
Protected environment
Housing for all
City-orientated, Doctor-orientated medical care
Adequate diets
Water and sanitation
Education for all
Hygiene
Village health care
Paramedics (barefoot doctor) service
Immunis- ation programme
Lower infant mortality
Family planning
Village health care
'Trickle-down' development
Low life expectancy
60–80 km radius
Lower birth rates
High infant mortality
Millions without medical care
Regional hospital
Longer life expectancy
High quality of life
15 km radius
Doomsday scenario
World population increases to over 10 billion by 2090; dwindling environment; low life expectancy; high birth rate; poor health care for majority; 'development' – a dream?
D Dispensing clinic
N Nursing/midwifery centre
P PHC unit/barefoot doctor centre
A new future scenario
World population stabilises at 7–8 billion in 2060; improved environment and individual human needs; longer life expectancy; low birth rate; development

GNP per capita (thousands of US dollars)

10 9 8 7 6 5 4 3 2 1

Industrialised

Developing

Year

1960 1965 1970 1975 1980 1985

Growth in GNP per capita, 1960–86

Under-five mortality rate (per 1000 live births)

240 200 160 120 80 40

Developing

Industrialised

Year

1960 1965 1970 1975 1980 1985

Decline in deaths in children under five, 1960–87

5.45 Wealth and and health?

5.46

A critical element in the development process is the WHO's plan for 'Health For All by 2000'. Its central tenet is the adoption by countries of a strategy of **primary health care** (PHC) based on a close association between local communities and their health workers (5.44). The quest for health in developing countries is far-reaching. There is an acute need for adequate sanitation and safe drinking water (pages 158–61). Funds for medical training, essential drugs, disease eradication programmes, health-care technology, and family planning services are in short supply. Some key approaches such as immunisation programmes and **oral rehydration therapy** (ORT) have proved very cost-effective but still require extensive back-up services and political support.

Primary health care is a programme to improve the health of children and the absolute poor in developing countries. It can cost relatively little but it demands a reorganisation of priorities: city-orientated, doctor-orientated administrations are converted into extensive local networks for community care. Many locals can be easily trained in hygiene and first aid to become visiting 'barefoot doctors' and local, traditional medicines can be incorporated into PHC schemes.

The drive toward health, however, must come from the locals. Their participation – in planning community services, in the introduction of clean water, in preventative programmes – is often the key to the success of any PHC scheme. Health is not only part of medical care provision but is integral to the development of society. The central aims of health promotion and health-care provision should be to improve health, eliminate poverty and inequality, spread education and enable the poor and underpriviledged groups to have a higher quality of life.

China, Sri Lanka, Mozambique and parts of India have already reduced mortality by these means. Although the gap between developed and developing countries has continued to widen in terms of wealth in the last decade, the gap has narrowed in terms of health (5.45). Improved health raises the quality of life: education, especially of women, and community-based conservation can raise it further – to a point where the birth rate begins to fall, and a new future is possible.

Ultimately, for both the developed and developing countries, quality of life is not measured by economic advance, industrial growth, or the introduction of high technology. For millions of the inhabitants of planet Earth, development means satisfying their basic human needs and improving the quality of the environment in which they live for their short lives (5.46).

Questions

Q LEVELS OF HEALTH

1 (a) Explain the link between poverty and ill health.
(b) Prepare two graphs, one for developed countries and one for developing countries, to illustrate the contrasts in life expectancy (5.17).
(c) How can investment in hospitals create more problems of ill health in some developing countries?
(d) Contrast mortality rates in developed and developing countries.
(e) Quoting specific examples, explain the term 'great neglected diseases'.
(f) Is there a geographical pattern to the growth of cancers?

Q MILLION KILLER MALARIA

3 (a) Illustrate and explain the world distribution of malaria.
(b) What exactly causes malaria?
(c) Describe the transmission of the disease.
(d) In which ways can humans influence the spread of malaria?
(e) Why has the WHO recently declared that global eradication of malaria is impossible?

Q AIDS

4 (a) What exactly is AIDS?
(b) Explain the link between HIV and AIDS.
(c) How can someone carry the HIV virus and not suffer from full-blown AIDS?
(d) Make your own copy of map 5.38 to illustrate the distribution of AIDS.
(e) Explain how the HIV virus causes AIDS.
(f) How is AIDS transmitted?
(g) What are the symptoms?
(h) How quickly does the virus spread?
(i) In which ways is AIDS best
(i) prevented *(ii)* treated?
(j) What is the predicted socio-economic effect of AIDS ?

Q MATTERS OF LIFE AND DEATH

2 (a) Explain what is meant by exogenous and endogenous diseases.
(b) Classify all the named diseases in diagram 1 into exogenous/endogenous.
(c) Write brief notes to explain the following types of disease: endemic, epidemic and pandemic.
(d) Give reasons for the geographical classification of disease (mention basic human needs, water, diet, etc.)
(e) Explain the links between ill health and the lack of clean water.
(f) What is the difference between starvation and malnutrition disease?

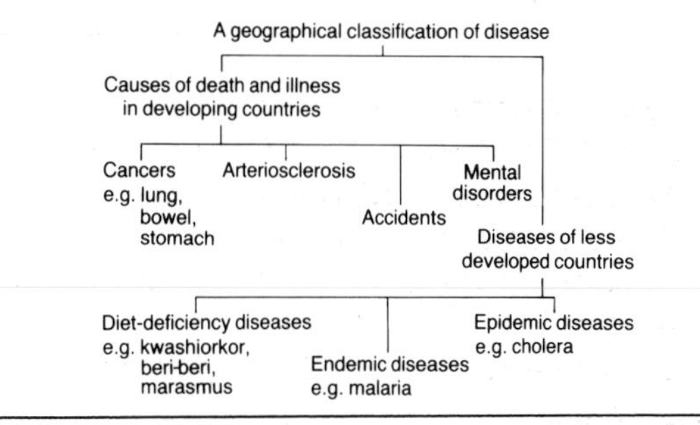

Q IMPROVING HEALTH: A BASIC HUMAN RIGHT

5 (a) In your own words describe the vicious circle of poverty.
(b) Write brief notes on each of the following: PHC, ORT, barefoot doctors.
(c) Why is improving health a far-reaching process in any country ?
(d) Using diagram 5.44, contrast the two approaches to development through health strategies.
(e) In your opinion, which is the more suited to developing countries? Explain your answer.
(f) Explain the link between development and health.

Research and Further Work

Select one disease listed in table 5.28 or 5.29 then carry out an investigation to find out more about it. Prepare a booklet covering its distribution, pathogen, transmission, symptoms, treatment, and socio-economic effects in developing countries.

INDEX

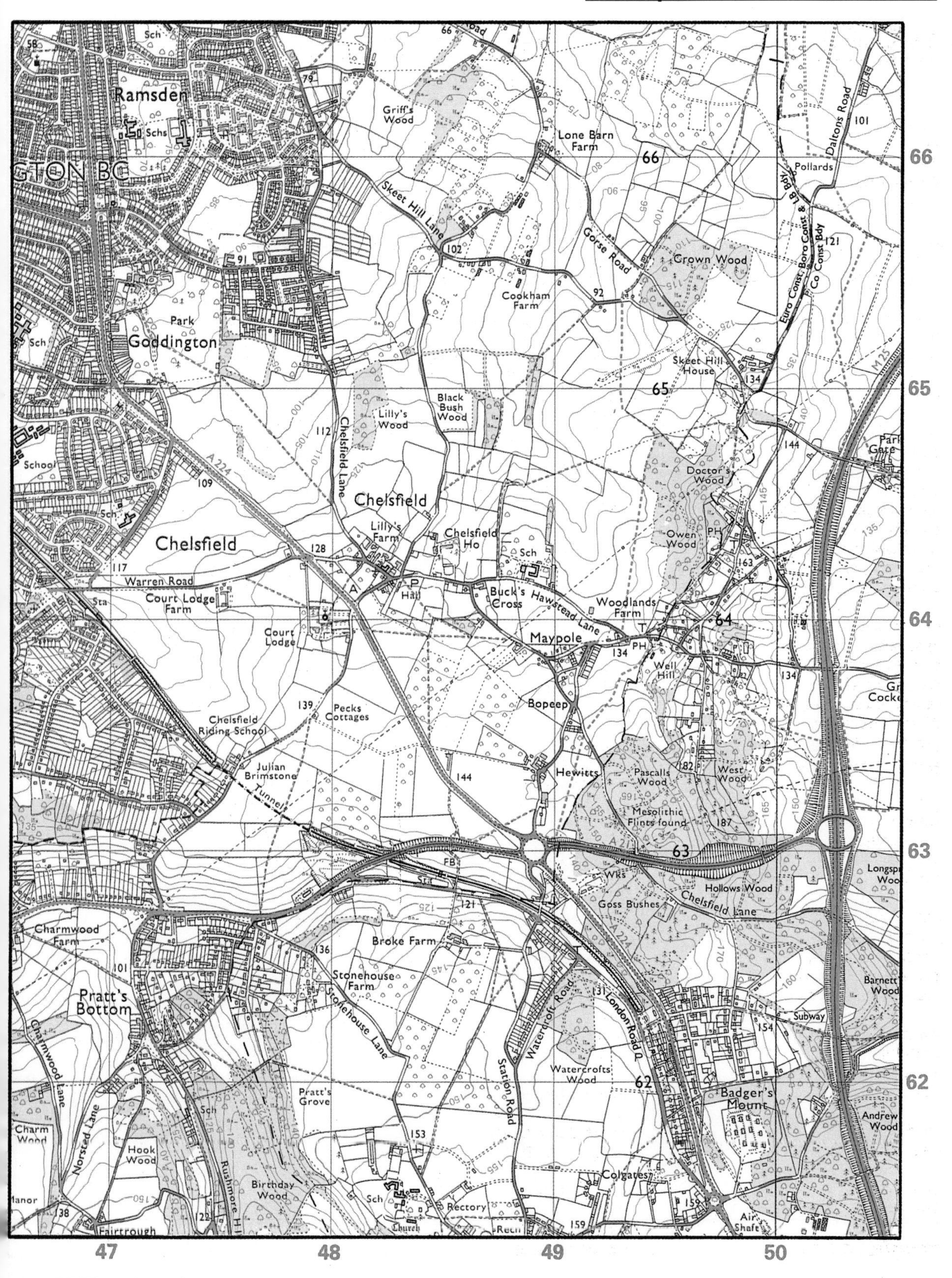

© Crown copyright 1991.

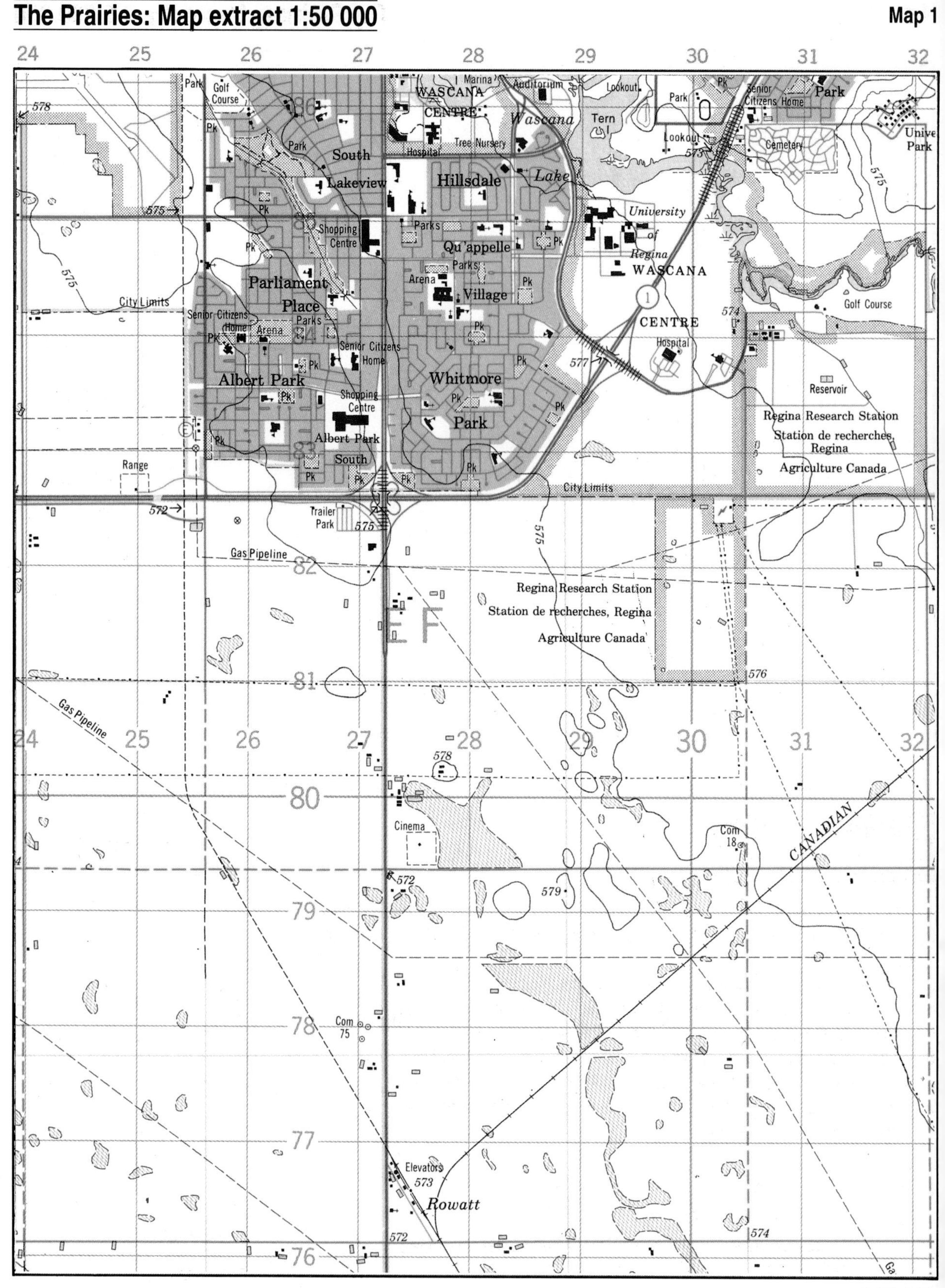
Marina
Auditorium
WASCANA
CENTRE
Wascana
Lake
Tree Nursery
Hospital
Lookout
Tern
Park
Senior Citizens Home
Cemetery
Golf Course
South
Lakeview
Hillsdale
Shopping Centre
Parks
Qu'appelle
Village
Arena
Parliament
Place
Senior Citizens Home
Albert Park
Whitmore
Park
Albert Park
South
University of Regina
WASCANA
CENTRE
Reservoir
Regina Research Station
Station de recherches, Regina
Agriculture Canada
City Limits
Range
Trailer Park
Gas Pipeline
Cinema
CANADIAN
Elevators
Rowatt
Com
Pk

1:50 000

Map 2

The Prairies: Map extract 1:250 000

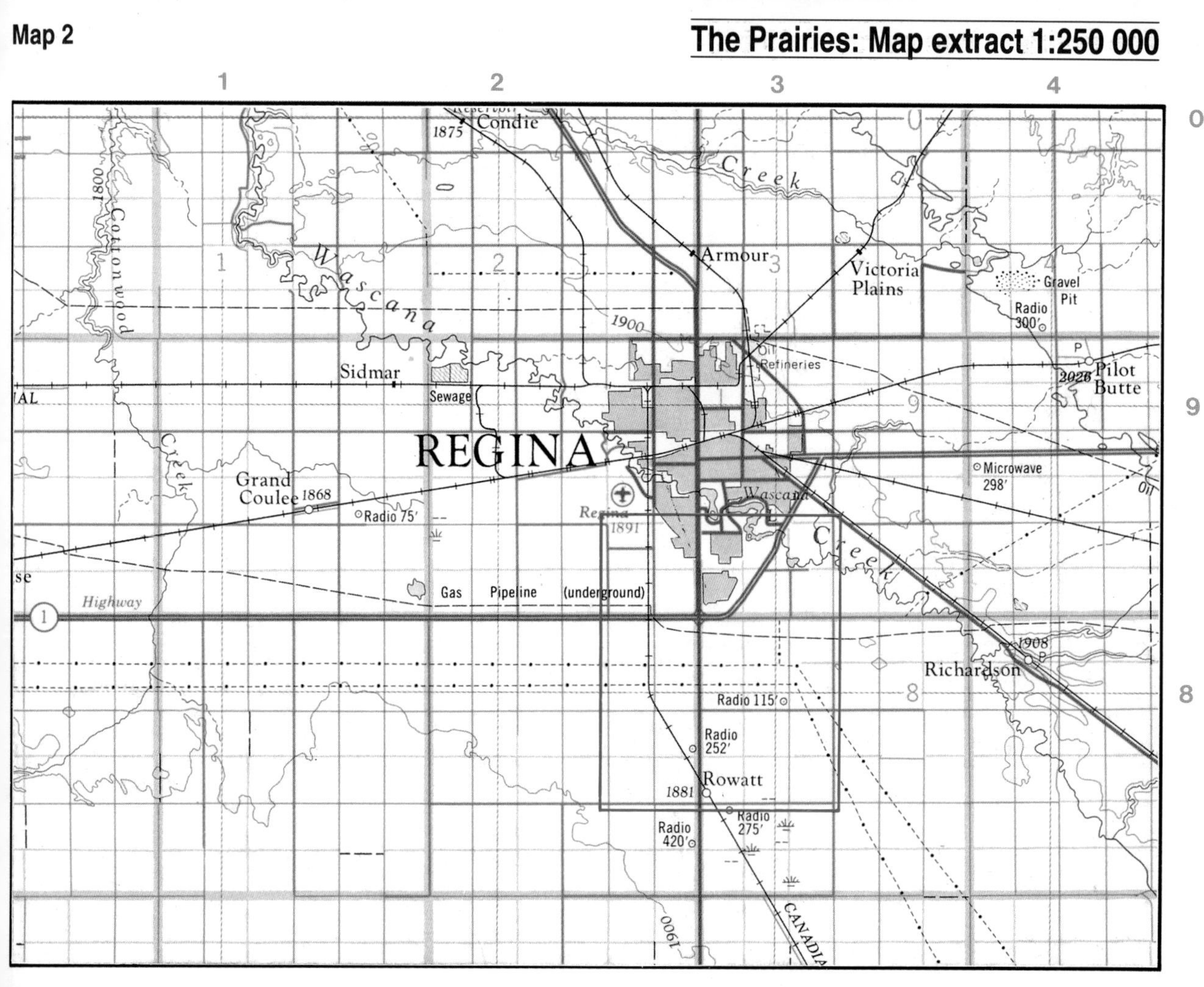

The two map extracts show part of the Canadian Prairies in the vicinity of Regina, Saskatchewan.

Area of 1:50 000 extract

1 Describe the physical landscape of the Prairies as shown on the two map extracts.
2 From map 1 describe the rural settlement pattern beyond Regina. Explain any patterns you detect.
3 What map evidence indicates that this area is an agricultural region?
4 Why are the railways important to the agricultural community in this region?
5 What map evidence suggests that Regina is an important regional centre?
6 The Prairie provinces have an important non-agricultural resource. What is there on the map extracts to indicate the identity of this resource and its importance?
7 Using the map extracts try to produce a sketch of the Prairie landscape and settlement which would serve as a model.

Key

Road

Railway

Home

Loose-surface unclassified road

Seasonally flooded land

Large building

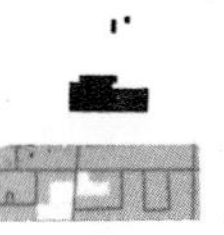

Building

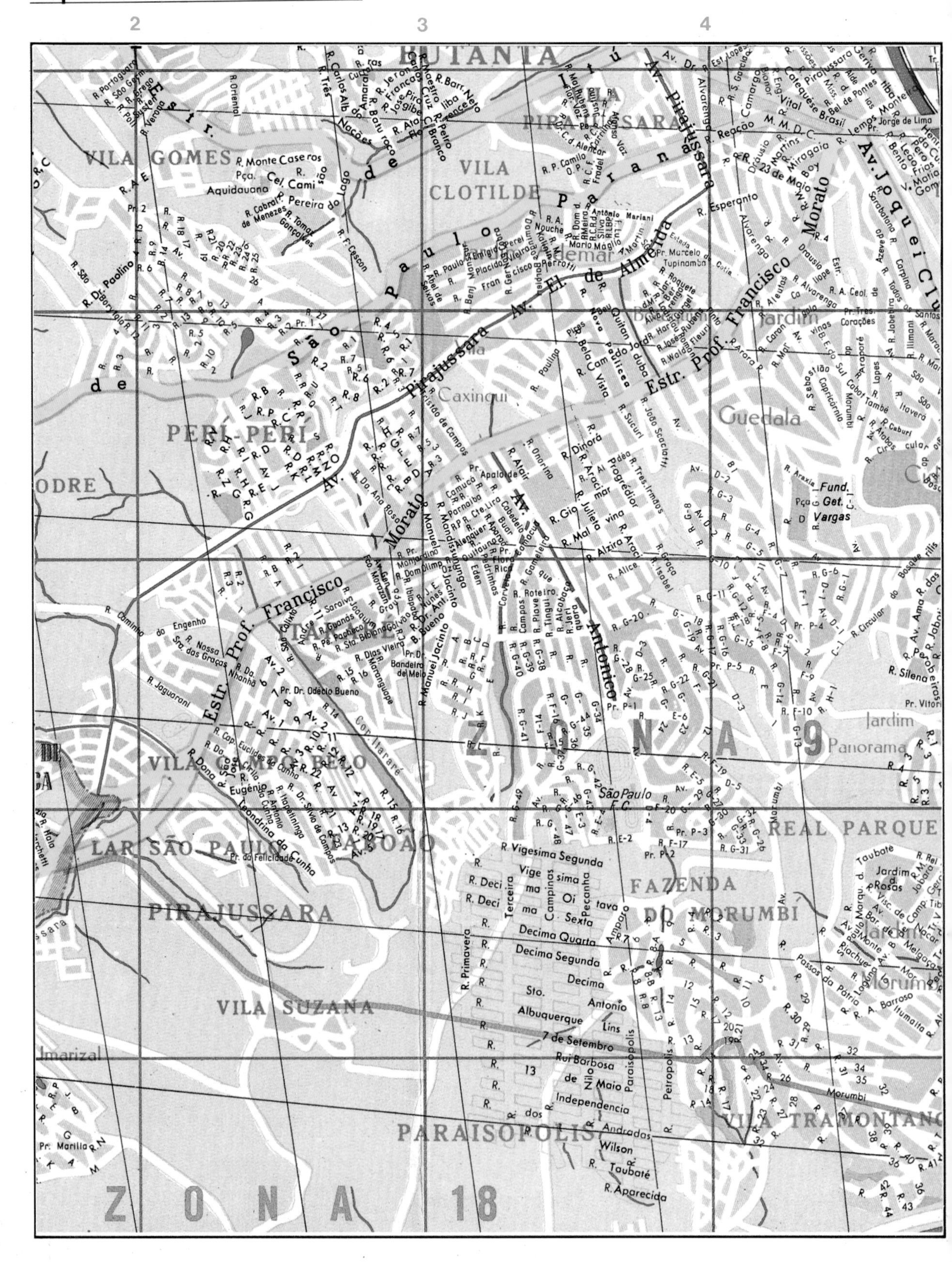
2
3
4
BUTANTÃ
VILA GOMES
VILA CLOTILDE
PIRAJUSSARA
PERI-PERI
Caxingui
Guedala
ZONA 9
ZONA 18
VILA CAMPO BELO
LAR SÃO PAULO
PIRAJUSSARA
VILA SUZANA
FAZENDA DO MORUMBI
REAL PARQUE
PARAISÓPOLIS
VILA TRAMONTANO
Jardim Panorama
Estr. de Itú
Estr. Prof. Francisco Morato
Av. Pirajussara
Av. El. de Almeida
Av. Morato
Av. Jóquei Clube
São Paulo F.C.
Fund. Get. Vargas
Morumbi